THE CHURCH AND REVOLUTION

THE CHURCH
AND
REVOLUTION

From the French Revolution of 1789 to the
Paris Riots of 1968;
from Cuba to Southern Africa;
from Vietnam to Latin America

by

François Houtart and André Rousseau

Translated by

Violet Nevile

ORBIS
BOOKS
MARYKNOLL, NEW YORK

Table of Contents

Preface

The subject of this book is a complex one which introduces us into a welter of historical and contemporary facts that are sometimes difficult to interpret correctly. And yet it is a subject we have to deal with, for it is impossible to live in today's world without being aware of the tremendous underlying thrust of social and cultural change of which the revolutionary movements are a sign. It is impossible for a Christian not to see the relation between the Christian message and the work of liberating mankind. At the same time it is impossible not to be distressingly aware of the paradoxical conflict between the two.

This conflict is situated not on the level of means but on that of ends. Why is it that Christianity, a proclamation of man's total liberation, historically finds itself in opposition to the movements which attempt to give concrete expression to this liberation and almost always identifies itself with the forces of oppression? Is Christianity itself and, perhaps, every transcendental vision of life, to be blamed for this as so many social reformers have taught? Is it the way in which Christianity has become institutionalized that is to blame? Is there a necessary link between radical social reform and the rejection of religion?

These are the basic questions that have inspired this book. It lays no claim to being an original work of history. We have used both secondary sources and direct experience, and the method consists in a description of a certain number of revolutions or movements for social change and of the Church's reaction to them. The descriptions vary greatly according to whether they concern historical events of the past such as the French Revolution or contemporary events such as the revolutionary movements of the Third World. The sources available are, of course, quite different in the two cases, and more elements of reflection can be introduced into the analysis of those situations which have already been scientifically studied. On the other hand the method used may seem unduly anecdotal, but we have deliberately quoted many facts and texts in order to provide the empirical basis for more systematic study.

Before describing specific cases, however, we should make some general comments about the sociology of revolution; these are given in the first chapter and should prove to be useful. The last chapter is a tentative sociological interpretation. It is still too early to speak of a genuine theory; we can only hope that this will gradually be elaborated.

We should also make clear what is meant by "Church" in this context. This study refers primarily to the Roman Catholic Church. The Orthodox or Protestant churches could also be studied in the same way, of course, and it is very likely that many general remarks in this book could be validly applied to them.

However, it is not sufficient to specify which church we are talking about; we must also be quite clear as to what we mean by that word. A sociological description of the institutional Church enables us to say at once that this concept is not coextensive with that of the ecclesiastical hierarchy. We are talking about the whole community of Christians of Roman Catholic obedience, members of an ecclesiastical institution which is clearly delimited and hierarchically structured. A social entity such as this has clear-cut stratifications and, as we shall see, the different strata within the community can take very different and, often, even contradictory positions.

The intention of this book is in no way to "recuperate" the revolutionary movements for the benefit of the religious institution. This tendency exists, it is true, in a number of contemporary works on the subject. "Recuperation" means, in this instance, restoring the Church to a role in new social movements similar to that which it played in the past. However, the concern which led to our choice of subject is linked to the conviction that Christianity does contain a message which is valid for the whole of mankind in search of liberation.

Several people have earned my gratitude for their contribution to this book: James Colliani, Secretary of the United States Liturgical Conference, who invited me to talk on this subject in Washington in 1968, and André Rousseau, associate at the *Centre de recherches socio-religieuses* in Louvain, who did a great deal of work on several chapters.

François Houtart

CHAPTER ONE

A Sociological Approach
to Revolution

More and more studies of the phenomenon of revolution are making their appearance. Most of them, however, have been made within the framework of political science, the sociology of power, the sociology of war, social psychology, and even the sociology of religion. The advent of a sociology of revolution is very recent and most of what has been produced so far has been based on the classical revolutions: the English, American, French, and Russian. To date, the most complete theoretical model available for analysis of these phenomena is the Marxist model.

It is becoming increasingly clear, however, that theories built on the historical cases mentioned, and even the Marxist theoretical model, must be developed further if we want to undertand contemporary revolutionary phenomena such as the cultural revolution in China, the revolutionary process taking place in consumer societies, and even the Cuban revolution or the war in Vietnam. Although much has been written, there is as yet no comprehensive synthesis.[1] This chapter is not an attempt to provide a synthesis. It will simply present a rapid overview of some classical elements of sociological thought and give some idea of contemporary discussion and research in this field.

The Notion of Revolution

Careful epistemological or sociopolitical analysis would be necessary to disentangle all the different meanings of the word "revolution."

The terms "urban revolution," "industrial revolution," or "scientific revolution," for instance, can only be used by analogy with the change in the political sphere (in the broadest sense of the term), which is the object of this study. The term revolution has also been applied to evolutive political change such as the experiment set in motion by the Christian Democrats in Chile.

Also, in examining the revolutionary phenomenon in relation to political change, we must make a clear distinction between a revolution and a *coup d'état* or a "palace revolution." The latter is often simply a struggle between persons or clans within the existing social system, which itself remains untouched; only the administration changes hands but without being modified in any way. The innumerable "revolutions" that have taken place in Latin America since the wars of independence have nothing in common with what took place in Mexico, and even less with what took place in Cuba.

When, in extreme cases, the notion of revolution becomes purely symbolic, it can even be used by counterrevolutionary forces to conceal their true intentions. The events of 1964 in Brazil are a striking example of this. National revolutions and minority movements of emancipation also need closer study, for in such cases the very term "revolution" can sometimes become a fetish or be usurped by an oligarchic power structure. We shall see an example of this when we discuss *la violencia* in Colombia.

Within a revolutionary movement the term can become the symbol of a permanent dynamic force, an ever-present renewal. Very different examples of this can be seen in the magnificently paradoxical "Institutionalized Revolutionary Party of Mexico," the "revolution within the revolution" of Régis Debray,[2] and the cultural revolution in China, not to mention the Trotskyist position.

Revolution is not synonomous with, although it implies, change. The notion of change usually connotes a linear process, and in this sense every society is in a permanent state of change and its stability depends on the way in which each element succeeds in establishing a harmony of balance with all the other elements. An entire social system can undergo metamorphosis, its elements realigning according to totally new patterns, without revolution.

The notion of revolution precedes change. It is the "project" of a new society. In phenomenological terms the idea of revolution consists of the birth within a society of an as-yet-unfulfilled intention; to carry out the revolution is consciously to will to overcome the "dichotomy between the real content of social relations and the ultimate exigencies inherent in these relations."[3] Lucien Sébag's definition takes us to the heart of the Marxist conception of revolution. In sociological terms it is a challenge to the collective values and goals of a society, and often on a deeper level, a challenge to its whole system of legitimation and its ideology. However, as we shall see, Marx qualifies this statement, and at this stage we mention it only as a hypothesis.

One fundamental element of the concept of revolution, however, can already be seen: the relationship between awareness and history. A revolution takes place when a population or a group or class of society becomes aware that they are capable of controlling their own history, when they "have the floor" as the saying went with regard to the events of May, 1968, in France.[4] When this occurs, people become acutely aware that new social structures can and must be created. This new awareness is, in itself, a cultural fact with far-reaching consequences in the sphere of social behavior; prerevolutionary and revolutionary periods are times of intense social creativity.

Revolution, therefore, cannot be reduced to an outbreak of violence or a seizure of power. It implies, first and foremost, the withdrawal of collective assent to the existing social system. It is a "process of collective reconquest of a common praxis, by men sharing a common project,"[5] rejecting the existing balance of production and overcoming the roadblocks to innovation. It is change, but it is radical, planned change. To quote Gaston Bouthoul, it is a "rapid application of new mental patterns in institutions, laws, and political and social organization."[6] Or, to quote A. Kroeber, revolution is a "change which takes place suddenly, more or less violently, which influences a whole cultural group and which spreads with a speed which is all the greater in proportion to the social backwardness that has prevailed."[7]

But it is in Marx's work that we find the broadest, most scientific analysis to date of revolution as a phenomenon; theoretically and in practice, his thinking is basic to an understanding of this phenomenon.

For Marx, revolution results from a contradiction between the growth of the forces of production and that of the relations of production (relations of property and superstructures). According to this hypothesis, revolution is inherent in the dynamics of dialectical reality. I would like to quote this key passage from Marx's *Contribution to the Critique of Political Economy:* "At a certain level of development, the forces of material production come in conflict with the existing relations of production or with their juridical expression, the relations of property, within which they have developed up to then." These are the necessary conditions for a "period of *social* revolution" to begin. I emphasize the word "social," which is central in Marx's thinking and which he distinguishes from "political revolution." In doing so, he indicates that the important thing in his hypothesis is not the revolutionary transformation of "ideological and state superstructures, etc. . . ." On the contrary, he explains that "one must always distinguish between the overthrow. . . of the conditions of production. . . and the juridical, political, religious, artistic or philosophical—in a word: ideological—forms in which men become aware of this conflict and fight it until it is suppressed." This is a major principle of analysis for Marx, and it leads to distinguishing, without opposing in revolutionary practice, the elements of knowledge or science and the elements of the will. "Just as we do not judge an individual by the idea he has of himself, similarly we cannot judge a period of upheaval by its own self-consciousness, but on the contrary we must explain this consciousness by the contradictions of material life and the conflict between the social productive forces and the relations of production."[8]

As we can see then, Marx offers both a theoretical definition and a method of analysis of revolution founded on the hypothesis that one can understand the revolutions of the past only by taking into account the real motivations which triggered them, that is to say, the contradictions existing on the level of the substructure. This general definition, which Marx constantly measured against history and existing practice, enabled him to hypothesize a revolutionary movement in which the protagonists are fully aware of the forces that determine them. With this Marxist concept as our starting point, it is possible to formulate a typology of revolution. Marx himself did this, not for the intellectual pleasure of it, but in order to elaborate a detailed project for the revolution of capitalism.[9]

All revolutions of the past have changed the forms of the ownership of property: feudal, corporative, capitalist. But they have only been "limited revolutionary appropriations."[10] "In all previous appropriations a mass of individuals remained subordinate to one instrument of production."[11] In other words, revolutions in the past had been "political," and had left "the pillars of the edifice still standing;"[12] that is, they had left intact the division of labor and class structures. Only one class had been liberated, although the revolutions had been carried out in the name of all.

> What does a partial, purely political, revolution like this rest upon? On this: A fraction of the bourgeois society emancipates itself and claims supremacy over all others; any given class, starting from its own particular situation, undertakes the overall emancipation of society. That class emancipates the whole of society, but only on the hypothesis that the whole of society is in a situation identical to its own, that everyone has or can acquire at will, for example, money and culture.[13]

Our study of the French Revolution is an excellent illustration of this statement.

If we now look at how revolutions actually happen, we shall be in a better position to understand the development of Marx's theory of revolution.

The Revolutionary Process

This preliminary investigation of the concept of revolution clarifies, we hope, the nature of the phenomenon. We must now attempt to describe the mechanisms by which it effects the transformation of a sociocultural system on the basis of new relations of production.

The prerevolutionary situation. Before going any further, we should note that factors which determine a revolutionary situation can be indigenous or exogenous and sometimes a mixture of both. In the case of Latin America, for example, it is evident that the internal contradictions of society have repercussions beyond the national boundaries of the individual states. This is equally true of the peasant revolution in Vietnam and of student unrest in Europe.

A prerevolutionary situation is one in which social structures lag far behind the collective aspirations of aware, dynamic groups within a population and when these groups recognize that the structures can be transformed. However, the locus of this necessary awareness, its link with any one class in society, and its modes of development can vary widely. Marx offers only working hypotheses on this point, and he himself continually subjected them to reexamination. After Marx, a great deal of work still remained to be done. From his own writings to those of Marcuse, including Lenin, Luckacz, and Mao Tse-tung, the problem of alienation and disalienation has been the terrain of lively discussion.

According to the Marxist model, then, there must first be a class consciousness; revolutionary action is precisely the praxis by which a class evolves from being a class "in itself" to being a class "for itself." Before a class can will to overcome its alienation, before it can be capable of overcoming its alienation, that alienation must have become an "unbearable force, that is, a force against which people will revolt. . . It must have reduced the mass of humanity to a mass totally deprived of property and which finds itself at the same time in opposition to a world of wealth and culture which really exists. And both these things presuppose a great increase of productive capacity, that is to say, an advanced stage of development."[14] What Marx and Engels describe here is important: For a group to become conscious of its alienation and capable of a revolutionary undertaking, it must not be in a situation of "overall poverty."[15] In other words, it must not be in a situation in which it is totally and definitively excluded from all social participation. Such a situation can give rise to revolts, but not to revolution. Alternatively it can give rise to a "professional" revolution which rapidly becomes the prisoner of its own institutions (e.g., Mexico). On the other hand many studies indicate that extreme destitution engenders myths or prophetic cults of liberation which secrete as much conservatism as revolutionary spirit.[16]

Nor is a subculture of poverty (a "residual poverty" as Decouflé calls it), as described by Oscar Lewis, propitious to the elaboration of a revolutionary project or a class consciousness. The gulf between this class and the dominant society leaves it without the means of offering any opposition to society. And this is all the more so where society founds its legitimation on egalitarian myths and the rule of majority representation.

The concept of political conflict provides perhaps a useful clue to the analysis of the birth of a revolutionary consciousness. Experts in the theory of conflict often make the distinction between a "problem-conflict" and a "political-conflict." A problem-conflict can be resolved by technical analysis (e.g., distribution of the national product, priorities in an overall plan, etc.). But a political-conflict opposes groups who identify with their class rather than with needs (e.g., political debate of the priorities of the overall plan). Perhaps the transition from the status quo to a revolutionary situation consists precisely in the transition from a conflict of interests to a political conflict or, in other words, to a conflict of values. The situation of the blacks in the United States and the movements for independence in the colonial nations are good examples of such a transition: A group ceases to clamor for a better lot in life and clamors for recognition as a social entity, for power.

The beginning of revolutionary action. How does a prerevolutionary situation develop into a revolutionary one? Historical analysis shows that a romantic revolutionary spirit is not enough. Revolution must be organized even if its origins are anarchic. It would be interesting, in this respect, to analyze the revolutions that have failed, or to make a comparative study of the revolution which succeeded in Russia in 1917 but failed in Germany, or the Mexican revolution and the Spanish civil war or the Cuban revolution in 1959 and the victory of counterrevolutionary factions in Brazil in 1964.

Credit must be given to Louis Althusser for some valuable original work in this field and for his analysis of the October Revolution of 1917. At that time, revolution had become feasible in Russia for reasons that reached beyond its borders: The imperialist war had plunged the whole world into a revolutionary situation. But revolution succeeded in Russia only because Russia was the most vulnerable spot in European capitalism. In the Czarist empire, all the contradictions present everywhere were exacerbated and compressed within the boundaries of one state. These were the determining circumstances which made the 1917 revolution possible; the absence of this constellation of circumstances explains why it failed in Germany in 1848, as well as why the Paris Commune failed in 1871.[17]

The revolutionary process always begins with some leaders, a common ideal, and organized groups seeking to inaugurate a new "golden age." The part played by groups in all revolutions—pressure groups, groups forming an illegal government, revolutionary groups, etc.—is worth noting. We can find examples in the "town meetings" in New England, which laid the groundwork for the American Revolution; in the *sociétés de pensée* in eighteenth-century France; in the nihilist groups in Russia; in contemporary student associations such as the March 22 Movement in France; in the groups of African intellectuals in Portugal; and even some Catholic Action groups in Latin America such as the JUC (Catholic University Students) in Brazil. It is also interesting to note that the historians of revolution can usually be divided, like the general run of onlookers, into two schools of thought: those who favor the theory that a revolution is sparked by "circumstances," and those who hold that it is the result of a conspiracy on the part of just such groups as those mentioned.

The actual process of revolution seems to unfold according to certain constants: Society crystallizes into two groups, the old and the new; there is a period of revolutionary euphoria and union between the "idealists" and the "realists"; there are struggles for power and a period of intransigence and "puritanism." It seems that all revolutions are inclined to be intolerant and go through at least one phase during which they cannot accept the slightest criticism. It is well known that Marx attributed great importance to this period of the "dictatorship of the proletariat," and that his thesis has led to a great deal of recent debate. There seems to be a dialectical pattern involved in which intolerance is necessary to begin with in order to reach the declared goals, but it later becomes an obstacle to attaining these goals. For when a process of institutionalization sets in at the same time, intransigence—ranging from terrorism to "stalinism"—becomes a fixed pattern, sapping the life force of the revolutionary project.

The protagonists of revolution. Marx's analysis also attributed great importance to the type of protagonist in the revolution, and both he and Lenin stressed the utility of active groups. The necessity of "awareness" and of scientific analysis is still one of the central themes of Marxist sociology today.

We have emphasized the importance of the prerevolutionary situation, but revolution does not automatically follow, as though it were the result of a blind determinism. Before a revolution can actually take place, a certain threshold must be crossed making the process irreversible, thanks to the awareness of leading personalities and groups. The events which took place in May, 1968, in France, demonstrated the importance of a group capable of rapid analysis and adaptation to circumstances. The role Lenin played in the success of the Soviet revolution and his tactical genius have often been emphasized. But Marx does not have too much to say about the "revolutionary advance guard" which Lenin favored so strongly; his main concern was to arrive at an exact definition of the concept of a revolutionary proletariat.

According to him, as we saw earlier, an authentic revolution must be led by a class which is really carrying out the emancipation of the whole society. The originality of the social revolution lies in its agent: the proletariat. Marx defined at length the characteristics of that class, the features which make it universal.[18] He sees it as a negative element of society, completely excluded from society. What Marx declared in 1843 to be a categorical imperative, he hails in the *Manifesto* in 1848 as a reality.[19] For, on the basis of his theory of increasing pauperism, Marx believes that "the bourgeois class produces its own opposite: the proletariat."[20]

The proletariat, then, is the antithesis of capitalist society, and it alone can carry out the revolution in the name of the majority and reorient the whole of society in the right direction. It will do this by taking possession of property, culture, and the state.[21] The whole of the old order is radically called into question by the proletarian revolution.[22]

If the essential act of revolution is the suppression of private ownership of the means of production, Marx and Engels were deliberately uncommunicative about the details of how this revolution was to be carried out.[23] The first practical measure mentioned in the *Manifesto* is the political dictatorship of the proletariat. They must take over all political power. In this connection, of course, Marx was thinking in terms of the social reality of his times and within the context of nation-states. A political framework is needed during the transition from a capitalist to a communist society. The dictatorship and social supremacy of the proletariat is the fundamental practical measure which provides the framework for the social revolution.

Historically, the Marxist schema is of the utmost importance, and it has given rise to endless debate. This is understandable if one remembers that Marx conceived this hypothesis within a given historical context, but that the same method can be validly applied in other circumstances. It is neither a dogma nor a prophecy. But we must also bear in mind the philosophical context in which Marx first formulated these concepts: Ideological practice still predominated over scientific practice.

Although Marx described the role of the principal protagonist of revolution in almost messianic terms, there is still room for other actors in the revolutionary process. It does not just happen. Nor can it take place without being preceded by a prerevolutionary situation. It is not the result of determinism. As we have already seen, circumstances lead to the crossing of a threshold beyond which the movement becomes irreversible and leading figures make their appearance. The essential backdrop of revolution is a social class which has reached a certain point of social consciousness or a certain degree of frustration. But revolution gets under way only when three other types of protagonists appear on the scene: leaders who catalyze and incarnate a movement; militants (or "agitators" according to the point of view) who serve as intermediaries; and groups. Intellectuals also play an important part in almost all revolutions, particularly in the prerevolutionary phase, through their critique of the sociopolitical system, their leadership, and their contribution to setting up a new regime. Sociologically it is they who are best placed to challenge a political regime, since they are not usually directly involved in political action and yet they are sensitive to innovation. This is also true of students today. It must be added, however, that the "scholarly" role of the intellectual often allows him to play a "clean" part, leaving others to "dirty" their hands.

The revolutionary process, then, can be described with some degree of accuracy, but what is important now is to see whether contemporary events correspond to the different stages we have described.

Contemporary statement of the problem. In our day the revolutionary movement is scattered far and wide and takes on an immense variety of forms.[24] In industrially developed countries one can find forms as different as the Black Power movement in the United States and the student movements in the universities of America, Europe, and Japan. In socialist countries, what connection is there between Marx and the "Czech spring" or the Chinese cultural revolution? In the Third World, the example of the Cuban revolution is spreading, but what do Latin American guerrilla movements have in common with African freedom fighters, the Palestinian resistance, and the war in Vietnam? Is there any revolutionary significance in the clamor for "self-management" in the industrialized countries? And what is the revolutionary significance of the Yugoslav, Cuban, Czech, and North Korean "ways"?

In theory one can still talk about world revolution, but it is increasingly difficult to grasp any one reality common to all the examples mentioned. Is it, indeed, still possible to speak of a common theory of revolution? A fortiori, is there any such thing as one common strategy?[25] Some thinkers like Marcuse go even further and ask whether the very concept of revolution as it was developed by Marx should not be revised.[26] The Marxist theory itself seems to invite such revision.

One of the most striking features of the current scene is the apparently national character of the revolutionary movements. However, we must look closer. In Latin America, as we shall see, the Cuban model—rightly or wrongly—is the common basis of all the guerrilla movements and attempts to unite them in an anti-imperialist perspective. On the other hand, there is a growing feeling among the revolutionary movements in Vietnam, Latin America, Africa, and even the United States that they are all engaged in the same struggle. And in Europe, the student movements seem to realize that nothing can be done to change the system if they restrict themselves to the national context. In fact Marcuse believes that

> the theoretical framework of revolution and subversive action has become a world framework.... Just as Vietnam is an integral part of the corporative capitalist system, so the national movements of liberation are an integral part of the potential socialist revolution. And the liberation movements in the Third World depend, for their subversive power, on the weakening of the capitalist metropolis.[27]

To speak of "polycentrism" in the international revolutionary movement simply means, according to Pierre Naville, that "every movement can and must have its own autonomous power of decision."[28] If this seems self-evident, we must remember that it is indispensable if a revolution is to be truly the people's revolution. In this sense revolution is never the same in any two countries.

As to the role of nature of the proletarian revolution, in view of the fact that opposition in the United States to the established system is taking shape essentially "among the ghetto population on the one hand and, on the other, among the intellectual elite of bourgeois background and, especially, among students," Marcuse believes that the form of the future revolutionary movement can be found here, provided that the working class will disassociate itself from the system and come to the support of the new advance guard. And Marcuse concludes his reflections on this topic by saying that "the Marxist concept of revolution, as a movement which has the support of the majority of the exploited masses and which ends by bringing the proletariat to power in a political dictatorship... this concept itself has been rendered obsolete by historical evolution...."[29]

This thesis, which some see confirmed by an analysis of events in May, 1968, in France,[30] brings us to the central problem of the qualitative difference between capitalist and socialist societies. If both societies manifest apparently similar phenomena once they have reached a high degree of technical and economic development, what is the qualitative difference between them? Marx used to speak of the "social soul" of the revolution, but historical revolutionary undertakings seem to have been strangely forgetful of this. Recent experiences in China, Cuba, and Czechoslovakia are urgent reminders of this question, which could also be glimpsed underlying the events in 1968 in France.

In China and Cuba and generally in the Third World, we have countries which are unable and unwilling to carry out their socialist revolution by the detour of capitalism. The specific contradiction on which Marxism is founded is, therefore, reversed: Property and social relations are more important than the forces of production, and the paths these countries follow often have little relation to the Marxist schema, especially as far as the use of ideology is concerned.

Mao Tse-tung, for instance, in opposing the Kuomintang, attacked the traditional order and launched his revolution from the rural areas, staking everything on the emancipation of the rural masses. In opposing Liu Shao-ch'i, Mao was rejecting the Soviet path of authoritarian development of the forces of production and the new bureaucracy in order to promote a new social entity and progress on the path of democracy and collective creation. Similarly, when Castro minimized the development of production and consumption and gave priority to the work of scientific and cultural education and the constitution of a nation in which every citizen would be worker, soldier, and student, he was seeking a socialism capable of "changing man."

But are these predominantly ethical and political revolutionary tendencies valid only for the underdeveloped countries? Are they useful only in the period that precedes economic "take-off" because they make the break with imperialism and its consequences as well as avoiding the pitfalls of Soviet-style development? The evolution of a country such as Czechoslovakia and the current social movements in the capitalist countries of Europe show, perhaps, that this is not so. But how can the "social revolution" once again be recognized as an imperative? It is being called for today in the form of self-management of the means of production by the working classes, and this is a resurgence of an old objective, which some say was largely disregarded by Lenin and utterly ignored by Stalin.[31]

Technical and industrial development has entailed profound changes in human relations and social awareness. Automation in production means that man is becoming less and less a "producer" and more and more a "consumer," and the need for a social revolution, for liberation, is accompanied by another need based on the same causes. In an advanced system of production, man's place is fundamentally changed: The work of wage-labor ceases to be the principal source of social wealth. Marx himself noted that

> It is neither the time spent at work nor the immediate work done by men which now appear as the principal foundation of the production of wealth; it is the appropriation of his overall productive force, his knowledge of nature and his ability to dominate it, in a word, the development of the social individual represents the essential foundation of production and wealth.[32]

The main contradiction within the system, then, rests on education, culture, and competence, which are monopolized by an elite and oriented exclusively toward production. Those who make progress possible are excluded from the enjoyment of the wealth they create and from any responsibility for what they produce. The division of labor that gives wealth and the power of decision to the few is in direct contradiction with the very nature of the process of production, which is more and more socialized. As Rudi Supek writes, "the essential contradiction of all capitalist development lies in the fact that the mode of work, the form of coordination, and the organization of productive functions have been socialized, while the producer or worker has become more and more isolated."[33] This is the contradiction, therefore, that must be revolutionized, and a radical transformation of the ownership of the means of production is still an urgent task: It is the key to the transformation of society.

The new contestation, however, attacks both capitalism and certain forms of socialism which have allowed a new bureaucracy to proliferate, and which, in turn, entails a new form of alienation, fundamentally different from that of the capitalist system but all the more poignant in that it represents the death of former hopes.

On a deeper level the task of the revolution is to challenge our scale of values. How can modern society, in possession of modern instruments of knowledge and production, also "produce" man and accomplish its own qualitative transformation? This is the question that the Chinese and Cuban experiments have attempted to answer. And, in other ways, Western societies are being asked the same question.

> It is not simply a matter of abolishing poverty and the slavery of work, but of rebuilding the social and natural environment in such a way as to build a universe of peace and beauty. . . . In short, it is a question of a total conversion of values, a transformation of the needs and goals we aim for, and it implies yet another change in the concept of revolution: a rupture in the continuity of the technical apparatus and of productivity. . . .[34]

Marcuse has focused his analysis on technically advanced societies. It seems to me, however, that a true picture should take in both the developed societies and those which go by the name of "Third World." More and more students of the subject recognize that the different contemporary situations arise from an identical conflict: that which opposes the capitalist economic system on the one hand, whose power and control over the world's resources by means of economic, political, and military domination is reinforced by technical progress, and, on the other hand, a portion of humanity which has become socially aware and committed to the struggle for the values of human liberation and which is more or less effectively supported by the socialist countries.

Such an analysis is not necessarily simplistic. It does not claim that the capitalist system is a homogeneous whole, governed by a few key figures, but a complex system of basic solidarities which manages to survive the violent conflicts arising from internecine struggles for influence. The growing solidarity of the freedom movements, whether in Vietnam, the Portuguese colonies, Brazil, or Palestine, is a recent phenomenon growing out of the realization that, in the last analysis, they are combating a common enemy. And this solidarity reaches beyond the boundaries of the Third World to the freedom movements and groups working for the emancipation of the blacks in the United States and, even, to some of the movements of social conflict in Europe. Nor is this analysis simplistic when applied to the socialist bloc. Everyone knows that a socialist monolith exists only in the mythology of the "free world," and that the socialist world is also rent by conflicts and rivalries which affect the support it gives to the freedom movements. In fact, in face of these two networks of solidarity, one might well say that the Third World War has already begun.

This is how the contemporary reality of the revolutionary process appears today: It is complex but unequivocal. The struggle for man's liberation follows the path of political revolution, which, in turn, is inseparable from a revolution of the economic system. The latter, however, though necessary, is not sufficient. The soul of revolution does not die, it takes on new life whenever man's liberation gets bogged down in routine and bureaucracy or the interests of one group. Marx rendered sociopolitical analysis the signal service of introducing the dialectical method. It is up to us to go on with the work he began by applying the Marxist analysis to post-Marxian society. He also situated his analysis in the perspective of history, and history did not come to an end in 1848.

Revolution and Violence

Our study of the revolutionary process brought up the question of the passage from a prerevolutionary situation to actual revolution and that of the protagonists involved as well as ways and means. One question which frequently arises in this respect is that of violence. Revolution and violence seem almost bound to go together, so much so that the terms are often used almost synonymously. And yet some *nonviolent* revolutionary movements do exist, and their action, illustrated by the work of people such as Gandhi, Martin Luther King, Jr., and Dom Helder Camara, is beginning to be analyzed. In fact the interest aroused by nonviolent struggle today calls for specific analysis by philosophers and theologians, psychologists and sociologists, who all approach the violence-nonviolence question from different angles. We would like to mention a few of the possible approaches to the question.

Analysis of nonviolence. The social psychologist who studies nonviolent action may attempt to fit it into a theory of behavior. This is what Paul Hare has attempted[35] on the basis of three attitudinal dimensions: domination-submission, positive-negative, and conformity-deviation, thus supplying a typology of nonviolent attitudes and behavior and making it possible, at the same time, to draw up a parallel typology of the reactions which nonviolent contestation arouses in the power structure or its representatives and in the general mass of spectators.

From a more strategic point of view the social psychologist studies the mechanisms of attitudinal change and can point out instances in which nonviolent action has a chance of meeting with some success.[36]

The sociologist, on the other hand, attempts to discern and describe the social condition of nonviolent action and, particularly, its ideological postulates.[37] In this way he distinguishes two forms of nonviolent strategy: One is based on the fundamental harmony of social relations and is opposed to every form of coercion or violence; this is *conscientious nonviolence.* The other flows from an evaluation of conflict, seen as a healthy element of reality, and of nonviolence as the least costly way of resolving it; this is *pragmatic nonviolence.*

Conscientious nonviolence is concerned more with the means than with the ends. It holds that conflict ensues from a lack of communication and must be resolved by a conversion of the heart. The flaw in this approach is that it runs the risk of failing to identify the real conflicts. It is inclined to attach more importance to psychological and ethical factors without a social analysis of the facts, and it is, therefore, blind to the causes of a given situation.

Pragmatic nonviolence does not seek to eliminate conflict, but practices "symbolic violence" and attempts to ritualize the struggle. Groups which opt for this form of contestation attach great importance to the communication of their objectives and values, and rely on collective action rather than on the individual witness.

The difference between the two options stems from two different notions of political action. The former seeks to resolve conflicts and injustice by establishing better communications. The latter seeks to influence structures. The former is based on a personal ethic, the latter on an ethic of responsibility and, therefore, on an analysis of society.

One might object to this typology on the grounds that history shows these two positions existing on the same continuum. If the basic element from which action flows is the social structure, then the very foundations of that order must be attacked and the first step in nonviolent tactics must be to call into question the norms and legitimation of the system. Nonviolent action becomes, therefore, a "transgression" which provokes a process of mobilization and awareness, leading to the control of the social machine by means of strikes and other collective action.

Gandhi's whole undertaking was based on an analysis of the colonial structure in which he lived.[38] His task was to undermine the consensus on which that order was based and oppose the violence of the mighty with the violence of the weak. His protest followed a strategy which developed progressively: symbolic resistance (marches, fasts, demonstrations); defensive measures (strikes, noncooperation, refusal to pay taxes or to serve in the armed forces), and, finally, offensive measures (boycotts, sit-ins, occupation of buildings, etc.).

In a totally different context the evolution of Martin Luther King's action is a clear demonstration of how nonviolence can develop from an ethical to a more and more political concept. In the same way the protest movements in the United States against the war in Vietnam combine a highly symbolic and dramatic character with an increasingly political and radical content.

The meaning of violence. An analysis of violence—in the same way as an analysis of nonviolence—must see beyond the naïve view which equates revolution and bloody confrontation or which sets nonviolence, as a sign of the "good" revolution, against violence seen as an odious reversion to primitive instincts. Just as nonviolence is more than a desire to keep one's hands clean, violence is more than an irrational reflex. Its meaning flows from the revolutionary process itself.

"No liberty for the enemies of liberty!" proclaimed a slogan in 1793, and in 1966 Mao's Red Guards declared that a "revolution cannot be carried out with elegance and delicacy or with much gentleness and magnanimity."[39] Analysis shows that revolutionary violence seems to be an answer to a twofold need: that of gaining a hold and that of strengthening that hold by inspiring fear. This is why a revolution sometimes moves from offensive violence to the use of gratuitous terror.

But there is also a ritual aspect, which is at least as important as the tactical aspect. Violence is a symbolic assault on the old order, a calculated provocation of the establishment which forces it to reveal its true nature. It can also contain elements of "savagery" in the sense in which Lévi-Strauss uses the term, and if this seems gratuitous, it is only because it is liberated, whereas violence is normally legalized and confined to certain accepted norms. But is not everything in revolution violent? Does it not set out to do violence to the ordinary course of society? Whether through violent rhetoric or physical force, there is always a ritual enactment of vengeance and purification. The symbols of servitude must be destroyed and banished from the new horizons. "An age-old memory of servitude erupts violently as an act of liberty."[40]

The tactical importance of violence is especially obvious in armed insurrection and guerrilla warfare. Not long before his death Che Guevara is known to have called for the use of more violence. But the Latin American *guerrilleros* often distinguish between institutional violence, which they judge to be indispensable, and the use of personal violence, which should be used only when there is no alternative. The history of the South Vietnamese NLF or of the freedom movements in the Portuguese colonies shows that they were not originally violent. They became violent because of the systematic opposition they met with in the first place and, later, in response to repressive measures used against them by the power system.

This is what Dom Helder Camara is talking about when he speaks of the "established violence" of social and political structures. Violence is triggered by police repression, which transforms a nonviolent movement into a violent one. Many moralists have failed to take this basic historical process sufficiently into account when pronouncing their judgments.

Marxist analysis has contributed greatly to the rationalization of violence in society, thereby easing the burden of culpability in a basically human situation. The will to grasp the real movement of history demythologizes realities and brings them back to the level of man, within the scope of responsible investigation and action. Engels, in his polemical discussions with Dürhing, shows that violence in itself is not quite so simple and fundamental as it may seem: Robinson Crusoe on his desert island gratuitously makes Man Friday his servant; is this a case of pure violence, a political relation as Dürhing claims? No, says Engels, Crusoe needs a slave to work for him. The relation is economic. The point of the allegory is to show that their unequal relationship—which is violent—in only possible because their wealth is unequal. Before the division of labor becomes a value, it has to be incorporated into the mode of production. Slavery in the United States, for instance, was less the outcome of human iniquity than of the cotton industry in Britain. And Engels applied the same argument to private property, which, in itself, results from the relations of production, not from robbery in the moral sense of the word; the work of thieves has never given rise to property in itself. And so the state uses coercion only because it is the state of the economically dominant class. Engel's reflections on *The Role of Violence in History* led him to the conclusion that political violence rests on an economic function in society and that it can take two directions: in the line of natural evolution, as in the revolution of 1789 in France which brought the bourgeoisie to power in reaction against the violence of the aristocracy; or against the natural, evolutive current as in the case of the social revolution.

Marxist thought looks beyond the outward appearance and seeks for causes: The violent struggles of history are not pure violence, but struggles for economic emancipation. It is in this light that we must see the Marx-Engels contention that "all history is the history of the class struggle." It has so often been concluded that Marx was an advocate of violence for itself, whereas, in reality, he saw it as a historical reality which can be organized and rationalized by knowledge in order to liberate the exploited majority. This struggle for liberation will be violent only in proportion to the resistance of the dominant minority class. The detailed studies that follow will be seen to bear out these contentions. To quote the MIR (Leftist Revolutionary Movement) in Venezuela: "If peaceful and legal forms of protest are countered with police brutality and growing numbers of dead, wounded and prisoners, [the popular movement] finds itself forced to transform itself into armed self-defense."[41]

It is important, therefore, to recognize that violence is not an end in the revolutionary process. No responsible revolutionary movement uses violence for its own sake. Violence exists in revolution just as it exists in the status quo. In the former it is often more spectacular and it does not benefit from the aura of respectability surrounding what Max Weber calls "legal violence." It is, therefore, "savage." It is the violence of the poor, of those who have no part in the power structure and who cannot, therefore, use "legal violence," which is less noticeable and better organized.

In a report dated July 31, 1967, the Guatemala Committee for the Rights of Man declared:

> The armed struggle in Guatemala, as in any other region where it may arise, can be understood only in terms of the destitution and injustice in which the majority of the urban and rural masses live. Who would think of organizing a guerrilla group in the Swiss Alps or in any country where other forms of struggle can be used for negotiation? A serious study should be made to see whether violence stems from orders received from abroad or whether it is the fruit of a revolt against the repression under which people live. What nonviolent means are available to the people of Guatemala to express their problems legally and peacefully?[42]

We would like to end this section with a mention of Franz Fanon's *The Wretched of the Earth*. In this book the author makes a striking analysis of the violence employed during the Algerian war, and although he believes that violence is an indispensable element in revolution, he emphasizes its terrifying cost and its dehumanizing action. The question arises, then: At what point does a revolution of liberation begin to destroy the very values it set out to promote? Is there a dialectical process here? Is man fated to live out periods of change in pain and suffering? Will violence be banished only when there is a classless society or when we have reached the threshold of Utopia or of the Kingdom of God?

The sociologist has no answer to such questions. He can only turn to the philosopher and the theologian. The philosopher will probably reply that man always lives in a state of tension between two levels of existence: the ideal he pursues of equality, fraternity, and universality and the reality of violence. That is the human condition. The theologian will probably speak of death and resurrection, suffering and glory, the archetype of every existence, or of sin and redemption.

Revolution and Religion

From a functional point of view many sociologists and psychologists consider the classic function of religion to be the promotion of social harmony and a stable social order. In support of this thesis it is pointed out that most religions, including Christianity since the fourth century, have been opposed to revolution except when the established order was hostile to institutionalized religion, or in the case of independent church groups that had broken away from the official body.

An investigation of concrete cases will often confirm this analysis, and yet it is valid only up to a point. The sociologist Henri Desroche has adopted Durkheim's original intuition[43] and relates three different functions of religion to three different situations in society. There are certain religious functions through which a society asserts itself (the function of integration); others through which it searches for its own identity (the function of criticism); and yet others by which a society revolutionizes itself (the function of protest).

Durkheim held that the birth of religion could always be traced to a society in turmoil and vice versa. Henri Desroche shows how religion can reactivate criticism and contestation of society in any social group. And a Marxist sociologist acknowledges that "closer study seems to indicate that both mysticism and heresies have stimulated and oriented the masses far more effectively and more profoundly than has materialism."[44] It would be interesting to attempt a study of the history of religion along these lines: the function of submission and the function of revolt. One has only to think of the Prophets of the Old Testament—and in our own time Camilo Torres offers an interesting example, which we shall have occasion to study more closely.

Our hope is that the historical analysis of concrete situations will shed some light on this problem of the relation between religion and revolution in the strict sense. We shall be analyzing the reasons which have so often led the institutionalized churches to resist social change: lack of an objective critique of the human condition; concern not to break with their conservative members; lack of a theology of political commitment; the traditional function as guarantor of the social system legitimized by religion (an order willed by God); fear for the survival of pastoral institutions; horror in view of the ambiguity of the revolutionary process and the violence it almost always entails.

Our analysis of the revolutionary project at the beginning of this chapter led us to define it as the will to fulfill the most deep-seated aspirations of a society, those which lie above and beyond all its falsehoods and pretenses: "To change life," to live in another world without becoming alienated in "the world to come." A comparison of this project with the religious project would have to be made with particular care for detail. G. Girardi has recently made a contribution in this area with an analysis of the conflict between faith and revolution.[45] According to him the conflict takes place "at the point at which the cultural solidarity which binds a religion to a given system appears to be the sign of a structural solidarity between that religion and a certain view of reality and values."

On the basis of this a comparative analysis can take several different directions. The conflict between religion and revolution can be on the level of historical ideals: The revolutionary wants to establish the "new life" here on earth, whereas the Christian is on his way toward a transcendent future and believes that the solution of history lies outside history. The conflict can also lie in the area of a notion of history: The revolutionary believes that man's role is to transform the world, whereas a certain type of Christian sees social reality as a gift of God which man has only to accept. The symbolic images are quite different: For the former, development is the only reality. The world can be changed. For the latter, all things come direct and already perfect from the hand of God. Finally, the conflict can lie in conflicting interpretations of history: For historical materialism, revolution must change structures in order to change man, whereas the spiritualist point of view seeks to revolutionize the heart of alienated, sinful man. But there are also areas of agreement: the emphasis on certain values; a thirst for justice; the defense of the downtrodden; and reference to a certain utopia. P. Blanquart, for instance, who offers another comparative analysis of the Marxist and Christian projects for humanity,[46] shows that the former contains a rationale or operative model, a utopia which mobilizes the whole human potential and an atheistic and scientific humanism. In the latter we find no operative model, but we do find a utopia expressed in mythical terms as well as a transcendent humanism.

This raises a question which will be treated from another point of view in the last chapter: At a time when a certain type of Marxist revolution is rediscovering its humanist origins and reaffirming its rigorously scientific foundations and the urgency of its action, are not the questions being raised by some of the revolutionary movements an invitation to Marxist sociology to reconsider certain of the hypotheses put forward by Marx and Engels which have all too often been treated as dogmas and which give a rather one-sided view of the connection between religion and reaction? Latin American Marxists seem to be closer to this than the Russians.

As far as Christians are concerned, this supposes that they identify with the struggle of the poor and that they undertake a critical, historical, and sociological appraisal of past and present bonds between conservatism and institutionalized faith, with the certainty that such a critique will necessarily change their way of believing and expressing that faith.

CHAPTER TWO

The French Revolution

It is both necessary and somewhat unfair to begin an analysis of revolutionary periods by discussing the French Revolution—necessary because it was, without question, a decisive turning point, which provided, as it were, a model for all revolutions that came after it, and unfair because it tends to overshadow other events, whether in France prior to 1789 and which were, sometimes, more radically revolutionary and popular, or, for example, in England and Germany. In spite of this, however, the French Revolution is a subject which must be squarely faced. We shall, of course, be running the risk of simply repeating facts which are common knowledge without contributing anything radically new, but this chapter is intended mainly as an introduction to those that follow. It is enough that the events of 1789 and the following years help us to understand many contemporary events.

The Prerevolutionary Social Context

The roots of the French Revolution lay, of course, in the economic and social structures of the old order, and it might be well to outline here the forces at work and the built-in contradictions of those structures.

Toward the end of the monarchy, in a pyramidal and sacral society in which rank was based on birth and the possession of land, an element of contradiction began to take shape. Control of commercial and industrial economy lay in the hands of a growing class, the bourgeoisie, whose wealth was negotiable and who had considerable intellectual influence. Traditional social structures no longer adequately expressed the economic and social forces of society. The Revolution, when it came, wiped out this contradiction by bringing bourgeois power to the fore.

Conditions in the different strata of society before 1789. The *bourgeoisie*, as we have said, held the reins of economic power and

27

were in control of both the most recent and the most promising areas of economic development. Theirs was the world of trade and finance. It has also been estimated that they owned approximately one-fifth of the land and were the prime movers in the transformation of agricultural methods of production. They were actively involved in all sectors of production, and it was inevitable that their influence should be considerable in the social order. They were also in a position to develop political ambitions and to envisage a new society.[1]

The *urban plebeian classes* did not yet constitute a proletariat. Most workers and guildsmen lived in close association with the craftsmen and little distinction was made between them. In 1793 workers, guildsmen, and craftsmen, as well as the poorer intellectuals, became the spearhead of the revolutionary movement, the *sans culottes*. Unemployment was widespread and the lower classes lived in conditions of extreme hardship.

The only unifying factor which bound the *peasants* into a class was their antagonism to the feudal system which weighed on them, maintaining them in conditions of abject poverty. It is true that there were a few prosperous peasant farmers, but there was also an immense rural proletariat whose only capital was their physical capacity to work. Many factors had contributed to the proletarianization of the lower strata of the peasant world, among them primitive agricultural methods, heavy taxes, the hazards attendant on every harvest, and the fluctuating prices of cereal crops. It was the peasants who bore the brunt of taxes imposed by the crown and by the ecclesiastical authorities. The rural community with roots in the distant past, was a sort of local democracy whose main function was the collective exploitation of commonly owned lands and the assessment of dues for the use of forests and fields. Time and time again in the course of their existence, these communities had had to do battle for economic survival and administrative autonomy. In fact, the history of the monarchy is studded with peasant revolts. But toward the end of the old order a series of administrative measures set stringent limits on the rights of the communities in such a way as to promote the interests of the wealthy farmers. This was the first step in the disintegration of the rural communities and in the transition from a subsistence to a capitalist economy.

The *aristocracy* was in a state of complete decadence. The power of the monarchy had both ruined it financially and imposed a political stranglehold on it. Since it was considered demeaning for an aristocrat to become involved in productive tasks, it was sinking, as a class, into poverty. The nobles at court ruined themselves trying to keep up appearances, while those in the provinces simply vegetated on their vast, underexploited lands. Unless they could stave off bankruptcy by obtaining an ecclesiastical benefice or a military commission from the king, their only hope of survival lay in extorting from the peasantry every last penny to which they were entitled.

The *Church* was an ideological as well as an economic force, thanks to its property, the taxes it collected, and the gifts it made to the crown. The clergy constituted an "order" within the nation, ranking even higher than those of noble birth. But the Church also constituted an administrative power through its general agents, its diocesan courts and officials, and through the virtual monopoly it enjoyed in the fields of education, social assistance, and civil records.

As a "subsystem," the Church, like the other classes, experienced a good deal of internal strife. A "high clergy," composed of the bishops and curial officials, were possessed of an aristocratic turn of mind and were recruited exclusively from the nobility. There was not one bishop in 1789 who was not of noble birth. The "lower clergy," on the other hand, were the "ecclesiastical commoners," often living in straitened material circumstances and with many grievances against the high clergy. Most of the religious orders were also in a state of moral decay. It was said of them that, "Here, the passions hold sway."[2]

Fundamentally, the Church was closely linked to the aristocracy for many of whom ecclesiastical orders provided a living. It was not uncommon to find bishops and abbots spending more time at court than in their episcopal sees or their abbeys.[3] They lavished more care on their administration of the provinces than on that of the sacraments!

In the cities, and even in the country areas, many of the clergy were highly educated men, but profoundly uninterested in theology. In fact, what was produced in the way of theology during this period was extraordinarily futile. The bookshelves of the clergy, however, were well furnished with the works of the Philosophers, and the *Encyclopedia* was very popular. When the lower clergy began to use theology in support of the rights they claimed from the hierarchy, they restored its full value to the "second order" and opened the door to the later developments, when the Church was reformed by the Constituent Assembly. The chapters of the Tours and Auxerre dioceses, which were in conflict with their bishops, declared: "It is we who constitute the presbyterium. . . . It is we who make up the collectivity of the diocesan clergy, the power of the keys is, essentially and fundamentally, ours together."[4] These were theological refrains which must have grated on the ears of the hierarchy of those days, but they were soon to be put to good use in the Civil Constitution of the Clergy.

The clergy reflected rather faithfully the tensions rife in society in general. The aristocratic and extremely wealthy hierarchy on one end of the scale was opposed by the lower clergy, who were poor and of common stock. Between the two was a kind of "bourgeoisie" made up of the diocesan chapters and the pastors of wealthy parishes. "The clergy is not an order, it is a body." So wrote Sieyès a little later. But the Revolution was to shatter all appearances of unity.

The church in the midst of institutional crisis, ideologies, and class conflict. With Louis XIV, the power of the monarchy had reached unprecedented heights and, with his death, died the principle of cohesion. "Despotism is rife but there is no despot." National unity was an illusion which existed only in the form of a centralized power system. At this time Mirabeau described France as an "unconstituted aggregate of disunited peoples." The administration was a jigsaw puzzle of intransigent autonomous entities. Over this situation of latent anarchy still hung the ideology of absolute power. The king, God's representative, was "King of France and Navarre by the grace of God." The royal anointing conferred a divine seal upon him, and his oath was to the Church and to his people. At his anointing the bishop pronounced the words: "Be thou blessed and made king in this kingdom which God has given you to rule." And on the day following his coronation it was the custom for the king to lay hands on the sick with the words, "The king touches you; may God heal you. . . ."

The theory of absolute power was eloquently proclaimed in the course of a royal session of the Parliament of Paris in 1776. In the name of the king, one of the counselors read the following statement: "Sovereign power, whose specific characteristic is the spirit of counsel, justice and reason, resides in my person . . . all public order derives from me and the rights and interests of the nation, of which some have the temerity to make a body separate from the Monarch, are necessarily one with mine and rest exclusively in my hands."

The Church considered itself the guarantor, defender, and legitimation of the concept of power as well as of the whole social order. Bossuet was to become the theoretician of this symbiosis. "The royal throne is not simply the throne of a man but also the throne of God," he declared. "The Prince sees farther and from a higher viewpoint. We have to believe that he sees more clearly and we must obey without reluctance, for reluctance is a disposition for sedition." In his *La politique tirée des propres paroles de l'Ecriture Sainte,* Bossuet became the theologian of the monarchy: "O kings, exercise your power boldly, for it is divine and salutary for the human race."[5]

The noted preacher Masillon was not to be outdone by Bossuet in defending the power of the mighty in God's name: "It is not by chance that you were born to might and power. From the beginning of time God has destined you for this temporal glory and he has placed on you the seal of his own power, setting you apart from the masses by the glory of your titles and human distinctions."[6]

By then, however, the royal power had, in fact, already been obliged to give up some of its independence. When it became necessary to introduce some fiscal reforms and put the finances of the country in order, the crown had to reckon with the combined forces of the aristocracy and the bourgeoisie.[7] It was the combined

opposition of these two mutually antagonistic forces which opened
the floodgates of revolution. Critics of absolute power began to
declare themselves. Whether aristocrats like Fénelon (he, too, a
bishop and theologian), or liberals like Locke, or aristocratic and
liberal at once, like Montesquieu, their common purpose was to
limit the absolute power of the monarchy either by strengthening
the intermediate structures or by dividing the center of power.

Although the nobility was hostile to the central power of the
king, it was also opposed to any kind of reform which might affect
its own privileged position. As a class, it was still the mainspring of
the social system, supplying the cadres for the army, the judiciary,
and the clergy, and it had every intention of retaining this position.
This was the context in which social antagonisms were going to
build up.

In 1776 the Parliament of Paris declared:

> A system which, in the guise of humaneness and the desire to do good,
> attempts in a well-ordered monarchy to establish equality of duties and elimi-
> nate necessary distinctions, would before long bring about disorder, the inevita-
> ble sequel to absolute equality, and would cause society to be demolished. The
> nobleman dedicates his rank to the defense of the state and assists the sovereign
> with his advice. The lowest class in the nation, which is not in a position to offer
> such distinguished services to the state, fulfils its obligations by paying taxes,
> and by its industry and manual labor.

The nobility had good reason to be so much on the defensive,
for they were the target of bitter attacks by both the bourgeoisie
and the landed gentry. The plays left by Beaumarchais are unri-
valled for the picture they reveal of bourgeois grievances against
the nobility. "Because you are a powerful Lord, you think you are
a great genius! What have you ever done to earn your good
fortune? You took the trouble to be born and that is all. . . ."[8] The
aristocracy, counterrevolutionary by birth as it were, won a part of
the Church to its side when the Church was, or believed itself to
be, endangered by the new regime.

The urban lower classes, although closely allied with the revolutionary bourgeoisie, became estranged from them in the course of
the revolutionary process. They were united in their opposition to
the aristocracy, but their attitude toward the successive factions of
the bourgeoisie which grasped the reins of government varied. The
masses felt that the simplest way to solve the problem of shortages

and the high cost of living was to establish controls, whereas the bourgeoisie clung to individual free enterprise. This conflict explains some of the vicissitudes of the Revolution and, in particular, the abortive attempt at establishing the "democracy" in the year II. The role of the masses in the campaign of de-Christianization of the period remains obscure. Was it really a question of the people following a rationally antireligious tendency of their own or was it not, rather, another instance of the way in which they acted as the pawns of the bourgeoisie, who were only too happy to see them sidetracked in this way?

The importance of the peasants in the Revolution should not be underestimated. The basic reason for their involvement was the question of feudal rights. The "great fear" of peasant revolts weighed heavily in the decision taken on the night of August 4, 1789, and the sudden change of ownership of national and ecclesiastical properties bound the peasants who acquired land irrevocably to the new regime.

However, it was the bourgeois ideology and its "project" for society which constituted the true nub of the Revolution. Two central themes, which were at the roots of the latent conflict with religious ideology, illustrate this.

Descartes, of course, was the man who had triggered the whole process when he broke with tradition: "It is possible to arrive at knowledge that can be very useful to life. . . instead of the speculative philosophy which is taught in the schools. . . . Knowing the power and the working of the bodies all around us. . . . We can also use them in every way for which they are suitable, and thus make ourselves masters and possessors of nature."[9]

The mastery of nature through the power of reason entails a break with tradition and with the principle of authority, for the past never repeats itself, but can be used as a steppingstone for progress. "Let us put a limit to our respect for the Ancients," says Pascal. "We can discover things that they could not perceive. . . . The endless succession of men who have lived in the course of the centuries must be considered as one man who lives forever and is continually learning."[10]

It was Descartes who liberated men's critical faculties. For two hundred years all philosophical thought had to take a stand for or against him. His influence was tremendous. In one way Bossuet was perfectly correct when he foresaw "preparations being made for a great battle against the Church, and it goes by the name of Cartesian philosophy."[11] And yet, in his *Discours*, Descartes was at pains to assert his respect for the established order and for religion. But alongside him there arose a bourgeoisie which, as opposed to the epicurean and mystical attitude of the aristocracy, saw man as owner and overlord of the goods of this world, an attitude which was in radical contradiction to the authoritarian and ascetic ideals of both Church and State.

"Once man dares to think," declares D'Holbach, "the dominion of the priest is destroyed."[12] Man's relationship to the world changes as his relationship to the sacral order changes. The bourgeoisie found that a religious ideology lay as an obstacle in the path of its plan to dominate nature and society, and this ideology was proposed and propagated by the ruling class, the aristocracy. It had to be opposed, therefore, on both scores: as an element in a system that must be transformed and as an obstacle to the legitimation of the new undertaking. The aristocracy, excluded from economic influence, had turned religion into a denial of the world and a justification of its own position of supremacy, a legitimation for the whole existing social order. The new class rising to power attacked the Church's role as guarantor of the status quo and religion as being alien to its vision of the world and incapable of finding any meaning in the world's values.

But what was the new system offered by the Enlightenment? What was its political plan? In reality it was nothing more than an "enlightened absolutism." No doubt it was an improvement on the absolutism of the old order in that it had a keener appreciation of individual man as an essence worthy of respect, and equality before the law was recognized as basic for the development of authority. It was an absolutism that was no longer tied to a religion. On the contrary, it was the enemy of positive religions and the friend of the freedom of belief.

In the philosophy of the Enlightenment, therefore, absolute power is called into question, but in its political conception power is still seen as the personal attribute of a prince. However, a prince is seen as taking his place at the head of a state which will proceed to eliminate the feudal system. With serene trust in the progress of humanity, the state is envisaged as the powerful servant of the natural order and, with the Constituent Assembly, the notion is applied to ecclesiastical reform even before the famous case of Josephism and the Christian state.

On the economic level the ideas of the Enlightenment were best expressed by the Physiocrats, Quesnay and Turgot. Since for these scholars, the best form of government is the one which most clearly corresponds to the natural and essential order of political societies, a new order based on the physical laws which govern society must be inaugurated.

But what of the arguments of the reformers when it came to attacking religion and the Church? Pierre Bayle (1674-1706) maintained that since everything human is subject to change, he saw no good reason why religion should not change also. Could one not conceive that beyond the religious moral law there existed a higher moral law based on psychology—the moral law of the "virtuous man," which knows neither obligations nor sanctions?

Bayle was a pioneer of many nineteenth- and twentieth-century secularist ideas about ethics, but he was by no means ahead of his times as far as his political ideas were concerned. His ideal was a strong government to maintain order. As he said, "France has such genius that the very worst fate that could befall her would be to live under a weak and feeble government." As a group, the Philosophers of the eighteenth century advanced these antireligious ideas while holding to political ideas which by no stretch of the imagination could be called revolutionary.

The fact that Voltaire had a keen feeling for all that is human and that he was in favor of freedom to speak and write as one pleased, never made him question the political system. He got along very well with unequal conditions and even expressed the hope that religion would serve to keep the masses (ingenuous enough to believe in it) in a peaceable and conservative frame of mind. His antireligious themes and his diatribes against providentialism (e.g., *Candide*) or fanaticism were aimed at established religion only insofar as it was the guarantor of a social order which did not correspond to his own aspirations or to those of his class.

It seems quite possible, in fact, that behind the concerted attack on religion there may well have been the secret wish to exploit or change it in order to control it and make it serve the rise to power of this new class.

In the last analysis, "the politics of the Philosophers can be summed up as the intention of putting the omnipotence of the state at the service of infallible reason, of making Reason the new reason of state."[13] The gerrymandering that Sorel condemns may very well have occurred also in what concerned the Church and religion.

The Church on the eve of battle: preliminary skirmishes with the revolutionary movement. An analysis of the complaints lodged by the clergy before the Constituent Assembly affords a good indication of the power of the lower clergy in this body. Their influence had already made itself felt in the regional preparatory assemblies. This is readily explained by the method of representation: Every pastor of a parish was seated, whereas chapters had only one representative for every ten members, and all the religious orders as well as the bishops had only one representative. The high clergy protested this invasion by the lower clergy, and the Paris chapter declared: "The Church is based on obedience to its first pastors and is in danger of being wiped out by despotic domination."[14]

After meetings which were often riotous and during the course of which the internal conflicts of the clergy were exposed for all to see, some form of compromise was reached with regard to the complaints registered. It was unanimously agreed that the reformation of the French Church should be effected, not by the pope but by the king. It was also unanimously agreed that the rights of religion should be protected by censorship, "religious police" in charge of public morals, the obligation to assist at Sunday Mass, etc. However, the pastors manifested their intention to supervise episcopal nominations and to form an association for the defense of their own interests. As far as the needs of society at large were concerned, the hope was expressed that the power of the crown would be restricted, but no mention was made either of freedom of conscience or of the privileges of the aristocracy.

On many points the clergy showed itself to be in agreement with the urban bourgeoisie, the so-called Third Estate. In particular, they had a common concern for the rights of religion and a deep distrust of the high clergy.

When Parliament opened, the clergy had 296 representatives, of whom 47 were bishops, 23 abbots and vicars-general, 12 canons, and 208 pastors. From the very beginning, with the verification of voting rights, it became clear that the interests of the clergy, led by the pastors, were in accord with those of the Third Estate. The representatives of the Third Estate urged the clergy to join forces with them and little by little they received a favorable response. Even some of the prelates, such as the archbishop of Bordeaux, gave their support to the trend. And when some of those who opposed it voiced their objections, a pastor replied: "This Chamber is not a Council. Parliament does not deal with religion. The clergy will never suffice to reform the clergy and regenerate the nation. What is needed for such a great task? Bishops? No. Vicars-general? No. Canons? No. Pastors? Again, no. What then? Citizens, nothing but citizens!"[15]

Another priest spoke in the same vein and even more forthrightly to the bishops: ". . . in this place we dare to say that we are your equals; we are citizens as you are; we are representatives of this nation as you are; your rights are no greater than ours and if our opinion is contrary to yours this does not mean that we are declaring a rebellion."

Finally the king himself begged the clergy to join with the Third Estate, and a contemporary observer declared: "The pastors are praised on all sides. They are being told that they have saved France and I am beginning to believe it myself." It is certainly true that it was they who set things in motion. The representatives of the clergy ceased to be distinguishable as such and became a part of the general picture; they ceased to be an "order." And in contributing to the destruction of an absolute monarchy, thus removing the Church from royal control, they put it in the hands of others: the increasingly powerful bourgeoisie.

On the night of August 4, 1789, under the threat of the "great fear" of peasant revolts and the capture of the Bastille, the clergy, together with the other representatives, abolished its own privileges. And this was not all: Talleyrand, at that time bishop of Autun, proposed that a "transaction be effected with the property of the clergy," putting it at the disposition of the nation in order to balance the national budget. In his mind the transaction would be quite compatible with a "very strict respect for the right of property" and with the spirit of canon law. From then on the nation would simply have to provide for the needs of the clergy.

This suggestion provoked very lively debate and there was tenacious resistance from the clergy. It is interesting to note who finally clinched the argument and the spirit that prevailed in the final agreement. It was Le Chapelier (who shortly after was to introduce a law against corporations which opened the door to free enterprise) who declared: "If the clergy continues to own property, they will continue to constitute an order within the nation." Parliament was impressed by this argument. The clergy had ceased to be a political entity and it was not fitting that it should continue to be a class of property owners. In accordance with its ideology, Parliament directed the state to promote and enforce, even in the ranks of the clergy, the right to individual property of private citizens as equals before the law.

There was a rush to acquire property, and pastors, chapters, and religious communities were no less avid than the landed bourgeoisie to buy houses and presbyteries. This did not, however, prevent them from opposing the Civil Constitution of the Clergy shortly after. In the west of France the future leaders of the Royal Catholic Army of Vendée seized the opportunity to round out their estates. And later many of those who acquired ecclesiastical properties supported the regime which had made landowners of them and opposed the democratic *sans culottes* as vigorously as they opposed all attempts at a restoration.

The Church in Conflict with the Revolution

The Civil Constitution of the Clergy. As we have seen, the clergy looked to the king to reform the Church, and not to the pope.

However, Parliament, which was dominated by the Third Estate, had a tendency to take over from the king all the reforms that needed to be carried out, including the reform of the Church. This is all the more comprehensible if one bears in mind that the realms of religious and political affairs were very closely associated under the old regime. A reform in the Church followed logically from a reform in the political order, and if any additional reason were necessary, the sale of ecclesiastical property stimulated the representatives' interest in the Church. The state, therefore, undertook to provide for the ministers of religion.

It is interesting to note that the prevailing mood of this reform does not seem to have been anticlerical. As we have already seen, the majority of the representatives, even the Voltairians, were certainly not anxious to destroy "religion." On the contrary, the influence exerted by the philosophers, combined with the residual influence of Gallicanism, prepared the way for the Church to be considered a matter for the state to deal with as an element in the new society that was being built.

On July 12, 1790, Parliament enacted the law of the Civil Constitution of the Clergy. The main clauses dealt with the number and size of dioceses. Henceforward their boundaries were to coincide with the new administrative divisions of the country, one to each department, and this implied a considerable reduction in numbers. More important was the stipulation that the bishops were to be elected like other civil servants by the electorate of the department, and the pastors of parishes were to be chosen in the same way, on the district level. The number of parishes, therefore, was also reduced and the notion of ecclesiastical "benefice" became more wholesome. A minister entrusted with the care of souls was recognized as having a responsibility for which he should receive suitable payment.

This constitution involved a fundamental change in the relationship between the French Church and the Holy See, particularly by reason of the change introduced in the method of choosing the bishops. It reinforced the old Gallican and presbyterian tendencies and created a truly national church. Pastors of parishes became civil servants and in the places assigned to them contributed to the reshaping of society. They were obliged, for instance, to read the decrees of the Sovereign Assembly from the pulpits of their churches. As natural leaders and elders in the community, they lent their full support to the new system.

Many objections were voiced, nevertheless, among the clergy, but it is difficult to see in them anything but reluctance on the part of the hierarchy to allow some of their authority over the low clergy to be wrested from them. Boisgelin, archbishop of Aix, reminded the Assembly of the "rights and sacred principles of ecclesiastical authority," but not a word did he utter about relations with the Holy See. The long-standing Gallican reaction of many of the bishops faced him with a conflict of interests; his response was to propose a national council to be constituted exclusively by bishops in order to regain control of the emancipated, revolutionary clergy.

It was the fear of precisely such authoritarian reaction on the part of the bishops that persuaded the Constituent Assembly to seek papal ratification of the Civil Constitution of the Clergy. The episcopacy, confident of Rome's support, made the same move in its *Exposé des Principes.* Cardinal de Bernis, who was instructed to put the matter before the pope, was firmly on the side of the bishops and certainly did not plead the cause of the Civil Constitution. But Pius VI gave no official response for eight months, and during this time unofficial expressions of opinion abounded, all of them clearly unfavorable. The pope's ties with the old regime, the fact that he had temporal power of his own, his recently expressed hostility to the Declaration of the Rights of Man as well as Spanish influence at the Vatican, all contributed to making any understanding on the question extremely difficult. When, in 1798, the pope finally condemned the Civil Constitution of the Clergy, the gulf between the hierarchy and the great mass of the clergy, and even more between the Church and the Revolution, was made wider and the Church was literally cut in two.

Only 7 bishops out of 160 took the oath of consent to the Constitution before the Assembly. Many went into exile. The ranks of the parish priests were split, but a fairly substantial proportion took the oath. A few striking personalities among them, won over by the ideas of the Enlightenment, made their influence felt among their disoriented and confused brethren who clustered around them. The precise number of "juror" priests is difficult to determine, but it must have been about 50 percent or more. In the Île-de-France the proportion was as high as 90 to 95 percent, whereas in more isolated regions such as the Massif Central or the Northwest, the majority remained loyal to the hierarchy.

Two outstanding factors influenced the clergy's decision. The first was fidelity to the new ideals which led them to unite with the Third Estate. The second was simply the voice of ambition: Positions hitherto open only to the aristocracy now became accessible to the low clergy, and out of 80 bishops elected according to the Constitution, 55 were pastors.

To many of the faithful, the true stakes in this dispute remained obscure. Their principal concern was to have a pastor to continue the service of worship and the traditional ceremonies. Those who were classed as "nonjuring" were essentially in rebellion against the Revolution. In fact some of the prelates admitted that it was simply their aristocratic prejudices which dictated their choice. As the bishop of Narbonne is reported to have said to La Fayette: "We have conducted ourselves like true gentlemen; for most of us one cannot truthfully say that it was for religious reasons."[15] And one can discern, behind the split between the "jurors" and the "nonjuring," another, much deeper split dividing Roman Catholic and counterrevolutionary tendencies on the one hand from constitutional and patriotic tendencies on the other. It was an instance in which the internal, social conflicts, both of the clergy and of society, were projected onto the ecclesiastical institution.

It must be admitted, however, that the Constitution never really worked. Parliament's point of view did not prevail, and it was obliged to try to maintain two churches in existence simultaneously. But from this time on, the question of the separation of Church and State had been posed. The solution, however, did not see the light of day for a long time. It was still far beyond the powers of imagination of the representatives. What they wanted was the clergy and the Church as a whole to serve the cause of "progress." For the population at large, also, the separation of

Church and State at this juncture would have been seen as an attack on religion.

In the long run this crucial period involved the Church even more deeply in the revolutionary process. Many of the faithful in the lower classes, fearing for their eternal salvation, refused to abandon the "good" priests, thereby putting themselves in the counterrevolutionary camp. It was in this context that the anticlerical and antireligious phase of the Revolution was born.

The Jacobins, intending to give support to the "jurors," launched an attack against Roman Catholicism which was supposed to nip in the bud any attempt to revive the old regime, by accusing the Church of fanaticism. *La feuille villageoise*, a revolutionary newspaper, wrote: "We have been accused of showing intolerance toward papism. We have been accused of not always sparing the immortal tree of Faith. But if one looks closely at this inviolable tree, he sees that fanaticism is so closely entwined in all its branches that one cannot strike at one without seeming to strike at the other."[16] There is no question about what was happening: By changing the Church the Constituent Assembly (mainly composed of bourgeois members) was changing an element in society which obstructed the bourgeois rise to power.

At the end of 1790 the Revolution was at grips with the aristocracy and the nonjuring priests on the right and a popular upsurge on the left, growing out of the clubs which outspokenly condemned the birth of a new form of feudalism. With the development of this popular movement the Revolution began, between 1792 and 1795, to be more decisively committed to a struggle against the aristocracy and to take a decidedly anticlerical turn. But what was the antireligious content of this trend?

Revolution, de-Christianization, and anticlericalism. The French Revolution has a reputation for having been violently anticlerical, principally between 1793 and 1795, but also during the Directory and until the advent of Napoleon Bonaparte. It is difficult to be sure that the meaning of this confrontation, the most bitter the French Church had ever known, has really been understood. In order to clarify the meaning, we shall first attempt an historical overview of the events in the hope that they will throw some light on the underlying logic that inspired them. A fuller sociological analysis of the whole revolutionary period will be needed before we can advance any hypothesis concerning the significance of these facts.

The foregoing analysis of the basic premises of the Revolution has shown the ties, whether explicit or implicit, between the non-juring priests and the counterrevolutionary forces and, in particular, the aristocracy. After the dissolution of the Constituent Assembly, events led even the "juror" priests and the constitutional Church to stand back somewhat from the Revolution, thus manifesting their attachment to order and the Church's status in the old regime.

Theoretically, with the end of the monarchy and the abolition of the Constitution of 1791, the constitutional Church ceased to exist officially, but the purpose of the bourgeois elite continued to be pursued, and the government, unwilling to alienate the great numbers of people who were staunchly attached to religion, continued to support the clergy while exercising strict control and seeking to exclude from its ranks all "nonpatriots."

New measures were taken in August, 1792, however, to confiscate whatever property the Church still possessed. The gold of the sacred vessels from the churches was very useful to the mint and the copper from their bells was invaluable for making guns. The new laws also broke the Church's monopoly in the field of civil records. This was a perfectly legitimate move in view of the prevailing disorder and the fact that many priests were no longer in their original parishes; but it also made it possible henceforth for the state to fix the impediments to marriage and, consequently, to authorize (and later, enforce) the marriage of priests and of those who had been divorced.

This development proved decisive for the constitutional Church: It was obliged to choose between loyalty to a new regime and its traditional institutional and theological position. The alternative was the loss of its own identity and a blending into the state, or reneging on its alliance with the Revolution and reverting to an attitude of opposition. The dilemma is typical of that which faces every church in which the institutional dimension has been allowed to predominate.

On the question of divorce, for instance, churchmen were divided. Some invoked the divine law by which marriage was indissoluble, while others maintained that the new legislation respected the consciences of both Catholics (who were not put under any obligation by it) and non-Catholics (whose freedom was thus recognized). The same lack of unity was evidenced over the question of marriage for priests. There were those who clung intransigently to the old law, while others reminded them that the rule of celibacy was a positive law of the Church which could be ignored by the state and even revoked by the Church itself.[17]

Faced with the Church's failure to reach a decision, the government's attitude became more intransigent, and instead of offering a choice, it very soon imposed its own decision: All those who refused to abide by the new legislation were to be deported. The Church was again divided in itself and an object of suspicion, and before long it came under open attack. For the time being, the Convention, swayed by personalities such as Danton, maintained a cautious attitude:

> France is being turned inside out by the precipitous application of philosophical principles which are very dear to me but for which the people are not ready. When the *officier de morale* has brought enlightenment into the people's cottages over a long period of time, then will be the time to speak to them of ethics and philosophy. But until then it is a crime against the nation to attempt to deprive the people of these men who can still offer them consolation.

So spoke Danton, and the fact that Robespierre shared this opinion is eloquent testimony to the true intentions of the government and to its relation with the lower classes.

Even those who were staunchly anticlerical could not imagine the state without a church or the people without religion. On the first anniversary of the taking of the Bastille, the Celebration of the Federation took place. It was the first official symbolic expression of the drama that was being enacted in the social order, and the clergy took part in the "religious" rites. But by August 10, 1793, the Celebration of Unity and Indivisibility took place without their collaboration. A cult of the "martyrs of freedom" was now beginning to develop and the assassination of Marat gave it added impetus. In the west of the country the people even venerated the "saints" of the Revolution. Pilgrimages were made to their tombs and it was claimed that they performed miracles.[18]

At the same time some revolutionary militants expressed their intention of "de-Christianizing" society and a new calendar was established in which the heroes of the Revolution replaced the saints. Everyday life was thus secularized according to the intention, at least, of the authors of this plan, one of whom was M. J. Chénier, who reported to the Assembly:

> Free from the prejudice and worthy of ruling the French nation, you will know how to build on the ruins of the superstitions that have been dethroned, the one, universal religion which has neither secrets nor mysteries, whose only dogma is equality, whose laws are its orators, whose magistrates are the pontiffs and which allows this immense family to burn incense before no other altar than that of the fatherland, Mother and God of us all.

Is this secularization or is it the first sign of a new religion? This is a question we shall try to answer during the course of our analysis.

At first, the campaign to de-Christianize the country was virulent only in the provinces and even this was almost exclusively the work of the ex-Oratorian, Fouché. His mission was to gain control of the provinces which had risen against the central government, and this required that the priests be very closely watched, for they were suspected of fomenting the counterrevolutionary revolt. Fouché went about his task by denouncing religious sophism from the pulpit of Nevers Cathedral, by obliging priests to marry (or, alternatively, to adopt a child or take care of an old person), and by ordering the destruction of all statues and religious objects.

From the provinces the movement reached the capital where the extremists were in power. On November 10, 1793, the Cathedral of Notre Dame in Paris was the scene of a "religious" Celebration of Freedom, and the sanctuary was "consecrated" to Reason. Before the month had ended, Catholic worship had been forbidden in all the churches of Paris.

Historians tell us that the cult of the Martyrs of Liberty was a movement springing spontaneously from the masses, replacing the Catholic religion, which was forbidden at the time. The government, however, remained deeply suspicious of this cult, whether from reluctance to consecrate the leaders who had preceded them or because they distrusted the popular agitation, it is hard to say.

Both the cult of the martyrs and the campaign of de-Christianization, however, were brought to a halt by the same gesture. Robespierre emphasized the danger of undue pressure on those who were still hesitant and warned of the advent of a new fanaticism: "The man who prevents someone from saying Mass is just as fanatical as he who says it."[19] Robespierre was doctrinaire and he detested both the Church and the clergy, but he was a Voltairian who believed in God and he was politically opposed to the extremists. He believed that the urban and rural masses were not yet ready for de-Christianization and he was anxious to ensure the stability of the government.

Freedom of religion was soon the object of yet another declaration, and little by little it was reestablished in practice, in spite of some ups and downs. The calm that ensued was a sure sign that it had been a wise move; the government had regained control of the country.

After Robespierre, the Thermidorian reaction was a sign of the triumph of the bourgeoisie, now the dominant class, imposing its own ideology and its own power. The bourgeoisie had been skeptical and anticlerical long before this, but their opposition to the Church had been principally on the intellectual level and they were careful to keep up appearances.

On May 30, 1795, the churches were opened again on condition that the clergy take an oath of loyalty to the Republic. Priests who were loyal to Rome hesitated to do this, although many observed that the gesture was no more than a ratification of the civil laws and a promise not to disrupt the social order. Nevertheless many remained bitterly opposed. Once again, then, on the eve of the Directory, the Church found itself rent in two and the government, threatened by forces outside the country, was again obliged to take firmer measures of domestic control and imposed new limitations on religious freedom.

We should also perhaps note the appearance, between 1798 and 1799, of a new religion, which appeared as a kind of shadow of the government. It was known as Theophilanthropy, a natural religion based on the existence of God, the immortality of the soul, tolerance, and solidarity. Its liturgy was a syncretic mixture of Socrates, the Gospel, and Zoroaster. The government, for its own part, also established a "religious" feast day, the "décadi," which was to replace Sunday, and on which day civil marriages and "baptisms" were to be performed.

Before going on to discuss these events from the viewpoint of ideology, I would like to synthesize the period between 1789 and the Concordat of 1801.

The Revolution attempted, at first, to replace a state established by "divine right" with a secular state, entirely separate from the Church. The status of Catholicism was changed; instead of being the official state religion, it was simply a religion that was favored by the state. The situation evolved all the more rapidly as a result of the schism caused by the Civil Constitution of the Clergy. Neither the nonjuring nor the juror priests were capable of recognizing the true nature of the sociopolitical metamorphosis that was taking place in the country, and their distrust and hostility toward the new regime provoked a reciprocal antagonism. The breach between Church and State was already a fact during the civil war and the campaign of de-Christianization, long before it was consummated by decree in February, 1795, when the state became more openly and aggressively secular.

The Revolution left the Church divided, disorganized, and hostile to the government. The Concordat, by which religion was restored to a position of honor, was both cause and effect of a need for social stability. Bonaparte saw religion precisely as the means for compelling social compliance and the Church served him by upholding his authority. The Church during the Consulate and the Empire was not a national church. Once again, it served to legitimate the regime almost as wholeheartedly as it had legitimated the monarchy.

Legitimation of the new power system. At the beginning and again at the end of the period we have just studied, the Church lived in peace, accommodating itself to the privileges of one class and serving as legitimation for its authority. In the intervening period it was thrown into the maelstrom of the battle between conflicting interests from which the bourgeois state was to emerge. It was not an easy task to interpret this period.

According to A. Aulard,[20] the "de-Christianizers" were not theorists taking advantage of events in order to apply their own preconceived ideas. The state of war with exterior forces and within the country and stubborn resistance to the new mentality, led inevitably to an attack on Catholicism. In this view, the campaign of de-Christianization was simply expedient for national defense, for to attack religion was to attack the life force of the coalition of the enemies of the fatherland.

A. Mathiez,[21] on the contrary, believes that the conflict cannot be fully explained by political reasons of expediency. He sees it as a religious conflict between two rival conceptions: Catholicism and revolutionary patriotism. The revolutionary ideology, as a blueprint for the regeneration of society, conflicted with that of the Church, which is based on a mistrust of nature and an orientation toward an extraterrestrial beatitude. This would explain the violence of the collision, the holy fury against traditional religion. It would also explain the enthusiasm for a new religion, to propagate and express the mystique of a nation reborn.

According to Daniel Guérin,[22] the revolutionary religious gestures are both myths and hoaxes, and the antireligious campaigns were simply diversionary tactics designed to keep the masses happy by setting them on the priests. In the meantime, on the political level, the Revolution, which the *sans culottes* wanted to make even more radical and permanent, had time to gain a hold. However, the consequences of these campaigns were considerable: "By daring to attack the Church and the priests head on," the revolutionary extremists "released the masses from themselves" and contributed, for a long time to come, to the disappearance of religious prejudice among the masses.

Albert Soboul, on the other hand, believes that in spite of the scope of the political upheaval, the Revolution did not destroy traditional religion. On the contrary, it precipitated an evolution that led Catholicism to adopt more popular forms, at least for a time. When the crisis had blown over, those who had adhered to the new religions simply reverted to tradition. In support of his thesis, Soboul notes that in the rural areas the cult of the "saints" of the Revolution grafted itself quite naturally onto popular religious sentiment. The traditional cult simply opened its doors to new heroes or was replaced by the new cult. In the urban lower classes the new cult, with a symbolism very similar to that of Catholic liturgy, simply replaced the old liturgy which was forbidden at the time.

> The *sans culottes,* brought up on Catholic practices, understood salvation to have a temporal as well as an eternal meaning. The *ex-votos* in the churches are sufficient evidence of this. Probably no *ex-votos* were dedicated to the "friend of the people" (Marat), but in the popular mentality the same result could be obtained by invoking Marat, martyr for freedom, because he had given his life for the Revolution and therefore for the whole of humanity. One may presume that for many of those present the funeral ceremonies in honor of Marat, which more often than not took place in the churches, were like Masses for the repose of his soul.[23]

Soboul submits this as a hypothesis because, without witnesses or documents to support it, it would be difficult to be sure of this transposition of Catholic beliefs to the new ceremonies. On the other hand he has no hesitation in recognizing that although the government was obliged to accept this cult, it managed to use it for its own ends. It is also interesting to note that "the militants of lower middle-class or middle-class stock, who had a classical education, referred to the traditions of antiquity" in their ceremonies, whereas "the *sans culottes* borrowed the elements of their new religion from Catholicism." Similarly one is struck by learning that the majority of those present at the officially organized ceremonies were women and children. One cannot help wondering, in line with Daniel Guérin's thesis, whether there are not two different levels of meaning in this phenomenon—the one being the need of the masses to live their social experience on a symbolic level, the other being the manipulation and canalization of this need by the political authorities in such a way as to guide it into purely ideological channels which constituted no threat for the government. It is extremely difficult to arrive at any definite conclusion about this.

There are other questions, however, which are more relevant to our subject. For example, how can one account sociologically for the impact which the redistribution of the social classes had on a Christian population with very strong institutional bonds with the Church under the old regime? Did the years of revolution only accelerate the de-Christianization of France, or did they cause it? Is one justified in seeing the various revolutionary ceremonies as new sects by means of which an overinstitutionalized Church might have been reborn?

If we wish to find the answer, or even elements of an answer, to these questions, we must not separate the religious from the social conflict.

Admitting that popular religiosity survived all the campaigns to uproot Christianity, one must also admit that anticlericalism legitimated the seizure of power by the new ruling class. The religious events of the Revolution illustrate quite as clearly as the sociopolitical developments that it was an affair of the bourgeoisie. The masses were simply being used to put it into effect. Many of the "anti-Christian" measures reveal their bourgeois origin: The "revolutionary calendar," for example, which professed to be a secularization of everyday life, was a response to one of the principal demands of the industrial bourgeoisie: to reduce the number of holidays in the year. "Instead of fifty-two Sundays and an infinite number of other holidays which used to rob labor and industry of one third of each year, there will be fewer days for rest and laziness which will add considerably, little by little, to our wealth. . . ."[24]

The fact also that Reason was proclaimed the new divinity, when one bears in mind the ideology of the Enlightenment, was a transparent indication of the class origin of this new religion and its hidden function.

Underlying the turmoil of events, the religious policy of the Revolution can be discerned in the fact that the elite, permanently in power, was deeply imbued with the ideology of the Enlightenment and bourgeois irreligion, which ever since the seventeenth century had had a tendency to recognize only the natural moral law and which paved the way for economic liberalism. In Napoleon's conciliatory attitude one can see an extension of Robespierre's policy, which protected the future emperor. Robespierre saw the Supreme Being as "a great idea which protects the social order." Napoleon expressed himself very clearly when the time came: "In religion I do not see the mystery of the Incarnation, but the mystery of the social order. Religion links heaven with a notion of equality which prevents the rich from being massacred by the poor."

The emperor of the French people restored both the nobility and the ecclesiastical hierarchy. Even in their most distant campaigns the bourgeoisie had a use for religion. In one of the emperor's reports can be found this passage: "Religious will be very useful to me in Asia, Africa and America. . . . I shall send them to obtain information about the state of the country. Their robes protect them and serve to conceal political and commercial designs."

And so, under the Empire the goal of the anticlerical bourgeoisie was attained: Without any fundamental transformations being necessary, the structures of the Church which served the goals of their class so well were made over to the new system. As Napoleon put it, "My police, my prefects, my priests. . ." and the Church did not contradict him. The National Catechism of 1806 had this to say about the Fourth Commandment:

> Christians owe to all princes who rule them, and we owe particularly to Napoleon I our emperor, love, respect and obedience . . . and military service. . . . We also owe him our fervent prayers for his salvation and for the spiritual and temporal prosperity of the state. . . .
> Why? Firstly because God . . . has established him as our sovereign. To honor and serve our emperor, therefore, is to honor and serve God himself. Secondly because our Lord Jesus Christ . . . has taught us what we owe to our sovereign.
> Are there no special reasons? Yes. Because it is he whom God has raised up in the midst of troubled circumstances to restore public worship and the holy religion of our fathers . . . he has restored and preserved order in the land. . . he has become the Lord's Anointed through the consecration received from the Sovereign Pontiff, head of the universal Church.

By way of conclusion I would like to try to answer two questions: Why did the Church allow itself to be manipulated in this way? What caused the birth of nineteenth-century anticlericalism and what was its significance?

No satisfactory answer can be found to the first question without a scientific analysis of the process by which the institutionalization of a religion falsifies its original message and turns it into a political ideology. Symbols which constitute the language of religion are uprooted from their native soil, often through lack of a living hermeneutic tradition in constant touch with a changing culture, and become prey to appropriation by the civil power. Religion becomes an integral part of the system of legitimation of society, which, in turn, provides it with what Peter Berger calls a structure of reliability, i.e., a social basis.[25] The universalism of the Church, for instance, worked in favor of the Roman Empire when it could be lived and expressed in a context in which Christianity was no longer in perpetual conflict with society but was admitted by society and on the way to becoming institutionalized.

In the period under discussion a certain osmosis had already taken place between religion and the legitimation of the power system of the old order. The sociocultural evolution of the seventeenth and eighteenth centuries did nothing to change the interpretation of the content of religion: Not one theologian of any standing arose to confront the philosophers of the day. Ever since the time of Philip the Fair a parallel development can be clearly seen between the relations binding the French Church to the sociopolitical system and the Gallican tendencies which were, later, to facilitate the establishment of the bourgeois state. The ambition, also, to be a "perfect society" had led the Church to attach more value to its hierarchical aspects than to the fact that it was a "communion," with the result that all innovation and dissent from within had long been stifled. Ten years of revolution changed practically nothing in the expression which the institutional Church gave to its relations with society or to its understanding of its own structures. From our vantage point one might think that the Church would have seized the opportunity of the Revolution to introduce an element of contestation into its own structures and in society. But no doubt the necessary objective conditions were not present. The opening ceremonies of the *Etats Généraux* in 1789 and the thanksgiving mass for the establishment of the Concordat on April 18, 1802, were presided over by the same ecclesiastical dignitary, Archbishop Boisgelin. This continuity is a symbol worthy of a Graham Greene novel: In 1802 the Church found itself virtually in the same role as that it had assumed before 1789.

The paradox lies in the fact that, in spite of appearances, the divorce between the Church and the prevailing cultural system seems to have been complete. And this is perhaps the point of view from which one must judge the antireligious crisis and the birth of popular anticlericalism.

On various occasions sociopolitical change had sparked an experience among the popular masses which sought for religious expression, that is, which sought for expression through the only symbolic system available: that of Christianity. This type of popular expression was ill-received in official religious circles and found itself in opposition to the explicit or implicit coalition of Church and State. In the existing socioreligious system any contestation of the social order was also necessarily a contestation of the religious order and vice versa.[26]

It often happens that social groups deprived of all power and in an almost anomic situation become aware of their situation through myths and religious symbols. Engels analyzed this phenomenon in the *Peasants' War*, a struggle led by the theologian, Thomas Munzer.[27] And Brazil, South Africa, and Korea all offer similar examples.

In theory this agitation could have been assimilated by the Church, becoming a contestation of its own structures and a critique of its social function. But the Church was not ready for this and that extraordinary revolutionary newspaper, *Le Père Duchène,* reproached it for having betrayed the message of its founder, "Jesus, the honest *sans culotte*."

As for the bourgeois power structure, it had manipulated, sublimated, and all but repressed the utopia of the lower classes, while at the same time hastening to use the Church for the legitimation of its own social power and offering it in return a new structure of reliability. When the time came for a popular social consciousness and a more systematic social theory to develop, both were already affected by anticlericalism and, even more profoundly, by the struggle against religion.

CHAPTER THREE

The French Worker Movement in the Nineteenth Century

Strictly speaking, this chapter does not deal with a revolution, although many revolutionary episodes were scattered throughout the history of the European—and particularly the French—worker movement. It is impossible, however, within the context of this study, to ignore what took place in the working classes in the nineteenth century, for the workers were both the principal protagonists and the symbols of a series of key events in the metamorphosis of the contemporary social scene.

"The working classes were lost to the Church in the nineteenth century." This oft-repeated lament seems to express an intuitive perception of a more basic and far-reaching fact: While Europe was in the process of being industrialized, something foreign and even antagonistic to the Church was born, something the Church was unable to understand, just as it was unable to keep in step with the movement of history or to redefine its own nature and vocation within a changing society.

In this chapter I shall try to see beyond the intuitive perception and describe the facts and determine their causes. The facts belong to the social history of France and Western Europe, and chief among them is the new impetus in the development of the capitalist system, which found itself faced with a revolutionary worker movement. With this as the context we shall try to understand the circumstantial and structural reasons which led the Church to remain a stranger to the issues of the day and why, when it did speak or act to those issues, it was almost totally ineffectual.

The period we shall be studying runs from 1830 to 1914 and the context is mainly that of France, which means that we shall be starting with the newly established bourgeois regime and following the progress of the first two phases of the Industrial Revolution.

Our first task will be to situate the dominant social class in relation to the Church and to analyze the stand taken by the Church throughout the sociopolitical transformations of the period. Secondly we must look at the birth of the worker movement and particularly the ideological structures of the movement in relation to the Church and religion. And finally a study of the growth of "social Catholicism" will allow us to analyze in depth the development of Christian thought in this period.

The Bourgeoisie in Power; Its Relations with the Church and with Religion

A rapid look at the developments which brought the bourgeoisie to power toward the middle of the nineteenth century will be followed by an attempt to describe the dominant cultural system in that period of strife and change, and the bourgeois attitude toward religion.

Bourgeois power. "The reign of the bankers is just beginning . . ." was the whispered comment at court when Louis Philippe came to power in July, 1830.

When the Empire had been overthrown, the bourgeoisie had not been in favor of the Restoration, and thanks to the poll tax suffrage—by which only those who paid a certain sum in taxes had the right to vote—they had managed to keep control of the regime. It was they alone who had money, they alone who were represented. Even royalist Vendée was represented in Parliament by a bourgeois liberal. Charles X set everyone against him by clinging to the attitudes of the old regime; the aristocrats, returned from exile after the eclipse of Napoleon I, "had learned nothing and forgotten nothing," and the clerical ways of the regime were a direct affront to the anticlericalism of the Voltairian bourgeoisie.

The spark which ignited the 1830 Revolution was the provision in the July Ordinance depriving merchants of the vote by suppressing the license tax which had previously been counted as part of the poll tax. The lower middle class fought back and in doing so found an ally in the upper middle classes and many intellectuals, teachers, and journalists, who were discontented because of measures against the press. It was this uprising of the middle classes and intellectuals that finally brought the revolutionary undertaking of 1789 to its conclusion.

The endless vicissitudes of French political history in the nineteenth century can be seen in the context of the advent of an industrial civilization. Landowners and the aristocracy found themselves replaced by a middle class in control of industrial and commercial capital, and using the state for its own ends. The beginning of the twentieth century was to witness the full flowering of this new society. But since 1789 a tremendous reshuffling had been going on in the areas of property, rank, and social influence.

The Declaration of Rights in 1789 legitimated the working class by attaching great importance to the value of individual initiative, thereby laying the foundations of economic liberalism. Individuals were protected against the group and society was protected against pressure groups. The Le Chapelier Law (June 14, 1791) suppressed corporations; another law in 1803 proscribed all activity aimed at changing salaries or working conditions. The Napoleonic Code ratified the economic, social, and political victories of the bourgeoisie. The Charter of 1814, in effect, ratified the new order.

The metamorphosis in the social order was, of course, inseparable from that which took place in productive methods. The ascendancy of the bourgeoisie heralded the dawn of mechanical industrialization: When the hand tool was replaced by the machine, human energy was liberated, transforming production methods as well as living conditions. The need to concentrate industry in areas close to sources of energy led to massive migrations and changed the balance of land distribution as well as the distribution of the socioeconomic factors. But until about 1870, the narrow framework of industrial development (the family) and the protectionism it entailed, especially in France, slowed the pace of technical and social progress and maintained high costs of production and wretched living conditions for the workers. This first generation of the new working class experienced a lower standard of living, with mean wages and intolerable working conditions.

Developments on the economic level were accompanied by a new political and social strategy. Liberalism, the political principle of the bourgeois class, taught that the public interest is the fruit of private interest. The social sector does not have to be organized, it must simply be studied as an entity. An understanding of the laws governing its development makes it possible to direct it more profitably. Crises in the social order were thought to be inevitable and dependent on laws that were quasi-providential.

The ruling classes were progressive in the sense that they had by their very nature the responsibility to promote growth. And finally free competition came into play in three different ways: On the money market the guiding principle was to place money where it would be most productive; in the commodity market the principle was to create consumers; and in the labor market productive power had already acquired negotiable value. As the English Prime Minister Pitt was quoted as saying: "If wages are too high, hire women and children." The nobility under the old regime had oppressed the rural proletariat; the bourgeoisie exploited what was to become the urban proletariat.

With the industrial era the history of France became, irrevocably, the history of its cities. The historic figures of the ruling bourgeois class were the bankers, merchants, and industrial magnates, and also professors; the reign of money went hand in hand with the reign of ideology.

The bourgeois cultural system. A circular from the minister of education to schoolmasters in 1833 gives an eloquent idea of the maxims they were supposed to inculcate into the minds of the young. "Faith in Providence, the sacredness of duty, submission to paternal authority, the respect due to the law and to the prince, these are the sentiments that the teacher will endeavor to cultivate."[1]

In the bourgeois regime, as in antiquity, the foundation of society was "paternal authority." One might equally say the "authority of ownership," for in the eyes of the law wages earned by a wife or child were considered as revenues from real estate. The image of the *paterfamilias,* austere and conscientious, was the archetype of the employer in a society in which all virtue was subordinated to the thirst for wealth. For a bourgeois, to live virtuously was to adopt Franklin's principle: "Always behave with equity, do good from fear of God and respect for all men, and you will succeed in all your undertakings. . . . Always keep God before your eyes and your heart, work with intelligence, such are the first rules of the art of becoming wealthy."[2]

The wealth of the aristocracy was in their personal fortune and their real estate. The wealth of the bourgeoisie was in negotiable personal goods and stocks and bonds which had to keep circulating in order to earn. The aristocrat enjoyed his riches; the bourgois calculated his profits, and thanks to those profits he could count on ascending the social ladder, a myth which he earnestly pursued. "The father was a peasant, factory worker, or ordinary seaman on a ship. If he was hardworking and thrifty, the son will be a farmer, a mill owner, or skipper of a ship. The grandson will be a banker, notary, doctor, lawyer, even a head of state. Thus the generations keep moving up, each one above the one before."[3]

It was in the urban development of the nineteenth century that bourgeois values were most clearly expressed, and this has marked France even today. The esthetics of the cities is a striking demonstration of a typically bourgeois distinction between the beautiful and the useful. Even today, in the manufacturing towns one can see signs of the destruction of the human environment that took place in the nineteenth century. Their layout clearly shows the ruling class's intention to set itself apart and protect itself from the proletariat. When the symbols of power—banks, hotels, and large private houses—were first established in the center of the cities, the working population lived in the basements and attics. But before long (in June 1848 and particularly with the Paris Commune) this proletarian presence in the cities was seen as an ever-present threat to the bourgeoisie. From then on, a deliberate class strategy was written into the replanning of urban centers. Broad avenues sliced through them making it possible to "rake Paris with machine guns," and residential suburbs were built in which, it was hoped, the workers would learn to become more "moral."[4]

In asserting its values, the bourgeoisie was acting in its own defense. Education, for instance, was a class affair. The *baccalauréat*, proof of the assimilation of "culture," constituted the level of "distinction" which had to be attained in order to belong to the bourgeoisie. At the same time it served as a barrier which a non-

bourgeois would have to hurdle in order to "raise himself" socially.[5]

Bourgeois society constituted an elite and its code of behavior,
applied in all the details of daily life, guaranteed the "distinction"
they sought, in the twofold sense of keeping up appearances and of
being set apart from others. The aristocracy had been "noble," the
bourgeoisie was "distinguished." One caste replaced the other.

The bourgeois attitude with regard to the political regimes of the
nineteenth century varied considerably, but the regime which
seems to have afforded the class its finest hour was the constitutional monarchy. The bourgeoisie was steadfastly opposed to democracy and this attitude never really changed even with the
Republic.[6] Casimir Périer asserted: "If there is no monarchy, the
system will drift toward democracy and then the bourgeoisie will
no longer be in control; but it must keep control for reasons of
principle and because it is best fitted to do so."[7] And the bourgeoisie did remain in control, in the serene conviction that it was
building "civilization." Even a thinker as outstanding as Auguste
Comte, speaking of his search for the laws that govern society,
revealed the self-centered attitude of his class when he declared
that he was interested only in a majority of the white race, since
other societies had quite obviously stood still on the path of progress. Saint-Simon, before him, had said that "research into the
history of the Chinese and Indians should not be a preoccupation
for trained minds. It is clear that these peoples have remained in
infancy."[8]

It is not surprising, then, that to the bourgeoisie, the proletariat
was a virgin forest, a strange and repugnant thing, a constant
threat which had to be exorcised by being thrust out of the way or
by being "raised up" and "moralized." "The barbarians that
threaten society do not live in Caucasia or on the Tartar steppe;
they live in the suburbs of our manufacturing towns." The bourgeois class cultivated the myth of the poor classes as an ignorant
and brutal mass of men, and attempted to allay their own fears in
face of this threat by prescribing efforts in the field of education,
while the women—loyal and maternal and imbued with the religious principles of their upbringing—practiced "charity" among

them. An excellent example of this attitude is given by Guizot, minister of education, who held that "to improve the conditions in which men live we must first of all strengthen and enlighten their souls," whereas his wife said that "the work of charity is the sweetest consolation in life's trials, the sweetest pastime in the midst of languors."[9]

Even in their works of charity the bourgeoisie had a sense of duty and of their rights. Adolphe Thiers in his work *On Property* wrote:

> You must not forget that it is not the rich man who made the poor, poor. If he had not become rich ... the poor would be even poorer. And his adorable benevolence did not begin by robbing the poor man in order to appear generous by giving back what was his. ... There are times of crisis in which some classes are destitute of everything and someone must come to their help. This is our opinion and our hearts are not made of stone. They must be helped, not in a spirit of restitution but in a spirit of brotherliness, which is a charming virtue when it is sincere.

Indeed there was no question of restitution. "Charity bazaars" provided the funds so badly needed for good works. Even when giving alms, the bourgeois was a business man!

This value system was legitimated both by science and by religion, which provided the intellectual and theological rationalization of the bourgeois social order. In his essay, "The Intellectual and Moral Reformation of France," Renan sketches the plan that should be aimed for:

> The universities should train a rationalist leadership for society, ruling by science and proud of its science and unwilling to lose its privileges for the benefit of the ignorant rabble. ... At the same time the masses should be elevated, their enfeebled faculties revived, and *with the help of a devoted clergy* loyal to the fatherland, they should be inspired with respect for science and virtue, the spirit of sacrifice and generosity. This would be the ideal.

Science, understood as the study of a measurable and quantitative object, as the knowledge of unchanging laws, legitimated the power system and provided it with the right to rule. Science, as the accumulation of objective knowledge, makes it possible to govern both men and the things of nature. Rarely has knowledge been the object of ideological attitudes such as prevailed in the nineteenth century scientism, both in the natural sciences and in economic and political sciences. The highest type of man, in this civilization, was the engineer whose social role bacame increasingly that of a prophet. This characteristic of nineteenth-century society seems to have been the fruit of the sociocultural thrust of the previous century: The ideology of progress taught by the Enlightenment had been vindicated by the industrial development that took place at the beginning of the nineteenth century. Liberal capitalism put a premium on instruction and science as opposed to the obscurantism of the old order. But by 1830 this high-flown optimism was given the lie by economic, social, and political upheavals, and the unfailing progress of humanity and the "naturally" harmonious development of society became objects of pure faith, utopian and voluntarist projections.

A veritable religion of evolution developed, whose high priests were a series of thinkers ranging from Saint-Simon to Auguste Comte and including Fourier and Buchez.[10] Starting with the notion common to all of a providential mission, this phenomenon took the most diverse forms. Joseph de Maistre first gave voice to this "faith" when he wrote, "Only wait until the natural affinity between religion and science brings the two together in the mind of a man of genius; the coming of this man cannot be so far away. . . . He will be famous and will put an end to the eighteenth century which is still with us."[11] These men dreamed not so much of a reversion to a lost harmony of the past as of a mission in the future to manifest the unity of the scientific, industrial, and religious potential. Saint-Simon, conferring this mission upon the man of the future, considered himself the forerunner of the new Messiah: "Princes, listen to the voice of God who speaks by my mouth. . . . "[12] His disciples took his work, A New Christianity,[13] at its face value and attempted to constitute a new church.[14]

In his Introduction to the Science of History (1833), Buchez gave an interpretation of the future in which he saw religion not only as the motive power but also as the crowning glory of mankind's moral and economic progress, as we shall have occasion to see later. And although Saint-Simon and his doctrines legitimated some of the most spectacular industrial undertakings of the century (canals, railroads, etc.), Buchez stands out as the foremost figure in the development of an ideology of the worker movement before 1848.

There is another aspect of this phenomenon, however, which at first sight seems surprising, and that is that parallel to the religious foundations of the system of legitimation of bourgeois power, ran a strong current of hostility toward the Church. This aspect calls for further study.

The philosophy of the universities, for example, as illustrated by the work of Victor Cousin, was on the defensive against both left and right. On the left it endeavored to ignore Rousseau—not only the democratic but also the materialistic current—while on the right it was at loggerheads with the Jesuits, Joseph de Maistre, and Catholic traditionalism. Between these two extremes there was room for a bourgeois idealism, open to spiritual and religious values and which broke away from its historical affinity with Descartes and the scientific spirit and produced an ethic based on duty to the economic and social imperatives of the dominant class.

The ideological situation of the bourgeoisie found an echo in many different areas. It is curious to see, for example, that relatively unified counterrevolutionary action can stem from different legitimations and rival institutions such as the university and the Church. For the theocratic school of thought, represented by such people as de Maistre and de Bonald, the system of government flowed from considerations of a religious nature: the will of God, the providential order of things, etc. The historic school of thought, founded by Tocqueville, reached identical conclusions on the basis of an analysis of the experience of different societies while challenging the validity of all theological or metaphysical prejudices.[15]

Another example was that of orleanism: the political expression of liberalism which constituted a whole philosophical system with its own metaphysic. René Rémond speaks of an "orleanist spiritual" in the same way as one can speak of a "republican spiritual" fifty years later. The former was loyal to the university, the latter to the "religious" authority of the schools and of Freemasonry. Simultaneously, liberalism, influenced by philosophical relativism, took an anticlerical turn, reviving the old quarrel between the Church and the spirit of free inquiry. The Protestant background of many outstanding figures in the intellectual, political, and industrial fields certainly had something to do with the quarrel. But philosophical liberalism seemed to coexist fairly amicably with the remnants of Gallican and Jansenist tendencies in a form of Catholicism which put far more emphasis on moral than on philosophical questions.[16]

And so there developed an implicit alliance between a secularized social philosophy in bourgeois liberalism and a theologization of society in Catholic traditionalism.

Bourgeoisie, Church, and religion. Catholic traditionalism, which had been very alive and active during the Restoration with the "ultras," remained active under the July Monarchy with the partisans of the House of Bourbon and made its mark on the whole nineteenth-century Church. The bourgeois liberals who came to power in 1830 allied themselves with this powerful faction, at least as far as conservative social practice was concerned. But we must not forget the deep-seated animosity that subsisted and which probably was primarily a cultural phenomenon. For what common ground could there possibly be between the "natural order" of the liberals and that of traditionalists like de Bonald or de Maistre? True, they both believed that "natural" laws exist and that man's intervention could only serve to upset those laws; but the "nature" of the traditionalists was that of an agrarian civilization, whereas that of the liberals was the function of an industrial, mercantile society.

It is possible that in this divergence can be found one of the basic reasons for the Church's attitude at the time of the Industrial Revolution. However that may be, for the time being it can shed some light on the religious attitude of the bourgeoisie.

Our analysis of the premises of the 1789 Revolution revealed the roots of anticlericalism and irreligion among the bourgeoisie. Ever after, the ideology of the emerging class attacked what it called the "metasocial guarantees" of the aristocracy. Bourgeois irreligion was a form of warfare, a political and economic strategy. The creation of a mercantile and industrial society was simultaneous with, and in fact caused, the disappearance of these guarantees: part of a process which Max Weber calls the "disenchantment of nature." Irreligion accompanied and legitimated the destruction of the traditional society, which was conceived as an immutable cosmos. The new modes of social and religious participation were still related to each other, but their meaning and function had changed.

The religious behavior of the bourgeoisie changed, however, when they came to power. Once they were obliged to face their own internal contradictions, and the problems raised by the growing worker movement, they tried to find endorsement in religion and began to institutionalize their own metasocial guarantees. The guarantees of the aristocracy, so hotly contested by the bourgeoisie, were ecclesiastical and political; those which they established in their turn were economic and social. The authority of those in power, which was legitimated in the past by religious power and later by absolute political power, was legitimated in the nineteenth century and long after by the laws of economics. Just as the absolute power of the monarchy found institutional forms to legitimate it in the established religion, the Voltairian bourgeoisie of the Restoration became orthodox again after 1848, and especially after the Paris Commune, and learned to use the Church for its own ends (especially in its educational policy). It was to revert to anticlericalism when it seemed expedient to do so in order to put the Republic on a firmer footing. We saw how, with Saint-Simon, religion was revived and became highly institutionalized in the bourgeois ideology, a religious role being attributed even to economic factors. At the same time the processes of identification gradually slipped toward subjective anxiety or a revaluation of the past. The romantics emphasized religious "feeling." "It's true because it's beautiful," said Chateaubriand, whereas de Bonald and de Maistre would have said, "It's true because it's part of tradition," but their stand would have been in defense of an aristocratic position.

If a critique of bourgeois humanism were to be attempted, it might well be along these lines. What could be more "religious" than the Rights of Man, proclaimed for the benefit of all by the dominant class, but in such a way as to make it impossible for the victims of their oppression to invoke these rights against them.[17] What could be more religious than their plan for a new society, conceived and presented as a mystical obligation, an imperious messianism, whose prophet was the bourgeois class, and which left such a profound mark in utopian socialism with Buchez, Fourier, and even Proudhon. The social ideas of the bourgeoisie had a mythic function, for they explained the social order in historical terms and justified it by giving a moral foundation to the role of social agencies.

As we saw earlier with regard to the image of the family and the economic enterprise, and now with regard to the works of "charity," the bourgeoisie borrowed a social form from the very heart of Christianity to guarantee its own order. Love became a negotiable stock, a defense in any possible assault on the unequal distribution of wealth. The Christian symbol of unity became a guarantee of social differences.

The Church in the Bourgeois Society

In this section, after an extensive analysis of the interactions between the Church and sociopolitical change, we shall take a preliminary look at Catholic attitudes with regard to social questions. This, in turn, will be a first step toward a study of the mental processes underlying the Church's activity at this period.

The religious question in the process of political change. The return to a monarchic system at the Restoration was consolidated with the help of the Church while, reciprocally, serving to reinforce the Church's status as a power in society after the onslaught of the Revolution. The very term "Restoration" is indicative of the mentality of those who returned to power. René Rémond describes this mentality and the symbolism: "A full cycle has been accomplished, a new world is beginning, we are at the dawn of a new era, like the man of old after the Flood. France has been purged of the stains of Jacobinism and restored to its royal, Christian vocation. . . . The Book of Kings is living again with Charles X; it is the Lord's anointed who is coming from Reims."[18] When they went into exile, the aristocrats were libertines; when they returned, they were chastened, devout, and pious.

The Restoration had endorsed the Concordat and even tried, unsuccessfully, to extend its scope. Divorce had been abolished

(1816) and a law against sacrilege made the dogma of the True Presence a legal truth. But what was far more serious was that administrative practice, the complicity of public authorities, and the infiltration of notoriously intransigent Catholics into the civil service had given substance to the notion that the government was wholly devoted to the cause of the Church and the faithful servant of what was known as the "Priests' Party."

The Revolution of 1830 reversed this trend completely; it was as emphatically anticlerical as it was bourgeois. The religious issue first began to crystallize around the educational question, which became the principal bone of contention in the quarrel between the "clericals" and the "anticlericals." Public opinion was divided: On the one hand anticlericalism had the advantage, if it can be called such, of being backed by the social power of the bourgeoisie and the clericalist policy of the previous regime. On the other hand Catholics constituted a pressure group of some importance and the clergy was becoming increasingly ultramontanist and, consequently, increasingly intransigent. The only way in which they could envisage the possibility of re-Christianizing France was by an explicit recognition of the divine rights over society and the restoration of the social prerogatives of the institutional Church.

No one, of course, even dreamed of recommending that Church and State be separated—with the exception of a few Protestants like Vinet and after 1830, a handful of Catholics, disciples of Lamennais. Although all idea of a return to the old regime was becoming more and more illusory, the adherents of two extreme, opposing positions continued to pronounce anathemas against each other, thus keeping public opinion divided. And, as is often the case in institutions, the hierarchy was unwilling to commit itself to the right or to the left and chose to do nothing at all.

The bishops had always bitterly resented the monopoly given by the Napoleonic regime to the state in the question of the universities. They were concerned about the liberalism that was so prevalent among intellectuals. In 1840 a group of bishops and laymen started a campaign against state monopoly in the control of the universities and a Catholic political party was formed with the watchword: "Freedom of Education." A lively polemic ensued and during the July Monarchy it was one of the most hotly debated questions in French politics.

Behind all this lay the fact that the Church could not decide what reception to give the 1830 regime. For a long time the regions which remained loyal to Charles X were those in which the clergy was influential. On the whole, however, it was not very long before the bishops rallied to Louis Philippe. At this stage it was a secular and bourgeois conception of the monarchy that took precedence. The consecration was replaced by an Oath to the Charter and the king took no pains to conceal his irreligious feelings. The bourgeoisie of this regime had nothing but scornful pity for the Church and Casimir Périer frankly told a member of the clergy, "The time has come when only a few old people will be for you."

For its part, the hierarchical Church seemed quite incapable of seeing anything but the age-old problems. The bishops obstinately concentrated all their attention on purely institutional questions, lamenting the days when the Church was honored as the keystone of society. Nothing, or practically nothing, was said of the restoration of values at a time when the bourgeoisie was distorting even the notion of charity. The fact of having lived under the protection of the Concordat had obliterated anything the Church had learned from the Revolution. It remembered only the violence and the social principles of the revolutionary movement in the distorted version of the anticlerical bourgeoisie. To the hierarchy it was these principles that seemed to be the source of all the Church's torment and the very embodiment of evil.

One could search the documents in vain for any intellectual appraisal of the new economic order that was gradually taking shape. And yet the Church might have done well to remind the faithful of the law (Canon 1543) about usury, and to try to revive the spirit underlying that law. As it was, in a note to the Sacred Penitentiary in 1830, the hierarchy declared that priests who had given absolution to a penitent who had lent money for interest should not be harassed. In 1873 a second declaration admitted that in virtue of civil law one had the right to receive interest on loans. It was not until the publication of *Rerum Novarum* that the official voice of the Church was raised against the "consuming usury" which is an integral part of economic liberalism.

There were no regrets at the downfall of Louis Philippe, but the Church, remembering 1793, was seized with fear of the new republican regime. The revolutionaries of 1848, however, seemed to be filled with Christian sentiments: "Long live Christ's Republic! Long Live Liberty! Long Live Pius IX!" The priests readily accepted invitations to plant or bless trees in celebration of liberty and Ozanam exclaimed: "Let's go over to the barbarians!" Lacordaire was eloquent in heralding the dawn of a new hope and Louis Veuillot wrote euphorically in *l'Univers,* "God in heaven, liberty on earth, that is the whole of the Charter."[19]

The archbishop of Paris had the prayer for the French king transformed into a prayer for the French people and there was good reason to hope for God's help, for universal suffrage was about to replace the exclusive suffrage of the anticlerical bourgeoisie with an overwhelmingly rural population with whom the clergy was still very influential. The Church and the new government were both gauging the fields of influence that would be theirs with the new system of voting. And, in fact, the voters sent a very conformist majority of representatives to the Assembly. The Church could see its own reflection in the new regime, born of a revolution but in favor of cooperation between the classes for the common good. When the congregations were also restored, the Church had still more cause for optimism.

The euphoria in ecclesiastical circles was accompanied by renewed prestige, for the events of June 1848, only a few months after the Revolution, revealed the deep discontent of the working masses, and the bourgeoisie came flocking back to the Church in alarm.

As though by instinct they adopted the attitude of Voltaire, who had become a pious member of his parish in order to ensure the docility of his peasants. In 1850 the Falloux Law established freedom of education, going even further than the clergy had hoped in regard to primary education.

Thiers went so far as to call on the Church to keep a close watch on teaching in order to keep it in the path of orthodoxy:

The teachers are 35,000 Socialists and Communists. There is only one solution and that is to entrust primary education entirely and without reserve to the Church. I ask the pastor to act vigorously, much more vigorously than at present, for I am relying entirely on him to spread the good philosophy which teaches men that they are here on earth in order to suffer.[20]

Montalembert, on the other hand, could now freely parade his hostility to democracy, while the group that put out the paper *Ere Nouvelle* (Abbé Maret, Lacordaire, etc.) became somewhat isolated in spite of being far more circumspect than in 1848. Louis Napoleon, elected president of the Republic, was strongly supported by Catholics whose natural preference went to a strong central authority, especially as he had promised to support the Catholic schools and to take the side of the pope in the Roman Question. When, on December 2, he took the reins of government by a *coup d'état,* Lacordaire, Ozanam, and Bishop Dupanloup expressed their energetic opposition. But Montalembert, in spite of his personal hesitation, advised Catholics to rally to the new emperor "to defend our Churches, our homes, our women against those who respect nothing."[21] As for Louis Veuillot, he felt that the only choice lay between the "emperor Bonaparte and the socialist Republic." Pius IX must have been overjoyed at this restoration of authority; the *Te Deum* rang out from all the churches and talk was of an "alliance between the army and the clergy."

Under the Second Empire, anticlericalism and the liberal tendencies in the universities still continued, even though the government censored the press, ordered the cafés closed during High Mass on Sundays, ordered the army to take part in religious processions, and seated the cardinals in the Senate. And though Catholics saw the Crimean War as a crusade against Orthodox Russia, they still felt that the regime was no better than a "bawdy-house blessed by the bishops." When the emperor concurred in the dismembering of the papal states, however, the attitude of Catholics stiffened considerably. The quarrel once again was between two institutions, each as imperialistic as the other, whereas the real issues of the time were the economic system and its repercussions in the social order.

The Church retained a great deal of influence in society, as much with the old aristocracy as with a section of the bourgeoisie which was opposed to the regime and which was soon to turn against it completely when France was defeated in the war with Germany. The generosity of those to whom the Church appealed enabled it to build up its wealth again and to extend its influence in the field of education. It also made it possible to finance charitable works by which the Church hoped to maintain its influence among the workers. And all the time, the type of priest that was being trained continued to fix in the public mind the image of one set apart, pious but uncultured, trained only to deal with problems of conscience and to absorb theological treatises which were still as meaningless as those of the previous century.[22]

The fall of the Empire and the short-lived drama of the Paris Commune again faced the Church and the whole country with choosing a political regime and with the problems of French society. For the bourgeoisie, the crushing of the Commune was a violent and symbolic exorcism of their enemy, the proletariat, and the elections sent a majority of honest country elders, as fearful as they were orthodox, to the Assembly.

The restored Republic, under the presidency of General Mac-Mahon, certainly earned its title of "Republic of moral order." The fear of socialism outweighed even the fear of the Jesuits, and even more than in 1848, the bourgeoisie once again had recourse to the Church. It was a living paradox in which the Church continued to mourn the "good old days of the Monarchy" while walking hand in hand with the Republic. In the meantime Catholic schools were flourishing and the public schools were experiencing great difficulties. Before long the Church received permission to open its own universities in which to educate Christian lawyers and doctors. The budget of the Churches at this period was two percent greater than the national budget.

As usual in periods of social upheaval, the Church looked for a religious explanation of what followed the Commune and found it in France's apostasy, the cause of all its misfortunes: The bloody events it had gone through were a punishment and a call to reparation. The Assumptionist Fathers skillfully orchestrated tremendous ceremonies of expiation and the consecration of France to the Sacred Heart took concrete form in the Sacred Heart Basilica of Montmartre.[23] The Catholics saw signs everywhere and interpreted them as a call to battle against the Enemy. For them salvation lay in a return to the regime that most ideally suited the "eldest daughter of the Church," the Monarchy. And from Rome, Pius IX continued to proclaim that the cause of all the evils of the times was the principles of 1789.

Only a small minority of Catholics failed to join in the general chorus, and they were looked on with suspicion by the hierarchy. Throughout this period the intellectual trends, and especially the worker movements, were developing very rapidly under the influence of the second Industrial Revolution and were becoming even more radical on the social level and more areligious on the philosophical level. Currents of social thought did develop in the Church in France and elsewhere, as we shall see, but in France the political question and the problem of anticlericalism seemed to absorb all the available energies in the Church. The whole of the latter part of the nineteenth and the beginning of the twentieth centuries was dominated by the struggle to consolidate the position of the Republic. In 1875 the new Chamber which was to defeat MacMahon was republican and anticlerical once again. Gambetta spoke for the whole Chamber when he declared that "the real enemy is clericalism."

This new wave of anticlericalism can be explained in the first place by the ancient ways of the Church, especially in the field of education: The hostility of the teachers had been roused to a furious pitch by the control exercised by the Church. But it can also be explained by the new government's need to assert itself in the face of royalist tendencies, which persisted for the most part in Catholic circles. To this one should add that, for a government which was very far from progressive on the social level, anticlericalism seemed a convenient alibi in face of the international worker movement. This, at least, is what many leaders of the worker movement believed when they were questioned about the tactical merits of this conflict with the Church, at the beginning of the twentieth century.[24] Most of them declared that the only enemy was capitalism: Quarrels with the clergy were all too often a manifestation of bourgeois double dealing. The bourgeois took good care not to inflict a death blow on the Church so that it could continue to use the moral force of religion as a weapon against the workers and incite them to anticlericalism, thereby turning their attention from the real issues.[25]

Under the pressure of this hostility Catholics soon found themselves beyond the pale in their own country, and their awareness of social questions was seriously retarded as a result: they interpreted all legislation enforced by the state as a direct attack against the faith and the worker movement as one vast campaign to de-Christianize the whole country. But here again a more detailed analysis of the problem is in order: If we explain the narrow attitude of the Church in the nineteenth century by the hostility from which it suffered, we are only postponing an intelligent understanding of the phenomenon. The question remains: How and why had the Church become a rival institution to the new society?[26]

The Church's attitude toward social problems before the advent of "social Catholicism." We are now in a position to offer a tentative answer to this question, with the help of elements to be found in the period preceding the institutional development of social Catholicism (c. 1870).

By 1830 one can detect traces of a nascent awareness among Catholics of the existence of a new problem: that of the fate of workers owing to the development of mechanical industrialization. Significantly, however, this problem was frequently identified with that of the poor, a fact which constituted an obstacle for a long time. Instructions emanating from the bishops at this time reveal the themes which would dominate all Christian reflection about the "condition of workers" for a long time to come. Even the literary style of these texts merits study, for it reveals a whole attitude and understanding of the social reality.

Cardinal de Croy, archbishop of Rouen, dedicated his Lenten letter of 1838 to the subject of respecting Sunday as a day of rest: He realizes that the working classes are often deprived of this day of rest by the demands of their work. The Church cannot remain indifferent to this unfortunate situation: "At all cost, the lives of the poor, of prisoners, and of the working classes must be made easier.... What is more worthy of admiration than this universal solicitude for the welfare of the working classes. ..."[27]

A description of the hardships of workers often goes hand in hand with a condemnation of the profit motive, the fundamental reason for the conditions imposed on the working classes, but the problem was more generally seen as being part of a life style which leads to religious indifference. Owners are reproached for losing their souls by their pursuit of material gain and by putting the workers into situations in which it is difficult to live in virtue. "Our temples are abandoned in favor of the workshop," declared Archbishop Delmas of Cambrai.

> More than ever before, money has become the idol of this century.... Workers are obliged to work on Sunday or to give up working on the other days of the week; the necessity of earning a living for themselves and their families becomes ... a temptation hard to resist. In this way, as though by contagion, the burning thirst for riches spreads; in this way first indifference and later contempt for religious duties spread; in this way moral corruption spreads among those who had previously been pure, thanks to the promises and threats of the faith which served to dampen the ardor of their passions.[28]

Condemnation of the profit motive was sometimes more direct,[29] but it is especially interesting to point out the frame of reference underlying the bishops' statements. Prelates of the old regime had no hesitation in castigating the aristocracy for being too comfortably ensconced in their riches. Time and again they reminded them of their duty to give alms and a good example to the poor. The prelates of the nineteenth century do not seem to have realized that the situation is no longer the same. They seem to identify profit motive with the thirst for pleasure, seeing it simply as morally wrong. At best they protest against the inhuman mechanization of work.[30] Since society is divided by nature into rich and poor, those who possess are in duty bound, "without abandoning their ownership ... to give back what belongs to all by sharing their profits...." So said Cardinal Giraud, Archbishop Delmas' successor at Cambrai, and Cardinal de Bonald of Lyons, although he deplored the "injustices" suffered by the silk workers, found it in his heart to congratulate the mill owners of Lyons who were "amply provided with the benefits of wealth" and who were still capable of being guided by "a prudence which takes into account the age and health of the workers, rather than by the barbarous cupidity which, elsewhere, pitilessly cuts down these young plants for the sake of a few rags of silk,[31] just when they are beginning to open to life."[32]

Since the evil is moral, the solution must obviously be to restore the inspiration of charity, which unites rich and poor: "There is only one way to have peace on earth," declared Bishop Affre, "and that is to spread the sacred fire of charity. It is charity, more than any laws or the forces of order, that binds the social edifice together."[33]

Without underestimating the real generosity which inspired these protests and the truth they contain, and without forgetting that men such as Montalembert raised their voices in Parliament to express the revolt of Christian consciences against child labor,[34] it must be acknowledged that the frame of reference of most of these texts is that of a preindustrial society—which is perfectly understandable at the time—dominated by the problem of scarcities and divided into rich and poor. The social ethic proclaimed from the pulpit can only remind the rich of their duty to improve the lot of the needy. The novelty of the situation had escaped the bishops who looked at industrialization with the eyes of Bossuet. And in no area was the gulf between their reading of events and the reality wider than in that of the class struggle. Social discontent and the propagation of the first socialist theories warned the bishops of the existence of a problem, but they were unable to grasp its true causes or its full import. They could only unanimously condemn those who put men into different categories and the theories which "sowed the seeds of deadly divisions and odious rivalries between brothers, as though the law of work did not apply to all men,"[35] invoking St. Paul's argument of complementarity of the members of the Mystical Body.

It was at this period that the Church developed its agencies of "assistance" both as a religious (theological) gesture and as a way of ensuring its continued presence and influence. When the workers claimed the right to work in 1848, therefore, it was virtually an insurrection against the economic dependency forced on them by both public and religious institutions of assistance—such organizations as the Convent Workshops, for example, in which gratuitous aid had been replaced by a strict framework of production and in which the workers were "protected" against immorality sometimes to the point of being cut off from the rest of the world.

For French Catholics, the 1848 Revolution posed both the political and the social problem. It will always be to the credit of such men as Ozanam and Abbé Maret that they saw and proclaimed this. But the mass of Catholics were not even aware of it. This could be explained, of course, by the fact that most practicing Catholics and their priests had a rural background while the bishops were from the aristocracy,[36] but this sheds light only on the circumstances. It still does not explain the pattern of their thought and its origins. We shall return to this point later.

The first realizations of what could be called "social Catholicism" were such organizations as the Society of Charitable Economy whose members were drawn from the ranks of the rightist Legitimists. Its prime mover was Viscount Armand de Melun, and the deep-seated hope of these societies was for the Church to monopolize all works of assistance.[37] There were some men at that period, however, influenced no doubt by Saint-Simon and Fourier as well as by Lemennais, who did connect political and social problems. The newspaper l'Atelier, inspired by the social thought of Buchez, counted some Catholics among its collaborators, but, as we shall see, it represented a challenge from outside the ecclesiastical communion rather than an awareness on the part of the Church of social problems.[38]

Under the Second Empire, charitable organizations continued to develop: the Society of Mutual Assistance, the Young Workers' Clubs, etc., and Maignen, the founder of the Young Workers' Circle, dreamed of reviving a Christian guild. Armand de Melun's group continued to flourish also, but the royalist tendencies of many of these organizations caused the government to look on them with suspicion.[39]

In Belgium the Mechelen Congress was also dominated by paternalistic trends and the refusal of state intervention. A minority, led by Ducpétiaux, whose thinking was opposed to the general trend, was vigorously attacked by the majority. The only solution that seemed acceptable was that of individual or collective action on the part of factory owners to improve the lot of their workers. And while Ducpétiaux declared, "Man has always been and still is subordinated to production... he has been treated as an instrument or tool....,"[40] the Mechelen Congress could bring itself to acknowledge only a "lack of harmony in the relations between employers and workers which is due, principally, to the neglect of the duties which religion lays upon workers as well as upon employers."[41]

When one remembers that from 1830 on, with such people as Owen in England, and Fourier and Proudhon in France, a critical analysis of capitalism was already beginning to take shape and that the *Communist Manifesto* appeared in 1847, one is justified in believing that the reason for the social blindness of the majority of Catholics must be sought not only in the morphology of the group but also in the overall pattern of their thinking and their belief. As we have seen, the weight of political circumstances was considerable in the case of French Catholics, but again this is not an adequate explanation.

The pattern of Christian thought in the nineteenth-century. We shall now attempt, therefore, a tentative study of the patterns of thought of nineteenth-century Catholicism. One of the first things that strikes one is that it seems to have been dominated by a conflict between two rival conceptions of the Church, politics, reason, and anthropology.

Eighteenth-century philosophy and the revolutionary crisis had left a deep mark on Catholic thinking. In practice, it had been necessary to rebuild the institutional Church, which had been so sorely afflicted materially. I speak deliberately of *necessity,* for Catholics had been divided over the question of whether rebuilding the Church meant a return to its former situation or whether some other reality should be born that would take heed of the lessons of the past. It seems that the only possibility that received any serious consideration was the former. Only Lamennais thought otherwise and he was immediately branded as heretical when he wrote with such feeling:

Give me a hut as a presbytery; take a boulder from your fields as an altar; let the barn which holds your harvest be your temple. Do you not think that God would rather be free with us, under a thatched roof, than be enslaved in a palace with his children? Do you think that the priest in his hut would be without a mother or a sister, or that his sackcloth would make him less independent than silk?[42]

The official, majority expression of the Church's thinking gives the impression of being exclusively interested in carrying on its polemical arguments with its old enemies. "It is all the fault of Voltaire and Rousseau," the Church believed, sensing their influence in all intellectual, political, and social movements.

It seems that there were two "ideal" types of Catholic in the nineteenth century. For one of them, the "modern world" was his own period of history, with its own institutions and values, and this was the world in which the Church should take flesh and be transformed. For the other, the "modern world" was synonomous with the anti-Catholic principles of the Revolution, and the Church could not live in peace with error, it could only combat it. Toward the middle of the century these two general categories had hardened until they constituted two rival parties.[43] On the political level they could be classed as Orleanists and Legitimists; on the level of ideas as Liberals and Traditionalists. The Liberals developed their ideas by observing contingent facts, which, it was accepted, should qualify principles. This was the Dupanloup group. The Traditionalists developed their ideas from the basis of immutable principles to which both men and material creation are bound to conform. This was the Veuillot group.

A brief look at the ecclesiology of the period shows the standing these two trends enjoyed and their relative importance in the mainstream of Catholic thought as it was expressed in the First Vatican Council. Two main theological trends converged to produce the Constitution *Dei Filius:* one, the trend of restoration, the other of renovation. The first, based on the role of authority, was expressed in France by Traditionalism. It was hostile to all democratic and Gallican tendencies and sought to restore a monarchical type of authority, both in the political and ecclesiological spheres. This trend was in harmony with an underlying theme in Bellarmine's theology, which emphasized an exterior view of the Church as in institution. Although it did not wholly prevail, this current was extremely influential during the Vatican Council.

Another trend, however, which drew its inspiration from patristic and romantic sources, had been developed particularly in Germany at the Tubingen school of theology and considered the Church not only as visible and hierarchical, but also as a people and a communion.

What is sometimes ambiguously known as "Catholic liberalism" must be clearly distinguished from "Protestant liberalism," which is a theological trend. In the Catholic Church liberalism was not a doctrinal stance so much as an attitude toward events, which led Liberals to welcome new ideas to the point, sometimes, of challenging the accepted values within the Catholic group. When the values they challenged were such things as the temporal power of the papacy and the partnership of Church and State, then one can well imagine that a challenge from within the institution, at least in the period we are concerned with, could not survive for very long. Lamennais' case is proof of this.

Lamennais' case, in fact, is particularly interesting, for it is an instance in which an unorthodox position was derived from a pure doctrinal tradition. It was Lamennais' philosophy of knowledge (i.e., that the basis of all certitude is the permanent fund of knowledge and not personal opinion) which provided him with his argument that the faith could be reconciled to the modern conception of liberty. The slogan used by his newspaper, *l'Avenir,* which appeared between October, 1830 and November, 1831, was "God and Liberty." In an article entitled "On the Separation of Church and State," he wrote: "We firmly believe that the development of modern enlightenment will one day bring not only France but the whole of Europe back to Catholic unity, which later on and by successive stages, attracting the whole human race, will make it one spiritual society through one faith." But this does not prevent him from clamoring vociferously for the separation of Church and State. He pleads that the Church must give up all its material and temporal prerogatives. At the same time he upholds the growing national movements in Belgium, Poland, and Ireland. We shall come back to Lamennais when we come to speak of Christian Democracy between 1893 and 1902. For the time being we can simply note that the Church rejected his political conclusions out of hand. The encyclical *Mirari Vos* (August 15, 1832) condemned rationalism and Gallicanism (as did Lamennais himself); it also condemned Lamennais' liberalism, for its consequences seem farfetched to the point of heresy.

The dramatic turn of events in 1848 served only to confirm Pius IX in his traditionalism, after a short-lived liberal phase. The ambition of the hierarchy was to remain under the protective wing of the civil authority (which asked nothing better than to keep it hostage). To this end it favored an authoritarian Catholicism within a state that was as officially "Catholic" as possible. Although not explicit, the Church's anxiety not to cut itself off from a following that was still predominantly rural and in which religion and family were still integrated, was no doubt foremost in this whole debate. There is no question but that it strengthened the Church in the fatal illusion that a culture is automatically Christian if it moves within the ecclesiastical orbit and clings to traditional forms. The encyclical *Quanta Cura* and the accompanying Syllabus endorsed this stance in 1864. It is quite evident from these documents that the pope was convinced that liberalism was the central error of the century and that it was his duty to condemn it.[44] A parallel development, which was to go on for a long time, was the process of centralizing the institutional Church. Rome began to intervene directly in the affairs of local churches; papal nuncios became more and more influential even in nondiplomatic questions; and Ultramontanism reached such proportions that shortly after the definition of the Immaculate Conception a French journalist wrote: "Louis XIV pronounced the famous words: 'I am the State.' Pius IX has gone even further: with more justification he has declared by his acts: 'I am the Church!' "[45]

A pessimistic and reactionary attitude was thus firmly established and the behavior of Catholics in respect to sociopolitical change bore its mark for a long time. Traditionalism, as Jean Lacroix points out,[46] is truly political in its motivations and results even if it draws on theological sources. Replacing the authority of facts with the fact of authority, it exalts humility and submission as the peak of virtue, the highest perfection of intelligence. And de Bonald wrote: "One should never allow men to gather together except under arms or in Church, for there they do not debate, they only obey." To think is to run the risk of dividing and fragmenting the social and ecclesiastical body, which can speak only the language of universal categories and in which all participation is defined according to a vertical scale. As Roger Aubert writes, Catholic thinking in the nineteenth century "clung to the oratorical techniques of romanticism in a time when people were more and more sensitive to the results of the positive sciences or the detailed analyses of historical criticism."[47] And Adrien Dansette writes that Renan's theses were contested only by "old dissertations by seminarians, which were totally powerless to convince anyone."[48]

Ecclesiastical authoritarianism can sometimes be accompanied by progressive ideas on the sociological level. But when this happens, the underlying theory of progress is often that of a value which Christian truth alone can inspire. The whole of "Christian sociology" has been influenced by this notion, and it is especially in this sense that Catholic liberalism is ambiguous. In the first place it is not simply a Christian version of the complacent bourgeois liberalism; sensitivity to injustice or at least to poverty has always distinguished Catholic liberals from the economists of the same name. Thiers was perfectly right in his evaluation of the situation when he declared: "The clergy must be resisted; we shall never by able to do anything with them. Some of them will be Socialists, never Liberals." But it didn't take much for someone like Thiers to class a man as a Socialist. In fact, in 1851 Montalembert, a Catholic Liberal, declared: "I have made my choice. I am on the side of authority against revolt; on the side of conservation against destruction; on the side of society against Socialism."

One last point deserves to be discussed, and that is the relationship between the bourgeoisie and the Church, who were what Marxists call "objective allies." It is very likely that when the Church was called upon to defend the status quo by its teachings, ecclesiastics took this as a gesture offering them prestige: The Church was being restored to its traditional place in society. Fortunately, however, the values defended by the Church and the legitimation it offered the regime were not completely identical. The Church, at least on the conscious level, did not back up the bourgeoisie as fully as it was asked to. But "objectively," nevertheless, the distance between them was small. Perhaps those who actually acted out this history are not so much to blame, but this does not alter the nature of the legacy they left behind them.

Before going any further with this phase of our analysis, we should take a closer look at the direction the worker movement was taking and its interaction with the Church.

The Development of the Working Class in France; Its Interaction with the Church and with Religion

We must begin this section with some remarks about the birth of the "worker movement" and how it became a challenge to society. After that we shall study a few of the theorists of the workers' struggle, especially in relation to the Church and religion. In closing I shall try to introduce some kind of order into the picture of the movement's attitudes toward the Church.

The phases of development of the worker movement. According to a rather simplistic schema, the working class owed its origin to a threefold development which was part of a global transformation of industry in the nineteenth century. Mechanical work took the place of manual work; big industries engulfed small industries; and the growth of the towns drained all vitality from the rural areas. In point of fact these changes took place extremely slowly, and at the end of the century the rural population was still in the majority.

What is called the first Industrial Revolution was first of all a considerable growth of small industries and crafts in those very towns in which the French worker movement was to see the light of day: Paris and Lyons. However, in industries of this category the line of demarcation between employer and employee was still fairly flexible. The worker dreamed of becoming an employer and there was nothing extravagant in such dreams. The true "boss" of production was business capital, and in fact the first blows were struck not between manufacturers and their workers but between manufacturers and merchants.

Before wage earners could demonstrate any collective consciousness, the notion that one day their power could be substituted for the power of management had to be expressed as a real possibility. When the ambition to gain creative control over what was produced first became collective instead of purely individual, it took the form of cooperatives and attempts to socialize the means of production.

A characteristic of the growth of big industries was the dependency in which the workers lived. Their living quarters close to the factory, their work records, certain social advantages—all these combined to make them members of a closed society, entirely controlled and ruled by management. It was a miserably poor society, and the social and cultural gulf between worker and employer made any challenge difficult.

As mechanization made greater strides, the big industries entered into competition with craftsmanship, which gradually ceased to exist. Industries clustered together, creating manufacturing towns, and railroads made it possible to transport both workers and ideas as well as goods, more readily. And, finally, the laws that govern the market in economic liberalism caused fluctuations in employment and the tide of the workers' discontent began to rise. Nevertheless there was no outbreak of violence until 1844 and that was an isolated case in which two thousand workers put the General Company of Mines of the Loire Valley out of operation. By 1869 strikes were already widespread and were showing the influence of the Workers' International. A class consciousness was beginning to take shape among workers at the time, and from then on the growth of the worker movement gained momentum, helped along by the concentration of industry, the beginning of labor unions, legalized in 1884, and especially by the development of labor markets which gave workers in different branches of industry an opportunity to learn the power of concerted action.

It was only toward the end of the century, therefore, that one could speak of the existence of a working class "for itself," that is, conscious of its own interests and working out plans for the reform or revolution of society. But hardly did it exist before the tradition and the strategy of its struggle were already elaborated.

The various ideological trends at work in this new class showed signs of the evolution it had been through. To begin with, the ideal was modeled on the guilds; it was friendly to the management of small industries and to craftsmen, and open to the ideologies and utopian ideas of the lower middle classes and later to utopian socialism. The growth of the big cities with their less integrated way of life was perhaps favorable in the beginning to the birth of a more revolutionary class consciousness, and at the same time to concerted action by the mass of workers. But the development of workers' residential suburbs, foreshadowing the later dormitory towns, began the disintegrating process of urban life, which had such disastrous effects on the life of the collectivity.[49]

The structural evolution of the worker movement was extremely complex and it would be beyond the scope of this study to attempt to follow up the different steps it followed. To observe the attitudes it adopted toward the institutional Church and religion in the nineteenth century as exactly as possible, however, we have to take into account certain principles of analysis, since the way in which different groups challenge society varies according to their respective structures.

In a traditional, strongly integrated society dominated by the problem of the scarcity of basic commodities, the members are integrated hierarchically and the subservient group finds its self-identity in its respect for the metasocial guarantees, whether religious or political, claimed by the dominant class or projected onto them by those they rule. This phenomenon has been analyzed by sociologists like Touraine, who calls it the "constituent consciousness."[50] As he is powerless in the face of nature, says Touraine, the subject "reverses the terms of his problem: he is powerless because creative power resides in nature which becomes a metaphysical entity." The myths of the ruling class reinforce this phenomenon. The individual can participate in history only vicariously by magic and a mythical language. The unsubdued elements in him are liberated in aggressive behavior with strong religious overtones, such as various forms of messianism.[51] The social and cultural systems of a society of this kind are stable and homogeneous. The plans any individual may formulate are predetermined by his background and his function in society. Change consists only in substitution of one privileged group for another. The monolithic nature of the cultural system (a compact body of legitimations upholding a compact body of norms and values which have been strongly internalized) inhibits the autonomy of the individual, and any suggestion of subculture would be considered alien and dangerous.

To break down a system of this kind, technical progress, which proves that it is possible to transform nature,[52] has to be accompanied by an awakening of class consciousness: The social classes must see themselves for what they are. It was the Industrial Revolution which gradually accomplished this transformation, begun in the eighteenth century.

A slow evolution from oppression to exploitation had transformed the consciousness of the subservient classes, and the birth of a working class and its development into a full-fledged worker movement expressed the gradual passage from a hierarchical form of social participation to "democratic" participation, which completely upset the accepted notions of power, its origins, and its legitimation. The workers' self-consciousness evolved very gradually out of the "constituent consciousness," and for a long time the doctrines which inspired their struggle bore the marks of the dominant cultural system from which they had sprung. As can be seen in the work of Fourier, Buchez, Cabet, and even Proudhon, they called on God to help them in their struggle against their masters.[53] In the beginning what Touraine calls their "proud consciousness" led only to revolt or to utopias. During the process of industrialization, but before the birth of an industrial civilization, the workers' complaint was based on deep dissatisfaction with a society that they recognized as inhuman once they had become aware of their own psychological disillusionment in a "disenchanted nature." It became revolutionary (with Marx, essentially) only when society was seen as a total system and criticized as such, with a will to change that left no room for regrets for the past. In this respect, as we shall see, Fourier and Buchez, for instance, projected their nostalgia for an integrated society (phalansteries, fraternities, mutual assistance associations) into utopias, and symbolized their dreams in religious terms.

The worker movement began by fighting for its rights and it appealed almost exclusively to a principle of identity,[54] i.e., the awareness of being exploited and a defense of its own interests. Its language was that of the prevailing cultural system and it did not name its adversary. In some ways it could be said to be a protest movement, limited and uncoordinated, until it began to express itself in a united and organized movement. Finally it developed into a movement of social thought, especially when it borrowed the bourgeois language of Saint-Simon or the ideas of "social Catholics."[55]

It is important to remember that the theoreticians and animators of the movement were men who possessed a principle of resistance to society by virtue of their education and professions. As Touraine points out, they came "not from poverty but from a trade." Buchez was a doctor; Proudhon was a skilled worker and self-taught intellectual; Fourier came from a family of merchants. The fact that these first theoreticians of the worker movement often had an intellectual background is worth emphasizing from the point of view of this analysis, for one would perhaps be justified in seeing it as the final outcome of a process of secularization, begun at the end of the Middle Ages when, for the first time, clerics were distinguished from intellectuals. As Marx remarked: "Bacon used to say that theological physics was a virgin consecrated to God and, therefore, sterile. He set physics free from theology and she became fruitful...." The evolution of social theory from Saint-Simon to Marx appeared in many ways to set social theory and practice free from religion. There was an emancipation from institutionalized religion toward a "new Christianity," or a return to the true religion of Christ; there was the violent destruction of paternal—and paternalistic—religion, and, finally, there was an emancipation from religion itself, as can be seen with Marx.

The torchbearers and interpreters of the socioreligious dimension. One cannot speak of the first social theorists of the nineteenth century without mentioning Saint-Simon. In view of what became of his doctrine under the Second Empire, we spoke of it earlier as an ideology. In point of fact, Saint-Simon was really a utopian and his synthesis clearly influenced the first rationalizations of reform of the budding industrial society.

Charles Fourier (1771-1837), like Saint-Simon, criticized unorganized production, but, unlike him, emphasized the distribution of labor and its products, and dreamed of a society which would live primarily off the land. A rural society without trade was his idea of the ideal order willed by God. By introducing the problem of pleasure in work, he testified to his awareness of exploitation but only to a utopian aspect of this awareness as it began to mature. His contestation was relatively primitive and orgiastic.

Etienne Cabet (1788-1856) considered himself a second Socrates or even a second Christ. He brought a new gospel to the world in the form of a novel: *Le Voyage en Icarie*. In it he envisaged a new religious reformation, and another of his works was entitled *Le vrai christianisme selon Jésus-Christ*. His influence was felt in the working class around 1848 and was particularly attractive because of his revaluation of brotherhood. The fact that the February 1848 revolution was so euphoric was certainly due to Cabet's influence. But the reaction that followed in June tore his dream of collaboration with the bourgeoisie to shreds.

Philippe Buchez (1795-1865) and his collaborators—virtually his disciples—in the newspaper *l'Atelier*, were a typical example of social criticism expressed in religious terminology or rather, based on a restoration of Christianity as a preliminary to reforming society.

Buchez was opposed to Saint-Simon, wanting to reconcile the latter's contribution with Catholic and democratic traditions. In fact it was his feeling for democracy which really set him apart from Saint-Simon. What he was really proposing was not a hierarchical society but an association. However, it was Saint-Simon's influence that brought him to Christianity,[56] although he never joined the Catholic Church. In his *Parliamentary History of the Revolution* Buchez attempted to demonstrate that Christian and revolutionary principles are identical, and in his *Introduction to the Science of History* he sets out to reconcile Christianity and progress.

The newspaper, *l'Atelier,* was typical of a characteristic phenomenon of nineteenth-century social theory: a small group (perhaps with the idea of reconstructing a community disrupted by the first stages of industrialization) animated by an almost religious fervor. The social theory elaborated within this group under Buchez's leadership, had mankind for its object and God for its support.[57] Religion was the cement that bound the members into a social unity; their analysis was built on the premise of the unity of mankind whose necessary destiny is progress toward a future, animated by the spirit of universal brotherhood. And since, according to Buchez, association is the social condition toward which Christianity is moving, the motive power of society's progress is the Christian ethic.

The "theological age of sociology," as F. A. Isambert so aptly calls Buchez's venture[58] was the last of its kind. After 1848 all the social theorists were either anticlerical or atheists. Isambert's expression, however, suggests a certain ambiguity which we must avoid: It would be incorrect to place Buchez in the category of Catholic social theorists. He represents the "theological age" in the sense in which Comte used this expression. The leitmotif of his thought was not theology seen as ecclesiastical dogma, but a religious view of the present and the future.[59] In *l'Atelier* of May 31, 1843, he wrote: "We are in agreement only with the principle of the Catholic institution."[60] Also, the way in which he used theology in his social theory provoked the institution to take issue with him: "If the Revolution claims to be Christian ... priests will find themselves with the choice of serving the undertaking or opposing it. If they oppose it, they will be considered heretics and will be prosecuted as such."[61] The argument went right to the heart of Christian doctrine when the paper habitually translated the Gospel text: "My kingdom is not of this world," as "My kingdom is not *yet* of this world." This was far more than a quarrel of exegetes and translators; it touched on the very meaning of religion: the emphasis of religious life was directed to this world. *L'Atelier* reacted against religious writings which had always used the text to turn believers away from the world, and reinterpreted Christ's words in accordance with its own social practice.[62]

In Buchez's writings, as it happens, one can find evidence that he saw the doctrine of Christ's divinity as a socially useful myth.[63]

A similar line of thought is evident in a short work by Corbon, one of the editors of *L'Atelier,* which took the form of an open letter to Bishop Dupanloup and was entitled "Why We Have Left You." "We have left you now," writes Corbon, "because for centuries you left us. . . . You have abandoned our temporal cause; your influence was even used to prevent rather than further our social redemption." Corbon accuses, in the first place, the good works of the Church. In his view the conflict between the Church and the Revolution is not just the result of circumstances. It reflects Catholic doctrine, "revised and syllabused," which contains less and less of the authentic Christian spirit. Corbon's faith and that of his friends had become more and more secularized and "detheologized." "In place of yesterday's religion, whose object was God and whose end was the salvation of souls, there is now a new religion whose object is mankind. . . ." They did not deny God; they simply maintained that true Christianity was no longer to be found in the Church but in modern society. These were Corbon's opinions and we must remember that he also held that "bold denials of God" were "weapons without a basis in scientific certitude."[64]

With Pierre Joseph Proudhon the whole argument moved a step further: "Evil is God," and "to restore religion we must do away with the Church."[65] His hostility toward the Church was in logical conformity with his hostility toward every form of authority: "I have always been in revolt against the Church as well as against the government." For there is an essential relationship between temporal authority and spiritual authority, which is illustrated by the idea, so repulsive to Proudhon, of Providence. So he preached that Christianity, as it had been fashioned by theologians, must be destroyed, for its "true foundation is intolerance." And yet this rabid anticlerical was, himself, a theologian who used their own weapons against the mighty with theological arguments against the civil and ecclesiastical powers. Culturally, though, he was always a conservative, using the prevailing idiom of his society, and for this he was criticized by Marx.

With Marx and Engels, social criticism acquired a very different scope. Even anticlericalism became a thing of the past, since a philosophico-religious explanation of society was outdated. The accession of the proletariat to the principle of totality means that to the extent to which it has been expelled from society it can challenge society all the more radically. The proletariat does not participate in the dominant culture; it is the "dissolution of the existing social order."[66]

If the workers' struggle is to be a radical critique of religion, if it is to become atheism, man must define himself exclusively in relation to his work. This is possible for the proletariat when not only this one class, but the whole of society is visibly determined by tangible social forces, and when the classes come into conflict, not over political or religious ideologies, but for the control of productive power and the profits of production.

The proletariat, "dissolution of all classes," takes on a universal character through its universal suffering and does not claim any particular right since it has not suffered any particular wrong, but a wrong "in itself." It opposes society "simply in the name of its own humanity," and it can be emancipated only by "emancipating itself totally from all other spheres of society and, consequently, emancipating them."[67]

According to Marx, when the challenge to society moves on to a deeper level, the worker movement becomes estranged from religion rather than hostile to it. The tide that sweeps it on toward the classless society also bears it toward atheism. For Marx this was not a prediction of future developments but an element in his analysis. And it is true that, to the extent to which proletarianization signifies not impoverishment but a break with bourgeois society and a struggle to the death against it, the mastery of language (that is, of the culture) through the mastery of work can lead to a radical secularization. For it means control of the religious language or, as I would prefer to say, of the "providentialist" language. In saying this I am not reducing Marx's criticism to the criticism of the language of a given period or of a particular theology, but accepting it as a criticism of all theological language, which was employed both in liberalism and in Christian social principles.[68]

In a sense Marx laid the foundations of a sociology of knowledge in his critique. What is the opposite of alienation? It is consciousness, the knowledge which transforms nature and the relations between men. And is it not true that the asymmetrical relationships of power are founded on unequal knowledge? For Marx atheism was not a theoretical problem nor an ideology; it was the end goal of ideological representations and, therefore, the control of language.

If Marx seemed to attach such importance to the criticism of religion, it is because the religious vocabulary typifies vicarious knowledge. According to this definition religion exists in politics just as politics is reflected in religion. "Atheism is a quarrel with religion in that it is a quarrel with the supreme ideology . . . of the eminent mechanism which traps knowledge in its own product." It is not a new philosophy replacing an old one, but the "presence of each and every man to all men." Marx's work could perhaps better be defined as a "critique of mediations." The criticism of sacred forms of mediation as well as the nonsacred. "I want to criticize religion within the critique of political conditions rather than criticizing political conditions in religion."[69] This is a critique of religion as a system of legitimation, or as a metasocial guarantee. The Marxist critique, then, was an authentic and radical secularization rather than "Christian truths run wild," as many have too hastily concluded.

The worker movement and the Church. Analyzing the religious themes treated by the press during the July Monarchy,[70] F. A. Isambert finds an expression of "marginal" forms of Christianity, ranging from the "quasi-Catholicism" of Buchez to the "near-atheism" of Cabet's fraternity.

In the "Christian socialism" which so deeply influenced the first generation of workers of the Industrial Revolution, one can see a splintering of the psychosocial components of religion. Religion challenges society and society challenges religion. Both past experience and plans for the future are dramatized through a religious vocabulary, and at the same time they call on the institution to supply and guarantee this language.

From a morphological point of view, the groups in which the new doctrines were being elaborated had many characteristics in common with sects. No doubt an ancient tradition of secrecy in workers' organizations had something to do with this; but from our point of view it is difficult not to think of a protest, or even a reform in the form of a sect, organizing its own private domain and its own language on the fringes of the prevailing religious system. The attitude of Buchez and Corbon seems to denote the challenge of one religious phenomenon by another.[71] It seems that the worker movement as they experienced and expressed it was, as it were, a more authentic branch of Catholicism. When one contrasts what the Church was teaching and practicing, with the affirmation of values in the nascent worker movement, one can understand the barriers that grew up between the institutional Church and the challenge offered from outside it.[72]

On another level, in view of the body of doctrines to which Buchez, Corbon, and even Proudhon subscribed, and the network of beliefs by which they translated it into norms and values, one can see that doctrine was being used to legitimate a system of norms originating not in the ecclesiastical value system of the period, but in the value system of the worker movement. And this explains the shifting of values that is so clearly visible in their statements as well as in their criticism of ecclesiastical norms. The "optical selection"[73] in the dogmatic system was the result of a social practice different from the Church's traditional practice which legitimated a traditional social order.

Following this hypothesis one can begin to understand the divorce, soon to be complete, between the Church and the world of workers. Occupying—or seeking to occupy—a key position in society, the Church continued to legitimate the hierarchical forms of social participation we mentioned earlier. The attempt to reconcile the two, implicit in Saint-Simon's work and characteristic of Buchez, was brought up short by an alien, impenetrable system. With Proudhon the divorce was already close at hand. A study of social Catholicism will enable us to judge whether the practice it introduced into the Church had any chance of modifying its value system.

From another complementary point of view, taking the worker movement in its relation to the ruling class, one might wonder whether the endeavor of thinkers like Buchez and Proudhon was not a response to the necessity of addressing the dominant class in its own language, the language of humanism. And this necessity could be explained by the fact that the worker movement was still in its initial phase, not yet detached from the prevailing cultural system. If this hypothesis is correct, then I would like to suggest that Proudhon's anticlericalism was closer to that of Renan or Loisy than to Marxist atheism.

Father de Lubac thinks that Proudhon was an "integrist theologian"[74] who might easily have been a disciple of de Maistre, Renan, or Comte, but who would have used the arguments they used in favor of the worker movement instead of the bourgeoisie. Proudhon's reaction to Renan's *Life of Jesus* is revealing: "Mr. Renan has conceived his hero as a pure mystic, idealist, even a quietist, revolutionary only because of irritation and by accident, against his will; whereas I believe him to have been, before all else, a moral teacher, a social reformer, in a word, a man of justice." And later he adds: "If Mr. Renan has made Jesus in his own image, how could I not make him to mine."[75]

We have here, I believe, two different ways of trying to find a new religious legitimation of social values. With Renan it was a case of bourgeois humanism, and with Proudhon, an anticlerical but religious, proletarian prophetism.

Finally, we must account for the birth among the workers of a practical, militant form of atheism, based on Marx's premises. We have to bear in mind that for Marx atheism is inextricably linked to the accession of the proletariat to the principle of totality. The new class consciousness has been made possible by the disappearance of metasocial guarantees. The social classes now emerged as economic entities simultaneously with the disappearance of the religious dimension. In this context institutional religion experienced a sort of "backlash": The sacred became more and more institutionalized and norms were fixed in the rigidity of outmoded

social forms (parishes, the liturgy, language in the broadest sense
of the term). This process was already well on its way in the
nineteenth century. Henceforth the Church, its symbols, and its
language appeared dysfunctional and alien to the social transformation that was taking place. By the time a class consciousness
had developed they were devoid of all meaning.[76]

Social Catholicism: Its Growth and Structure

We must now investigate the social ideas which developed
among Catholics in the nineteenth century, thus rounding out what
we have already seen of the patterns of Christian thought in this
period. It is here, I believe, that the ultimate reason for the
Church's failure in the Industrial Revolution is to be found.

The evolution of ideas. Apart from Lamennais and the *Ere
Nouvelle* group (Montalembert, Lacordaire, and Maret) between
1830 and 1850, it was only in 1870 that any attempt was made, in
France at least, to systematize social theory and practice.[77] In 1809,
in his earliest writings, Lamennais had shown that he was fully
aware of the necessity of studying contemporary history and the
progress of the human spirit. But he had also shown a tendency to
reduce everything to a question of religion. Until 1829 he was
fiercely royalist and intransigently Catholic. Only later did he
begin to advocate the separation of the Church from the ruling
power, and this was in reaction against state control of the university. As we have already seen, his ideas were ambivalent. When he
was condemned for them, he left the Church. In 1836 he declared:
"I abandoned the Christianity of the pontificate to join the Christianity of the human race."

In his social writings he questioned the right to private property
and advocated the participation of workers in government, free
schooling, and worker ownership of the means of production. The
high clergy was solidly opposed to his views and only a small
minority was moved by his writings to a greater sensitivity to social
problems. During the July Monarchy Catholics were divided, as
we have already seen, into two factions: those who remained loyal
to the lawful king and those who showed some sympathy for
"socialist ideas." However, the optimistic euphoria of the latter did

not survive the riots of June, 1848, and the two camps became one again in their reaction. Only Lacordaire remained reticent, while his friends took up the battle cry of a "Christian order."

We should also mention the work of Villeneuve Bargemont, whose research into the working conditions at this period awakened many intellectuals, Catholic or otherwise, to the true state of affairs.

In Germany Catholics were rather less absorbed in political questions, but were just as conservative as in France. If they did not ally themselves with the bourgeois Liberals and create a party to maintain order, it was primarily because they were more concerned with a return to the traditional order and with crafts and agriculture. Only a few, such as Baader and Buss, raised their voices as early as 1837 to condemn the destitution in which the workers lived and to demand that the state intervene. But thanks to these men, the idea that industrial problems should be studied was introduced into the Catholic Congress. In 1846 Father Kolping set up the first social organization to seek the active participation of the workers. Archbishop Ketteler of Cologne had considerable influence in this area and was probably one of the first to elaborate a theory of this type of social organization based on cooperative action, which was to constitute the central theme of Catholic social teaching for more than fifty years. Leo XIII called Archbishop Ketteler, who died in 1877, "my illustrious predecessor."[78]

Under the Second Empire the spirit of paternalism triumphed in France. The fact that, as we have seen, the clergy came from a rural background and the bishops from the aristocracy—which was still bogged down in political and institutional questions—made it all the easier for Louis Veuillot's influence to spread. Proudhon was considered an anarchist, while Fourier offended all the conventional ideas in the domain of sexual and family ethics. Armand de Melun's influence was very small and any real thinking on the doctrinal level was almost nonexistent.

Only in 1871, with the Paris Commune, did a coherent theory and practice begin to emerge, with Albert de Mun and Patrice de La Tour du Pin. The horrors of the Paris Commune in which

Albert de Mun (1841-1914) was an officer, and an encounter with Maignen, founder of the Workers' Circles, launched him into the field of social action. The Workers' Circles answered a twofold need: ethicoreligious and social. Their aim was to bring together a dedicated elite and the workers whom they were helping, uniting them in justice and charity. They did not conceal their intention of combating the revolution, which de Mun accused of "founding society on the will of man rather than on the will of God," and of putting the "sovereignty of human reason in the place of divine faith." De Mun's work, based on such premises, constituted "a final effort to save the people and hasten God's return to a workshop regenerated." Subversive doctrines were to be answered by the teaching of the Gospel; materialism by the spirit of sacrifice; the cosmopolitan ideal by the ideal of the fatherland. In 1876 Albert de Mun declared to his constituents: "In the social as well as in the political order, the Catholic faith is the necessary foundation of all institutions and laws. It alone can be a remedy against the revolutionary peril and dissipate its effect and ensure the salvation of France."

This was the policy he pursued in the Chamber of Deputies and he was persecuted for it by the rightists as well as by the Catholics, led by Bishop Freppel. After the publication of *Rerum Novarum,* examining the concept of corporatism as a social system, he began to investigate the limits of the role of corporations:

> Are they to own all the fruits of their work, without appropriating anything for capital or, at least, for profit? The most logical say yes, and unless they are Christians in intention and in deed, I cannot see that they are very different from Socialists. Others hesitate, beat about the bush, and evade the question. The former are no longer reformers; they are revolutionaries. The latter are neither one thing nor the other. . . . All things considered, I am afraid that that is the danger we are in, of abandoning the idea of reforming society and presuming to substitute the idea of founding a new society.[79]

What better expression of the inner conflicts of Christian social thought: The systematic opposition to progress seems culpable, but the revolution seems contrary to nature, hence the only acceptable solution is reform. We are reminded of the texts prior to 1848, mentioned earlier.

La Tour du Pin, who died in 1924, was more of a theorist than de Mun. His ideal was to establish a Christian social order in

France, based on the monarchy. He accepted *Rerum Novarum,* but the papal recommendation to rally to the support of the Republic was qualified by him as "august splutterings." Whereas de Mun briefly entertained the idea of founding a Christian political party and only gave up the idea at Leo XIII's insistance, La Tour du Pin was categorically opposed to any idea of a Christian democracy. His ideas about property were based exclusively on an almost feudal conception of land ownership, and his ideas about the industrial order were, at best, a rehashing of Saint-Simon: "The contractor and the worker have not acquitted themselves in all justice when they have exchanged the price agreed upon for the work done unless, to the extent to which it is their responsibility, they have also given each other what they need in order to live honestly in their respective states of life." Written in 1882, these words foreshadowed *Rerum Novarum.*

In Belgium, the Liège Congress of 1886, 1887, and 1890 saw a very moderate expression of interventionism. Charles Woeste (1837-1922), speaking to the participants in 1886, declared: "The solution to the worker question must be sought, above all, in action by individuals and associations. . . . We should examine our legislation to see if it is, in some way, defective regarding the social questions, but . . . it is important to limit the action of the state as much as possible, and not to hinder individual action."[80] And Monsignor Rutten, vicar-general of Liège, considered that the "worker should understand that he must resign himself to his lot and bear the consequences of the inferior state in which God has placed him. And to convince him of the truth of this we need arguments that only religion can supply."

In 1887 the same Charles Woeste, having agreed that there was a need for social legislation, hastened to add: "What must be opposed is a false democracy which is a destructive doctrine. . . . That democracy would have the workers believe that all men have a vocation to wealth or, at least, to ease. This is just not so!" And how can the workers be persuaded that it is not so? "There is only one way and that is by charity, for, in the words of Scripture, charity fills up valleys and levels mountains."[81]

Between 1886 and 1890, however, those who were to be the pillars of Christian Democracy (e.g., Fathers Daen and Pottier) had begun to make themselves heard in Belgium, and the mood of the third Liège Congress in 1890 was more openly interventionist. But even then the emphasis on the revival of corporatism witnessed to a nostalgic hankering after the past, which seems to have been peculiar to Catholics at this period, even when they were "social minded."

With Léon Harmel (1829-1915), the theory and action of French Catholics took another turn. In 1854 Harmel was running the family factory in Val des Bois near Reims, and it was here that he put his theories into practice: a board, apprenticeships, a canteen, a cooperative, etc. The workers were whole Christian families transplanted from other areas and geographically isolated. Religious and social action was perfectly integrated and yet, although it might well have degenerated into the purest paternalism, Harmel's experiment remained truly democratic. His method developed, from 1884 on, into the Workers' Circles in which he insisted that the autonomy and responsibility of the workers be respected: "Everything for the good of the workers, but never without them and, a fortiori, never against their will." Harmel soon realized the limitations and ambiguities of such organizations as the Association of Catholic Employers of the North and their declared policy of "elevating the workers." He even broke off his association with the "mixed" unions to which both employers and workers belonged, advocating unions composed exclusively of workers.

Social methods of this kind inevitably led to certain theories and options on the political level. Harmel and the Workers' Circles organized regular conventions from 1893 on, and became the moving force in what was called the "second Christian Democracy" (1891-1902), following the first attempt by the Ere Nouvelle group. But plans for a Christian workers' party encountered the hostility of Leo XIII, who refused to envisage any form of democracy that was anything more than "good works for the benefit of the people."

Before pursuing the story of Harmel's experiment, we should perhaps pause to examine some of the main points of Rerum Novarum. The encyclical, published in 1891, had been prepared with great care and at great length by German and Swiss Catholics (especially by the school of Fribourg and Monsignor Mermillot).[82] The document was a résumé of the Church's thinking to date, and at the same time it was a new point of departure for further developments.

The encyclical declared:

> The violence of political revolutions has split the social body into two classes and has opened a great gulf between them. On one side are the all-powerful rich: a faction in absolute control of industry and commerce, directing the flow of wealth entirely toward itself . . . on the other side is the impotence of poverty, a vast multitude with bitterness corroding their souls, always on the verge of violence.

According to this document, one of the causes for this state of affairs is the fact that the Revolution only destroyed former social structures, leaving nothing in their place. "Workingmen have been given over, isolated and defenseless, to the callousness of employers and the greed of unrestrained competition."

The immediate cause for the publication of this letter was the mounting tide of socialism,[83] and the doctrine of socialism is condemned several times in the text:

> . . . Religion teaches . . . never to employ violence . . . nor to engage in riot and disorder; and to have nothing to do with men of evil principles, who work upon the people with artful promises and raise foolish hopes which usually end in disaster and in repentance when too late. . . . It is impossible to reduce human society to a level. The Socialists may do their utmost but all striving against nature is vain. . . . To remedy these evils the Socialists, working on the poor man's envy of the rich, maintain that private possession of goods should be overturned . . . but their proposals . . . would cause complete confusion in the community.

To withstand this danger the pope proposes a notion of the right to property founded on natural law and insists on the social function of this right: "Man should not consider his outward possessions as his own, but as belonging to all, so as to share them without difficulty when others are in need."

"It is just and right that the fruits of labor should belong to him who has labored." This is a point that should be emphasized: Leo XIII deals with the whole social problem in terms of justice. Salary is a right; rest is a right; and the state has a duty to intervene in social questions.

Not once did the pope use the word "union." With a view to rebuilding the fabric of society torn by revolution, he insists on the

need for associations of workers, or of workers and employers, and
he shows a perference for the latter. But the recognition of associations of workers did not mean that he accepted the class struggle.
The Church proposes something "more perfect": Its aim is to
strengthen the union between classes through the bonds of friend-
ship.

In short, *Rerum Novarum* seems to have been a mixture of
liberal ideas with a sprinkling of interventionism and corporatism
and distinctly hostile to socialism. Although they were new to
Catholics at the time, Leo XIII's contentions were decidedly behind the times in comparison with contemporary ideas in the
worker movement. Twenty years had passed since the Paris Commune and twenty-five since the founding of the first International.
The first workers' organizations had been formed several decades
earlier. In fact this encyclical was new only in contrast to the
utterances of the preceding popes. The polemical attitude it
adopted with regard to socialism was the voice of fear, and its
understanding of property still bespeaks a confusion between the
ownership of personal property and an exact notion of private
ownership of the means of production. This confusion reigned in
the Church for a very long time. The astonishment which *Rerum
Novarum* caused in the ranks of Catholic employers should not
mislead us into thinking that is was more progressive than it really
was.

Nor should it cause us to forget a phenomenon which followed
very soon after: the second Christian Democracy. Albert de Mun
saw the work of the "Circles" as the "dedication of the ruling class
to the popular classes." Harmel saw it as "an elevation of the
people through the restoration of initiative and responsibility."
Rerum Novarum put a stamp of approval on the former, whereas
Graves de Communi in 1901 was to condemn the Christian democracy that had emerged from the latter.[84]

This movement began in about 1891 or 1892, when the workers
took the initiative in forming groups called "Christian Social Study
Circles." The spirit and structure of these groups was democratic,
if by that one understands only the primacy that was attributed to
the responsibility of the members who were workers. When in 1896

4 8 1 2 0

the Christian Democratic Party was formed, its constitutions stipulated that "to be a member of the National Council, one must be, or have been, a wage earner."[85]

The choice of "Christian Democracy" as a title and the formation of a political party are evidence of a practice that had evolved into a doctrine. It is also an indication of the members' intention to make a clear distinction between themselves and the "social Christians," who, to them, were Christians who "engage in social affairs." The underlying feeling at the origin of the Christian democracy was, quite clearly, that the people should take charge of their own affairs: "the government of the people by the organized people." But no sooner was the political party organized than the word "democracy" was condemned by the pope and dropped, and, far more significantly, the whole thing drifted into being simply a Christian vision of society.

In 1902 the basic intuition of the group was taken up by Marc Sangnier (1873-1950), who founded the *Sillon,* a popular educational movement which gravitated around the Study Circles and which also created the People's Institutes in the major cities, which were open to all students and workers, whether or not they were Christians. Sangnier spoke of himself as "a fearless Christian and an unequivocal democratic Republican." His movement was never given any permanent structures. It began as a Christian movement with social tendencies and evolved, from 1906 on, into a movement which was still Christian in inspiration but political and open to nonbelievers. This development alarmed the hierarchy and the days of the *Sillon* were numbered in 1910 when Pius X called them to order.

The terms of Pius X's letter, incidentally, make fruitful reading in the context of this study. He writes: "We know very well that they [the members of the *Sillon*] flatter themselves that they are elevating human dignity and the condition of the working classes, which is too miserable . . . and we do not reproach them for this." But the pope believed that

By wounding the vital organs of society and shattering the framework of its activities, we urge human beings on, not to progress but to death. And yet this is what they want to do with human society. Their dream is to change the traditional and natural foundations and to promise a new city for the future, built on other principles which, they dare to say, are more fruitful and beneficial than those on which the Christian city is built today. . . . One cannot build the city except as God has built it. . . . No; civilization no longer has to be invented, and the new city no longer has to be built in the clouds. It has already been built, it already exists: it is Christian civilization, the Catholic city. It only remains for it to be established and constantly restored on its natural and divine foundations, against ever renewed attacks of unhealthy utopias, revolt and ungodliness. . . .

The point that had particularly aroused the wrath of the hierarchy and led to this condemnation was the accent Sangnier and his friends put on the autonomy of the civic conscience: They had the intention of joining in united action with all Democrats and running their movement quite independently of the hierarchical Church. Sangnier's political ideas led him to call for the decentralization of government in order to facilitate the fuller participation of all citizens. He advocated workers' unions whose aim would be to transform society, and he had very serious doubts about the validity of Christian trade unionism. According to him, democracy is not "Christian," it is political, and it is not only Christians who should promote it.

Patterns of Christian thinking and the social problem. In this part of our analysis[86] we shall study two questions. The first concerns the reasons that led Leo XIII to speak of "new things" when they were already fifty years old. The second concerns the evolution that took place in Christian thinking with the appearance and assimilation by Christians of the democratic value system. Why was it so long in coming and why did it meet with such opposition from the Church?

Several times already we have distinguished between the circumstantial and the structural reasons which determined the attitude of the Church in any given period. We must have recourse to this distinction again here. There was, of course, the Roman Question, which caused so many Catholics to neglect the social question. For French Catholics there was also a major political question on the domestic scene which distracted their attention from the world of workers. But these facts in themselves explain nothing. The real question still remains as to why the Church became so hypnotized by the problem of its own temporal power. Why did French Catholics take so long to get the republican question out of their systems? Why were the first forms of social Catholicism corporatist and paternalistic?

On the level of the facts we can see that Montalembert, Lacordaire at least partly, and La Tour du Pin were royalists in their politics. The value system to which they subscribed belonged, as we have seen, to a preindustrial, traditional society, in which plurifunctional social structures produced a hierarchical type of social participation. The Church was present in all areas of life in this society, and endorsed existing social relations as sacred and "natural."

Social problems caused these men to bend their efforts toward new objectives, but they were still impregnated with the old value system. A feudal landowner could be a conservative and still be deeply concerned with social problems; it was part of a long tradition in which the master's concern for "his people" was a value acknowledged by society. On the other hand, liberalism went against the grain of all their political convictions. The solutions they proposed were dictated by their experience and were in keeping with their culture: the patronage of the ruling classes and corporative organizations of a decidedly antirevolutionary style, based on the assumption that only the Church holds the key to the social problem.

Going a step further, we might ask how it was that *Rerum Novarum* favored this trend to the point that it became for a time the *summum* of Christian social doctrine. Our attempt to reply to the second question posed above will shed some light on this. For if we can understand why the Church rejected democracy as a political motivation for Christians, we shall at the same time discover the patterns of thought and the value system endorsed and promoted by the theology of the day.

In his thesis *Conscience religieuse et démocratie*,[87] Maurice Montuclard sets out to show that behind the antagonism between social Catholicism and the Christian Workers' Circles between 1891 and 1902 lay a twin constellation of Christian thinking, resulting from two quite different practices.

With the help of Montuclard's material[88] we can now pick up the
threads of the analysis, begun in the second part of this chapter,[89]
of the principal themes of the Church's social theory in the nineteenth century. This theory continued to be based on religious and
social images of the past: The world was conceived as being an
integral part of the religious scheme of things; social questions
were interpreted according to patterns handed down from a preindustrial society in which men were of two classes—the rich and the
poor—and in which the function of ethics was to compensate for
this inequality by the practice of charity while, at the same time,
legitimating it by reference to a supernatural order in the world to
come, thereby putting a premium on resignation. As we have seen,
those who opposed this ideology, whether in the worker movement
(Buchez, Corbon, etc.) or within the Church itself (Lamennais, the
Sillon), did so at the price of becoming marginalized or of being
rejected outright by the Church. This description of the dominant
ideology leads directly to the question that has haunted these
pages.

We have already seen[90] how the Holy See condemned Marc
Sangnier and his associates in the *Sillon,* accusing them of seeking
to change the very foundations of society: "No; civilization no
longer has to be invented, and the new city no longer has to be
built in the clouds. It has already been built, it already exists: it is
Christian civilization, the Catholic city." With this declaration Pius
X clearly and solemnly declares that society has no consistency of
its own, that the social order comes from God, and that only the
Church is qualified to interpret God's will and guide men in their
temporal options as well as in their supernatural vocation. In other
words Christendom was still the ideal which inspired the ecclesiology and the social ethic of the Church in the nineteenth century. It
was still trying to resist the intellectual thrust which, ever since the
sixteenth century, had tended to see it as an entity distinct from its
social environment.[91] It persisted in harking back to the time when
it was perfectly integrated into the social order entrusted to its care
by Constantine and took refuge against contemporary "error" in a
scholastic approach proper to a society in which the metaphysical
implications of religion still had significance in the social order.

Buchez quarreled with Thomistic scholasticism precisely because, as he said, it opposed progress and expressed a civilization which conceived the world as immutable, and he pointed out that the conceptual instrument of Thomism, the syllogism, is designed for argumentation but not for an understanding of new situations.[92]

The Syllabus was no stranger to the elaboration of a social doctrine which tended, above all, to affirm that there was a "Catholic solution" to all social problems. But in practice an apparent paradox can be seen in the strong emphasis on institutionalization, which coexisted with a narrowing of the scope of Christian ethics to the domain of interpersonal relations.

If the world's problems can be solved only by God himself through the instrumentality of the Church, then the Church is under an obligation to make an active and concrete contribution to their solution. A long-established tradition, therefore, associates Christianity with works of charity, and within this tradition can be found both fundamental values and accidental institutional aspects. There is nothing to be gained by judging the good will of the people concerned. What interests us is to try to understand the logical connection between ideology and practice. The Church's creation of welfare agencies in answer to immediate needs at the beginning of the industrial era and its insistence that specifically Christian solutions could and must be found for the organizational problems of industrial society are inspired by one and the same vision of reality. Hence the creation of "mixed" unions in which workers and employers came together to resolve the adventitious effects of a system, but without questioning its basic premises. Two unconscious values justify this practice and make it seem reasonable: a theology which includes the whole of the social order in the religious (i.e., in practice, in the domain of "charity") and a refusal to acknowledge explicitly that there could be conflict between the faithful of different social classes.

Perhaps we should go even further, however, for it seems that certain ambitions of domination were not altogether foreign to the birth of a social doctrine. Giuseppe Toniolo, one of Leo XIII's collaborators in the preparation of *Rerum Novarum,* admits that "we cannot even accept a vague and deceptive social neo-Christi-

anity for it is a deformation of Christianity. Our aspiration is to re-
create the social order that the Catholic Church alone can give us
and we ask, therefore, that the Church be restored to exterior,
social liberty so that it may resume the government of society and
civilization"[93]

This ambition was translated into concrete form even in details
as, for instance, when the Association of Catholic Employers of the
North undertook a campaign to "moralize" the factories: A priest
had access to the factory and a chapel was put at his disposal, the
employer's wife exercised her "charity" among the workers with
the aid of the "Little Sisters of the Factories," the workers were
given religious instruction and were subject to control and assistance in every facet of their lives, by the benefactors who employed them.[94] Certain Jesuits justified this practice by a theology
aptly summed up in this passage: "Imbued with the teachings of
the Holy Father, we must remind Catholic employers of the extent
of their duties. . . . At the same time we are endeavoring to fashion
the hearts of the workers to their life of submission and labor. . . .
We are showing the example of our divine master to all men and,
in the words of Jesus Christ, we declare for all to hear: *Quaerite
primum regnum Dei et Justitiam ejus. . . . Diligite invicem. . . .* In
this, we believe, lie the elements necessary for the solution of the
social question."[95]

On the broader level this tendency was expressed in the rejection
of state intervention or, at least, in a deep distrust with regard to
any intervention by government in the social area. But this particular point can be fully understood only if it is seen in the context of
the conflict between the Church and a society which had grown up
outside and in opposition to the Church.

At this stage we must look at the Church's point of view concerning the bourgeois ideology. As we have seen, the bourgeoisie
set great store by its attempted restoration of "religious" and
spiritual values, considered to be the best way of bolstering its own
authority, while at the same time carrying on a running battle with
the Church. As a group the bourgeoisie feared the traditionalism of
the Church, which was, in effect, hostile to every form of idealism
and even every form of spirituality which did not express itself in

orthodox Catholic theological terms, for they opened the door to "natural religion" and a formulation of faith which could not be controlled by the institution. Louis Veuillot eloquently voiced the Church's mistrust, which extended even to any independent philosophical project, when he said to Victor Cousin: "You are not and never have been a materialist. And yet materialism is one of the things I hold against you, because you represent philosophy and whatever rights you claim today, materialism will also claim when its time comes . . . and its time will come very soon."

Seen in this light, the dispute about state control of the universities is understandable: The Church was the hostage of a besieged social class fighting for its own interests against the industrial bourgeoisie. In a later phase, when the bourgeoisie had consolidated its power, it used the Church in its interest to protect society against the challenge of the worker movement.[96] Since the latter had built up its ideology outside and in opposition to the Church, the same reflex by which the Church rejected all independent thought came into play again, causing it to refuse the autonomy of the collective social project. And so the Church stood opposed to all influences which tended to subvert the established social order as well as to all attempts at control by the political arm. On this point at least Leo XIII's encyclical was a decided break with tradition, but the fact went largely unnoticed by Catholic employers, so concerned were they with the encyclical's attack on socialism and democracy. And this ambiguity led Catholics to adopt completely contradictory positions in all good faith. Lacordaire proclaimed from the pulpit of Notre Dame: "In the conflict between the strong and the weak the oppressor is freedom," whereas the theologians of the Association of Catholic Employers felt that "in France, legislation is often no more than a weapon to be used against freedom, society and the Church. . . . It would obviously be foolhardy to promote new laws at this juncture or even to arouse a movement of public opinion in favor of legislation."[97]

By default, the Christian ethic became a single-minded preoccupation with individual consciences and interpersonal relations, from a strictly religious point of view. "The factory, properly understood and wisely organized, must make a worker a better man and help him to get to heaven just as much as it must fulfill his temporal needs and, if possible, help him improve his situation."[98] This led to the paradox of a holistic institution which offered no outlet for the collective social project. While ideologies such as those of Saint-Simon and Buchez tried to interpret Christianity in terms of a collective project in the future, capable of integrating change and progress, the official Church put a premium on society as it already existed, cold-shouldered anything that smacked of change, and saw the individual as subjected to a ready-made history and the established social order. On what theology of history, on what interpretation of reality did the Church base its reaction? Basically, as we have said, the Church's ideal image of society, even in the nascent industrial society of the period, already transformed by the tool of collective production, was that of a simple, stable society of the past. It envisaged the problem of pauperization as a problem of scarcity, and it still held to a sacral notion of social relations.

In a society dominated by the problem of scarcities, Christianity made social life possible by emphasizing the value of asceticism and the painful nature of work. At the same time it cultivated the charity of the wealthy in order to remedy the destitution of the poor. This was still the viewpoint of the Catholic Employers of the North: Christianity is the answer to the social question for within the framework of Christianity "everyone has a happy life insofar as this is possible on this earth; the established order, wealth, has its own God-given uses: it comes to the aid of the poor and sanctifies the wealthy. . . ."[99] "A worker can be happy only because his wants are modest and, above all, because he is capable of sacrifice,"[100] whereas "a thirst for pleasure nourishes perpetual discontent in the soul because of the situation in which providence has placed the worker."[101]

Charity was considered the best possible solution for present conflicts. A passion for justice would have undermined private property and social inequality and the social order was based on respect for these realities. When workers organized and started their own provident societies, the Church warned against the dangers of this solidarity which would corrode the bonds of dependency linking the poor to the rich. "It is a mistake to believe that the workers' needs will ever be ensured by such institutions. The patronage of their betters will always be their principal means of security."[102] And if there was any doubt as to the providential necessity of the established order, there was always one argument that clinched the matter: "How can there be room for Christian charity in a situation in which the keystone of all organization is social equality? The more room there is for equality the less there will be for charity: the two are mutually exclusive."[103]

By promoting these norms the Church was in fact promoting the preservation of old values and the conservation of the existing social system. "God has made the employer the pastor of his factory,"[104] his authority, therefore, is by divine mandate and can neither be divided nor contested. His very function is part of God's plan, for "although the employer may seem to be pursuing only his own advantage or his own legitimate satisfaction, he is the instrument of providence and, thanks to his capital, he can give a living to many workers who would be in dire straits without him."[105]

The foregoing synthesis, although it illustrates the predominant aspect of the Church's thinking in the nineteenth century, does not give the whole picture. Various groups from different social classes had developed other theories antinomic to these, but they had never really been accepted by the institution. The Christian Workers' Circles, for instance, were diametrically opposed to the Catholic employers on such questions as the relation between the social and the religious or between justice and charity: "Many of us seem to think that man is only a soul. The pope has reminded them that he is also a body, that he is made for life on earth before heaven, and that his daily bread should not depend on alms: it is important even for his eternal destiny."[106]

This line of thought recognized that society has its own autonomy and that it cannot be called Christian simply because the Church includes it in its holistic view of reality. If "Christianity is not a question of sword or scepter,"[107] then one has the right to say that "to restore order in society it is not enough to Christianize it," and that "a society in which all the individuals are Christians is not, ipso facto, a well ordered society."[108] A well ordered society is one in which *justice* reigns. If Christians concern themselves with social problems, it must not be in the name of charity but in the name of justice, for "charity does not substitute for justice, it presupposes it."[109] Justice can be established only through a fraternity which tends toward liberation. The Congress of Workers' Circles declared: "Our goal is social elevation which will enable the people to look after their own rights, thus safeguarding the dignity of their own lives. . . . The day the worker can draw strength from his union he will have found his place in the sun; moreover this is in keeping with the plan of God who has no desire to crush the lowly and the humble."[110]

These values make it possible to integrate and recognize the zones of conflict within society and among Catholics: "Catholics worthy of the name give sympathy and help to anyone who rebels and struggles against poverty."[111]

However, the attitude we have just briefly described prevailed only in groups which had become marginal to or were completely excluded from the institutional Church. We have come across this phenomenon more than once in this period and the fact that it was the case of those who first felt the need to reconcile their Christian commitment and their loyalty to the workers' cause is a clue to one of the most important aspects of the impact social change had in the Church. It highlights the conflict between the "establishment" and any group which adopts new values. We shall be in a position to come back to this aspect of the phenomenon and to look at it from a more fundamental sociological point of view when we have seen how it comes to pass in different circumstances.

We shall conclude quite briefly, therefore, with three related observations. First, the Church of the nineteenth century was a stranger and sometimes an enemy to the metamorphosis that was going on in the society of the day. It was incapable of allowing itself to be affected by the class struggle and the worker movement and introduce changes in its own structures, simply because it failed to understand or even recognize these phenomena for what they were.

Secondly, the Church's failure can be partially explained by the prevailing circumstances, but more profoundly by its own attitude, its time-honored method of action, and the structure of its cultural system. Throughout this period it was in the position of a subculture threatened at all times by the rising class, first the bourgeoisie and then the workers. I have tried to point out this phenomenon by describing the ideological implications of the conflicts opposing the institutional Church and society. The Church's religious view of society and its steadfast conviction that it was the key institution within that society meant that its ideology became a hothouse of ancient values and a ready prey for the dominant classes.

Finally, this second point raises the questions of the relation between the Church as institution and society and that of the function of its theological discourse. Every time we realize, with Merleau-Ponty, that "Catholics are poor conservatives but unreliable revolutionaries,"[112] we are brought up against this fundamental problem. We shall come back to it at the end of our study.

CHAPTER FOUR

The Cuban Revolution

The Cuban revolution is perhaps the one important contemporary event which has most influenced the thinking and action of people interested in the social transformation of today's world, not only in Latin America but all over the world. The revolution is more than ten years old now, and in spite of international opposition it is still in control. The relations between the Church and the government are better than they were, but much can be learned from studying the evolution of the movement and seeing why Church-government relations deteriorated so rapidly at the beginning.

The Church in the Sociopolitical Evolution of Cuba before the Castro Revolution

Until 1898 Cuba was a Spanish crown colony. As the last remaining piece of Spanish real estate in the New World, it was jealously guarded and every effort was made to guarantee the perpetuation of its colonial status. One of the means used to this end was the Catholic Church. The bishops and most of the priests were Spanish and, it must be added, the clergy was not always of the highest caliber; the island often served as a "refuge for sinners" for priests who had had difficulties of one kind or another in Spain. The native clergy, which had existed in the beginning of the nineteenth century, had dwindled to almost nothing, as no effort had been made to encourage Cuban vocations but rather the contrary. In return for lending its influence in support of the colonial regime, the Church was given social status and political power, which enabled it to keep up an appearance of vitality and an ecclesiastical apparatus out of all proportion to its true strength.

It is not surprising that the first few years of independence were unhappy ones for the Church, deprived of its hierarchy as had happened in the majority of Latin American countries after independence. After only a few years, owing to the dearth of local clergy and the fact that relations with the old metropolis had been partially normalized, Spanish priests began to work in Cuba. At the time they were almost all members of the religious orders. The Cuban people were not very fervent and the Church's prestige was at a low ebb. The number of men who practiced their religion was infinitesimal. The clergy, applying the methods they had always used in their own country, began to build up a relationship between the Church and the state similar to that which existed in Spain, and gradually the Church won social prestige, not because of its concern for the poor but because of its alliance with the rich.

The history of independent Cuba has always been eventful. The political vacuum created by the withdrawal of Spain and the fact that its powerful neighbor, the United States, had presided over the birth of the new state, did nothing to foster a sense of political responsibility among the population. Cuba was ruled by a series of regimes, all of them of more or less dubious repute. In 1933, however, Antonio Guitera launched his program of social reform: an eight-hour working day, social security, nationalization of the American Electrical Society, etc. Sumner Welles, then United States ambassador to Havana, advocated a military intervention according to the classic practice of the time in the Caribbean and Central America. But American diplomacy chose a different weapon: It supported the army chief, a certain Fulgencio Batista, in his attempt to win control, first through the intermediary of a third party and, in 1940, in person. In 1944 Batista lost the elections, but he was returned to power in 1952 after the totally corrupt regime of Rio Jocarrás. He was finally overthrown at the end of 1958.

For nearly twenty years political disintegration had practically become an institution characteristic of Cuban society. The peasants, who—in contrast to other Latin American countries—constitute only 45 percent of the total population, lived in abysmal poverty, exploited by the owners of the immense sugar plantations. Industrial workers were not very numerous, and the sugar mills functioned only a few months out of each year. A large category of the population was crowded into the towns, living on disproportionately extensive service industries, on the foreign, mostly American, tourist trade, and on the administration. Political corruption was one of the principal means of social promotion.

Gradually the Church became more diversified, and in 1928 Catholic Action was founded. Although it was still imbued with a triumphalist mentality, it was gradually coming into its own with a certain religious elite, mostly from the middle classes, who were beginning to practice their religion and acknowledge themselves as loyal members of the Church. The preferred area of pastoral activity, particularly among the religious orders, was education. More and more colleges were founded for both boys and girls, in the cherished illusion that this was the best way to re-Christianize society. After 1945 the Jesuits organized the YCW (Young Christian Workers), and in the space of five years, from 1948 to 1953, the movement provided more candidates to the Society of Jesus than Belén college with its two thousand students.[1]

In 1953, when Catholic Action was celebrating its twenty-fifth anniversary, Havana, with at least one million inhabitants, had sixteen parishes with an average of two priests per parish. There were also two hundred priests in the secondary schools, mostly run by religious. The majority of these were Spanish and some of their schools earned substantial revenues for their congregations in Spain. This was also the case with some of the parishes in the residential areas of Havana, which is the reason the archbishop never managed to divide them into smaller parishes.

Most Cuban seminarians joining a religious order would receive their training in Spain, but there was no more than a tiny trickle of vocations, although, thanks to Catholic Action, the situation improved slightly in the 1950s. The diocesan clergy, with very little social prestige, had even fewer recruits than the religious orders. But it was the rural areas which suffered most from pastoral neglect. All these elements served to identify the Church with the upper middle classes, whose main concern was political stability. When Fulgencio Batista took over the government in 1952, he did so with the support of Cardinal Arteaga y Betancur. Canon (later Cardinal) Cardijn, founder of the YCW, visiting Havana for the twenty-fifth anniversary celebrations of Catholic Action, was horri-

fied at what he saw of the situation of the Church and especially of
the bishops' lack of awareness. He could only repeat: "They don't
know what's in store for them. They don't know what's in store for
them."

The Church in the Different Phases
of the Revolution

Liberation from tyranny. Fulgencio Batista's regime became
more and more dictatorial and arbitrary, and political arrests and
assassinations were frequent occurrences. On July 26, 1953, Fidel
Castro led an abortive attack against the Moncado Barracks in
Santiago. Castro was arrested, but, thanks to the intervention of
Bishop Pérez Servantes of Santiago, he was given a regular trial.
One year later, after his release from prison, he went into exile.

The hierarchy was divided on the attitude they should adopt in
view of the way the situation was evolving. Bishop Pérez Servantes
and Bishop Martín of Matanzas were outspokenly opposed to
Batista's regime, whereas the aging cardinal continued to be on the
best of terms with it and the bishop of Camaguay felt that the
Church should have no opinion in the matter. Until 1958 the
hierarchy made no official pronouncement. By then, however, the
struggle was being carried on openly in the Sierra Maestra, militant Catholics were on the side of the rebels, and many priests had
joined the underground as chaplains or were helping the rebels in
other ways. On February 10, 1958, the pastor of Holy Spirit parish
in Havana condemned the regime in strong terms from the pulpit
and the following day Catholic Action organizations took a stand
against arbitrary political power. Before this, a few scattered statements had been made by militant Catholics, most of them urging
the necessity of an agrarian reform.

On February 25 an incident occurred which was characteristic
of the situation:[2] Bishop Pérez Servantes convened a secret meeting with his fellow bishops in the hope of bringing pressure to bear
on Batista to resign. The bishops, however, failed to reach agreement on this, and what seems to have been a compromise solution
was adopted: They published a text, which is worth quoting:

> We exhort militants on both sides to renounce the use of violence and to find,
> as quickly as possible, an effective solution which will restore the physical and

moral peace our country stands so much in need of. To this end we have no doubt that those who really love Cuba will find a way of winning merit in the eyes of God and of history by unhesitatingly accepting all the sacrifices necessary to establish a government of national unity, capable of restoring a peaceful and normal political life to our country.[3]

President Batista immediately made known his agreement with this proposition, for he was already hard-pressed. But Fidel Castro, in a letter dated March 9, wanted to know what the bishops meant by a government of national unity and whether they really thought that any honorable Cuban could participate in a government presided over by Fulgencio Batista. Bishop Pérez Servantes made known his own disagreement with the published text; the only solution he could envisage was the resignation of Batista. The bishop of Matanzas, on the other hand, visited the dictator and urged him to resign. Batista's answer was not long in coming: Catholics were victims of vicious reprisals, which took the lives of labor leader Sergio Gonzalez and several other outstanding Catholics.

As the Catholic hierarchy still did not protest officially, other voices began to be heard, especially from the ranks of the clergy. At the beginning of December, 1958, Father Belarmino García publicly reproached the hierarchy for their indifference, which was an encouragement for the repressive powers wielded by the government. The majority of Catholic militants were opposed to the tyrannical regime and collaborated in the struggle for liberation. In January, 1959, a few days after his victory, Fidel Castro declared: "The Catholics of Cuba have given their most vigorous collaboration to the cause of freedom."[4]

Freedom yes; Revolution no. The struggle for freedom from tyranny had not been inspired by any one ideology. The Communist party had not been willing to trust a young lawyer of aristocratic background in the beginning of his revolutionary adventure, and it rallied to his side only very late in the day. The bourgeois and middle classes had suffered greatly at the hands of Batista's regime, and the last few months had become unbearable for many of them. Catholics too had suffered many injustices. All were united in the common struggle against the dictatorship and against those who had taken advantage of it to line their own pockets.

Having accomplished the first phase of the actual liberation, Fidel Castro intended to remain only the charismatic leader of the movement; he did not want to assume public office. On January 2 he installed Manuel Irruia as provisional president of the Republic, and José Miró Cardona was chosen to form a government. On February 15 Cardona asked Castro to be president of the Council and two days later Castro accepted. He was, admittedly, in a difficult position: How could anyone else really govern the country if all popularity and prestige were invested in his person? On the other hand, Castro had probably been overly optimistic and had underestimated the reconstruction that would have to be undertaken. He realized now that certain radical measures were called for: transformation of social structures, particularly in the field of agriculture and land distribution; the creation of a new political ethic; liberation from the stranglehold of foreign capital, etc.

Gradually, as the liberation became the revolution, opposition to Castro began to crystallize. The first signs of it came in March, 1959, among government employees, especially those who had joined in the struggle against Batista and who now felt they were being betrayed by Castro. Manuel Artima, who was to head the invasion a few years later, was one of them. In August, 1959, the *latifundistas* (big landowners) conspired in an attempt to bribe the press. As early as June, part of the American press—particularly *Time* magazine—began to attack Castro, accusing him of communist tendencies. In the middle of October, Cuban crops were bombed from bases in Florida, and at about that time a counterrevolutionary movement took shape in Havana, drawing most of its adherents from the Ministry of Agriculture. The movement was led by Catholics who reproached Castro for accepting the collaboration of the Communist party and who found themselves completely disoriented by the preparations that were going ahead for an agrarian reform which, to many of them, seemed inspired by a collectivist ideology.

The Communist party had been the only party to refuse its participation in the last elections held under Batista. It was, therefore, the only one that seemed "pure" to the new regime. Apart from it, the political scene was void. On the other hand, Cuban

Catholics, even the best, had been so rigorously trained in anti-communism (ten years earlier the Holy Office had excommuni-cated anyone who took part in the activities of the Communist party or who voted for their candidates) that the slightest hint of a compromise with the party or any of its goals seemed to them absolutely opposed to Catholic principles. It was at this period that the confusion between social reform and communism arose, as well as the confusion between the interests of certain classes and of religion. Some went as far as to say that "at least Batista was anticommunist." A current of opinion gradually grew to compel Castro to declare himself opposed to communism. A Catholic journalist, Francisco Paré, wrote at that time that the aim of communism was the "destruction of the pillars that uphold the Cuban capitalist, Christian and democratic society." Fortunately there were other Catholics who took a different stand. Andrés Valdespino wrote that a distinction must be made between the social reforms proposed by communism and its ideology. Angel del Carro felt that the Church had nothing to say in the present circumstances and that the communist threat could have been averted if the Church had thrown itself wholeheartedly into the revolution.[5]

The clergy was becoming more and more distrustful of the regime and yet, when the educational system was reformed, the bishops asked for and obtained the inclusion of obligatory reli-gious instruction in the curriculum of the public schools. This had never been done before. In May, 1959, the Agrupación Católica declared its opposition to the agrarian reform, but Bishop Evelio Díaz of Havana gave it his approval, saying that it "enters fully into the spirit and meaning of Christian social justice" (Declara-tion of May 29, 1959).

At the end of that year the American government pressured a certain number of noncommunist countries to withhold support of Cuba, and Castro was obliged to conduct his struggle on two fronts: inside the country against rapid political disintegration and outside the country against growing pressure from the United States.

At the end of the autumn of 1959 the bishops seemed to be more and more opposed to the regime, mostly for reasons concerning its foreign policy: Nonalignment seemed to them incompatible with the Christian faith.[6] Pressure from the United States was growing, for many American interests had been affected by the agrarian reform. On November 28 and 29 the National Catholic Congress met in Havana with close to one million participants; many different opinions were expressed and a great number of voices were raised in warning against communism.

This was the signal for a more rapid development of the situation. In January, 1960, a group of religious superiors gathered at the Spanish Embassy were assailed by Castro, who declared that the clergy harbored reactionary and counterrevolutionary elements. On February 5, on the occasion of the visit of Anastas Mikoyan to Cuba, Catholic students demonstrated in protest.

The year 1960 saw relations between Cuba and the United States deteriorate still further, while a rapprochment was effected with the USSR. In May diplomatic relations were established between Havana and Moscow, and on May 16 this move was publicly criticized by Bishop Pérez Servantes, the Christian Democratic party was dissolved, and its leaders sought refuge in the United States. When the American oil refineries, which refused to process Russian oil, were nationalized, Bishop Eduardo Boza Masvidal protested against abusive state control of social and economic life.

The conflict with the United States came to a head when, in July of that year, the U. S. Congress decided to refuse what remained of the Cuban sugar quota for the current year. Two days later Castro nationalized American property, saying that compensation would be paid out of the revenues from future sugar sales to the United States. Meanwhile the domestic situation was very tense. On August 7 a joint pastoral letter from the bishops denounced the "growth of communism in our country." On August 9 Bishop Díaz, who had previously shown a very liberal attitude toward the regime, threatened to close the churches in protest and to declare the Church to be in a state of persecution. To this Castro replied that there were some priests in the service of the poor, but that others of a higher rank were in the service of the rich. And he added, "I would like to see a pastoral letter condemning the companies which exploit our people and the imperialist aggression against our country."

Bishop Pérez Servantes continued to give voice to his protest. In October he wrote in a pastoral letter, "Cubans yes, slaves no," and in November he condemned Catholics who collaborated with the regime. On December 4 came yet another letter from the hierarchy. This time it was an open letter to Fidel Castro, urging him, for the last time, to repudiate communism and expressing the hope that the Lord would "enlighten him." On December 16 Castro replied that the government was not answerable to the bishops. A few months later, referring to this incident, he said: "Have you ever seen a pastoral letter in defense of the peasants on the sugar plantations? Or calling for schools for the peasants' children? Or condemning the murder of worker- and student-leaders? Have they ever protested against the profiteers who stockpile foodstuffs, or against high rents and fraudulent practices?"

An open struggle against the socialist revolution. By 1961 the conflict between the Church and the Castro regime could no longer be contained. On January 3 the United States broke off diplomatic relations and imposed an almost total economic blockade. The Church was denied access to public channels of information and restricted to the use of its own papers. On April 17 the fiasco of the Bay of Pigs occurred.

The abortive invasion was led by two factions: the partisans of Batista and a group of Catholics. Manuel Artima, the leader of the Catholic group, was also in command of the operation. The three Spanish monks who accompanied him had prepared a declaration for their arrival in Cuba:

> We come in the name of God.... The assault brigade is composed of thousands of Cubans who are all Christian and Catholic. Our struggle is the struggle of those who believe in God against atheists, the struggle of spiritual values against materialism, the struggle of democracy against communism. Ideologies can only be vanquished by a superior ideology and the only ideology capable of defeating the communist ideology is the Catholic ideology.... Long live Christ the King!

On May 1 Fidel Castro published a harsh declaration in which he did not blame the Church itself, but denounced Spanish fascism working through the intermediary of "its priests." In consequence, the status of every foreign priest was to be examined on its own merits. He also claimed that "falangist" priests were engaged in counterrevolutionary propaganda in the Catholic schools frequented by the children of the rich. Accordingly he decreed the nationalization of all schools in order to establish free public education: Henceforward religion was to be taught only in the churches. Religion and the revolution could coexist, declared Castro, but some people were using religion as a pretext to resist justice.

The nationalization of the schools provoked a mass exodus of Spanish religious and clergy. Many of them could not envisage the reorientation of their work without schools; others feared a repetition of the Spanish civil war and preferred to leave before that happened. The exodus reached such proportions that the Vatican sent a special envoy to try to stem the tide, but by the time he arrived more than half the priests and about three-fourths of the religious had already left the country.

On September 10, 1961, there was an incident in which a religious procession of several thousand people from Bishop Boza's parish turned into an anticommunist demonstration. One person was killed and several wounded. Two days later Bishop Boza was arrested, and within a few days he and 135 other priests, 45 of whom were Cubans, were put on board the *Covadonga*, a Spanish ship bound for Spain. On September 19 Fidel Castro declared that from then on religious processions were banned. Ceremonies were to take place inside the churches only. Priests who behaved themselves and confined themselves to the service of worship, which was their true mission, would be respected. On September 20, during a public audience in Rome, John XXIII expressed the hope that a "sincere desire to preserve the values of a Christian civilization would prevail over hasty decisions."

The rapid succession of events suggests how difficult it must have been for the hierarchical Church and the Catholic community to understand the historical evolution that was going on. Whether Fidel Castro's Marxist convictions had always been the same, as he himself declared, will be for historians to show. It seems more likely, however, that the complex circumstances of the birth and development of the revolution led him inexorably to model it on the pattern of Leninist socialism. And even if he had preferred to avoid this, the attitude of the United States would probably have forced him in that direction.

The opposition of many Catholics, belonging mainly to the upper and middle classes, was not motivated only by doctrinal anticommunism. It was also, often unconsciously, the result of their incapacity to extract themselves from a sacral mentality characteristic of medieval times. This phenomenon is so similar to some of the other cases studied in this book that it is worth noting[7] and, needless to say, it is present also in many other cases. Contemporary Europe can supply several examples, not only in Spain and Portugal, but also in Italy and, in fact, in certain aspects of the "school question" in Belgium. In Asia the attitude of Christians to decolonization was characterized by similar tendencies; the Church's reaction to the political evolution that took place in Ceylon between 1956 and 1960, for instance, was similar to that which prevailed in Cuba.

The year 1962 was a sorrowful year for Catholics in Cuba. Large numbers had left the country; many others were in prison; and those who remained were all suspect. Out of 800 priests there were only about 250 left to minister to the needs of about 7,000,000 baptized Catholics. The number of religious had dwindled from 3,000 to 300. There was some discrimination against middle-class Catholics, especially when their children wanted to enter secondary schools and the university. Education had made great strides, for it was one of the sectors that was most dynamically reformed by the revolution, and it now became officially Marxist. Although there was no official widespread antireligious campaign, there were frequent incidents on the local level.

At the beginning of 1963 the Vatican appointed Bishop Cesare Zacchi chargé d'affaires at Havana. His attitude toward the regime was distinctly innovative and he established a personal relationship with its leaders. Because of this, however, many Catholics considered him a traitor and even the bishops cold-shouldered this prelate who had had no first-hand experience of the events and who was now establishing a new style of relation with the regime. In that same year the incident of the nuclear missile bases on Cuba shook the world. (Only three years earlier, on November 13, 1960, Bishop Pérez Servantes had declared in a pastoral letter: "It is thanks to the generosity of the American people, who in the last fifteen years have contributed the fabulous sum of $365 billion to win world security, that communism has not invaded the entire world.")

Coexistence and Gradual Acceptance

It was not easy for the Cuban Church to recover fully from the traumatic experience of the revolution. All concrete hopes of a counterrevolution gradually faded even from the minds of those who still dreamed of it. The bishops accepted the *fait accompli* and made an effort to face up to the new situation. In mid-1963, for the first time since September, 1961, the priests of the Havana archdiocese met informally at the chancery to hear a visiting priest from abroad give them news of developments taking place in the Church in other Latin American countries. At the end of the meeting a circular was distributed, inviting the priests to a meeting at the seminary in honor of the *motu proprio* restoring Latin as the official language of instruction in the seminaries. The program was to include a speech in Latin by one of the seminarians, celebrating the merits of that tongue in the life of the Church.

The situation remained tense until the end of 1963 in spite of certain concessions obtained by Monsignor Zacchi: Some of the priests who had been exiled were allowed to return; foreign priests were admitted, mostly French and Belgians; priests were allowed to import Bibles, cars, paper for their catechism classes, etc., duty-free. But the situation lacked stability: At times feelings ran high in the different regions of the country. The atmosphere of a revolution, which has to keep up a white-hot enthusiasm in order to overcome very difficult conditions, is hardly conducive to a sense of relaxation in those who are not in wholehearted agreement with the revolution and who are constantly aware of the ideological conflict involved.

In 1963 John XXIII's encyclical, *Pacem in Terris,* was published in Cuba in an edition of ten thousand copies, and a group of government members took it as a basis for a series of discussions. When John XXIII died, later in the year, a mourning period of three days was decreed throughout the country and the government was represented at the official requiem Mass for him. The diplomatic corps was also present, including the representatives of most of the communist countries. In the sanctuary the Knights of the Holy Sepulchre, draped in their white capes, provided the sad spectacle of a Church obstinately triumphalist, apparently unaware that it represented next to nothing in Cuban society.

Gradually, however, a new generation of young priests and Christians has grown up. Although they are not yet very numerous, they have adopted a progressive new attitude toward the revolution. In February, 1966, when Camilo Torres was killed in the Colombian guerrilla war, he at once became a symbol of the social revolution in Latin America. Fidel Castro has spoken about him more than once, and at the beginning of 1968 he declared that Marxists should not be dogmatic and should recognize that Christians too can be true revolutionaries. In September, 1969, Castro invited the theologian González Ruiz to give a course on Christianity at Havana University and, further signs of the times, on April 29 of the same year the Cuban bishops published a joint letter condemning the economic blockade of their country.

Coming after the conference of Latin American bishops (CELAM) at Medellín, this first pastoral letter after nine years of silence deals primarily with development. Pointing to the need for a renewal of the social ethic along the lines of the documents elaborated at Medellín, and reminding the faithful that man has a vocation to development and that his work makes him the chief protagonist in the process, the bishops then take up the subject of what they see as the major obstacle to the development of their country: the American blockade.

> We are all aware of the difficulties of every kind that lie in the path of development: Difficulties from within, stemming from the novelty and technical complexity of the situation as well as from the sins and failings of men; difficulties also, and not the least, from without and which are related to the complexity of the factors determining contemporary relationships between nations and which are unjustly detrimental to small, weak and underdeveloped

countries. Is not this the case in the economic blockade to which our country has been subjected and which makes things more and more difficult for us as it is prolonged?—difficult, that is, especially for the rural and urban workers, the mothers of families, children and adolescents, the sick; in a word, for so many families who are separated from their loved ones.

Seeking the best interests of our people and faithful to the service of the poorest according to the commandment of Jesus Christ, and to our commitment, renewed at Medellín, we condemn the injustice inherent in the blockade which contributes to unnecessary suffering and makes the path of development more arduous. Consequently we appeal to the conscience of all those who are in a position to resolve the problem and urge them to undertake firm and effective action to bring these measures to an end.

Vatican II, which ended late in 1965 and which most Cuban bishops had attended, has also been a factor in this gradual transformation. Cuban Catholics took part in the World Congress for the Lay Apostolate in Rome in 1967, and innumerable Catholics have visited the island in the course of the last few years, including even a few European and Latin American bishops.

All this does not mean that the situation has been fully normalized, but at least the period of open conflict seems to be a thing of the past. A state of mutual tolerance has taken its place. The Church is no longer a threat to the Cuban government and attitudes have changed among Catholics, particularly among the hierarchy.

Has the Church really accepted a new mode of existence? Unfortunately this does not seem very likely, for the universal structures still make it impossible. Before that can happen, there will have to be a "revolution within the revolution" within the Church itself. In the final analysis, however, the Cuban Church is in a better position than many others to blaze new trails, which must, one day, be those of the universal Church.

CHAPTER FIVE

The War in Vietnam

If we want to understand the Vietnamese conflict and the attitude the churches have adopted in regard to it, we have to see it as part of a much vaster whole. Our study of the Church and revolution has now reached the heart of the problem of contemporary ideologies at work in a complex situation lying between the poles of American imperialism and communist dogmatism and involving all the principal contemporary myths.[1] It is essential, therefore, to see the Vietnamese conflict in the overall context, before analyzing the reactions and attitudes of the churches.

That myths are very difficult to kill off is a well-known sociological fact. They lead men to model their attitudes and behavior on what they believe to be reality, rather than on reality itself, and the more closely a myth touches on the vital values and interests of individuals and groups, the more powerful it becomes. After a time it is not only present facts which are explained by myths: Even historical events of the past are reinterpreted so that sometimes the very best-intentioned people, believing themselves to be entirely objective, accept mythical interpretations of reality without criticism, even when these contradict their opinions of a few years before.

None of this would matter very much if the phenomenon were confined to the fine arts or literature or local politics. But it is something which has invaded the dynamics of the international community, and in a world that is increasingly interdependent myths have become exceedingly powerful. Once they are established—often by the ideology underlying the social, economic, and political systems—they become substitutes for facts and constitute the only principle of analysis.

Experience has shown that men cling to their myths and that exceptional courage is needed to refute them. It is extremely rare, therefore, that someone with a responsibility in the political arena undertakes to do so. The first attempt to explode a myth usually comes from intellectuals or popular leaders, and even if the trend seems purely marginal to begin with, from the point of view of those who cling to the prevailing myth, it is a far greater threat than any other innovation; the power structure usually takes very severe measures against it.

A well-balanced study of any situation, therefore, must always try to grasp it in its reality and to point out the mythical nature of some of the convictions involved; in the case in point these convictions have plunged part of the world into war.

Revolution for Development

At the risk of oversimplifying the problem, we can state that development depends on two considerations: the responsibility of each people for its own growth and the responsibility of the international community to foster conditions which favor development. Although the basic responsibility for development belongs to the peoples concerned, it is still important that other nations refrain, at the very least, from putting obstacles in its path—and in present conditions of imperialism there are many ways of doing this. The whole of Latin America with the exception of Cuba, all of Africa and a great part of the Asian continent, with the exception of China, North Korea, and North Vietnam, are economically dependent on the capitalist system. The fact of decolonization has not altered this fundamental fact. The present capitalist system, however, is powerless to do away with the obstacles to development it has itself created. Fixed prices, international contracts, markets— most of the apparatus of international relations as well as private investments—are still products of a form of economic liberalism, the validity of which has been called into question for a long time, even in the nonsocialist developed countries.

The encyclical *Populorum Progressio* makes this comment:

> It is unfortunate that on these new conditions of society a system has been constructed which considers profit as the key motive for economic progress, competition as the supreme law of economics, and private ownership of the means of production as an absolute right that has no limits and carries no corresponding social obligation. This unchecked liberalism leads to a dictatorship rightly denounced by Pius XI as producing "the international imperialism

of money." One cannot condemn such abuses too strongly by solemnly recalling once again that the economy is at the service of man.[2]

This economic system entails still other consequences, however. It brings pressure to bear on Asian, African, and Latin American countries to maintain the status quo of economic relations. This is done in many different ways, and the economic pressures are reflected in the political regimes as well as in military alliances. Practically every country in the world is involved in a network of military pacts: NATO in Europe, Pact of Rio de Janeiro in America, SEATO in South and Southeast Asia, CENTO in the Middle East, ANZUS in Oceania, not to mention the myriad bilateral pacts (Japan, Philippines, etc.). This system has gradually built up a powerful network of solidarity, which weighs heavily in the scales of political relations and on the side of the status quo in both internal politics and international relations. Military considerations are often preponderant in certain political decisions and military ambitions combine with economic and industrial interests in an ascending spiral. A vast international arms trade has grown up—largely controlled by the governments themselves—and plays an important part in the balance of payments of some countries with the result that they are reluctant to put a stop to it.

Although problems are not identical in the different continents, the solidarity that has been created in the process of domination prevents any state from intervening in so-called local conflicts unless it is directly implicated. None of the Latin American countries, with the exception of Cuba, has raised a protest about the war in Vietnam, nor did any European country object to American intervention in the Dominican Republic. And in the meantime, when General Westmoreland, onetime Chief of Combined Operations in Vietnam, became chief of staff of the American armed forces, he was entrusted with the command of all counterinsurgency operations in Latin America (meeting of September, 1968, in Rio de Janeiro); in 1969 General Goodpaster, second in command of American troops in Vietnam, became chief of staff of SHAPE, the military facet of the NATO alliance.

The new imperialism is more complex than the old, but it is just as real. One of the ways in which it grows and is perpetuated is by means of bilateral aid agreements, which result, whether this is directly intended or only tolerated, in the maintenance and sometimes in the consolidation of existing social structures. A whole volume could be written about this aspect alone—and the chapter concerning the corruption among the elitist groups in power would not be the least voluminous.

The division of the world into two blocs, which we shall discuss later, also has serious consequences; and in this the "free world" shares the responsibility equally with the "socialist world." On the one hand, the expansionism of a capitalist economy and the bulwark that it has tried to build against the "communist plot of world domination" has brought about alliances with political systems that are very far from democratic. This, in turn, has slowed or completely halted social reforms (in Guatemala, for instance). On the other hand, extremist ideologies (Stalin and Mao), the reemergence of centuries-old expansionist tendencies, and the support given to certain subversive movements by the socialist bloc, have all served to increase distrust and, consequently, to multiply opposing alliances.

This, of course, is the situation which led to the Cold War and the arms race, morally justified by the necessity of peaceful coexistence. The two blocs together spend about $100 billion a year on arms, while the developing countries continue to stagnate because of the obstacles to international trade; and foreign "aid" programs, including loans and investments, barely top the $10 billion mark.

China can afford the effective application of a theory of development without foreign aid because its population and territory are both so immense—which means that its market is also immense—and its natural resources and the traditions of its people combine to make it possible. But China is an exception. Very few countries can claim as much. When President Nyerere, in the Declaration of Arusha, emphasized the ambiguities of foreign aid, whatever its origin, he did so primarily to assert that he would prefer to do without it rather than to see the people of Tanzania become slothful and its leaders corrupt.[3] Concerted planning on a world scale is necessary in order to make aid multilateral, to regulate international trade,[4] to arrive at joint programs,[5] and create a "world fund"[6] and a strong supranational authority from which no nation is excluded.

All of this may seem visionary and yet nothing could be more realistic. The technical solutions are difficult enough to find without further complicating the situation by clinging to myths.

The Myths Behind the Vietnamese Conflict

It is, of course, a delicate business to attack myths when they form the basis of highly emotional behavior and to touch on problems as serious as war and peace. Myths are built up around a commonly accepted basic doctrine and serve to reinforce it by supplying it with the arguments necessary to its continuance long after the facts have ceased to correspond to the theory. For the myths we are speaking of here do have a basis in fact. They are not of the same type as those of ancient or modern mythology, which attributes human weaknesses to various gods.

To demythologize means to expose the mythical character of a policy that has been adopted and defended. And as public opinion is very important today, such an exposure can be really effective only if it is accepted by public opinion. There are two ways in which this result can be achieved. One consists in acting directly on public opinion through different media: publications, declarations by public figures of different tendencies, by demonstrations, etc. This is the slow way, however, and it can fail if, and to the extent to which, the public is very attached to its myths (because of the psychological and moral security their rationale affords) and refuses to see them exploded. The other way, which is more efficient, is for the political leaders to make an about-face and publicly reverse their stand.

The first way is usually adopted in the Western world, in which the communications media are highly developed. The second is more widely, although not exclusively, used in the socialist societies in which public opinion has far less direct influence.

There are also two different methods of revising or "rewriting" myths. The first is to show how the new attitude not only is in keeping with the basic theory, which, of course, remains unchanged, but that it even expresses it more perfectly. The second is

for new men to arrive on the political scene and simply to overthrow the myths of the past. An excellent example of the latter
method was that of General de Gaulle during the Algerian crisis in
France.

Of course, one might well ask to what extent humanity can get
along without myths. They seem to be an integral part of man's
most ancient heritage, and even the most rabid movements that
have arisen to do away with them have wasted no time before
creating new ones. This can be seen in all the major revolutions:
French, American, Russian, Egyptian, or Chinese. Political real-
ism, therefore, lies in containing myths within certain limits, toler-
ating those which can cause no harm, using those which help to
mobilize men's energies for development and peace, and destroying only those which feed warlike passions or passivity. The temptation arises, of course, to invent wholly new myths and in periods
of crisis this often happens.

And now let us turn to some of the myths which have direct
bearing on the war in Vietnam. It is not easy to discuss the myths
which have brought about one of the most tragic realities of our
times and to give only a brief description. I would like to emphasize that this attempt has been made only with a view to shedding
some light on the reality and with no desire to ridicule anyone.
and with no desire to ridicule anyone.

The myths of the "free world." Both here and when we speak of
the myths of the socialist bloc, we must first of all discuss some
general myths and the theories that have given rise to them, in
order to understand those which directly concern the war in Vietnam. The basic theory is that the world is divided into two zones of
influence and that its stability depends on maintaining the status
quo. The "free world" is determined to keep its freedom in the
teeth of threats from an aggressive communist system. Here we
cannot do better than quote from an article by Eugene V. Rostow,
who expresses the position of the political authorities in the United
States with admirable clarity.[7] Concerning the basic theory, he
writes:

> Our ultimate aim in South Vietnam is not obscure even if it is disagreeable: it
> is a question of continuing a policy which Ambassador George Kennan called,

for the first time eight years ago, "containment." Kennan's idea—mutual respect of existing frontiers between the communist and the free worlds—is a
necessary, if not a sufficient, condition for peaceful coexistence. . . . The communist movement, presently shaken by rivalry for supremacy, is seeking to increase
its area of control, especially by rushing into the gaps created by the political
near-vacuum in the new nations of Asia and Africa, and by identifying itself
with their aspirations for progress.

A whole series of myths feeds on this theory and we shall look
first at some of general interest and then at those directly related to
the situation in Vietnam.

World communism is seen as a monolithic, militaristic force.
Hence the frequent parallel with Munich and the conviction that
firmness is essential in order to discourage the aggressor. In reality
the unity of the communist world could be achieved today only by
a threat of mortal danger and even then it would not be easy. The
Russo-Chinese disputes, the demonstrations of autonomy in the
European and Asian satellites of Yugoslavia, Albania, Rumania,
and North Korea are signs of something less than a monolith.

On the other hand the real power of communism is social rather
than military, and this is what attracts persons and groups in the
developing countries, which are often mired in social stagnation.
So the danger is not one of invasion, as in the case of Hitler, but of
subversion (or wars of national liberation, depending on one's
point of view). For the most part, the national communist movements have no desire to lose their national autonomy even if they
are ready to accept help from other communist countries. Fidel
Castro's declarations are evidence enough of this, and North Vietnam's attitude surely proves that it intends to maintain its independence, for, in spite of being at war with several countries of the free
world, it still has not asked for help from Russian or Chinese
troops. Moreover, communist regimes established through external
military or political pressure have never proved to be very endur-
ing. The Russians are fully aware of this and it explains their
European policy.

As for the danger of military invasion, this happens only with a
powerful expansionist nation, and political analysts are all agreed
that that is not the case with Russia today even if, as many believe,
it was so twenty years ago. It is true that China has shown expan-

sionist tendencies in its invasion of Tibet and the attacks on the Indian frontier. But even if China has expansionist designs, we must admit that they have nothing to do with any plan for world conquest by international communism; Russia sees to that. North Korea shows its independence; North Vietnam has carefully avoided asking for Chinese troops; the Indian Communist party has shown a united front with the rest of the nation in protesting the Chinese invasion, which was, incidentally, disapproved of by the Russians, not to mention various border incidents between Russia and China.

To all this we should add the slow but far-reaching change that is going on within the different communist regimes. *Pacem in Terris* called attention to this point: "Once a doctrine is fixed and formulated it does not change whereas the movements whose object is the concrete and changing conditions of life cannot help but be very much influenced by this evolution."[8]

World communism can be met and challenged only on its own ground, the ground of social and economic reality, and this is particularly true in the developing countries. It is not military might which erects a barrier—but the myth that this is so conveniently justifies the perpetuation of the accepted policies.

The "special mission of the United States" in the world is another general myth. Simply because it is the most powerful nation of the "free world," the country somehow feels that it has a special function to safeguard the balance of power in the world and to act as a global policeman. E. V. Rostow's article illustrates this point: "We are also a world power with many responsibilities and we are the chief advocate when it comes to enforcing the ban on aggressive war, proclaimed in the Charter of the United Nations."[9]

All this is part of the general basic theory, added to which there is a deep-seated conviction that the United States has some kind of special moral mission in the world which it, alone, must carry out. And yet it is less alone than ever. Perhaps the isolation experienced in the struggle in Vietnam has served to reinforce this myth.

This sense of special mission justifies the United States' intervention in the internal affairs of others, which is so fiercely contested by its adversaries. Such interventions, however, do not all follow the same pattern. They can be direct and open, without benefit of rhetorical camouflage, as in the case of the Dominican Republic; carried out through a third party, as in Guatemala or Cuba; secret, as in Iran; or with massive military involvement, as in Vietnam. Such a mission also justifies ill-matched alliances with military dictatorships, corrupt and corruptible political systems, and despotic oligarchies, which means that in particular instances the United States is in the position of defending values directly opposed to those it is championing before the world. It also justifies the bypassing of international agencies, for, in view of their inefficacy, the United States feels compelled to step in. Finally, it justifies the use of the veto and political pressure to block Communist China's entry into the United Nations.

"*The benefits of the capitalist system*" is another popular myth. The United States is keenly aware of its own economic development, made possible by capitalism. Only very recently have some nagging doubts as to the internal cohesion of American society begun to surface. All in all, however, the conviction is widespread that the rest of the world would also find happiness in the same system, and so the defense of the "free world" is designed to permit the functioning of a "free" economy. This, by definition, is what will make it possible for the developing countries to reach their goal. "The Western nations, and especially the United States, have tried to contain the expansion of the communist movement and to help the nonindustrialized countries to master the secrets of modern wealth. . . . We and the other powerful nations of the free world must contain communism and give the peoples of Asia, Africa and Latin America time to achieve their own process of modernization and liberalization."[10]

In reality the situation is quite different. Liberal capitalism, "left to itself, works rather to amplify the difference in standards of living, not to diminish them: rich peoples enjoy rapid growth whereas the poor develop slowly."[11] It is quite clear, from this passage of *Populorum Progressio,* that what is being called into question is "the fundamental principle of liberalism."[12]

If the struggle the "free world" is carrying on manages only to perpetuate a political and economic system which is totally incapable of solving the problem of development either on the international level or on the level of individual countries, it is passing sentence on itself.

We come now to the myth of "*invasion by North Vietnam.*" The American thesis is that it was the North Vietnamese government that broke the first and most basic law of peaceful coexistence: that the border between the two zones should not be changed arbitrarily or through military action.[13] "The long-standing tradition of international law justifies South Vietnam's right to strike back in its own defense against this oppression,[14] and the legal and moral right of the United States to help it in this task."[15] Consequently "our aim in South Vietnam is purely defensive."[16]

At this point we are already involved in a case in which facts have been interpreted in accordance with a myth: The United States, as upholder of morality in the world, cannot be in the wrong. The aggressor is the "bad guy"; therefore, the aggressor is someone else.

It is sufficient, however, to consult a few dates and figures to see that this simplistic view cannot be taken at its face value unless one accepts the myth that sustains it. Guerrilla warfare began in the South as long ago as 1958, as a result of a complex combination of social conditions and in reaction against a regime which had become unendurable for the peasants. American aid was increased in order to help the government control the guerrilla forces, but this only served to promote communism. The elections, provided for by the Geneva Accords, did not take place since the Saigon regime, which had not been a party to the Geneva agreements, refused to allow them. President Eisenhower said in his memoirs that the experts all agreed that if elections were held, 80 per cent of the population of South Vietnam would have voted for Ho Chi Minh. Consequently Washington agreed that it was better not to have any elections.

In order to keep control of the internal situation, President Diem was obliged to impose his authority with increasing harshness and to rely heavily on the army. But the army stood in need of reorganization and so the American military advisers became more and more numerous. All this took place before any troops started infiltrating from the North. Infiltration began in 1959 with men from the South who had fought with the Viet-Minh and had thrown in their lot with the North, in accordance with the provisions of the Geneva agreements. According to the American white paper on the subject,[17] eighteen hundred men infiltrated back into the South in 1959-1960. Prisoner accounts tell of the long march of several weeks that they had had to undertake before joining up with the guerrilla troops in the South. On September 30, 1960, the Communist party in the North officially agreed to help the Southern guerrillas and launched an appeal for the liberation of the South from "American imperialism." But it was not until July, 1963, that Chinese arms were captured in the field. For a long time the war in the South had been fought with French and American arms captured from the Southern army.

American intervention solicited by the Saigon government provoked increased aid from the North, which, in turn, brought more American aid for Saigon. Long before the term was invented, the situation was caught up in a vicious circle of escalation. But the myth of the invasion of the South by the North is still a simple and convenient explanation which legally and morally justifies the American position.

The equation Vietcong-North Vietnam-China. The NLF[18] quite patently originated in the South as a coalition of organizations of various tendencies, including Communists, who have a leading role in it. Because of the myth of invasion from the North, not much attention has ever been paid to the revolutionary movement in the South. It is not given credit for its own existence, but seen simply as an emanation of Hanoi with no real autonomy and with whom, therefore, it is impossible to negotiate.

As for North Vietnam, it is considered a satellite of China, and once again we are back where we started with the old myth of world communism. The facts that China is Vietnam's traditional enemy and that North Vietnam has manifested its independence of China, if only by refusing the help of Chinese troops, are never taken into consideration. According to Rand Corporation experts, Lin Piao's declaration to the underdeveloped world in 1965 was a warning to the Vietcong that it "would have to rely primarily on its own resources and its own revolutionary ardor."[19]

A Christian crusade. This is one of the most distressing myths: It represents the war as a crusade for the defense of Christian civilization and the cause of God. In fact, the "defense of Christian civilization" boils down to the defense of a particularly unjust and ineffective economic regime which prevails in the "free world" and its zone of influence.

On the other hand, the immoral means employed in this war—bombing nonmilitary objectives, poisoning crops, torturing prisoners—make any identification with a Christian crusade a sacrilegious farce. A number of American churchmen of various confessions have emphasized this very clearly.[20]

We could speak of other myths of the "free world," but it would lead us too far afield. We have already looked at the principal ones, so we can now turn to those "on the other side of the fence," in the communist world.

Myths of the communist world. The Western world has no monopoly on myths; they abound in the communist world as well. It will be enough for our purpose, however, to mention only a few.

Communism is the only model for development. Not only does Marxism teach this, it also teaches that communism is the ultimate goal and the fruit to which certain intermediary phases must inevitably lead both in industrialized and nonindustrialized countries.

This theory justifies a policy of aiding and abetting every revolutionary movement, wherever it may be, as long as it shows some chance of succeeding and leading to communism. When success seems unlikely, the same theory engenders considerable distrust toward these movements. This is perhaps the reason why the North Vietnamese Communist party did not support the NLF much sooner, that the Cuban Communist party gave its support to Fidel Castro only on the eve of victory, and that the Colombian Communist party withdrew its support of Camilo Torres.

An analysis of social facts indicates that, to date, communism has acted as the motive power of development and industrialization in the same way as capitalism. The social and human cost has been extremely high in both instances. In the case of communism, however, the aim and motivation is man and not profit, as in capitalism, and this is what gives it its unquestionable advantage. In the take-off phase of development, communism shows itself to be really effective, although somewhat hampered by obvious contradictions—which are normal, up to a point—but it is always accompanied by a psychosocial conditioning of individuals which is often painful and dehumanizing.

However, once this initial phase is past, the imperatives of development are seriously hampered by the rigidity of the system. This, in turn, leads to the gradual transformations that we can see taking place in the socialist countries of Europe.

In theory there are other models of development, but in practice, unfortunately, they are all too few. None of those we could mention is entirely free of ambiguities, nor entirely successful. We would have to make a comparative study of Cuba, Formosa, Israel, North Vietnam, Tanzania, the Ivory Coast, Japan, Mexico, and Chile to reach a more adequate understanding of the factors at work in development.

International communism. The "free world" myth of world communism has its parallel in the communist world. The latent conflict between the USSR and China has at times erupted openly, but the myth had already shown itself in other instances, for example, in Yugoslavia. Nationalism, cultural differences, and variations in the pace and type of development have contributed to the formulation of different doctrinal and political theories. One might have expected the much-vaunted and much-feared unity of the communist world to express itself more clearly and in more forceful action in behalf of North Vietnam by the other communist countries. To say the least, their attitude was equivocal. Even if North Vietnam had no desire to extend the conflict beyond the level of a national war with the introduction of troops from other communist countries, support based on the unshakable unity of the communist world should have made a better showing.

American imperialism. This is the constant target of communist declarations and propaganda. The term is sufficiently vague to allow different interpretations, and for the most part it is used in a very general way, making no distinction between different situations and underscoring the American will to achieve total domination.

American imperialism, even if it is an undeniable fact, must nevertheless be qualified. Economic imperialism is an inherent part of liberal capitalism and, as such, a reality as far as America is concerned. For evidence we need to look only at Latin America, where the economic domination of the United States is almost total and where it has not hesitated to overthrow regimes which have tried to free themselves of its yoke.[21] On the global level, the role of defender of freedom and the moral values assumed by the Americans have also inevitably led to imperialism. In this case it shows itself on the political level, and is frequently accepted and endorsed by some states in order to guarantee their own security. Military superiority also leads to interventionism, whether direct or indirect, and this is linked to a policy of arms supplies and military alliances in which, of course, the stronger partner always has the last word.

But American imperialism is not a colonial policy like those of the nineteenth and early twentieth centuries. It has no ambition to plant the American flag in all the capitals of the world—not even in North Vietnam. It is much more subtle.

Religious alienation. This is a far more fundamental myth in communism, bearing as it does on its philosophical underpinnings. It is based on a factual analysis which was unquestionably correct to a great extent when it was made. The same analysis today, however, would certainly lead to different conclusions. We shall have occasion to come back to this point later.

The attitudes of the churches to the war in Vietnam

The history of the Vietnamese conflict is so well known that we do not need to summarize it here. We have already seen it in its proper context: the worldwide problem of development and the antagonism between two major political and economic systems. It is obvious that no other explanation can account for the calvary the Vietnamese people have been forced to live through. To attempt to take it out of its context can only further confuse the issue. Toward the end of 1969, an editorial in *la Voix des Boud-dhistes Vietnamiens* declared:

> We Vietnamese do not approve of the war that is being waged in our country and which is destroying the fabric of our society.... Not only do we disapprove of it but we detest it.... We are only too well aware that we are victims of an international conflict.... We have been trapped in a war-machine and we know that that machine will only stop functioning if the whole world forces it to stop. But our voice is drowned by the noise of bombs and mortar-shells, stifled by dishonesty and repression. We are not free to express ourselves.[22]

A worldwide movement of solidarity has gradually grown, but it is well-nigh powerless in face of economic, political, and military oppression. The hopes of North American pacifists were raised when one President withdrew, but his successor has done no more than change tactics: Escalation has been replaced by "Vietnamization." From Vietnam the conflict has spread to the whole of Indochina and perhaps to the whole of Southeast Asia.

It is important to keep this international context in mind if we are to situate and understand the reactions of the churches in relation to this reality.[23]

The position of Paul VI. Pope Paul VI's gestures in relation to the war in Vietnam must be seen in the light of three different factors: the renewal begun by Vatican II; his own ideas concerning peace; and the present conflict in the Catholic Church, particularly insofar as it touches on the pope's role.

Paul VI has frequently made public statements about Vietnam. He has even offered his services as peacemaker and has actively intervened more than twenty-five times in his writings and addresses between February, 1965, and January, 1968. This is a fact which must be seen in the context of the dynamics of the Catholic Church and the papacy. The pope's first gesture in behalf of peace was his Christmas Message of 1965 in which he referred to the Vietnamese conflict but without naming it. Not long after he sent telegrams to the heads of state concerned, expressing the hope that the Christmas cease-fire might be a step in the direction of a peaceful settlement. On January 31, 1966, he recommended that the United Nations intervene.

On September 19 of the same year, in his encyclical *Christi Matri,* he proposed a world day of prayer and condemned both parties to the dispute. On October 4, after sending a representative to Vietnam, he again called for negotiations and in his Christmas Message and in an allocution to the cardinals he reiterated his distress and his hope that negotiations might lead to a just and lasting peace. In February, 1967, he intervened with President Johnson for a cease-fire. Mr. Johnson refused, and President Ho Chi Minh, who had also been urged by the pope to show a conciliatory spirit, replied, stating the preliminary conditions for any initiative on his part: the withdrawal of American troops. On April 7 Secretary-General U Thant met the pope and discussed the Vietnamese situation with him. On May 24 the pope called for a halt to the bombings and to all infiltration from North to South. At the end of September he renewed his appeal to the United Nations Organization to act as peacemaker. In his Christmas Message of 1967 the pope seemed very discouraged as he called for a "peace offensive" for Vietnam.

This enumeration of some of the pope's principal gestures in view of peace in Vietnam shows his perseverance and his concern to act as peacemaker, apparently in the role of an impartial diplomat. But this exterior view entirely misses the significance of Paul VI's gestures; his words and his acts are meant as signs and can be understood only if they are seen together, as a whole. This is true of the visits he has made to different countries and it is true of his speech at the United Nations; he is presenting himself before the world as an "expert in humanity," the prophet of the humanity of the future. On January 29, 1966, the pope explained that his action was not a pretext for "meddling in political questions or temporal interests" outside his competence, but that, "urged on by the love of Christ," he wished to bear witness to justice "without preconceived preferences but out of love for all men."[24] Paul VI intends his attitude to be an illustration of the Vatican Council pronouncements, a sort of commentary on the introduction to the *Pastoral Constitution on the Church in the Modern World:* "The joys and hopes, the griefs and anxieties of the men of this age, especially those who are poor or in any way afflicted, these too are the joys and hopes, the griefs and anxieties of the followers of Christ. Indeed, nothing genuinely human fails to raise an echo in their hearts," and the pope abundantly expresses his anxiety about the state of the world and all its suffering. He speaks of Vietnam because, in his own words, he wants to "be one with suffering humanity."

But the pope has not confined himself to echoing contemporary feelings and sharing the universal desire for peace. He has made a personal contribution to the formulation of a plan for peace, understood as a quest for justice and the construction of a more harmonious social order. His attitude toward Vietnam is an application and an illustration of his ideas about peace. When he advocates peace in the midst of belligerency, he is advocating a peace based on respect for the rights of others, "a peace whose true foundations are justice and love."[25]

The peace which the pope hopes to promote in Vietnam is a situation in which the Vietnamese will find "freedom, order and prosperity."[26] This was his wish to the Vietnamese bishops in a message on September 30, 1966. And he expresses the hope that their faithful might soon go back "to the peaceful and tranquil works of the fields, and realize social and political reforms."[27] What he wants is to "hasten the day when all arms will be laid down and the Vietnamese people can devote itself to the reconstruction of their fatherland in serenity, freedom and independence."[28]

But when someone adopts an entirely new role, there is always a risk that he will fail to keep a proper balance. Paul VI has not really made a choice between arbitration, prophetic proclamation, and institutional involvement.

In his encyclical *Christi Matri,* for example, he calls on all concerned to weigh their responsibility in the conflict; in doing so, he is deliberately assuming the role of arbiter. But is the Catholic Church in a position to act as arbiter? Quite apart from the role he himself played in the first stages of the affair, what about the militia recruited by the Vietnamese bishops to oppose the Vietminh's agrarian reform, which fought alongside the French in 1946? And what about Bishop Ngo Dinh Thuc's part in the appeal which his brother Diem made to the United States? What about the massive involvement of Catholics in the Diem regime? And, not to mention Cardinal Spellman, what about the Catholics who called for a resumption of bombing raids of the North, in April,

1968?[29] What reactions can the pope expect when, as head of the Catholic Church, he sends "good wishes and blessings" to the World Anti-Communist League, at whose assembly he is represented by an archbishop of Formosa?

On July 20, 1966, Pope Paul declared: "We have recently received assurances of good will from one of the parties involved in Vietnam; we dare to hope that equally good dispositions will be shown by all."[30] But in March, 1965, even the *New York Times* had expressed the fear that "faith in the word of the American government" was "one of the countless casualties of the Vietnamese war."[31] The arbitration proposed by the pope seems dangerously subject to exploitation by both sides.

One of the major questions, however, is whether the Vatican has adequately analyzed the nature of the war it is trying to stop. When one sees that in February, 1967, it sent messages to Washington, Hanoi, and Saigon, but completely ignored the NLF, this seems highly doubtful. And yet just at that time U Thant had emphasized the fact that the Front had to be recognized as interlocutor if any solution was ever to be reached.

Similarly, when the pope cries out against the bombings "in the name of innocent people who are the victims of such deeds,"[32] one wonders whether he would not make a much more cogent criticism if he realized that those bombings were part of a deliberate strategy to destroy a country. And why, on the other hand, does he call on the other side to "cease their acts of terrorism," as though they were exactly the same brand of villainy as the bombings? This leads us to a fundamental question: Can one really believe that the Vietnamese war is nothing more than an "antagonism between nations,"[33] and that it would suffice, therefore, for "all men to want simultaneously" for the war to come to an end and the honor of the combatants to be saved?[34] It seems that the pope's appeal to the "goodwill" of those involved is totally out of touch with the true nature of the antagonisms at work here. This does not imply a negative judgment of his prophetic intentions but only that there are limitations to those intentions. The facts give ample evidence of this. For instance, when Paul VI asked the governments of both Vietnams to "take a step toward the foundation of a just and fraternal peace," Ho Chi Minh and Nguyen Van Thieu both replied with an explanation of the political theses they defended.[35]

And finally, how should we interpret the fact that, just at a time when dissent was growing visibly in the United States, the pope's call for peace in December, 1967, contained a thinly veiled attack on the peace movements? In his message for "Peace Day" he accompanied his exhortation with an urgent—albeit not very explicit—warning against pacifist movements, which, he says, run the risk of encouraging "inertia in those who are afraid of having to give their lives in the service of their country and their fellow-men, engaged in the defense of justice and freedom." These people, the pope believes, simply seek to evade their essential responsibilities and the risks inherent in "every great duty and every dangerous enterprise."[36] We could have hoped for a deeper understanding of civil disobedience thanks to the war in Vietnam, but the pope's statement leaves room for many misunderstandings, which have been skillfully exploited by those who stood to gain.

Has the Vatican now realized the quandary it was in or did it feel it had achieved its ends when the belligerents took their places at the negotiating table in Paris in May, 1968? However that may be, it has been extremely reserved about Vietnam ever since. The pope has continued to manifest deep concern for peace. This is still the principal theme in his public statements. But although his calls for peace are still urgent and plainly delivered with deep feeling, they are now couched in more general terms. He appeals to the conscience of men and, so far as one can see, seems to have reduced his diplomatic overtures considerably since President Johnson's visit.

All in all Pope Paul's action for peace in Vietnam leaves us with the impression that a figure of great authority attempted to intervene in the debate with great generosity but without having correctly gauged its true nature. What is even more striking is that during the pope's visit to Bogotá, which was intended as an encounter with the Third World, no mention was made of the role of the United States in that part of the world. Perhaps the key to Paul VI's attitude is the difficulty of analyzing the objective connections between different phenomena. He is so deeply troubled by the tragedy that he does not seem to recognize, in its effects, the signs of a system. His protest is moral and the solutions he advocates have no bearing on the causes of the evil. It must be admitted that the ambiguity of his attitude reflects on the prophetism which forms the basis of his good intentions.

The World Council of Churches. On February 16, 1967, the executive committee of the WCC published a declaration[37] expressing regret at the resumption of air raids over North Vietnam after the Christmas cease-fire. Undertaking an analysis in depth of the conflict, the text expresses the hope that the conditions essential to Vietnamese self-determination can be achieved on the basis of a withdrawal of all foreign troops. It gives a detailed list of the factors that would have to be present for a negotiated settlement: a halt to the bombings, a reciprocal gesture from North Vietnam, recognition of the NLF by Saigon, resumption by Moscow and London of their role in the Geneva Accords, the mobilization of public opinion, and the cooperation of United Nations Secretary-General U Thant.

One of the striking things about this document is its precise and practical style. A few months later Dr. Eugene Carson Blake emphasized the danger for all humanity of American policy and action in Vietnam.[38] He pointed out that it is alienating even those who have allied themselves with the United States in its struggle against "communist aggression." "The more we use force the more empty our ideals become." He also condemned the policy which led to abandoning the fight against poverty and which provides a pretext for delaying assistance to Latin America and the rest of Asia. In conclusion he appeals to the government to stop the bombings, to understand that peace cannot be imposed by military victory, and to agree to negotiate.

The reply of WCC leaders to Paul VI's suggestion for a world "Peace Day" provided an opportunity for them to make clear what they understood by "action to promote peace."[39] They wrote: "To promote peace we must be aware of the dangers and snares contained in actions for peace. We must support every constructive step toward understanding and international cooperation." The thrust of this message appears to go one step further than the pope's, and the WCC unhesitatingly emphasizes that the cause of the present "agitation" is injustice and tyranny. Two paths are open for action: the development of international and supranational organizations, and the formation of individual consciences, showing the possibility of acting in defense of justice by refusing military service.

Although the WCC's gestures in the debate over Vietnam have had less repercussion on the political scene than those of Paul VI, their statements seem more practical and less cautious about analyzing the aims and responsibilities involved. The WCC benefits from the excellent work undertaken with such sincere commitment by the Church and Society Conference in 1966. It seems to be less concerned with its diplomatic role and freer, therefore, to give voice to a moral judgment. At the same time certain limitations are imposed on it by the fact that it must safeguard the cohesion of an institution which exists solely on its membership. The fact that certain member churches have reduced their financial contributions, for instance, is partly due to the outspokenness of the WCC on the subject of Vietnam. But this did not prevent the General Assembly from taking a very firm stand at Uppsala in 1969: "The frightful situation of the Vietnamese people today is an example of the kind of tragedy the unilateral intervention of one of the great powers can lead to."

If declarations emanating from the WCC are few and far between, it is because of the great freedom of expression enjoyed by the different member churches and local communities, both on an individual level and on the level of their national synods.

In the rest of this chapter we shall study the reactions of local churches: American Christians, Vietnamese Christians, groups, and prominent spokesmen in the rest of the world.

American Christians. To begin with, I would like to examine two texts emanating from "official" sources. The first was published by the National Council of Churches[40] and the second by the United States Catholic Bishops' Conference. I shall then attempt a systematic synthesis of the various positions adopted by American Christians.

In a declaration about Vietnam dated February 23, 1968, the National Council of Churches analyzed the false suppositions on which American policy is based. The text attacked the simplistic view of a world divided into two camps, the communist and the "free" world; the illusion that the United States has a special mission to defend the free world; and the illusion that peace can be won by military force, since such means can only serve to maintain the status quo and in the meantime the country is depriving itself of the means to cooperate in the development of Latin America and Africa. In conclusion the text states: "We believe that further intensification of the American military effort would be useless and would contribute to the destruction rather than the realization of American objectives." And the NCC, after this attempt at a critique of accepted values—the originality of the attempt is worth emphasizing—called for an immediate halt to the bombing of North Vietnam as a first step toward peace talks.

The basic text of the U.S. Catholic Bishops' Conference was published on November 18, 1966,[41] and takes a doctrinal approach. Peace, the bishops say, is possible only if it is based on the order intended by God, that is, on the "demands of human dignity." And referring to Paul VI's teaching, they continue: "As Catholics we are members of the Church that the pope has called 'messenger of peace.'" The bishops also mention the "strong words of the National Council of Churches, the Council of American Synagogues and other religious denominations." Putting their own text into this context, they say: "We all have the same starting point: justice; and the same goal: peace." Although they decline to enter into a discussion of a political analysis, they nevertheless consider that they have the "clear duty to insist that the problems be constantly subjected to moral reexamination."

The bishops' statement is based on three principles inspired by the Church's teaching on war and peace: A distinction must be made between true and false patriotism; every country has the right to legitimate defense—and they add: "What one country has the right to do in its own defense, it also has the right to do to help another in its struggle against aggression." The third principle concerns the moral limits that must necessarily be respected when waging war; not all means are licit.

In applying these principles the bishops establish, first, that "Americans can trust the sincerity of their leaders as long as they continue to work for a just peace in Vietnam." They add, incidentally, that the efforts the administration has been making in this domain are "well known." Then, having specified that "divergent opinions in moral matters" do occur and that they do not claim to be capable of "solving these problems with authority," they go on to state their opinion that "it is reasonable to think that our presence in Vietnam is justified," adding, "we share the anguish of those who are responsible for decisions of life and death. . . . We praise the valor of our men in the armed forces and express our gratitude to them ... but everyone—our leaders as well as our citizens—must be ready to change our path whenever changing circumstances make this possible."

The fact that they appear to know nothing and say nothing about the causes and aims of the war; their concern to show that they are aware, and especially that they are loyal and trusting citizens; and their application by rote of a doctrine to the debate on means and "circumstances," leads them to adopt a strictly "conformist" attitude, in line with official government theories and the generally accepted myths.

The rest of the text formulates recommendations. The bishops emphasize that people have the right and the duty to inform themselves; they call on the faithful to ensure that the government seek ways to solve the problem, saying: "We should protest whenever the escalation of the conflict is in danger of going beyond morally acceptable limits."

In the last analysis, one can say that the bishops followed both the line taken by Paul VI in his declarations and the United States government line. The stand taken by some individual bishops has further accentuated the conformist attitude of the hierarchy as a whole, but this has been counterbalanced to some extent by more outspoken criticism on the part of some others.

In their declaration of December, 1968, the Catholic bishops again dealt with the subject of peace at some length. They paraphrased *The Church in the Modern World* and treated the prob-

lem of disarmament in greater detail, but they still did not venture
to take a stand on the Vietnamese question. Their conviction of the
moral justice of the American cause can still be sensed in the text:
"Despite and even because of the provocation in Eastern Europe
and elsewhere, the United States must continue to take steps to
create a better climate for these discussions. . . ."

We shall now attempt a systematic investigation of the attitudes
adopted by American Christians in general. Everything turns on
an analysis of the events: whether one has a conformist notion of
the causes and goals of the war, or whether one questions the
underlying values which determine it. Among those who criticize
the basic American policy as well as in the ranks of those who
criticize the means used, there are many shades of opinion. Christians who have taken part in protests against the war have primarily used moral arguments. The various attitudes and declarations
can be grouped under three main headings: defense of a just war;
protest against an unjust war; criticism of the means employed in
the war.

A just war. The official thesis that the Americans are in Vietnam
to help the country against communist aggression is, at first sight,
liable to be well received by many Christians since it postulates the
intrinsic evil of the communist regime. This is the thesis of Father
Daniel Lyons, S.J., in his radio talks. And Father Patrick O'Con-
nor, basing his arguments on those of the Catholics who fled to
South Vietnam in 1954, concludes that "for men who love justice
and freedom, nothing would be solved if the United States gave in
in South Vietnam."[42]

Michael Novak took a slightly less categorical position when he
conceded that the NLF was not entirely communist and the Saigon regime not entirely democratic. But he went on to conclude
that "the United States is in Vietnam to defend its own interests,"
which, according to him, are to contain communism.[43]

A positively Manichean view was expressed by Cardinal Cush-
ing when he asserted that "the war in Vietnam is the only means of
establishing peace in a hard world. . . . It can be love in disguise.
. . . The American heroes of Southeast Asia . . . are working hard
for peace. . . . There are times in history when evil men and evil

means can only be opposed by force; if the good abdicate evil triumphs."[44]

This position was, of course, overwhelmingly endorsed by Cardinal Spellman during his visit to Vietnam at Christmas, 1966. "I believe that the Vietnamese war is a war in defense of civilization. ... As our President and our Secretary of State have said, one cannot go halfway in a war... any solution other than victory is inconceivable." When he made this kind of statement, the cardinal was simply giving the troops the official government harangue and proving himself a good patriot. But he went even further and legitimated and blessed the undertaking "imposed on" his country. "We pray that victory may soon be won." The United States was "the Good Samaritan to all nations," and "our men are not here only as soldiers of the American army but as soldiers of Christ" to defend "the cause of justice, the cause of civilization, the cause of God."

To be quite honest one must question whether the cardinal's voice was quite as anachronistic as it may seem, or whether he was not simply expressing the logical conclusion of certain principles already enunciated and endorsed by the U.S. Catholic Bishops' Conference only a month earlier. One must remember that the conference expressed confidence in the government, judged that the American presence in Vietnam was justified, and praised the generosity of the troops. Cardinal Spellman only said explicitly what his fellow bishops had left implicit: The American presence is justified because it is a defense of Christian civilization. He also went further than most of the bishops in identifying the Church and the nation. He was, after all, chaplain general of the American armed forces.

We also have to remember that this apparently mystifying attitude was probably fostered by the quasi-religious respect with which many Americans (and many othes throughout the world) regard the pronouncements of experts and technicians. Any opinion that does not match the line taken by the administration and the "competent" people is classed as politically naïve. The myth of competence is perhaps even more important in defending the

Vietnamese war than the myth that the world is divided into "good guys" and "bad guys."

"I do not know one single priest whose opinion on Vietnam is competent," said Msgr. George Higgins, director of the Social Action Department of the U.S. Catholic Bishops' Conference.[45] And the Episcopalian pastor, Albert Mallagan, declared that he was astounded by the "naïveté of ecclesiastical declarations which deal with complex and agonizing questions, accomplish nothing and only serve to discredit the Church."[46] In support of this attitude, some cite the ambiguity of past ages "when religious leaders decided national policies of war and peace."[47] But surely the ambiguity still persists when the hierarchy, instead of deciding national policies, is content not only to conform to the government line but to endorse and bless it?

All this at least has the merit of clearly posing the urgent problem of the critical function of the churches in a society in which they no longer have the monopoly of providing legitimation and moral norms. How can they resist trying to sell their "commodity" to the "consumers" of religion by allowing themselves to be annexed by the dominant ideology thereby legitimating it and sacralizing the existing social system?

The protest against an unjust and unjustifiable war. The extreme position described above could not fail to provoke reactions from an active minority which already had its doubts about the causes and aims of the war. On the whole it is striking that those who represent this tendency pose the problem in practically the same terms as their adversaries. Only their conclusions differ.

Father Philip Berrigan, for instance, was basing his argument on the theology of a just war when he wrote: "Even if one does not accept the apostolate of truth and love the Gospel asks of us, let him at least believe in the strict application of the theory of a just war. Neither of these demands justifies the present policy of the United States in Vietnam or in the Cold War."[48] The allusion to the Cold War is worth noting, as it seems to open up the debate to at least one of its real dimensions.

Also, Gordon C. Zahn believes that "at least three and perhaps four of the necessary conditions for a just war have been violated or, at least, ignored."[49]

Father Daniel Berrigan explained the conditions in question in an interview with the *National Catholic Reporter.* According to Thomistic criteria, every other possible means of reaching an agreement should have been exhausted first, "but we ignored the intervention of the United Nations"; violence should be kept to a minimum in order to keep the door open to a just solution, "but we have used maximum violence." Finally, "if we want to justify our own presence as self-defense, we should take a close look at the Vietnamese' right to defend themselves."[50]

Father George Tavard took a major step forward in the analysis when he wrote: "Every people has the ultimate right to carry out a revolution without intervention from a foreign power."[51]

There are many Christians among those who claim that the right to self-determination should be restored to Vietnam, or at least that the U. S. should give up any hope of a military victory which would do nothing to improve the situation in Southeast Asia.[52] But this trend of opinion often comes closer to criticizing the means used in the war than the grounds of its justification.

"We run the risk of ruining all chances of peace and peaceful collaboration with the Soviet Union in Asia and of thrusting the North Vietnamese into the arms of the Chinese," wrote *Christianity and Crisis,* and although this brings the debate down to its fundamental political dimension, it is still only the means that are being called into question. Others, like Father Peter Riga, seem to go further; he analyzes the Vietnamese conflict as a civil war based on class antagonisms, but he then goes on to regret that the United States has failed to export its own brand of revolution to the Third World.[53] Or there is Father Daniel Berrigan again, who sees a form of racism in the American intervention.[54]

As we have said, the basis for most protests by religionists against the war has been moral, resting on an ethical option and partially evading, therefore, the necessity for a totally logical argument. It has often been a reaction of dignity in the face of widespread criticism of United States policy from other countries; a call to disobedience, founded on the illegal nature of the war; or an ethical option for nonviolence which opposes all wars. Often the three elements have been mixed.

The appeal launched by hundreds of university students and clergymen, for example, on July 7, 1965,[55] observed that a "growing number of young people feel the Vietnamese war was such a gross affront to their moral and religious conscience that they cannot envisage having any part whatever in it." The appeal also declared that the war was "unconstitutional," as it has never been declared by Congress; illegal according to international agreements; and immoral as to its means. Consequently the signers demanded that the religious and moral convictions of those who are opposed to the war be respected and they encouraged everyone to "choose the form of resistance that his conscience and circumstances dictate." They also appealed to the churches to support the resistance movement.

The 1968 annual meeting of Pax took a stand along similar lines, adopting two resolutions addressed to the Catholic hierarchy.[56] One called on the bishops to condemn the bombings. The other asked them to affirm publicly that it is morally objectionable to participate in such acts of war or at least to endorse every individual's right to decide the matter in conscience for himself.[57]

Although this trend seems radical in its gestures and public utterances, it still lacks a rigorous analysis of the causes of the war. As an idealistic, even utopian, trend it is still very close to the general mentality. Not that we have any cause to complain if American messianism changes its tack and preaches nonviolence instead of a holy war, but does not this protest deprive itself of the means for analyzing the true causes of the conflict, that is, the dominant position of the United States in the world, which has become an ideology? Such self-criticism is, of course, very difficult. And yet many American Christians have discovered that the Vietnamese war is a moral problem, not only in respect to the means used but also in respect to the morality of the whole society, and this is the first step in the right direction.

Criticism of the means. The third main trend of opposition to the war seems to be more widespread. It criticizes the methods used without explicitly calling into question either its justification or its aims.

In July, 1965, nine bishops reacted to George Ball's statement that Hanoi could not expect to remain a "sanctuary" immune from air attack. They declared that to "bomb purely civilian centers would be a flagrant violation of the Christian ethic and must be condemned as immoral."

At the same time the Catholic Association for International Peace, while approving continued military action, stated that "deliberately to bomb civilians, or to compete with the Viet Cong in the use of terrorist tactics, would be an immoral use of legitimate power." A similar opinion was expressed a little later by a Catholic paper:[58] "The means employed ... have not always been commendable, or even morally permissible. ..." But then it goes on: "Whatever its ambiguities, the Vietnamese war is quite obviously a confrontation with Chinese communism as well as with the North Vietnamese nationalist movement which is dominated by the Communists."

In this group the frequent calls for a halt to the bombings and for negotiation follow the same line of reasoning. This is also the case for the trends described in an article in *Time* magazine in 1968.[59] The Catholic magazine, *The Critic*, thinks that "it is now obvious that the war can no longer be regarded simply as a political question; it is a moral question." For the Presbyterian theologian, Robert McAfee Brown, "we must escalate the protest." And in January, 1968, a group of Protestant theologians opposed to war met to study the moral problems involved.

Once one begins challenging the norms, however, one is led to challenge values. The Jesuit theologian, Father Daniel O'Hanlon, for instance, questions the United States' mission to resist the threat of communism, and observes that the theory of the holy war has been officially rejected by the Church, adding that both Paul VI and John XXIII have proposed dialogue as a better way of combatting communism. The Lutheran pastor, Richard Neuhaus, believes that "there is no proportion between the aims of the war and the means that are being used in its conduct."

These positions are very similar to that of the clergymen and theologians who signed the manifesto *Negotiation Now,* [60] which called for an immediate and unconditional halt to the bombings, negotiations as the only means of stopping the war, a reciprocal gesture from the enemy, and a more concilitary attitude on the part of South Vietnam.

It is unquestionable that these positions, whatever their limitations, are evidence of something quite new, especially for American Catholics who have been so inclined to manifest an unimpeachable patriotism. In this sense the Open Letter on Vietnam to the Catholic Clergy and Laity of the United States[61] was a timid attempt to incite the bishops to adopt a more radical position. The Catholics who signed it recognized that "acts of terrorism have been committed by the Viet Cong," but they believed that the time had come to make some concrete suggestions. They condemned bombings which make no distinction between civilian and military targets, the destruction of human life by napalm and fragmentation bombs, the destruction of crops, and torture.

And yet, among Catholics at least, a false conception of group solidarity and the relation between faith and ethics still constitute major obstacles. In October, 1966, Cardinal O'Boyle of Washington instructed his priests to offer Masses for peace, but forbade them to express their opinion about American policy in Vietnam.[62] One might ask what the preaching of peace consists of under these conditions. Is it simply a criticism of the methods of war, leaving those who are "elected for that purpose" free to decide on specific policies?[63] And, if we push the analysis a little further, must this preaching leave untouched and sacrosanct the hidden values which motivate political decisions? This seems to be implied by Father Daniel Berrigan's expressed hope that Vietnam become "an immense laboratory" in which the efficacy of the "new frontier" politics can be clearly demonstrated.

In conclusion, neither trend of criticism situates the problem within the context of America's dominant role in the economic and political sectors in the world. There is an almost "casuistic" attempt to see moral implications in the *fact* of war (is it more immoral to kill people with napalm than with other weapons?), but an ethical investigation of the causes that have led to this situation is all too rare, even on the part of Christians who are convinced that the United States is making a political mistake.

The nature of the prophetic role of the churches and the question of its fulfillment remain a problem. But in all fairness one should not underestimate the courage and audacity of some individuals and groups in adopting an attitude that is frankly "deviationist" in relation to the attitudes of the institutionalized churches and of society as a whole.

As time goes on, it seems that the elections at the end of 1968, the new administration in 1969, and the first withdrawals of American troops have been signs of a new way of conducting the war rather than a new path to peace. The first part of 1971 brought no change in the policies either of the churches or of the United States. Pacifist groups are discouraged by their evident powerlessness to change the course of events and Christians who were actively committed are now at a loss to define a course of action since the defeat of Senator Eugene MacCarthy and in view of the fact that nonviolent action seems to have grounded to a halt. As far as religious authorities are concerned, it seems they have resigned themselves to silence, perhaps in the hope of concealing dissent in their ranks.

The Vietnamese Church. The attitude of Christians in both North and South Vietnam is, naturally enough, largely determined by their standing in the country and their history since 1954. The great differences in these two factors—their group history and their position in relation to the regime—have made the two Vietnamese churches very dissimilar.

The Geneva Accords allowed three hundred days in which the population could choose which side they wanted to be on. This provision enabled the Vietminh to evacuate members of the resistance and other young men to the North, but it triggered a far more extensive movement of migration in the other direction. According to later counts, more than 800,000 North Vietnamese crossed the seventeenth parallel, and 80 percent of these were Catholics. Within the space of those few months, five bishops, more than seven hundred priests and almost all male religious, the majority of women religious, and half the lay Catholic population had fled the North.

But the sociological aspect of the exodus was as important as the numbers. Entire villages followed their priests into exile, often because their attitude toward the Vietminh and the fact that many of them had formed private militias and fought on the side of the French, made them fear reprisals. Those who left the cities were mostly the upper classes. The Church found itself in a very precarious situation: The archbishop of Hanoi threatened priests who fled to the South with ecclesiastical sanctions, whereas other bishops, who had organized their own militias in the rural areas, told their people it was their duty to leave.

The Christians who did stay went through some very hard times. But United States aggression was largely instrumental in helping them to reintegrate into the nation, which was obliged to muster all its energies in the struggle for survival.[64] Under the bombings, in spite of the good intentions of the "Good Samaritan" who had ordered them, the Catholics of the North reacted as loyal citizens of their country. As David Schoenbrun observed after a visit to the North:

> They gave me the distinct impression of being on very good terms with the regime and of being free to practice their faith. Like all the Vietnamese, they were united in the struggle against the aggressor. The American bombs have made the enemies of the regime unite with it.... People who are being bombed cannot have much fellow feeling for those who are bombing them even if they are Christians like themselves.[65]

Whatever one might think of this journalist's interpretation, the fact remains, and it is important.

The North Vietnamese Church is still very isolated from the rest of the world and it does not seem likely that this will change very soon.

The situation of Catholics in the South and their prevailing attitudes are very different. Many of them came from the North, led by their priests in 1954, in a state of religious panic in which it is hard to distinguish what was genuine from what was the result of irrational exploitation. They resettled in clusters, as they had come—as, for example, in the diocese of Xuan Loc, which numbers 265,000 Northern Catholics. Before long they constituted the most loyal body of supporters of President Ngo Dinh Diem, himself a Catholic, who recruited a considerable percentage of his administration and military personnel from among them. The continued hostilities often drove them to seek refuge in the fortified villages or in the suburbs of Saigon.

Since they had acquired this relative security at the cost of their heartrending exodus, it is very understandable that they should be reluctant to jeopardize it: "Is it the moment to clamor for negotiations, to beg for a cease-fire, to pray for peace at all costs? We have too much to lose."[66] Some have even reached the point of envisaging a new exodus to Australia; others talk of going underground and organizing their own defense in guerrilla groups. The most extreme positions are usually found in the rural areas, for in the cities contact with many different ideas has usually engendered more flexible attitudes with regard to the Viet Cong as well as with regard to the Buddhists. But even in the cities the more open-minded groups have not made much headway with the general Catholic population.[67]

One of the major obstacles in the way of an evolution in attitudes is, no doubt, the fact that much of the Vietnamese Church is still dependent on outside help. Colonial support and protection has been exchanged for that of the dollar. And this means that the Church has, if not a feeling of power, at least a feeling of security which does not correspond to the reality. In Vietnam's misfortune, gifts from foreign churches have poured in to the schools and welfare agencies from which the clergy acquires its prestige and because of which it expects the gratitude of the people. "The Church gives but does not receive. It alleviates ills, but does not cure them. It succors the poor but never condemns the causes of their poverty."[68]

The most die-hard faction among the Catholics as regards continuing the war is, to a certain extent, a reflection of some of the most traditional aspects of the Vietnamese Church. This faction was led for a long time by Father Hoang Quyng, a refugee from the North. His Committee for the Defense of the Catholic Faith gained notoriety more than once by criticizing the Catholic and

Buddhist peace movements in the name of the struggle against communism[69] and by clamoring for a stronger centralist government.

This tendency received a new surge of vigor when Cardinal Spellman made his famous declarations in 1966. At that time most of the Catholic press was engaged in a lively polemical debate with *Song Dao,* a magazine published by a group of the most liberal Catholics. In January, 1967, the Saigon Catholic daily, *Xay Dung,* published an open letter to American Catholics who opposed the war:

> You are strangers, of good will certainly, but very far from the present Vietnamese reality. . . . The aggression is inspired by a communist regime, that of North Vietnam. . . . The ultimate aim of that aggression is, unquestionably, to force a communist regime on South Vietnam. Do not cooperate, especially in the name of religion, in imposing a communist regime on us.[70]

The declarations and gestures of Paul VI, however, and the general climate of Vatican II, have contributed to the development of more flexible attitudes. Signs of moderating influences have become increasingly apparent, especially in the relations between Catholics and Buddhists. The clamor for a strong government is gradually becoming a clamor for a government more widely representative of the people, and support for the war is dwindling in the face of a longing for the peace, which is so much in the national interest.[71]

Some smaller, more strongly critical factions also exist, but they are obliged to be very circumspect in what they say. This however, did not prevent a group of eleven priests from publishing a manifesto in January, 1966, asking the "authorities of both North and South to take all necessary steps to put an end to this fratricidal war." They observed that the disorder "engendered by the war, and the presence of foreign soldiers, puts the masses in economic, social and moral conditions unfit for man."[72]

This testimony from another priest is even more forceful: "In the South, the Americans are defending neither religion nor the Vietnamese. They are defending their own interests. They are trampling our traditions underfoot, upsetting the balance of our economy, and holding in power men who do not have the support of the people." And saying that it is easy for the Russians and Chinese to declare themselves "ready to fight to the last Vietnamese," he calls on the other nations to allow the Vietnamese "to resolve their own problems."[73]

A minority faction believes that the anticommunist struggle is simply a pretext for maintaining an authoritarian regime, which is itself alienated from the Americans. "We must have the courage to be realistic. War cannot stop communism.... It is a fact that the NLF exists." And on the hypothesis of a negotiated settlement with the NLF, the priest who exposes this viewpoint believes that "the poor people, who could not be any worse off than they are today, could all of a sudden be of the utmost importance." Is the Church ready to accept a socialist revolution? "You'll see; if the Americans offer us ships the priests will be the first to climb aboard. Or, rather, No. They have plenty of money; they won't be there any longer. They'll already have taken a plane." The same priest adds: "How is it that we don't see that in five or ten years from now everything is going to change in the world; that economic systems are going to be metamorphosed, crumbling away or being transformed, and that what matters is that we be here?" And he concludes: "We shall go through some difficult years.... I would say we deserve it. We had it coming to us."[74]

Somewhere, in a middle ground between the two most extreme tendencies, the bishops give the impression of uttering words completely unrelated to contingent realities. Even when they attempt to echo the words and the stand taken by Paul VI, their fear of offending those in high places has made them stick to generalities about peace. Their appeal of June 10, 1965, reads like a compromise between two rival factions: "The Catholic Church, represented in Vietnam by the bishops, can only be a principle of unity and peace. It always stands outside and above all political parties." With this as a starting point, the rest of the statement comes as no surprise:

> Every loyal member of the national community has a duty to participate actively in building the nation and in making it prosperous, to serve the common good, to spread the evangelical ideal of peace.... All the faithful must

abide by the laws of the state. And when it is necessary to defend legitimate interests, may it always be in view of the common good and in due respect for truth, justice and charity.[75]

On October 8, the following year, after a visit from the pope's personal envoy, Bishop Sergio Pignedoli, the bishops joined with the pope in calling for negotiations and reiterated the main points of Paul VI's ideas on peace as a work of justice. The doctrinal part of the text is followed by an urgent appeal to Catholics to commit themselves to work for peace in non-Catholic as well as Catholic organizations.[76]

In January, 1968, the tone of the bishops' statements seems to have undergone a slight change. They renewed their call for immediate negotiations, but they also expressed their alarm, in no uncertain terms, at the state in which South Vietnam found itself through the fault of those "whose lives are out of touch with the thousands of victims of the war," and who "even exploit poverty and loneliness."[77]

Their declaration of January 4, 1969, simply describes the conditions necessary for peace without specific reference to the political and military situation. Beginning with a reminder that peace cannot be bought at the cost of freedom, the bishops add: "Peace must be taken seriously and lived in conformity with the commitments that each side has made, both of them respecting the other's word."[78]

Like their fellow-citizens, the Vietnamese bishops are caught in the tragic dilemma of their country. For a long time their Conference was presided over by Archbishop Ngo Dinh Thuc, President Diem's elder brother;[79] for a long time they hesitated even to mention peace since to do so was considered subversive in South Vietnam. All things considered, the stand they are now taking is courageous even if they still speak mainly in terms of general principles. In view of the fact that such a large percentage of their flock are refugees from the North and still strongly in favor of the Saigon regime, they might well have taken the point of view defended by Cardinal Spellman.

European Christians. The attitude of Christians in the rest of the world provides an absorbing case study in the relation between faith and politics. In the texts we shall be looking at attitudes very widely between the two poles: "fear of politics" and "the Gospel in the event." Between these two extremes we find positions that have crystallized around criticism of the means, as in the United States itself, and pressure to stop the fighting; but there is no serious critique of the basic issues involved.

The fear of politics. How many Christians have been solicited, since the beginning of hostilities, to contribute to some charitable work on behalf of either North or South Vietnam? This reaction of rallying to the support of those in distress is very frequent in Christian circles. Charity is the favorite refuge of those who are fearful of commiting themselves on a political level. If I emphasize this, it is certainly not with a view to disparaging anyone's goodwill; but we must recognize that charitable organizations always have to take endless precautions before undertaking any direct action and that the peace movements often seem to be at a loss to articulate their analysis of the cause of wars. Charitable organizations are very much concerned with the equitable distribution of their gifts, while the peace movements are concerned with balancing the acts of appeasement they ask of the belligerents. All of this is perhaps based on something which is incontestably true: The victims of any one side should not receive preferential treatment and Christians must show that they are one with all men. But one cannot help wondering if this ambivalence does not also have something to do with the fear of studying the facts of the case a little more closely. I would like to mention just two episodes in illustration of this point.

On September 11, 1966, Archbishop Gouyon of Rennes, president of the French branch of Pax Christi, expressed the question in his mind as to whether all Christians were not murderers,[80] guilty of "refusing assistance to persons in danger." And he added: "It will always be difficult to judge the origins and development of the war in Vietnam. Each side has its own version and both have some verisimilitude; an objective and critical mind hesitates to pronounce itself. Some people make an option, however, but more from prejudice than because they are well informed."

Archbishop Gouyon believes, however, that one is in a position to judge the means that are being used, and condemning terrorism, "which makes it impossible to enjoy freedom," and which seems to him "no better than banditry," he adds:

> But can one sanction the bombing of North Vietnam any more readily? If we question it this does not mean that we are questioning the justification for an American presence in South Vietnam. . . . We would have to forget that many of our Catholic brothers are involved in this tragedy, and that at this moment, if the Americans were simply to withdraw, it would mean a massacre of many of those for whom they are fighting. What Christian could lightheartedly accept such a possibility?

The second text was published in *La France Catholique* [81] and was occasioned by a campaign for "A Boat for Vietnam." [82] Having made it clear that the campaign was inspired by communists and that it hoped for the victory of North Vietnam, the text goes on to say that "this is patently a political stand and it has a clear objective: to help the North in its fight. How far this is from Paul VI's declarations, which unfailingly insist on peace without victory, that is to say, peace through frank and honest negotiation in all justice."

I have chosen these two texts to illustrate my contention because they seem to me typical of two presuppositions in which Christians are steeped with regard to Vietnam and every other political reality. The first postulate is that it is impossible to judge a political problem in depth. Such is their complexity that an objective judgment, as Archbishop Gouyon has it, cannot be made. The only thing to do is to evaluate the *means*. For an objective mind this is a remarkable abstraction and an astonishing neglect of an elementary rule of ethics according to which one cannot judge acts isolated from—or if one is ignorant of—their aims and their sources. The second postulate is that no one can form an unbiased political judgment and that one is, therefore, necessarily the accomplice of certain interests, in whatever stand one may take, thereby adopting an equivocal attitude which cannot be founded in reason or theology.

This is not the first time we have come across these two theories. We have already seen them at work in other circumstances, and the problem they represent seems to be particularly acute in our times.[83]

A radical moral judgment. Another characteristic attitude consists in a revolt of the moral conscience at the horrors of war. "Every impartial observer," writes Cardinal Villot, then Archbishop of Lyons, "every serious and objective reporter agrees in describing the atrocious suffering of the Vietnamese people. No one has expressed the mind of the Church on this matter more eloquently than Paul VI himself: 'War, never again.' "[84] Cardinal Spellman's declarations elicited many reactions of this kind: Bishop Schmitz of Metz, for instance, evoked the passage of the Gospel which speaks of the suffering of families afflicted by war, and reminded his readers of the Council's condemnation of the "destruction of whole cities or vast regions, with all their inhabitants."[85]

In the same vein, Pastor Niemöller declared in 1967, "The Americans in Vietnam are murderers, not soldiers."[86] But this is a statement which has already gone beyond the simple expression of a feeling of revulsion; it implies an analysis and a subsequent moral judgment. This has not always been the case with the statements of those who, in line with the Council, have condemned war as a means of resolving conflicts. Cardinal Lercaro warned of this on January 1, 1968, saying that "the Church cannot be neutral in face of evil, whatever its origin. . . . It is better to be criticized now than to earn everyone's reproaches in the long run, for having failed to help in avoiding the most tragic decisions, or at least in guiding men's consciences in the light of God's word."

Several months before, having reached the age of 75, Cardinal Lercaro had submitted his resignation to the pope who had refused it. Now, only a few days after this declaration and following on indirect but very real pressure from Washington, the Vatican virtually forced the Cardinal to repeat his offer of resignation as archbishop of Bologna.

Similarly, Bishop Méndez Arceo of Cuernavaca, Mexico, emphasized that the Vietnamese war, "in its useless and atrocious prolongation," has greatly contributed to the growing feeling that, by rights, war is something that just should not exist. And he went on to underline the fact that the Church, by reiterating this, can help to announce prophetically a reality of the future, a necessary utopia.

This attitude must be interpreted as an expression of an "ethic of conviction," and interpreting it as such makes us realize how limited it is, for it is extremely difficult to make the step from an ethic of conviction to an ethic of responsibility, that is, an ethic which lies within the framework of a range of options limited by institutional needs or by the role of arbitrator. The problems begin when, for the prophet, the imperative lies in the direction of the utopia and, for politics, in the direction of present reality.

It would be totally impossible to give an exhaustive account of everything Christians have done in an attempt to put a stop to the bombing and to obtain a negotiated settlement. Almost all of the examples we have quoted included this request, and the international movement, Pax Christi, has directed all its work for Vietnam to this end. We mention this attitude on the part of Christians at this point because it is often a consequence of the moral indignation mentioned previously. However, it rarely has any serious significance except in the context of the analysis that has or has not been made of the event.

The Gospel in the event. Under this heading we would group all those texts which have shown particular concern to adopt an attitude toward the Vietnamese war in which the exigency of the Gospel, conceived as an a priori ethical option, is allied to a political analysis of the event, inadequate as this analysis and the options it leads to may be.

This option is based on the conviction that the way of peace cannot be proclaimed in each and every context. In this sense it is the exact opposite of the attitude described above, in which Christians fear a political involvement. The Christians we are talking about now believe that "by trying to avoid all politics, one only succeeds in practicing very inferior politics."[87]

This is the position of the Conférence Chrétienne de la Paix, according to which the "Vietnamese war is a war of aggression by which a military political power is leading humanity to the brink of atomic disaster."[88] The resolution which offers this analysis of the Vietnamese war was accompanied by a letter to Christians in the United States, enumerating the political options involved in the conflict. It is a remarkable document by reason of its competent sociopolitical analysis as much as by the quality of its theological reflection.

The Semaine Sociale at Nantes in 1967 also adopted a resolution about Vietnam, challenging the "superpower which claims to be the defender of the world order—and which is its greatest beneficiary—in order to crush the revolt of the poor by force of arms. . . . The Gospel does not offer a political solution, but it throws light on what is at stake in the conflict. . . . We reject all references to Christianity that have been put forward to justify the American intervention."[89]

Mention of Dr. Martin Luther King, Jr., is in order here, for his option for nonviolence was always associated with a positive analysis and concrete gestures. "We must," he declared, "unite our ardor for the civil rights movement with the peace movement. We must demonstrate, teach, preach, and organize until the very foundations of our nation are shaken. . . . We are engaged in a war which is trying to turn back the tide of history by perpetuating white colonialism. . . . In truth, the hopes of a great society have been killed on the battlefields of Vietnam. . . . The bombs from Vietnam are exploding in our own country."

Ambiguous judgments. In conclusion, we can now see how very different and even contradictory are the positions Christians have adopted with regard to Vietnam. We can also see how difficult it has been, in general, to arouse them to form any opinion on the problem, since they have been unable to see it in its full dimensions. As for official Church opinion, either it has expressed a simplistic Manichean judgment or it has refrained from judging the causes of the war and concentrated on attenuating the suffering it entails or exhorting both sides to lay down their arms. In its anxiety not to involve the faith in temporal questions, the Church has, in point of fact, refused to recognize what is at stake and where the injustice lies. Using the ambiguity of the situation as a pretext, it has kept strictly to general principles in spite of the fact that principles exist for the human community only in application to concrete situations. We must not forget that Vietnam has to be understood in the light of events in Latin America, and this is to be our next step, in the following chapter.

One can hardly fail to be struck by the parallel between the position of Catholics toward the Vietnamese conflict and the one they adopted in the nineteenth century. Now it is "Western civilization," the natural heir to bourgeois society, which consciously or unconsciously has become the principal frame of reference.

CHAPTER SIX

The Revolutionary Movements in Latin America

Latin America today is the scene of a twofold confrontation: A society with archaic socioeconomic structures is in the throes of far-reaching change, and the minority elite in power is faced with a rising tide of opposition from the people.

These two areas of confrontation are not completely coextensive. In some countries, in fact, the military power structure is actively concerned about economic development and a more rational organization of administrative and social affairs, but sociocultural change in these countries is accompanied by a political void and a total absence of popular participation in society.

The different situations in Latin America can be grouped into four main categories. First, there are the sociopolitical power structures which, for various reasons—military dictatorships, dependency on foreign economic interests, etc.—are still very attached to traditional forms. These countries, generally the smaller ones, live in a state of social stagnation.

The second type includes the very big countries like Argentina and Brazil, in which the military power structures freeze all social evolution while attempting to stimulate economic development. In general they achieve their objective only at the price of increased economic dependency on the United States.

A third category includes several different type of social experiments, ranging from minor concessions to popular pressure (e.g., vague plans for agrarian reform) to more radical changes, such as those in Mexico or, more recently, in Chile and Venezuela. In these countries there is a genuine desire for change, at least on the part of some of the leading figures in the country, but the patterns vary. In some countries concessions have been made in order to safeguard the basic social structures; in others, fundamental and

169

far-reaching reforms of the economic and social structures have
been attempted. In yet others the revolution has become institutionalized and been unable to resist the seductions of foreign
capital, and little by little a new dominant class is emerging.
Finally, there is a fourth type—which some consider the only
Latin American model for change—represented by Cuba. This is
the swift and sudden revolution which sweeps away all previous
structures and gradually proposes a new model for society.

It would be a mistake, however, to believe that the evolution of
the Latin American continent can be understood without reference
to its place in the international context. Everything revolves
around the economic factor. The major problem of the deteriorat-
ing exchange rates between industrial societies and countries
which produce the raw materials for industry or a preponderance
of agricultural products is sufficiently well-known. Latin America
is one of the victims of this process, and at the Geneva conference
of UNCTAD, and even more at the Algiers and New Delhi conferences, Latin American solidarity with the rest of the Third World
was very explicitly affirmed.

If the "American challenge" is very real for Europe, how much
more so is it for a continent like Latin America, 60 percent of
whose foreign trade—and in some cases 80 percent—is dependent
on the United States.

This economic bondage, which is also visible in massive American investment in key industries, only serves to strengthen its
political bondage. The attitude of many states, often in direct
contradiction with their true sympathies, in the affair of the Dominican Republic, is only one example of this political bondage.
Another is the United States' successful control of many of the
internal policies of Latin American countries. Major American
economic and military interests frequently pressure the administration in Washington to use the pretext of security or the principle of
free trade to cover their interventions, which are not always very
discreet. One only has to remember the innumerable interventions
in Central America within the last few years, especially in Guatemala; the abortive invasion of the Bay of Pigs; the more carefully
camouflaged interference in Bolivia, etc.[1]

On the economic as well as on the political level, Latin America is at the center of contemporary international geopolitics. The war in Vietnam is the violent expression of this situation: When Che Guevara advocated an irruption of "Vietnams" all over Latin America, he was not merely using a figure of speech.

The "free world" championed by the United States is no longer capable of guiding its own development in the direction it would like. More importantly, it is no longer capable of accepting the economic and social changes necessary to ensure the development of the rest of the world. It is fighting a battle on two fronts in an endeavor to prevent the spread of communism: by "containment," a policy which has led, for example, to the Vietnam tragedy, or by supporting reactionary power structures in order to guarantee the survival of a social order necessary for the development of a capitalist or neocapitalist economy. Even in terms of the latter policy, Vietnam is a particularly striking example; one of the original causes of the conflict was precisely a popular uprising against just such a power structure.

It is in this context that we must examine the present efficacy and the future prospects of the revolutionary movements in Latin America.

Present Problems and Future Prospects of the Revolutionary Movements in Latin America

The major problems—and the principal topics of discussion—of the Latin American revolutionary movements are, first, their isolation within the society in which their struggle is going on, and, second, their difficulty in defining the most suitable "model" for their revolutionary combat and their own particular situation. These two fundamental problems are further complicated by the shortage of trained militants and the fact that they have to stand up against the combined pressures of the Latin American and North American governments.

Many of the movements, influenced by the Cuban example and the pressure of government repression, take the form of guerrilla groups. Under the influence of the recent Cuban revolution and sometimes with its help, most of the guerrilla groups began in the early 1960s. A brief sketch of the history of this development will be useful here.

Venezuela. The overthrow in 1958 of the dictator, Marcos Pérez Jiménez, brought Rómulo Betancourt, leader of the Acción Democrática, to power. His party applied a reformist policy, which became the target for attacks from both the extreme left and right. At first the Venezuela Communist party (PCV), just emerging from a long clandestine period, supported Betancourt, but before long it was accusing him of a conciliatory attitude toward conservative and American interests. In 1960 the PCV joined the ranks of the opposition. The same year a branch of Acción Democrática broke off from the government coalition and founded the Movimiento de Izquierda Revolucionario, the Leftist Revolutionary Movement or MIR, and President Betancourt found himself faced with a two-headed radical opposition.

In 1961 and 1962 there was a series of violent incidents and some pro-Castro demonstrations and rioting. The hard-line wing of the Communist party managed to win the whole party over to a policy of armed struggle. In 1962 there were six guerrilla centers in the mountains, constituted of students, members of the MIR and of the PCV. In the spring of that year two of these centers seemed to be solidly entrenched, one under the leadership of Juan Vicente Cabezas in the state of Cabral, the other under Douglas Bravo in the state of Falcón. A plan for armed insurrection, in collaboration with urban groups, was discovered and defused and the government clamped down on the MIR and the PCV and declared their activities illegal.

In 1963 violence reached a paroxysm and the opposition began to plan for direct confrontation; the rebellion was becoming organized. On February 20, the Armed Forces of Liberation (FALN) was formed, and a little later a body of political control was established: the National Liberation Front (FLN). The government was powerless to stop the movement; on the contrary, there was increasing collusion between political leaders and the revolutionaries. In October of that year Douglas Bravo declared that the regions of Falcón and Lara had been "stabilized." But the discovery of a cache of Cuban arms and a plan to capture the capital finally prompted the government to act. President Betancourt lodged a complaint with the Organization of American States (OAS) and ordered preventive arrest of members of the MIR and the PCV. He also outlawed the two movements, thereby preventing their candidates from running in the presidential elections planned for December.

The elections, virtually a referendum against violence, were won by Raul Leoni, with the support of the labor unions and the peasants, and Leoni pledged to continue Betancourt's policies. The MIR and the PCV did not, however, conform to the order to abstain from participating in the elections. At the beginning of the new regime there was a lull in subversive activities and the leaders of guerrilla centers took advantage of it to plan their future tactics. Early in 1964 their plan began to crystallize around the ideas advocated by Guevara: "insurrectional focal points" and "protracted warfare." Two new fronts were opened in July, 1964, and in November the FALN opened an office in Cuba for contacts outside Venezuela. Acts of violence became more frequent and the repressive measures became increasingly harsh: "mopping up" operations, bombings, mass evacuation of the inhabitants of whole areas, etc. Urban operations were also very daring, but always entailed heavy losses for the rebels, and sometimes the whole group was wiped out.

The second national conference of the FLN was held in March, 1965. It spent several days studying its own aims and methods, its differences of opinion with other revolutionary movements (especially the Communist party and the Trotskyites), the attitude of the political power structure of the country,. and the contacts that had to be maintained with liberation movements in other Latin American countries struggling against a common enemy.[2] Their tremendous intellectual output is one of the striking characteristics of the Venezuelan revolutionaries, who seem to have made a more substantial contribution in this area than any other Latin American movement. The four volumes of Documentation compiled by Alejandro del Corro and published by CIDOC[3] is eloquent testimony to their work, which deals not only with organizational and methodological questions but also with theoretical questions. They have developed studies of national and international social conditions; the role of violence in the struggle for liberation; the political education of the masses; and the construction of a socialist state. It is evident that what was simply a revolt is now a full-fledged revolutionary war. A document published by the MIR on August 25, 1964,[4] makes this abundantly clear: It will be a long struggle—there can be no illusions on that score—but even then, in 1964, Vietnam was a frame of reference.

Among the opposition were some who favored violence, while others favored legal opposition. The former were energetically supported by the Tri-Continental Conference in Havana in 1966, at which the Communist party was not represented. When renewed violence broke out in 1966, it was met with political repression, which was later accompanied by military action.

From 1965 on the Communist party openly broke off relations with the guerrillas, calling for a return to mass political action and the preparation of an election campaign, and the party even established contact with the government. But revolutionary leaders like Fabricio Ojeda and Douglas Bravo were of the same mind as Cuba and believed in the necessity of an armed struggle. Bravo was demoted from his position in the upper echelons of the PCV.

In June, 1966, Bravo and Ojeda were arrested and the latter killed himself while in prison. In 1967 the PCV and Cuba finally broke off relations, and in May of that year a small group of Cuban and Venezuelan commandos were intercepted in an attempted landing. Their aim had been to inject new life into the guerrilla movement. When President Caldera came to power in March, 1966, there was a general call for social peace and the PCV was reintegrated into the political life of the country. Since then, although violence has broken out again, there seems to be little chance that it will lead to any new developments.

Venezuela is a typical example of the conflict between three forces which is taking place almost everywhere in Latin America: the government, the traditional revolutionary forces, and the guerrillas, the latter often divided into different factions.

Guatemala. The guerrilla conflict in Guatemala grew out of an abortive military coup against the president, Ydígoras Fuentes, in

November, 1960. The authors of the coup, Yon Sosa and Luis A. Turcios, found themselves obliged to go into hiding. The roots of the struggle, however, go back much farther. In Honduras, in 1954, the Americans supplied arms to Colonel Castilla Armas, who overthrew President Arbenz, author of the agrarian reform which had so offended the almighty United Fruit Company. The story of that intervention, as well as those which preceded and followed it, is so flagrantly "colonialist" that it is hard to believe that it happened in the second half of the twentieth century.[5]

The guerilla movement began to spread only when liaison was established between the groups active in the rural areas and those in the urban centers. Yon Sosa was the building spirit of the November 13 Revolutionary Movement, which is Maoist, and the Green Berets of Southern Command have done their best to put a halt to its activities in the rural areas. Turcios, in the meantime, founded the Armed Revolutionary Forces (FAR) and collaborated with the Communist party (the Guatemalan Labor Party). His groups operated almost exclusively from urban bases. When he was killed in an accident, the leadership passed to César Montes.

On April 24, 1962, the Guatemalan bishops published a joint pastoral letter in which they warned the population against "the grave danger of atheistic, materialistic, and totalitarian Communism" and urged them to safeguard "our Christian heritage." The communist threat, they declared, "has become greater in the course of the current year in several Latin American countries, thus impairing Catholic unity which embraces the majority of the people of our continent." The bishops reminded the faithful that although the Church has nothing to do with politics, it still has a "duty to defend Christian faith and morals in state structures and institutions." Finally they pleaded for Catholics to "cooperate in restoring public order . . . in face of Communist effrontery. . . , to defend the principal of respect for legally constituted authority. . . and to unite their efforts in an attempt to save the sublime mission of the Church. . . , seeking first of all the kingdom of God and hoping that God, our Lord, will free Guatemala from atheistic, materialistic, totalitarian Communism."

All this is part of a highly confused and lethal situation in which militaristic and extreme right regimes follow each other in rapid succession. The army is equipped, trained, and advised by American teams of specialists in counterinsurgency, some of them veterans of the Vietnamese conflict. A secret organization of the extreme right, *La Mano,* carries out missions which the official agencies prefer to avoid. The murder and torture of prisoners is common practice. Anything that smacks of leftist leanings is suspect, from the intellectuals to organized workers. The president of the YCW was assassinated. The guerrillas are pursued by Guatemalan rangers and bombed with napalm. And yet all of this is only the surface disturbance of a deep-lying revolt that has been repressed for generations. Perhaps the Cuban revolution has given the people of Guatemala an illusory glimmer of hope. César Montes, for example, has declared: "The peasants need land and no one gives it to them. They need houses and the government builds houses for the military. The fury that has been contained for centuries is about to explode, is in the process of exploding, in Guatemala."[6]

The Catholics of the country are deeply divided. The dominant bourgeoisie and the big landowners are all Catholics. President Méndez Montenegro, elected in 1966, is a Catholic liberal, but his regime was completely paralyzed by the army and turned out to be one of the most violent Guatemala had ever experienced. The campaigns for the elections of March 1, 1970, were particularly eventful. The Christian Democrats, with the support of a coalition of the left, presented a candidate for the presidency, but the revolutionary movements decided to intervene in the hope of radicalizing the positions, with the result that the candidate of the extreme right, Colonel Arana Osorio, was proclaimed President by Parliament. And so the struggle goes on, with the kidnapping of public figures such as Sean Holly, an American diplomat, the Minister of Foreign Affairs, the West German ambassador, etc.

Just before he was abducted by a commando of *La Mano* members (in a remarkably poorly organized operation), the new archbishop of Guatemala City, Archbishop Mario Casarriego, had published a pastoral letter in association with the other bishops, in which they described the social situation in the country. "No one can deny that our social and economic reality is terribly unjust and unequal.... The present unjust distribution of the national income, the disparity in salaries, ... the *latifundia* system which gives 70 percent of the arable land in the country to only 2 percent of the active population: ... All this calls for courageous and definitive change."[7] This declaration was, itself, courageous, but it was content to state a certain number of observable facts, seeming to imply that the classes in power would not be deaf to the voice of justice and would put certain reforms into effect. The internal dynamics of the situation are such, however, that the struggle will probably be prolonged and arduous. But it is already too late for it to be stopped. The social situation will change only when political power changes hands.

The religious factor is not foreign to all these events, and its influence is sometimes felt in unexpected areas. Although the Indian peasants have adopted Christianity, it is often no more than an addition to their own traditional religion. And yet many very fine militant Christians of the left have been recruited from among them. On the right so many well-intentioned Catholics still live in a world that is completely out of touch with present reality, as in the case of the lawyer from Guatemala City who spoke about his work during the catechetical congress at Medellín in 1968. Having declared that political assassinations and torture were common practice, he went on to describe how, a few weeks before, he had accompanied a young man whom he believed innocent, to the gallows. The boy was from the lower class and had received no religious instruction. Taking a big crucifix from his pocket, the lawyer reenacted the scene with deep emotion: "Although he had barely set foot in a church in his life, at my suggestion he offered his life for the freedom of Catholic schools." But the right also includes the MNL (Movement of National Liberation), an extremist group with the slogan: God, Country, Freedom;[8] the NOA (New Anticommunist Organization), which proclaims: "A communist unmasked is a dead communist," and which called on members of the Catholic University, in March, 1967, to stand up to those who are hostile to "the constituted government, the Catholic religion, the forces of labor, trade, the banks, industry and agriculture;"[9] and the CADEG (Anticommunist Council of Guatemala), which accuses the communists of "pressuring the peasants and workers to become the enemies of capitalism, society and the Catholic religion."[10]

Three American missionaries, two priests and a nun, have been expelled from the country for siding with the *guerrilleros,* being well aware, as they put it, of the responsibility of the United States in the present situation. When the German diplomat was abducted, it was the Apostolic nuncio, dean of the diplomatic corps, who served as intermediary, and the ambassador's family intervened with the Guatemalan government, arguing that their refusal to comply with the demands of the abducters for his release was contrary to Christian principles. All this may seem to be mere folklore, or rather to symbolize a civilization of the past. There is a fairly new element involved, however, and that is the tendency of several leaders of the revolutionary groups to give a religious interpretation to events, based on the Christian tradition of the South American continent and stimulated, perhaps, by the fact that some priests, such as Camilo Torres, have been involved in the revolutionary project.

At the beginning of 1968, the November 13 Movement, led by Yon Sosa, and the FAR came out with a joint declaration that signified the end of the dispute between them, a break with the Communist party,[11] and the expulsion from their ranks of Trotskyite elements: "The existence of two parallel movements can no longer be tolerated since they both recognize that history points to armed struggle as the only way to obtain freedom, justice, and progress." At the end of the declaration they add: "Our decision makes it possible for us to offer strong armed solidarity to all those people who are fighting for their freedom, and particularly to the heroic people of Vietnam who have shown us the way to victory through armed struggle."[12]

And yet, just as in Venezuela, there seems to be no prospect of a medium-term solution. All power is in the hands of reactionary conservative forces. The "long march" has begun, with its endless caravan of suffering and its implacable dialectic.

Peru. Until 1960 there was no organized social agitation in Peru. At that time a group of farmers and sharecroppers, under the leadership of Hugo Blanco, organized a movement in the Cuzco region and succeeded in gaining control of part of the province of Convención. Early in 1963 the influence of the movement was destroyed by repressive measures, and in May of that year Blanco was arrested. It seems that the conservatives profited most from the fiasco, but at least it had been proved that it was possible to organize a mass movement. At about that time there were numerous incursions by peasant groups against big landowners or North American agricultural holdings. Taking over the land, the peasants declared that it was a case, not of invasion but of reclamation. In the words of Hugo Neira:

> It is not only an act of juridical rehabilitation or a change of ownership. It is an act of justice, an ethical undertaking. The intuition of moral values so deeply rooted in the ancient Indian race is not dead. It is a question of squaring the accounts. The gigantic assemblies that gather on a piece of land after it has been occupied is a sort of "people's tribunal." The theme of debate is the land. One after another, men and women, leaders and followers, all have their word to say.[13]

The lands were occupied peacefully and with moderation. The peasants never claimed the entire property, leaving part of it for the owner and awaiting the arrival of government authorities to whom they made known the extent of their claim.[14]

Since 1963 a group led by Luis de la Puente, the MIR, has taken up the struggle and attempted to lay the groundwork of a revolutionary organization, but it places less confidence in the peasant masses and is made up principally of revolutionaries from the cities and universities. Three guerrilla groups were active in 1965 in the north, center, and eastern regions of the country. After some inital success these groups were wiped out by the vigorous reaction of the army. La Puente was killed in October, 1965, and his assistant, Lobaton, disappeared in January, 1966. The failure of this group seems to come from underestimating the repressive power of the government. Also, public opinion had not been prepared to give them support, the *guerrilleros* were cut off from the masses as well as from the leftist political movements.

Hugo Blanco had been keenly aware of this danger. In 1964 he wrote: "The armed struggle stems from the struggle for the land,

and armed groups ... will spring up as an emanation of the mass movement. ... At this stage it is pure adventurism to open up guerrilla fronts or focal points cut off from the action of the masses."[15] It was a direct allusion to the strategy of the MIR.

What followed is well known: The reformist president, Belaunde, failed to carry out his political and social program and was eventually removed by a nationalist military junta, which launched far-reaching social reforms, particularly in the area of land ownership. The main drawback of this is that everything is decided at the upper echelons: The resulting political vacuum is not the most effective way of integrating the masses in a social revolution.

Bolivia. Since November, 1964, the country has been governed by a military junta supported by the army and peasant militia. The worker movement has been held on a very tight rein. In 1967 a guerrilla training camp was discovered in the gorges of the river Nancuahaza. In this country also, the movement, which has been supported from Cuba, has lacked the support of the peasants. After a few violent skirmishes with the army the group scattered. In the beginning the army's counteraction was ill-adapted to this kind of fluidity, and with the active presence of Che Guevara and Régis Debray, the armed struggle was very effective for a time. But the government has since regained the initiative. Debray and Che have both been eliminated, and the guerrilla groups are being vigorously "contained."

Paraguay and Argentina. In the other Latin American countries the revolutionary elements have not been particularly effective. In Paraguay General Stroessner's dictatorship has been punctuated by several abortive coups d'état rather than by guerrilla activity, particularly since 1960. In 1963 the Communist party came out in favor of carrying on the struggle through legally recognized channels. Since 1968 imprisonment for political dissent has become increasingly frequent. In 1969, when some priests were the victims of repressive measures, the bishops reacted energetically, and for the first time Sunday Mass was suspended in protest against political oppression.

In Argentina some small revolutionary groups were dispersed in 1963 in the northern regions. But the main thrust of the social struggle is in quite another area: that of labor unions. Cordoba has been the scene of several conflicts in which university elements were involved. Opposition to the military regime has rarely taken the form of freedom movements, and conditions are very different from those of, say, Venezuela, Guatemala, or Colombia. Early in 1970, however, a mail train was attacked and the army discovered a relatively small guerrilla training camp at Lujan, not far from Buenos Aires. The Paraguayan consul was abducted by the FAL (Argentine Liberation Front), and a rightist movement calling itself *La Mano* (Argentine Organized Nationalist Movement) has appeared and in March, 1970, declared a state of civil war in reaction against the revolutionary movements.

Brazil. The military coup d'état in 1964 brought to power a regime which aims at efficient economic development and believes that the best way to achieve this is by means of strong and highly centralized government control. With this in mind it has even tried to force its policy on certain big property owners whose land was greatly underproductive, but at the same time it has stifled all popular movements, even when they have been started by the Church. The regime has its theorists—in particular General Golbery do Couto e Silva—and it would be a mistake to believe that it is nothing more than a military dictatorship. In conformity with its policy it has opted for a close alliance with the United States, with all that that implies on the economic, political, and military levels.

The repression that followed the political coup in 1964 caught the leftist movements off their guard, and it was several years before they began to show renewed signs of life. In 1968 and 1969 revolutionary incidents occurred more frequently, usually in the form of hold-ups or spectacular kidnappings. In 1969 the American ambassador, Burk Elbrich, was kidnapped, and in 1970 the Japanese consul at Sao Paolo. Marxists and Christians found themselves working together in what was increasingly recognized as a common cause. The Popular Action movement, which had been started by Christians, went underground very soon after the coup d'état, and the popular leader Carlos Marighela broke off from the Communist party and organized his own revolutionary movement. He was assassinated in November, 1969. In March of the same year Captain Varlos Lamarca deserted from the army and joined the revolutionaries.

The Brazilian Church is divided in itself, with an avant-garde faction under the leadership of Dom Helder Camara, which has taken a very progressive stand. On April 30, 1963, the central commission of the Brazilian episcopacy, of which Dom Helder was secretary, issued a statement which the conservative press refused to publish. In it the bishops declared: "No one can ignore the miserable conditions, unfit for human beings, in which thousands of our brethren live in the rural areas, cut off from any possibility of sharing in our development." The declaration concluded with the remark that "expropriation in the interests of society is not contrary to the social doctrine of the Church."[16]

At about the same time two bishops, Archbishop Geraldo de Proença Sigaud of Diamantina and Archbishop Oscar de Oliveiras of Mariana, took a stand diametrically opposed. In a joint publication, which received wide publicity—"Agrarian Reform, A Matter of Conscience"—they emphasized the natural right to private property and the special (quasi-divine) mission of property owners. At a press conference during the Eucharistic Congress at Bogotá, Archbishop Sigaud declared he would excommunicate any Catholic who accepted land distributed through agrarian reform. Reactions like this were no surprise, coming from the authors of the "anticommunist catechism" published not long before by the two bishops, in which they claim that Satan is the father of all revolution, for he knows that "the best way of getting people to damn themselves for all eternity is to get them to rebel against the order established by God" (article 34). Two other articles give a description of that divine order: "God does not want this world to be a paradise. He wants it to be a place in which we shall encounter great suffering as well as pure joy, so that we may be sanctified by carrying our cross [art. 95]. . . . Does God want there to be rich and poor, nobles and plebeians? Yes. It is in conformity with God's will that there should be the poor and the rich, the lowly and those who are important, as long as this hierarchy is based on justice and charity" [art. 96].

After the coup d'état the Church was radicalized. The "revolution" was preceded by massive demonstrations organized by the Brazilian Society for the Defense of Tradition, Family and Property, and one year later, Cardinal Rossi, then archbishop of Sao Paolo, gave a homily in which he declared that "a great debt of gratitude unites us today as we gather around the altar. We are commemorating the fact that, one year ago, the Brazilian nation, faithful to its historic vocation with the help of God and the courage, pride and strength of its sons, thwarted the communist conspiracy that was on the point of dragging this great nation into the sorrowful zones of silence. . . ." In the meantime Dom Helder Camara was being attacked on all sides; Father Antonio Henrique Neto, student chaplain, was assassinated at Recife; arrests and torture became more and more common and neither priests nor nuns were immune. Toward the end of 1969 it was discovered that the police had organized a school for instruction in methods of torture. A secret organization on the extreme right, almost certainly encouraged by the police, was responsible for a series of assassinations, and a bishop declared that those who carried out these assassinations were excommunicated.

Pressure from various directions sought a reaction from the Holy See, and Cardinal Roy, archbishop of Quebec and president of the pontifical Justice and Peace commission, publicly condemned the practice. On March 25, 1970, Paul VI referred to a personal intervention he had made, saying: "For the honor of certain nations very dear to us we cannot but hope for a denial of the charges of torture levelled against them." Dom Helder Camara had visited the pope at the end of January, on his way to a meeting of the World Council of Churches in Montreux.

Many groups, however, felt that this was inadequate and continued to press for a more cogent expression of the revulsion of Catholics in the face of such practices. The secretary of the Justice and Peace commission, Monsignor Gremillion has, however, replied that "the firm action that the Holy See and the Brazilian bishops intend to carry on in order to prevent further deterioration of the situation and to bring about radical improvement can sometimes be more effective if it is discreet and not surrounded by publicity."[17]

One has the feeling that these are the reactions of well-intentioned men, paralyzed by the existing structures which make it impossible for them to speak out clearly (the Vatican has diplomatic relations with Brazil), or terrified of the repercussions their words might have on the Brazilian Church and its pastoral institutions, or even fearful that a condemnation of "legal violence" might be interpreted as an endorsement of "illegal violence." Perhaps all these reasons combine, but however that may be, the only reaction from Brazil's president, General Ganastaza Medici, was a declaration on April 1, 1970, in which he said: "We remain faithful to our vocation as a Christian nation that loves democracy."

The Dominican Republic. After the downfall of Trujillo, political events followed what has become an almost classical scenario. Every serious attempt at social reform has been crushed by a coalition of the right wing, who have no intention of losing their privileged status or the services (and the troops) provided by the government of the United States, and who are prepared to do everything in their power to prevent a second Cuba. But here too, especially under President Joaquín Balaguer, more and more people simply vanish, arbitrary jailings are innumerable, political assassination is an everyday occurrence.[18] At the beginning of 1970, the kidnapped American military attaché was exchanged for some political prisoners, who were handed over in front of one of the downtown churches to a commission of three, which included Archbishop Hugo E. Polanco Brito.

Uruguay. Social disorders have not been lacking in Uruguay, home of the much publicized revolutionary group: the Tupamaros. The Tupamaros have not only indulged in terrorist activities, but have carried out hold-ups to finance their work. One of their most spectacular exploits was the release of thirteen prisoners held for subversive activities.

The Liberation Movements in Colombia and the Part Played by Camilo Torres.

Colombia is treated separately, for Camilo Torres is of special interest in the context of this study.

A prerevolutionary situation. Colombia must be seen within the overall context of the Latin American continent with its twofold pattern of conflict and confrontation. Like the other countries of the continent, Colombia achieved independence at the cost of much fighting. But the struggle against Spain, in spite of Simón Bolívar's own ideology, never became a revolution. The *caudillos* became property owners by decree of the Republic and took over the role played by the Spanish kings. Today, in spite of industrialization of certain regions, Colombian society has still not taken the step into the modern era. The apparent vitality in the center of the capital city of Bogotá is offset by the sorry spectacle of numerous beggars and the sordid "shantytowns" that surround it and all major cities. There is 1 doctor for every 2,500 inhabitants. Many peasants live practically on a subsistence level, for even when they own three or four acres of land it is often divided up into several smaller lots.[19] The agrarian reform which was carried out more than seven years ago has still not changed the fact that 3 percent of the population owns 70 percent of the land. One out of two adults cannot read or write, and 38 percent of the school-age children have no school to go to. The population is 75 percent rural, and only 20 percent of the gross national product comes from industry. Four percent of the population enjoys 40 percent of the national revenue. The bourgeoisie, however, and the lower middle classes in the cities, in spite of many difficulties, seem content with their lot and constitute the backbone of the present regime. In the last elections in 1967, only 30 percent of eligible voters went to the polls.

In Colombia, as in all the other areas of Latin America, the domination of the United States can be keenly felt. Colombia is one of the six countries which "benefit" from 90 percent of the American military aid to the southern continent.[20] Nearly 80 percent of Colombian oil production is in the hands of American companies. Coffee represents 65 to 70 percent of their total exports, and most of it goes to the U.S.A.; when the price of coffee drops by only one cent per pound on the New York market, the economy of Colombia loses $8 million.[21] This foreign economic domination has found natural allies within the country, especially among the big property owners who produce goods for export. The army has ceased to exercise direct control over the government since 1958, but with the aid of American military advisers, it has been extremely effective in its fight against the guerrillas.

From the point of view of social dynamics several morphological and historical facts are of importance. The population of Colombia is composed of only 2 percent Indians, 5 percent blacks, 23 percent mulattos (black and white parentage), 20 percent whites, and 50 percent mestizos (mixed parentage, mostly Indian and white). The Spanish domination completely wiped out the Indian civilization and replaced it with a Spanish, Catholic culture. The fact that the mestizos are very numberous and that they speak Spanish has not done away with social and ethnic barriers. Property owners and all preminent figures on the cultural and political scene are white.

The independence won by Bolívar hardly changed the social stratifications at all. The peasants, armed by their overlords in order to defend their lands, became a maneuverable mass in the struggle between two rival factions of the wealthy, the Liberals and the Conservatives. The political parties, which served the interests of the ruling classes, mobilized the peasantry in conflicts which were of no concern to them and while accustoming them to violence, succeeded in making them into a politically amorphous mass. "The liberal-conservative conflict has anesthetized political conscience by its factional struggles for power, envisaged as a goal in itself."[22]

In the 1940s Jorge Eliécer Gaitán attempted to stand up to the oligarchy. He was assassinated on April 9, 1948, and his death sparked spontaneous rioting among the population, causing three thousand deaths in Bogotá alone. The masses were, at last, awakening, but they knew only one method of action, *la violencia*.[23] For nine years fierce fighting went on between "conservative" and "liberal" villages, while the central government tried in vain to stem the flood of violence. The take-over by General Rojas Pinilla in 1953 and his incredibly brutal campaign of "pacification" initiated in the rural areas still did not manage to put a stop to the peasant guerrilla movements. In areas under "liberal" control at that time, zones of self-defense were set up in opposition to the central government and several of them, such as the Independent

Republic of Tiquendame or, later, the Peasant Republic of Marquetalia, soon fell under the control of the Communist party and organized their own government. In other areas violence simply degenerated into banditry, as with the notorious *Bandoleros.*

In 1958 the Liberal and Conservative parties joined forces to overthrow the military dictatorship and form a coalition government. But there was still no cessation of violence in the villages. The explosive expression of frustration, which had been going on for ten years and had cost the lives of more than two hundred thousand people, continued to disrupt the balance of Colombian society and destroy its traditional political and religious framework. The mentality of the peasant masses was changed. Ever since then the National Front has been in power. Banditry has been reduced, but guerrilla war goes on, and in the beginning of the 1960s newly organized movements began to make their appearance.

The first of these, the MOEC,[24] formed by former Communist militants and young intellectuals, attempted to launch guerrilla warfare in the Cauca in 1961. The attempt failed. In 1964 the army wiped out the Peasant Republics and in 1966 the *guerrilleros* who had escaped formed the FARC,[25] a revolutionary peasant movement. Finally, the ELN,[26] founded in 1965 and led by Fabio Vásquez, carries out its own, original type of guerrilla war, quite different from the Cuban model, in the region of Santander. All these groups, closely in touch with the local populations, are considered "leftist' by the Communist party.

The Communist party of Colombia, for its part, is being increasingly criticized for accepting a compromise with the liberal wing of the bourgeoisie. As a legally constituted party with 13,000 members, it still clings to the notion of "self-defense," which greatly contributed to making the Peasant Republics so vulnerable to government repression. The Communist party sometimes gives the impression that its ties with the guerrilla movements are only a gambit in its negotiations with the bourgeoisie, and it is criticized by the far left for its empty revolutionary rhetoric. Following Soviet policy, its electoral strategy is becoming more and more highly developed.[27]

The Communist analysis of the situation, based on the hypothesis of a conflict of interests between a section of the wealthy classes on the one hand, and the property owners and the United States on the other, does not seem to be borne out by the facts: Liberal governments have not succeeded in overcoming the innate contradictions of Colombian society, nor have they managed to get its economy off the ground.

This, briefly, is the context in which Camilo Torres undertook his revolutionary action, and I would like now to outline the salient features of his life and, subsequently, his actions and ideas in an attempt to discern the originality of his contribution.[28]

Camilo Torres' life. Camilo was born in a wealthy family and his childhood and youth were spent in comfort. Before World War II has father was ambassador to Berlin and young Camilo spent some time as a student in a college in Belgium.[29]

Unlike most priests in Colombia and other Latin American countries, Camilo never entered a minor seminary nor did he enter the major seminary until after he had acquired a degree in law from the university. At this period he was hesitating between the religious life and the diocesan clergy, and this uncertainty persisted almost up to the moment of ordination. He finally chose to join the diocesan clergy.

After ordination he was sent to Louvain, where he spent three years studying social and political science. During this time he did a great deal to help other Latin American students, working with a Belgian-Colombian association giving hospitality and aid. He also collaborated in the formation of a group of Colombian students who were anxious to put their intellectual training to good use for their country. When he had completed his studies, he was invited to stay on for another year in Louvain as vice-rector of the Latin American College, founded only a few years earlier.[30]

Back in Colombia in 1959, he was appointed chaplain of the National University of Bogotá, and at the same time taught sociology and pursued his own research.[31] In 1962 he left the university. A strike triggered by the expulsion of ten students had led him to intervene and propose a solution; the students, who were strongly influenced by his personality, chose him as rector, whereupon

Cardinal Concha, archbishop of Bogotá, ordered him to give up his university posts.

Several important factors should be noted about this first part of his life. Generous to a fault and temperamentally inclined to extremes, he continued to be plagued by the conflict between the religious life and the diocesan priesthood. His experience at the University of Bogotá was also his first real conflict with an institution. When he became chaplain, he soon found this official post altogether too comfortably established and he was ill at ease in the ambiguity of his role, which made him a sort of delegate of the authorities. He preferred his post as professor since it gave him a more normal relationship with the students and other professors. Another significant factor was his remarkable influence on the students and his exceptional intelligence. The sociological work he produced during these early years is of a high quality, but he was still oscillating between a commitment to theoretical research and a concrete involvement. His influence with the students was probably due, in large measure, to his capacity for grasping things in their totality, even with very different kinds of problems and when dealing with very different kinds of people.

When he left the university, he served as dean of the Institute of Social Administration, a section of the School of Public Administration.[32] His job required him to meet frequently with high-ranking government officials, and he began to be personally acquainted with those in power and with the obstacles standing in the way of the development of his country. He was also busy with some very practical questions, such as preparing mobile instruction units to spread information about agrarian reform.[33] He worked out the method to be used in the course of instruction and took part in training the rural leaders and administrators.

In all this work Camilo was exploiting his theoretical skills, but he also made good use of his convictions as a sociologist dedicated to social change and especially to studying the mechanism of social change. Already his language was outspoken and very much to the point. He seemed to have a singular gift for blending the qualities of theoretician and analyst with those of a militant. During this period he was getting to know his country in depth. The utter destitution of the rural populations moved him deeply and, even more important, he began to perceive the structural, ideological, and political causes.

In this context he began to associate more and more closely with political activists and he became more deeply convinced of the necessity of uniting all the leftist groups in the pursuit of clearly defined goals, with agreement on common action. Toward the end of 1964 his plan began to take shape and he contacted more and more people to work out a program. It was this program that was published—prematurely and apparently against Camilo's better judgment—in March, 1965, under the title: Platform for a Movement for the Unity of the People. It elicited an unprecedented response throughout the country.

This was the beginning of the conflict that was to grow up around him. For Camilo Torres was a griest, and although his entry into the political arena seemed to him perfectly logical, it could not fail to raise some thorny questions about his relationship with the institutional Church. Camilo's political work and his conflict with the Church will be examined in greater detail in the following section of this chapter. At this point a few more facts will help to complete this rapid overview of his personal evolution.

The United People's Front succeeded for a while in serving as a rallying point for all the progressive forces of the country. Camilo found himself led to ask for laicization, thus freeing himself for a fuller commitment to the political struggle. But other difficulties soon arose: Some members defected and the Front met with great hostility and distrust from the traditional political bureaucracies on the left as well as the right. As he gradually found himself isolated, Camilo realized that he had to choose between leaving the country or risking political assassination. Some friends urged him to return to Louvain to present his doctoral thesis in sociology, and to take the time to reevaluate his action. But Camilo chose instead to put his loyalty to those whose hopes he had stirred up above his own safety, and at the end of 1965 he joined a guerrilla group. On February 15, 1966, Camilo Torres was killed by government forces in the mountains of Colombia.

Camilo Torres' ideas and work. Camilo's bourgeois background and the fact that he was a priest were severe handicaps to be overcome in order to commit himself as he did to the revolutionary struggle. The social sciences furnished him with the critical instruments he needed; his own generosity and honesty did the rest. His most valuable quality as a revolutionary was probably his gift for combining conviction with a careful and objective analysis and a sound practical knowledge of the realities of Colombian society. As he said: "It is indispensable that the doctrinal foundation of every social action be rooted in a positive investigation of reality."[34] His own thought and action were dynamically unified. From the beginning of his intellectual career he had unstintingly applied his exceptionally broad culture to the investigation of social reality and especially to the ways in which it changes. As a young professor he founded a "Movement for Community Improvement" through which he worked, with his students, in one of the slums of Bogotá. It was in this setting that he discovered the importance of the people themselves as agents of change in their own lives and also the value of action as a means of transforming people's awareness of problems. While he was dean of the Institute of Social Administration, this zeal was the motive power in his work and research.

His political action stemmed not from any one theory or conviction but from his total personality. As he put it, "I am a revolutionary as a Colombian, as a sociologist, and as a priest. . . . As a Colombian I cannot be a stranger to my people's struggles. . . . As a sociologist, thanks to the knowledge I have of reality, I have arrived at the realization that technical and effective solutions will be be obtained without a revolution."[35]

This is no place to discuss the legitimacy of a "committed" sociology such as Camilo Torres practiced. The important thing is that he was able to combine the exigencies of scientific exactness with his own personal convictions. If there is any criticism to be made, it is only concerning the type of action he chose to pursue.

In his own studies of the Colombian situation, Torres "subordinated the economic explanation to the political explanation. . . . His analysis of the political causes led him to seek political solutions."[36] In the conviction that he could exercise his profession as a sociologist only on the basis and within the context of his own options, he took up the cudgels of his people in their age-old struggles, trying to understand the forms these struggles had taken and the causes that had given rise to them. This led him to a critique of their failure and then to an examination of the nature of the power structure and the adoption of a personal stance in relation to the power structure.

In his address, "Economic Programming and the Demands of the Apostolate,"[37] he mentioned that one of the obstacles to democratic and effective planning is the "nonexistence of a policy of development." "In the underdeveloped countries," he explained, "the different elements of power are usually concentrated in the hands of the few. The means of production as well as a superior level of culture are the appurtenances of a minority ruling class," which "exercises political power, directly or through a group of politicians. . . . In these countries the only justification for the army is to maintain interior order, that is, to maintain the dominant structure."

In March, 1965, when he presented his Platform for the United Front, his analysis, his objectives, and his method were, apparently, already clearly formulated in his own mind, but he presented them as a working hypothesis for discussion and experimentation in action. His basic convictions were as follows:

> 1. If Colombian politics are to be in the interest of the majority and not the minority, some essential decisions will have to be taken by those who are now in power.
> 2. But those in power are a minority whose strength is their wealth.
> 3. They are incapable of working against their own interests.
> 4. We must do away with the obstacles impeding the necessary decisions.
> 5. This being the situation, it is indispensable to change the structures of political power.
> 6. Today the majority rejects the political parties and the existing system, but has no political apparatus capable of taking power into its own hands.
> 7. The political apparatus we need must seek maximum support from the masses, must have technical planning, and must be built on principles of action rather than on the leadership of one man.[38]

With this analysis as his starting point, Camilo soon moved on to formulate the fundamental alternatives: No change of structure can be accomplished unless the people exert the necessary pressure; the chances of peaceful revolution are directly dependent on the foresight of the ruling classes. But Camilo had already had experience of the incapacity for foresight of these classes. The oligarchy with its monopoly on ownership and the domination of the North American economy were, therefore, the major obstacles to be overcome.

It is worth noting that Camilo tried to avoid turning the Front into a "sect." The need for a broad base of support prevented him from excluding anyone, even the Communist party. He saw his undertaking as a balance of forces against the government, and his attitude toward violence as well as his refusal to engage in a struggle for votes were a consequence of this choice. But to him the most fundamental element in the program was the education of the masses.

Camilo spent the last weeks of his life in an intensive effort of explanation. He explained clearly and honestly the situation of the Colombian social classes; he explained their history, their goals, and his reasons for choosing in favor of one rather than the other. The essence of his message at this time has been preserved in the publication *Frente Unido*.

Addressing himself to students, whom he considered to possess a special capacity for revolution thanks to their powers of analysis and their relative freedom from the system, he called their attention to the class-ridden university system and its teaching. At the same time he told them frankly that their dissatisfaction was often "too sentimental or the result of a feeling of frustration. It is too seldom a rational nonconformity."[39] And he urged them to be both competent and logical: Competent—that is, to be critical, always carefully measuring their scientific learning against the yardstick of reality; logical—that is, to carry through on their revolutionary declarations, above all by establishing a true relation of solidarity with the people.[40]

He himself was doing what he asked other intellectuals to do. He had absolutely no desire to play the role of advance guard for the masses. What he was aiming for was to build a popular revolution, starting with the building-up of class consciousness in the concrete, daily struggles that are entailed. This is why, when he wrote to the labor unions, he refused to associate himself with the extremist position in favor of insurrection any more than with the exclusively unionist strategy interested only in short-term gains in working conditions.

> A partial struggle for immediate improvements must not blind us to the fact that the overall triumph of the workers' demands will never be won until power is in the hands of the masses, the majority of the Colombian people. . . . Every struggle for short-term advantages will strengthen the revolutionary struggle, for it unites and organizes the Colombian workers and strengthens their sense of belonging to a class.[41]

Convinced, as he was, that pressure from below is the determining factor in introducing change, he was anxious to broaden the base of his movement as much as possible. He even addressed some remarks to the army with this idea in mind, reminding the soldiers, used as tools for the repression of movements among the people, that they too were the victims of repression, that they too were members of the proletariat.

> I have often seen peasants and workers in uniform; never has a member of the ruling classes been seen in the ranks. . . . The members of the armed forces are very poorly paid. Generally speaking, soldiers are not allowed to undertake studies which would enable them to earn their living if they left the army. . . . And yet one-third of our national budget is used for the armed forces . . . it goes to pay for the hardware we buy from the United States.[42]

Naturally enough, however, his first concern was to give the rural masses an awareness of their identity. In his opinion the period of *violencia* had already prepared them for the movement. "The diffuse civil war, which lasted for years in our country, is always called 'violencia' or 'terror.' In fact, it was an unorganized, empirical, unconscious change of structures. . . . It was the peasants who changed during that long period." The essential merit of the attempts at independent republics was, according to Camilo, the fact that they introduced a "new power system into those regions alongside the power structure of the central government. . . . This new situation completely changed the peasants' attitude about all institutions. . . . They no longer see private property, the government, and the Church as immutable elements in life."[43]

He was also, however, very much aware of the limited value of certain tactics of self-defense which did not aim far enough. "The peasants accepted the existing relations between the villages. . . .

They bowed before the material superiority of the army, and so once again they fell into the power of the dignitaries, the traditional leaders, guardians of our semifeudal ways."

His study of history, of present circumstances, and of the prevailing social system had convinced him that change could be achieved only by force. But his understanding of the problem of force was that of a sociologist.

> They have often told me that I preach violent revolution; but it is interesting to see why the ruling class portrays me as an advocate of violent revolution. You have realized that my proposals can be reduced to this: that the majority exercise power and that government decisions be taken in favor of the majority rather than of minority.... The ruling class knows who will decide ... whether the revolution is to be peaceful or violent. The decision is not in the hands of the lower class but in the hands of the ruling class. And since the lower class is beginning to organize itself courageously and with discipline and decision, and since we are not organizing for elections, they assume we are organizing for violent revolution. This is why the minority ruling class intends to unleash violence against the majority class.... Those who choose violence are those who can afford it.[44]

Similarly he felt that guerrilla warfare was, first and foremost, a social problem and should be a training in social awareness. But he applied the analysis to the past rather than to the present, and this being the case, one wonders why he chose this way for himself. The program of the United People's Front had met with enormous success and had raised great hopes,[45] and Camilo's personality certainly had something to do with this. By throwing himself so openly into the combat he laid himself open to attack by the hierarchical powers—including those of his Church—and the traditional bureaucracies.[46] Above all, the premature publication of his platform had left the problem of creating a party or a social movement unresolved.

And so his decision to join the *guerrilleros* was motivated by a combination of circumstances: the rifts dividing the Front and its failure to set in motion a social movement within the framework of legality. He also felt that the prospect of providing the armed groups with rational assistance could be meaningful in the long run, and an outstanding example could be contagious. It is also probable that his innate tendency to overcome obstacles by ignoring them and to thrust aside unforeseen complications, played a part in his rapid decision. But these are psychological factors which must be used with discretion in forming an opinion.

Is it possible, at this point, to hazard some kind of an evaluation of Camilo's work? Equipped with a "committed" sociology, he gave precedence, both in practice and in theory, to the problem of power, to the struggle against the oligarchy in power. In all his messages he condemned it for what it was and for what it was doing to the people.[47]

He did not want to found a political party to carry on this struggle, but a social movement based on serious scientific analyses and with a special concern for education. Perhaps success came too soon? Perhaps his ideas needed more time to mature? Perhaps, too, he had not yet been sufficiently schooled by the discipline of action to face the obstacles that arose? One highly regrettable fact is that when he disappeared he left no trained leaders behind him to carry on such closely reasoned work. And we must not forget that in his personal conflict, the attitude of the Catholic hierarchy was an important element.

To conclude this tentative appraisal, we must add that Camilo Torres' great achievement remains the fact that he took the revolutionary struggle out of its traditional home (the universities) to the masses, still unorganized but already becoming aware of their world. He failed, however, to give them an organization that would outlive him. Only the future will tell whether his ultimate decision to take up arms in the guerrilla forces was reasonable for him. But to his honor it must be said that he contributed to making a more human future a little more possible. His death became the symbol of a struggle in which man's most essential values are at stake.

Camilo Torres between the Church and the revolution. The Church was introduced into Colombia with the Spanish conquest and firmly established in a key position in society, which has changed only superficially in the course of history. To be Colombian is to be Catholic, and 99 percent of the population is baptized.

During one of their periods in power, the Liberals separated Church from State: The archbishop of Bogotá no longer chooses the president of the Republic as he did as recently as 1930. But in other ways the separation is not really noticeable. The Catholic Church is intimately associated with every aspect of the life of the community and the Concordat gives it many important advantages. Its influence can be seen in the cultural system, molded by a popular, rural religion which tends to be fatalistic and moralistic. The religious institutional system is a prisoner of the cultural religiosity of the people, but at the same time it manages to use the latter in order to play a major role of social control: in the field of education—all of which is directly or indirectly under its control; and in the political arena—all political parties are careful to keep on the right side of the Church. As the story goes in Colombia: "Who is the most important person in the country? The president of the coffee growers' union. And the second most important? The cardinal. And the third? The president of the Republic if the other two have no objections!"

In a number of recent social experiments, the Church has had a very active part, but this too has often been ambiguous because of the overall situation and because of the very "clerical" color of the experiments themselves. The Radio Schools of Sutatenza, for instance, which reached some 211,000 students in 1964, are directed by Monsignor Salcedo. Another priest, Monsignor Gutiérrez, launched the experimental Community Center of Fomeque, a kind of Christian kibbutz, which includes a peasant cooperative of 1,400 members. "God's Minute," a television program directed by another priest, solicited the generosity of viewers to contribute to the construction of a workers' township, etc.

Often the Church has taken the initiative in these ways in order to compensate for the government's failure to do so, absorbed as it was by its programs of "pacification." No doubt many of its financial backers in Colombia and elsewhere are quite content to leave this work to the Church so long as it never calls into question the existing social and political system and simply contributes to a gradual evolution in social conditions to improve the lot of the masses. This type of "solicitude" for the poor is a rich man's virtue and the Church, closely allied to the ruling classes—by reason of cultural solidarity more than by reason of its wealth or direct political power—has this virtue in common with the rich.

There are some signs, however, to indicate that the bishops are becoming more aware of certain questions. At least they no longer openly support the established order as the best possible one. But in the conviction that socialism is not the perfect solution and that revolution is a thoroughly bad one,[48] they still seem to fluctuate between conservatism and reformism. In 1961 the primate of Colombia considered that "any attempt to overthrow the legitimate government is condemned by natural law; ... it is illicit when it entails disobedience, rebellion, or the overthrow of power legally constituted."[49] Even after the 1968 meeting of the Latin American bishops at Medellín, the attitude of the Colombian episcopacy does not appear to have changed, and more than ever foreign priests are being expelled from the country and others, who have been too outspoken, are being transferred, quite patently as the result of agreements between civil and religious authorities.

Camilo Torres subjected his Church to the same honest critique that he made of society. And one of the first things he noted was the existence of a "stratification" in the Church similar to that which prevailed in Colombian society as a whole. "The Church seems to consist of a majority who practice but do not know their faith, and a minority who know their faith but practice it only exteriorly."[50]

This was an unorthodox but militant interpretation of the ecclesial reality: It is the people—the majority—whose faith is often mixed with a magical conception of the universe, who practice the commandment of love. They are part of the Church, but the Church has no room for them. All available space is taken up by the oligarchy—the minority—which is instructed in the faith, but which has turned it into a pure formality and which is damning itself (that is, cutting itself off from the Church) by its own egoism. This reversal of the accepted meaning of traditional terms was a revolution, announcing the revolution Camilo set out to achieve in the Church itself and in society. He reproached the Church for aligning itself with the dominant values and especially for behaving as though conformity were the only criterion by which to judge the aptitude for authority.[51]

In order to change all this and to purify itself, he felt that the Church should get rid of its material wealth. "I am in favor of expropriating Church property, even if no revolution takes place."[52] And with a passion worthy of Lamennais, he advocated a poor Church that could really be one with the poor.[53] The Concordat, he felt, was being used by the Conservatives to shackle the Church to their own regime for their own political purposes, while the Liberals used it to win votes for themselves, by clamoring for it to be revised. He felt, therefore, that it should be done away with altogether. He also felt that the Church should give up its almost total monopoly in the field of education and accept pluralism. To see the Church as an active element in the class conflict was a distinctly nonconformist attitude for a sociologist—at least for one who was a member of the institution in question—as Camilo was well aware. When in 1965 he had been offered the opportunity of pursuing his sociological research as a member of the diocesan curia, before submitting a plan for action he took the precaution of telling his bishop: "When I began thinking about how I should direct my studies, I encountered a number of theoretical problems and I believe that my solutions to these problems will be different and even contrary to the direction the hierarchy might want this research to take."[54]

We have already mentioned Camilo's attitude toward his function as university chaplain, indicating the difficulty he experienced when he had to work in close collaboration with institutions which reflected the authority of the established order.

After the publication of his political platform in 1965, pressure was applied to his superiors to dismiss him from the Institute of Public Administration. It was then that he first envisaged asking to be "reduced" to the lay state. He even got to the point of writing the cardinal to this effect, but the letter was never sent.[55]

Before we can understand his own inner conflicts about this, we must describe what took place exteriorly between him and the institution. Although rumor had it that he had been obliged to resign his teaching post, it was in fact his own decision to do so, in order to devote all his energies to the political struggle. This led the cardinal to publish a statement of the facts. But the cardinal's statement also added: "In the platform for political-social action presented or supported by Father Torres, there are points which are irreconcilable with the doctrine of the Church."[56] This statement, proffered without proof or evidence to support it, provoked Camilo to reply. He wrote a personal letter to the cardinal, asking him two questions: "To which sociopolitical platform does Your Eminence refer in your statement of May 25? What points which I have subscribed to or defended does Your Eminence consider as incompatible with the doctrine of the Church?"[57] The answer came, also in a personal letter: "I do not understand—or rather, I would prefer not to understand—the motives which have induced you to ask such a question. You know perfectly well the teachings of the Catholic Church concerning the points which you have treated in your programs and which have been knowingly removed from these teachings. . . ." Then comes the crux of the argument, and the real reproach: A priest may not intervene in politics.[58] Later, in a statement to the press, the cardinal made his reprobation known to the public.[59]

In view of this unjust attitude in which public accusations were made without substantiating proof, Camilo realized that he had to choose between his own convictions and his affiliation with the institution as a priest. On June 24 he asked to be laicized and published a statement explaining his decision:

> When circumstances prevent men from giving themselves completely to Christ, the proper function of a priest is to combat these circumstances, even at the cost of celebrating the Eucharist, for the eucharistic sacrifice can be celebrated only if it represents the offering of all Christians. The present structures of the Church make it impossible for me to continue to exercise my priesthood as far as external acts of worship are concerned. . . . I was chosen by Christ to be a priest forever, because I desired to commit myself totally to the love of my fellow man. As a sociologist I wanted that love to become effective. . . . I found that revolution is necessary in order to feed the hungry and give drink to the thirsty. . . . I believe that the revolutionary combat is a Christian and priestly combat. . . . It is the only way, in the concrete circumstances of our country, for us to love our neighbors as we should. . . . And yet it is a task which is still at odds with the present discipline of the Colombian Church. I have no desire to go against that discipline, but neither do I want to betray my conscience.[60]

Later the polemic became even more embittered and some of the cardinal's statements gave the impression that he felt himself obliged to expel from the ecclesial community any Christian who subscribed to such ideas.[61] It was as though the institutional Church was scandalized at the idea that one of its members could believe that revolution was necessary.

But what was Camilo's inner reaction to this conflict? One thing that is certain is that his close affiliation with the institutional Church—and this is especially true in Colombia—meant that for years he had lived apart from the world of the poor he wanted so much to love "as a Colombian, as a sociologist, and as a priest," and he had felt this separation very keenly. His intuition urged him to redefine the role of the priesthood, as distinct from the "ontological" reality of the priestly character, and this intuition led him into conflict with a Church that was not ready to understand him.

His way of resolving the conflict—just as he resolved the conflict in his political action: by going around it—is due no doubt to his willful and impatient temperament. In both cases similar causes— a prophetic intuition unacceptable to his social group—provoked similar effects. However that may be, Camilo Torres has brought both the Church and society, unequivocally, face to face with the question of revolution, and he has done so by providing a model in the moral sense of the term, a man capable of choosing and of accepting the logical consequences of his choice. Probably he was better aware than anyone of the ambiguities of his options, but he always chose according to one overriding criterion: to be on the side of the poor. On this level "his existence is a clarion call" both for the Church and for society.

But the story does not end with Camilo's death. It is true that the various guerrilla groups have been reduced to silence by the armed forces, but they have not disappeared. They now use different techniques. Those who were most deeply committed have carried out their self-criticism. They know now that the struggle will be a long one and that they must establish solid bases among the popular masses. They also realize that they must develop their revolutionary theory and their leadership training. A veritable underground university is now functioning in the mountains. In the meantime armed action has not ceased completely, although it is mostly defensive, and in February, 1970, the ENL captured a helicopter. President Carlos Lleras' regime is a liberal one, func-

tioning within the traditional framework of the established oligarchy. It is in no way comparable, for instance, to the regimes of
Guatemala or Brazil. It has undertaken certain reforms, but it is
incapable of resolving the fundamental problem of transforming
the whole social fabric. After a few years in exile, General Rojas
Pinilla is again active on the political scene and his movement is
gaining ground, especially in the middle classes. But the general
mass of the population seems to be more aware than a few years
ago, and a new balance of power seems to be in the making.

The evolution within the official Church, however, is far from
encouraging. Some very outspoken statements have been made,
but there has been absolutely no sign that the Church's status in
the society of which it is an integral part is being called into
question. Several priests who have thrown in their lot with the
slum-dwellers of Bogotá and Medellín have been repudiated by
their bishops and four of them who received prison sentences are
in forced residence in a convent, owing to the intervention of the
archbishop of Medellín, in view of their priesthood. In 1968 a
group of priests and one bishop gathered at Golconda and published a statement advocating a socialist regime as the only solution for the country's social problems. Many of the priests involved
were removed from their posts, others have been suspended, and
the foreigners among them have, to all intents and purposes, been
expelled from the country.

In 1970 four of the Golconda group joined the liberation movements, among them Father Domingo Lain, a Spaniard who had
been expelled, and on March 24 Father René García, who had
been suspended by the archbishop of Bogotá, announced the creation of a popular front in opposition to the government, adding:
"If power is handed over to the people peaceably, then the change-
over will be peaceful. If, on the contrary, the system opposes it,
then it will be a violent revolution. We priests have a political
commitment and anyone who declares that that is not so is a
pharisee. The only commitment is to the revolution."

The Sociopolitical Circumstances

This is not the place to attempt a critical evalutation of the
various revolutionary endeavors now extant in Latin America. The

guerrilla groups are significant of the whole revolutionary movement, linking as they do subversive methods with a positive program of development. Their aims combine the violent negation of
existing society and the affirmation and preparation of alternative
types of social relations.[62]

Marginal groups. Being minority groups functioning with no
institutional framework, these movements have to grapple with a
problem of first importance: how to forge and maintain bonds
with the rural and urban populations that will adequately articulate their values and enable them to find help and support. This is
a particularly thorny problem when the rural masses which the
guerrillas are trying to awaken to the new values include a majority
or even a strong minority of Indians. In four out of seven Latin
American countries where guerrilla warfare is now going on or
is an imminent possibility—Ecuador, Peru, Bolivia, and Guatemala—this constitutes a major problem. There can be no decisive
awakening of the masses and in the long run no victory for the
revolution without the adhesion of the Indian population, living at
present in a state of subhuman destitution. For them the white
revolutionaries are utterly alien, both in their language and their
culture.[63] To provide the rural masses not only with trained leadership, but also with an identity, is going to be a very lengthy task,
similar to that undertaken by the NLF in Vietnam; it can only be
carried out with success by those who have a profound understanding of the social reality of the country.

On a short-term basis, the isolation in which the revolutionary
movements find themselves makes it easier for the existing power
structure to liquidate them, or at least to render them harmless.
But they are, nevertheless, already in a position to effect something
in the way of political education and information, and this is some
guarantee of future success. This is the provisional task which
seems to define the purpose of the armed struggle: to give the
peasantry an awareness of itself and of its rightful place in the
national picture.

International solidarity. In addition it has become evident that
some form of coordination between local movements is indispens-

able, and in spite of immense difficulties this is the need that the national movements are trying to fill. On the international level they have created the Latin American Organization of Solidarity (OLAS) with offices in Havana.[64]

The first task of the revolutionaries—to establish a firm footing among the rural masses—is directly related to their other major problem: that of defining a "model" of revolutionary struggle adapted to Latin American society. Encouraged by Castro's success in Cuba, the other Latin American movements have often obstinately tried to create "Sierra Maestra's" all over the continent. But after eight years of repeated failure—for many different reasons—this way now appears more and more illusory. The Castro method—of multiplying the "focal points" of revolution until a network had been created, strong enough to take up armed combat and sweep the unorganized masses along with it until it gained control of the whole country—cannot be reproduced in other countries. In the first place, Cuba, unlike most Latin American countries, was a relatively homogeneous society. Also, Castro received considerable backing from the petty bourgeoisie and it seems highly unlikely that this will be forthcoming in other countries. And, finally, the United States is ready to stamp out incipient revolution either by direct intervention or by supplying effective antiguerrilla training.

Another illusion consists in the temptation to revive a past rich in messianic tradition.[65] Past glories can lead the revolutionary movements into the false position of announcing imminent victory without taking the necessary steps to bring it about. This failing has been fairly frequent and Che Guevara was well aware of the danger of it when he warned: "The duty of a revolutionary is to *make* revolution." Verbal extravagance is typically Latin American and the fact of being a revolutionary has not always sufficed to change this.

Guevara's notorious declaration in 1967, calling for the creation of other Vietnams in Latin America, was founded less on any objective possibility of this coming to pass than on the key realization that all revolutionary struggle is anti-imperialist: In Latin America the power structures which must be overthrown are shored up by United States imperialism. This dimension of reality must necessarily condition a realistic strategy. In the light of their own experience and under the influence of theorists such as Régis Debray and Che Guevara,[66] the guerrilla movements are also in the process of abandoning the pattern of self-defense advocated by the Communist parties,[67] which made them so vulnerable to repressive government action. The tactic they are now turning to is one of "pockets of expansion," formed basically of mobile units which seek the cooperation of the peasants while sharing their life, speaking their language, and conducting both a defensive armed struggle and a program of basic political education of the population. This method is already a long way from the Cuban model, as well as from the forms adopted by the Communist parties which are more concerned with keeping within the law.

Faithfully reflecting the Soviet policy of peaceful coexistence and apparently unmindful of the anti-imperialist nature of the struggle, the Communist parties are of the opinion that conditions are not ripe for an armed uprising—and in this they are not altogether wrong—but they are not doing very much to cause the situation to mature. Although they sometimes have recourse to arms—often vicariously—they do so above all as a maneuver in negotiating their own legal status within the existing political system.[68] To this end they seek to ally themselves with the most progressive elements, particularly with radical Christians. This attitude of "biding their time" seems to have been induced by Moscow's clearly expressed decision not to support another Cuba.

The Tri-Continental Conference in Havana in 1967 showed little interest for the internal conflicts of the communist bloc and considerable sympathy for the Vietnamese model. This is reflected in the work that is being undertaken with the masses with a view to a "long march" in clandestine combat until a point of sufficient maturity has been reached. In this type of long-term strategy, a lack of leaders is a very heavy handicap, all the more so because a peculiarly Latin American romanticism often seems to induce the leaders to run great risks. The disappearance of leaders like Che Guevara, Camilo Torres, and others cannot fail to have grave consequences. By contrast the NLF leaders in Vietnam show admirable prudence and are thus able to ensure continuity in their work.[69]

As things stand today, the guerrilla movements are plagued with too many ideological problems and are still too vulnerable to repression to be fully efficient. Ideological divergencies abound; revolutionary energies are being dissipated in Trotskyist, Castroist, Maoist, and communist tendencies. The theoretical disputes have rarely led to any coherent strategy and this is probably the principal weakness of the revolutionary movements as it spurs them on to action before they have fully evaluated the repressive power of the establishment.

The powers of repression. The repressive powers of the establishment have been considerably enhanced by the organization of the struggle against subversion on a continental scale. Repeated calls for armed insurrection from the Tri-Continental Conference in Havana in January, 1966, and the OLAS conference in 1967, brought reactions from the governments concerned. Peru, Colombia, Venezuela, and Uruguay convened an extraordinary meeting of the OAS in January and February, 1966, at which a statement was published condemning the communist states for meddling in Latin American affairs and appealing to the United Nations. In 1967 the OAS condemned Cuba and recommended economic sanctions; it rejected, however, a proposed inter-American peace force. The United States is sole coordinator and source of military supplies in the struggle against the guerrillas.

Southern Command, established in Panama after the Cuban revolution, consists of staff headquarters with five to six hundred officers in charge of large stocks of equipment, and special training schools, which, by 1968, had trained more than twenty-five thousand Latin American officers. The Special Forces, or "Green Berets," receive antiguerrilla training at this center and, in 1965 alone, they carried out fifty-two special operations. In 1966-1967 they intervened in Guatemala, Bolivia, Venezuela, and Nicaragua. Little by little the Alliance for Progress is also sliding toward becoming this type of military assistance program. The failure to carry out the idea of an inter-American force means that the

United States, with the consent of the governments concerned, is becoming the principal guarantor of the continued stability of the existing regimes. In every one of these countries, the United States ambassador can call on a military group under the control of Southern Command. Since he left his post in Vietnam, General William Westmoreland is in charge of coordinating the military forces of the whole South American continent; his Vietnamese experience is proving useful to the United States for the defense of law and order in the southern hemisphere.

The existing power structures in Latin America are, therefore, in no immediate danger—in fact they are in less danger from the revolution than from the traditional disputes of rival oligarchies—and rural guerrilla activities have come to a stop, at least for the time being. The student movements, on the other hand, still have many internal contradictions to resolve, foremost among them being their relation to the urban masses. New techniques of urban warfare are being developed: hold-ups, kidnappings, etc., but they only lead to more highly developed techniques of repression. Their principal virtue seems to be that they serve to alert world opinion.

The problems of the ruling classes, however, are not becoming any less complicated. In 1980 Latin America will have 350 million inhabitants. By the year 2000 the populations will have reached 600 million. The contradictions within these societies will soon have reached such proportions that the revolutionary movements—provided they avoid the snares of romanticism and passive waiting on the one hand and of repression on the other—will be in a position to prepare the ground in such a way as to make it impossible for these contradictions to be overcome within the existing framework. Things will have to change.

I believe it is not unrealistically optimistic to look forward to the day when this will be true. The iron hand of the United States is very strong, but here again, the example of Vietnam offers the movements a well-tried methodology and proves that even tremendous military strength, if it is at the service of an arbitrarily imposed political regime, can be defeated by a popular revolution.

The Religious Factor

As we have already seen, religion is an extremely important

factor in Latin American society. Traditionally the Catholic Church has been a power structure, and it was in close alliance with the colonial power during the conquests of the fifteenth and sixteenth centuries. The movements of emancipation from the colonial power, although they were often led by members of the low clergy, usually took an anticlerical turn, which led the institutional Church to oppose them as well as all liberal parties. This opposition expressed itself through strenuous support of the traditional social structures, even though the liberal movements were very far from posing any radical challenge to them.[70] The resulting situation seems complicated to a Cartesian mind, but it is perfectly logical when seen in its historical context.

Only within the last twenty years has some change been apparent in the Church's attitude, and it has sometimes been both rapid and radical. There is no doubt that a large percentage of Catholics are still conservative and even reactionary. But the Church of Latin America can no longer be wholly identified with its conservative elements. A certain number of outstanding religious leaders have shown themselves to be decidedly progressive, so much so, in fact, that a new kind of anticlericalism is beginning to appear, this time in the circles of the old or neocapitalist oligarchies. Attacks on the progressive bishops of Brazil and Colombia are more and more frequent; more and more priests are being arrested in Argentina, Colombia, and Brazil; more and more foreign priests are being expelled; cases of torture and even assassination of members of the clergy are becoming more frequent in Brazil. The repression which was originally aimed at militant lay people is escalating. The revolutionary movements are trying to recruit support from leftist Christians, and the first Latin American meeting of Christian revolutionaries at Montevideo in February, 1968, dedicated to the memory of Camilo Torres, is a sign that they are meeting with some success. The existing governments are fearful of the actions and reactions of the Church. This is particularly true in Argentina, where the power structure has succeeded in gaining the support of the hierarchy—at least provisionally—and in Brazil, where even the president moves with caution for fear of arousing the opposition of the dynamic minority among the Brazilian bishops.

The attitude of Christians. Latin American Christians can be grouped in four main categories with regard to their attitudes toward social change. A first category holds that the existing social system is fundamentally good, not only in theory but also in practice, and must, therefore, be supported by the Church. This position is held by a minority of lay people, clergy, and bishops. The lay people concerned are, for the most part, members of the old established oligarchies, whose privileges and monopoly of power would be threatened by change. Others belong to the new industrial bourgeoisie, and in general, government officials and officers in the armed forces identify with this position. The new elite classes model their behavior on that of the traditional ruling classes. From the religious point of view, this attitude has sometimes led to the foundation of "integrist" groups such as *El Muro* in Mexico or the Youth of Christ the King in Brazil, or to local manifestations of international movements. The group of army officers who came to power in Argentina, for instance, had received their religious formation in the *Cursillos de Cristiandad,* and several of them are known to be connected with the *GT catholique.* A certain Colombian bishop (now retired) is an example of the reactionary attitudes of these minority groups, openly opposed to the spirit and decisions of Vatican II. In 1961, in response to a proposed agrarian reform, he wrote of ". . . an impious and truly apostate attack against the beautiful Catholic social organizations which are doing so well . . . under the care and guidance of the bishops."[71] Another example, this time from Argentina is this: In 1966 the military regime which had just taken over the reins of government designated a colonel, governor of the Province of Buenos Aires, as their representative at the opening ceremony of the CELAM conference at Mar del Plata, which was to discuss the social situation of Latin America. In his address the colonel explained how their revolution had been faced with the choice of being for God or against God. It had chosen to be for God and the best guarantee of this option was, according to him, an alliance between the "sword" and the "cross." This was the government that obliged Dom Helder Camara, who was assisting at the conference, to cancel all public speeches.

A second category of Latin American Christians believes that the present social system is good, but that like all human institutions it could be improved. However, many of these people think that the Church should not concern itself with temporal questions. All it can do is organize charitable works to compensate for the defects of the present system. This passive attitude is widespread among lay people and even more so among the clergy. For the most part it seems to stem from a fear of change and its consequences, and many priests seem unaware of the changes that are already taking place. They continue to apply time-honored methods based on ecclesiastical control of society. Others, who are more aware of social problems, criticize the system, but still vigorously oppose any idea of social revolution.

A third category includes all those who realize that the present social system falls far short of the demands of development and justice. They believe that swift, effective action should be taken. The Church can participate by being an inspiration to Christians engaged in political, social, economic, and cultural work, and by developing some social organizations of its own. This is the attitude of many lay people engaged in politics—the Christian Democratic party in Chile, for example—labor unions, or simply in various forms of the apostolate. It is symptomatic that these people hailed the decisions of Vatican II with enthusiasm and have eagerly embraced the ecumenical movement.

Various shades of opinion can be found among the clergy and bishops of this category. Some accept the need for social action, but feel that the institutional Church should avoid direct implication. They do not see that change must also mean a redefinition of the priest's role and of his relations with lay people as well as the complete restructuring of ecclesiastical organizations, new liturgical expressions, and even new forms of ttheology. There is also a nascent "leftist clericalism." In the name of progress, the latest methods of cultural and social action (radio schools, cooperatives, unions, etc.), are highly organized and used as instruments in gaining a new hold on the masses and exercising new forms of social control.

On the other hand many priests and bishops believe not only that social change should involve the Church, but that, parallel to the changes in society, attitudes within the Church must be renewed. This supposes a real transformation in the whole conception of the relationship between the Church and society. Within ecclesiastical institutions a new relationship will have to be forged between the laity and the clergy. And it is in the light of this that a liturgical reform must be envisaged in such a way that it will contribute to forming a truly "incarnate" spirituality in which social responsibility will be one with the religious life.

These different shades and trends within the third group have given rise to many different ventures within the decade of the 1960s, such as agrarian reforms carried out with diocesan lands and, in the Northeast of Brazil, the creation of unions and cooperatives. In the sociopolitical context of that area a few years ago, the Church was probably the only institution that could have taken the initiative in this way with some chance of success. But this has not prevented the government from taking repressive measures against the leaders of these movements since the "counterrevolution" in 1964.

The Catholic Bishops' Conference of Latin America, held at Medellín in 1968, endorsed the type of awareness just described and made it "official." One of the preparatory documents declared: "The fundamental idea in the Church's contemporary mission is its commitment to poverty.... Faced with the existing conditions of poverty and social injustice, the Church has not been sufficiently energetic in exercising its role of condemning inequalities and inspiring needed reforms. On the contrary, in the past it has often identified itself with the status quo." And the document adds: "There is a grave danger that the future construction of the continent, which is in conformity with the divine will, will be carried out not only outside the faith, but in opposition to it."[72]

There is also, however, a fourth category of Latin American Christians, who believe that only violent revolution can effectually change the situation and that Christians should commit themselves to the revolutionary process even if this implies collaborating with the Marxist movements. Numerically speaking, this is still the position of a minority, mostly made up of young people, particularly students and university graduates whose special point of reference is the Cuban revolution, However, a certain number of priests are also of this opinion and some have joined guerrilla movements, especially in Peru, Venezuela, Colombia, and Guatemala. Camilo Torres is the best known of these. More and more people are being forced to the conclusion that revolution is the only possible answer, and while not necessarily joining an armed movement, they give them moral support in the social role they are filling. Naturally, such divergent attitudes cannot coexist within the Latin American Church without creating all kinds of tensions. The social stagnation of many of these countries makes the Church's position more difficult and, in some, more ambiguous.

Medellín and beyond. The concluding statement of the Medellín conference condemns "the tremendous social injustices that exist in Latin America. These injustices keep the majority of our peoples in woeful poverty, which in most cases goes so far as to be inhuman misery."[73]

The official statements are unequivocal: "Faced with the necessity for an overall transformation of Latin American structures, we believe that this transformation calls for political reform. . . . The exercise [of political power] and decisions of this order in Latin America very often turn out to be in support of systems which are contrary to the common good or to benefit a privileged minority."[74]

Although several national conferences of bishops have endorsed the findings of the Medellín conference, various groups of priests and laymen have expressed disappointment with their meager influence on concrete situations in their respective countries. The bishops' conference in Peru took a stand on several issues and the cardinal followed with some concrete gestures involving Church property and his own residence. The bishops' 36th Assembly had the courage to declare: "This situation of injustice . . . is the result of a process that has worldwide dimensions. It is characterized by the concentration of political and economic power in the hands of a few and by the international imperialism of money, which operates in league with the Peruvian oligarchy."[75]

Various priests' groups have been formed, among them the Priests of the Third World, who are particularly numerous in the southern regions of the continent and in Argentina and Brazil. These groups have been formed to express the solidarity of their members with the Message to the Third World published on August 15, 1967, by eighteen bishops from America, Africa, and Asia.[76] In Colombia they are known as the Golconda group, from the name of their meeting place. At its second meeting the Golconda group elaborated a text in which they exposed their basic position. It began: "Reacting against certain false interpretations of the present situation in Colombia, we must point out clearly that the present condition of tragic underdevelopment is the historical result of economic, political, cultural, and social dependence on foreign power centers that is exercised through our ruling classes."[77] The document explains this point of view with a review of the principal elements of the Colombian situation and, having demonstrated the contribution of Christian reflection on the question, it offers some guidelines for action: the elimination of conditions incompatible with human dignity; support for the various forms of revolutionary action combatting imperialism; an option for a socialist type of society; the radical transformation of pastoral methods and methods of evangelization, particularly in the areas of liturgy and catechetics. "The absence of authentic evangelization often leads to a situation where the religious attitudes of our people act as a brake on personal initiative and integral development."[78] The first signature to this document, dated December 13, 1968, was that of a bishop, Gerardo Valencia Cano, bishop of Buenaventura. Among the priests who also signed, approximately one-third had been expelled or jailed or had joined a liberation movement by the beginning of 1970. One of them had been suspended by his superiors.

On March 9, 1968, another group of priests, this time in Peru, published a declaration which was to serve as the basic charter of the ONIS movement. The declaration denounces in particular the agrarian system and the economic liberalism which controls the economic exploitation of the country's resources, but it also touches on many other problems such as education, the moral crisis, means of social communication, etc. It concludes with an acknowledgment of the fact that Christians have not fulfilled their mission as the prophets of justice and calls on priests and laymen to change their ways.

Many other documents could be quoted. There is the letter signed by 300 Brazilian priests in August, 1967; that signed by 80 Bolivian priests in 1968, which, among other things, deplores the fact that some bishops had seen fit to lead a demonstration against the guerrilla groups, and that none of them (with the exception of the bishop of Cochabamba) seemed to "take sufficient cognizance of the cry for justice that motivated the guerrillas."[79] There is also the letter signed by the Latin American provincial superiors of the Jesuits at their meeting in Rio de Janeiro in 1968, which opens with the statement that the majority of the inhabitants of the continent live in conditions of destitution "which cry to heaven for vengeance."[80] This letter calls for a thorough review of all sectors of the apostolate in which the Jesuits are engaged and, in particular, greater efforts in the area of social problems. Finally, we must mention the letter signed by 900 Latin American priests, addressed to the Medellín conference and entitled: *Latin America, Continent of Violence*. Describing the situation, the letter declares: "Because the privileged few use their power of repression to block this process of liberation, many see the use of force as the only solution open to the people.... This light [of the Gospel] shows us clearly that one cannot condemn oppressed people when they feel obliged to use force for their own liberation; to do so would be to commit a new injustice."[81] This letter calls for an unequivocal condemnation of unjust violence and the recognition of the right of an oppressed people to legitimate self-defense.

Dom Helder Camara, who is all too well aware of what the present escalation means, was inspired by Dr. Martin Luther King, Jr., to launch his movement for justice and peace in 1968. At Easter, 1970, he published a joint appeal, with Rev. Ralph Abernathy, Martin Luther King's successor, for a "nonviolent protest against the political, economic and social structures of the world which subject so many to destitution or the constant threat of war." Dom Helder's position is not quite as simple as some might believe: Violence is escalating; the violence of the oppressed is in response to institutionalized violence and it provokes, in turn, further repressive violence. Where will it end? Are there enough people of good will in the world to undertake a process of true development based on social justice? Dom Helder insists that violence begins with those who have wealth and power; that one must understand and respect the options of people such as Camilo Torres and Che Guevara; that violence leads to violence, and that in present circumstances, because of the tremendous power of the forces of repression, violent protest is bound to fail. Only a powerful movement of all those who, out of love for mankind, agree to struggle without using violence against persons, will one day achieve positive results, will, as Dom Helder puts it, bring down the walls of Jericho.

Paul VI at Bogotá. We must also mention Pope Paul VI's ideas, as he expressed them during his visit to Bogotá in 1968. Everything he said during this visit was directly addressed to Latin America. The pope used his own encyclical, *Populorum Progressio,* as his starting point, making a commentary on it for the intention of those who were most closely concerned.

In the first place his visit was intended as an encounter with the poor of Latin America. He told them: "In our wandering mission we wish to personify the Christ of a poor and hungry people."[82] Speaking to the *campesinos* of Colombia, he assured them that he was totally on their side. "We bow before you. . . . We have come to honor Christ in you."[83] "We wish to express our solidarity with your just cause, which is the cause of the humble, the cause of the poor."

Then, speaking of the conditions created by poverty, he said: "In the vast continent of Latin America development has been unequal . . . while it has favored those who originally began the process, it has neglected the great masses of the native population. . . ."[84] When an observation like this, pertinent though it may be, is proffered without any analysis of the factors that have contributed to the situation, it simply draws a veil over the fundamental historical reality of exploitation which has existed in the continent, from the Spanish conquest and the subsequent oligarchic system down to the present domination by foreign, particularly American, capital.

Finally, still without a word as to the causes of the situation, the pope observed that today the "poor" are conscious of their poverty and that this further complicates the situation.[85]

Speaking of solutions, the pope first of all vigorously affirmed the "human and Christian dignity" of the poor and their right to "gradual participation in the benefits and responsibilities of the social order."[86] Then, turning to those "in charge," to all "the governments of Latin America," and to the "ruling and property-owning classes," he condemned "unjust inequalities between rich and poor, administrative abuses and the misuse of authority" and hailed the "new organic plans for the working classes and especially for the rural classes."[87]

The pope affirms, therefore, both the rights of the poor and the duties of the rich, but given the circumstances it seems too much to expect that the latter will provide for the former. And yet this is what he seems to be saying in his appeal at Bogotá to the generosity of the rich:

> What can I say to you, men of the ruling class? What is required of you is generosity. This means the ability to detach yourselves from the stability of your position which is, or seems to be, a position of privilege, in order to serve those who need your wealth, your culture, your authority.... You, lords of this world and sons of the Church, you must have the genius for virtue that society needs. Your ears and your hearts must be sensitive to the voices crying out for bread, concern, justice and a more active participation in the direction of society....[88]

Because of his faith in this point of view, the pope categorically rejects violent revolution as a means of creating a new society. He rejects it as "contrary to the Christian spirit...."[89] Violence is not evangelical, it is not Christian."[90] He also rejects it as odious because it entails want and ruin and "civil and religious decadence," and because it inevitably ends in a "burdensome dictatorship."[91] And finally he rejects it as inefficient: "Sudden and violent changes of structure would be deceptive, inefficient of themselves."

Paul VI's reasoning seems to be based on the objective situation, which is such that violent change of government would not give the masses any greater part in the definition of a new society. And it is perfectly true that this is the lesson to be learned from the history of certain countries.[92] There is no doubt that a popular uprising would inevitably provoke a repression reaction, which would, indeed, lead to want and mourning.

But this being so, should not the repressive nature of the power structure be the target of his condemnation, rather than the revolution? And on a deeper level, when the pope seems to advocate gradual change as an alternative to revolution, his proposition seems to rest on a very questionable foundation, for any such gradual change means a long-term work of educating the masses and this, in turn, supposes that the powers-that-be are willing to effect gradual reforms and to do whatever is necessary to carry out this educational work. It still remains to be proved, however, that they would allow the masses to be organized, even in view of a peaceful revolution. And what type of new society would they tolerate?

Until some concrete proof of the oligarchies' good intentions is forthcoming, those who are most closely in touch with the social realities of the populations in Colombia, Brazil, and elsewhere, consider that in fact, if not in intention, the pope's words in Bogotá placed him on the side of the powers-that-be. The reason is two-fold: first, the lack of an analysis of the causes of poverty and nonparticipation, and, second, the pope's identification with the civil, military, and religious representatives of the established powers, which was only too visible during his visit to Bogotá.

To this must be added the fact that the management of the Populorum Progressio Fund, with proceeds from the sale of Vatican property in Paris amounting to $1 million, had been entrusted to the Inter-American Development Bank, as a fifty-year loan without interest; the bank is controlled by the Latin American governments, with the exception of the Cuban government.

Theological reflection on the analysis and the praxis. The texts and statements we have studied have all been from official ecclesiastical sources—which is abundant proof that the Church is not a monolithic structure. Groups of lay Christians have also taken widely varying positions and engaged in different forms of political activity, among them the YCW, whose leaders have been imprisoned or assassinated in Guatemala, Brazil, and Argentina; the

Young Christian Farmers and Rural Workers, who have also suffered reprisals in Brazil and Argentina; the Young Christian University Students who have also been active—and actively repressed. It is not easy for the Latin American Church to cooperate in social transformation. Having been the traditional guarantor of society for so long,[93] it has great difficulty in accepting the idea that the old system must go and that this will not happen if it is left only to the goodwill of the oligarchies in power; the lesson of the French Revolution and of the European worker movement attests to that. But a new factor is present today: international solidarity and the part played by economic, political, and military imperialism in repressing the revolt of the people.

In 1969, an American specialist in antiguerrilla warfare in Vietnam became one of the Brazilian government's chief advisers. In 1968 the heads of the various Latin American armies were able to benefit from General Westmoreland's experience in Asia, through the coordinating committee of the Rio de Janeiro Treaty, of which he is the chairman. Is it not true to say that the Third World War has already begun, the war of the poor against the rich, of the oppressed against their oppressors? It certainly seems so when one realizes that the Vietnamese peasants can virtually overthrow an American President, and when a group of Guatemalan *guerrilleros* can shake the West German government.

A situation as new as this demands equally new attitudes. Catholics in general find themselves ill-equipped to analyze present problems, as can be seen in some of the texts we have studied. Some of them take their cue from the social encyclicals, in spite of the fact that their constructs were elaborated in reference to European problems and cannot, therefore, be applied wholesale to the concrete situation in Latin America. Others, fortunately, are based on analyses of the local social reality. Great strides have already been made in this domain in Latin America in recent years. Thanks to the momentum given it by Bishop Manuel Larraín of Chile and Dom Helder Camara, two vice-presidents in its first years of existence, CELAM has always based its judgments on scientific studies of social change in Latin America and the impact of change on the Church. This tradition of socioreligious research has been continued and much of the material studied in the bishops' conferences is prepared in advance with sociological analyses, or at least with documents which attach importance to an analysis of the facts. This was the case at the Medellín conference.

Analysis, however, is not enough. The results must be interpreted. And it is the interpretation that is showing signs of being Marxist, that is, of expressing the situation in terms of a struggle between those who have a monopoly on power and those who are oppressed. Many Catholics are ill at ease with this interpretation, fearing that it will simply fuel the fires of antagonism in their adversaries, but in spite of their reticence it now seems to have become very widely accepted. For the most part, Catholics seem to realize that a Marxist analysis need not be accompanied by a Marxist philosophical interpretation. What is needed now is a new theological language, and this is beginning to appear. Some theologians have launched into a theology of revolution, but this has too often been akin to an attempt, by the development of a certain vocabulary, to "recuperate" something which is escaping from the Church. More than that is needed and the Peruvian theologian, Gustavo Gutierrez, has attempted to provide it with a theology of liberation.

For Gutierrez theology is not a doctrinal a priori, elaborated theoretically through a process of deductive reasoning. The task of theology is to deal with the human reality as it exists in the here-and-now. But there are deep-seated contradictions in the emancipation taking place in contemporary history and in which man is the artisan of his own destiny. This is strikingly true in Latin America. It is not enough, nowadays, to talk of development. The word has become devaluated. The term "liberation" seems more adequate, for it indicates that what is involved is a process of emancipation. It better expresses the aspirations of the oppressed and is used in a context which accepts conflict as a fact of life.[94]

Gutierrez believes that this outlook is more in keeping with biblical thought also, since it shows that creation and salvation are inseparable:[95] The plan of salvation includes the whole of man. This means that the eschatalogical promises are seen in the context of a transformation of unjust social structures.[96] Christ, the libera-

tor, frees us from sin, which is the root of all social injustice.[97]
Hope thus becomes creative when it comes into contact with social
reality.[98] The Church's mission is to remind us that all human
social constructions are provisional; in this sense the Church liber-
ates us.[99] But it must do more, for its mission is not only intellectual. It must also call constantly for a radical political commitment.

Gustavo Guierrez is well aware that this kind of theology can
contain inherent tendencies to deviate, and he asks: Is theology on
the way to becoming ideology again? The great thing is to find the
middle way between "Christian politics" and a total abstention
from politics, and this way will be found only by those who have
already set foot on it. "Some chapters of theology are only written
after the event."[100] Gutierrez has been greatly influenced by an
American Protestant theologian, Richard Shaull, who elaborated
his own theology while working in Latin America. In a speech at
the 1968 annual meeting of the Catholic Bishops' Committee for
Latin America at Davenport, Iowa, Shaull developed a similar
theme. Human history, explained Shaull, is the history of man's
liberation, and he pointed out the wealth of biblical references in
support of this view and called on Christians to plan their action in
this light.[101]

But all this implies a critique of the institutional Church and the
way it exists and functions in Latin America today. The role
attributed to it in history has led it to serve as a bulwark to the
traditional order, supplying it with many of its symbols, endorsing
its power, organizing the means of ensuring the propagation of its
values, and fostering a spirit of submission to the existing social
system in the masses. In their letter to the bishops, the eighty
Bolivian priests referred to this situation: "The very structures in
which we operate often prevent us from acting in a manner that
accords with the gospel."[102] And they go on to enumerate some of
the obstacles they encounter: payment for religious services, the
"class consciousness" of Catholic schools, the pointless construction of huge churches, civil privileges for the Church, etc.

Gustavo Gutierrez also tackles the problem: Whether openly or
secretly, consciously or unconsciously, the Church is in fact bound

in a thousand ways to the existing system.[103] "The times demand a creative spark from us, which will allow us to work up and create new ecclesial structures, new ways for the Christian community to be present in the world."[104] This theme was studied at Medellín, but only incidentally. The result is that one has the impression that Latin American society was being judged from a position outside itself, as though the Church was not really part of it.

But the problem of adopting a praxis, and especially a revolutionary praxis, will not be resolved by studying the various analyses of the situation. If a Christian can and must be a revolutionary in the face of present conditions, and if the duty of a revolutionary is to make revolution, what are the specific options he is faced with? This is the question which faces laymen and priests alike, and the object of so much discussion and conflict. More and more Christians, both lay and clergy, seem already to take for granted that they must commit themselves to the revolution. Many leaders of Catholic Action groups have opted for the revolution, thus coming into conflict with the hierarchy who believe that these movements should stick to religious questions and not take a stand on political matters. And, as we have seen, many priests have openly declared themselves in favor of a social commitment, and some of them have acted on their convictions and joined the *guerrilleros.*

It is at this point that the question of violence has to be faced. We cannot deal with it in detail, but I would like to give a general picture of the different positions on the question. At Bogotá, seemingly dismayed by the interpretations being put on a passage in *Populorum Progressio* which states that violence cannot be condemned in certain extreme cases, Paul VI insisted on the need for nonviolence. He has been followed in this by a majority of the bishops. The Medellín conference, however, preferred to use the terms of the encyclical, thereby refusing to condemn violence as illegitimate, a priori. However, the published statement declares that in the present circumstances, in view of the tremendous forces of repression and the probability of foreign intervention—however illegitimate it may be—the evils that would follow in the wake of violent revolution would be greater than those it set out to remedy.[105]

Dom Helder Camara's stand is well known: Analyzing the escalation of violence in the present situation, he sounds an alarm, calling on all men of goodwill to unite in nonviolent action. He does not take this stand on moral grounds; he carefully avoids any condemnation of those who choose the path of violence. His action has two facets: On the one hand he challenges the efficacy of violence; on the other he utters a prophetic call, reminding men of the dimension of love for which they are made. His critics accuse Dom Helder of being politically unrealistic, for he offers no concrete program for a praxis of revolutionary change.

Some Latin American moralists have studied the problem of violence. Luis Carlos Bernal, whose work is unpublished, comes to the conclusion that a revolution which is almost bound to result in violence cannot be condemned out of hand. The question as to whether such a revolution is opportune or not cannot be the object of a moral judgment. It is a question for the positive sciences: "Sociology, economics, law, and political science should tell us whether we should choose gradual development [desarollismo] or whether we should opt for a radical change of structures."[106] In a series of lectures given in Argentina, Robert Bosc developed a similar point of view, saying: "Without a social study of reality there can be no doctrine. . . . No decision can be taken on the level of values. The danger for many Catholics, for priests, and for almost all those who publish statements about violence is that of ignoring the sociological aspects. That is what is called 'moralism' "[107]

A good deal of reflection on the analysis and the praxis is going on, then, in Latin America and it has the advantage of an existential experience which exists nowhere else. Because of this we have every reason to hope for a profound theological renaissance. Latin American Christians cannot afford to wait until everything has been logically systematized before making their options and launching into actions. No sooner was the notion of a theology of liberation mentioned than it was snapped up and used in official texts—by the Peruvian bishops, for example—and widely diffused.

In March, 1970, for instance, Gustavo Pérez organized a symposium on the subject at Bogotá, which was attended by more than one thousand people, and other discussions are being organized throughout Colombia.

Finally, in this reality fraught with so many contradictions, it must be said that ecclesiastical organization is often less than prophetic: The progressives are called to order, but not the others. A certain number of consultants, invited to address the CELAM conference at Medellín in 1968, were simply struck off the program by order from Rome, and conservative and even reactionary bishops are still being given key appointments.

CHAPTER SEVEN

The Revolutionary Movements in Southern Africa

A major phenomenon in contemporary African history and one that has been largely overlooked for a long time is the situation created in the southern part of the continent by the joint efforts of several political regimes to maintain white domination even after the majority of African countries obtained their independence in the early 1960s. In reaction to this manifestation of "white power" in the black continent there has been an upsurge in African revolutionary movements. A substantial part of this chapter will be devoted to a historical summary and analysis of this situation, which is, unfortunately, very largely unknown.

Origin and Development of the African Revolutionary Movements

The Portuguese colonies. Anticolonial reaction in these territories dates back as far as 1920, when the African League was founded in Lisbon. The League was a branch of the Pan-African Movement and its members were mostly students and intellectuals. In 1931, also in Lisbon, a center for African studies was created, forming a bond among the intelligentsia of the African colonies and thereby laying the foundations of a movement for emancipation. It was not until shortly after World War II, however, that the movement of opposition began to gain in intensity. In 1957 a consultation and study session was held in Paris, with a view to promoting the struggle against Portuguese colonialism. This meeting gave rise to the Anti-Colonial Movement (MAC), which in 1960 moved its headquarters to Algeria and changed its name to African Revolutionary Front for National Independence (FRAIN). More recently, following the Casablanca conference of the National Organizations of the Portuguese Colonies in 1961, a bond was forged between the African and the Goanese movements and a new organization was founded, also with headquarters in Algiers. The function of this movement is to help the various member-movements define both their internal goals (a common front on the national level, total liquidation of colonialism, the social aspects of the struggle, etc.) and their external goals (African unity, nonalignment, a united front in overseas representation of the movements, etc.).

Inside the Portuguese colonies, the resistance movements began to take shape in the early 1950s. Before we describe them, however, we should perhaps do well to recall some of the landmarks in the history of these colonies.

Before the arrival of the Europeans, the kingdom of the Congo flourished at the mouth of the Congo River. It covered a territory which is today divided between Angola and the two Congos— Kinshasa and Brazzaville. When the Portuguese arrived on the scene, the Congo was prosperous. Its capital, Mbanza Congo, which the Portuguese renamed São Salvador, was a city of one hundred thousand inhabitants. The first contacts between the kingdom and the Europeans, at the end of the seventeenth century, were peaceful, but the situation deteriorated rapidly when the slave traffic became systematic. In 1665 the Portuguese army invaded the kingdom of the Congo, which collapsed, decimated by military expeditions and the predatory slave raids.

The kingdom to the south, Mbundus, fared no better. The struggle began almost from the first day of the Portuguese presence and went on until in the nineteenth century Angola was completely taken over by the Portuguese. By that time the war and the slave trade had considerably reduced the population. Some estimates put the number of slaves taken from the Angolan territory to America as high as 4 million. For a long time this trade accounted for 80 percent of the total exports from the colony. Although Portugal officially abolished slavery in 1836, the trade still flourished, albeit illegally, until 1880. The end of slavery, however, did not mean an end to African resistance. In 1872 the revolt of the Dembos broke out and was finally put down only in 1919, after several expeditionary forces had been sent out. It was the direct result of the occupation of their territories by the Portuguese, following the partition of Africa among the European powers at the Berlin Conference in 1886.

In 1900 not more than about 9,000 white people had settled in Angola, and it was only after World War II that substantial numbers of immigrants began to arrive from Europe. In 1930 there were 30,000 Europeans in Angola; in 1950, 78,000, and in 1967, 350,000, including the soldiers. Until 1961 the Angolan native population was represented in the administration by the "assimilated," who numbered barely 0.5 percent of the total population of some 5 million Africans.[1]

It was only in 1953 that the first African political group was born, inaugurating a new era of energetic action with a view to emancipation. In 1956 the Party of the United Struggle of Africans of Angola (PLUA) and the Movement for the Independence of Angola (MIA) combined to form the Liberation Movement of Angola (MPLA) under the leadership of Dr. Agostinho Neto. In 1958 they were joined by the Movement for National Independence of Angola (MINA).

An attempt to unite the MPLA with a movement begun by Roberto Holden at Kinshasa in 1954 failed, and in 1962 Holden founded the Revolutionary Government of Angola in Exile (GRAE), the political arm of the National Liberation Front of Angola (FNLA). This government was recognized by the Liberation Committee of the OAU in 1962, but in 1968 recognition was withdrawn and now only the MPLA is supported by the OAU.[2] In 1966 the National Union for the Total Independence of Angola (UNITA) was born, headed by Jonas Savimbi, a hereditary tribal chief and ex-minister for foreign affairs in the GRAE.

By 1959 the Portuguese authorities had begun to react with great harshness. Several national leaders were imprisoned, among them Agostinho Neto, in 1960. On February 4, 1961, the MPLA launched armed resistance with an attack on the prison of Luanda in an attempt to free the imprisoned nationalist leaders. Immediate repression followed and 3,000 people were killed in Luanda and a few days later several thousand more at Baixa de Cassange. The Portuguese reprisals drove thousands of Africans to take refuge in the neighboring countries, particularly in the Congo (Kinshasa). David Grenfell's Baptist mission estimates that between 1961 and June, 1965, 372,000 refugees entered the Congo alone. They also estimated that between 25 and 30 percent of the refugees were killed in their flight. The flood of refugees is still going on and, including those who fled to Zambia and the Congo-Brazzaville, their total number can be estimated at approximately 500,000. They are in very dire straits, and the help they have received from the international community has been very scanty.[3]

In the meantime, the fighting has been going on in Angola, with two main zones of guerrilla activity—one to the east of Luanda and the other covering the east and southeast part of the country (the Moxico region). The MPLA claims to have liberated about one-fifth of the national territory and to have set up a social administration in the liberated zones. The Portuguese army, together with the Provincial Organization of Volunteers for the Civil Defense of Angola, the Political Police (PIDE), and the security forces of the mining companies, number more than 150,000 men.

The story of Mozambique is similar to that of Angola. For a long time only the coastal strip was settled by the Portuguese. Sporadic attempts to penetrate into the interior met with considerable resistance on the part of the Africans, but the forays, aimed at collecting slaves, became more and more frequent toward the end of the eighteenth century when the population of Angola began to decline. In the beginning of the nineteenth century some agricultural development began in the Zambezi region, and throughout the century fighting with various tribes went on ceaselessly. In 1897 the last remaining kingdom was brought to its knees, but the country as a whole was "pacified" only in 1917. Except for the Zambezi region, the settlement of the country by white people is quite recent. In 1900 there were 1,500 Europeans; in 1968 the number had risen to 150,000.[4]

The prehistory of the Mozambique liberation movements goes back to the beginning of the century with the creation of legal organizations claiming equal rights. The leading organization of this type was the Gremio Africano, but all these movements were short-lived. In 1949 secondary-school students formed a clandes-

tine movement, the Core of African Secondary Students in Mozambique (NEMO). This movement proved to be a nursery for
several future leaders of the Liberation Front of Mozambique
(FRELIMO), founded in 1962 by an amalgamation of three existing movements. These three groups, which had tribal origins, were
united under the leadership of the sociologist Eduardo Mondlane,
who was assassinated at Dar es Salaam in 1969. Shortly after its
foundation, disputes of various kinds, some of tribal origin, broke
out among the members of FRELIMO. Another coalition, the
Revolutionary Committee of Mozambique (COREMO), also existed, composed of five different movements.

In 1948 the first uprising took place in Lourenço Marques, and
several hundred Africans were subsequently deported to the island
of São Tomé. In 1956 a dock strike, also in Lourenço Marques,
ended with a death toll of forty-nine. On June 16, 1960, the Mueda
uprising led to the massacre of several hundred people, and in 1963
another dock strike in Lourenço Marques provoked further bloody
repressions. On September 25, 1964, the armed conflict was officially recognized as having begun. The number of Portuguese
soldiers rose to 30,000 during that year, and the war began to
escalate in intensity. In 1968 armed guerillas were estimated at
10,000, while Portuguese troops numbered 50,000. The FRELIMO
claims to have liberated the two northern provinces of Cabo Del-
gado and Nyasa with their 800,000 inhabitants. In the south guerilla operations are more sporadic.[5]

The first Portuguese contacts with the people of Guinea also
date from the fifteenth century. The slave trade began very early in
these territories, the slaves being taken from Guinea to Cape
Verde, which was administratively joined to Guinea-Bissau as one
colonial territory. Fifty years of practically uninterrupted fighting
went on in these two territories from 1870 to 1936. White settlers
are few and far between: about 3,000 out of a total population of
800,000. About 30 percent of the native population are Muslims,
the rest are Animists, and the Portuguese use the Muslim elements
as village chiefs in the Animist regions. In the Cape Verde Islands,
the population numbers about 200,000, of which 3 percent are
Portuguese and 30 percent Africans. The rest are of mixed blood.

The economy is based on the monoculture of coffee, carried on by a small number of large property owners. This economic and social system, strongly reminiscent of Northeast Brazil, has had the same effects as in that country when the islands have been scourged by long periods of drought. In the twentieth century alone, between 1901 and 1959, it is estimated that seven separate droughts have caused 210,000 deaths from starvation. This explains, at least in part, why the population in 1950 was no higher than in 1900.

In 1921 a group of intellectuals proposed that the Cape Verde islands should federate with Brazil. (The notorious Tarrafai concentration camp is located there.) In 1956 the African Party of Independence of Guinea and Cape Verde (PAIGC) was formed, taking the place of another movement founded two years earlier. In 1958 a clandestine labor union was formed, the National Union of Workers of Guinea (UNTG). In 1959, in exile in Dakar, yet another movement, the Liberation Front of Portuguese Guinea and Cape Verde (FLGC), was founded, but it never amounted to anything. Under the leadership of Amilcar Cabral, agronomist and native of Cape Verde, and founder of the PAIGC, a new coalition was attempted: the United Liberation Front of Guinea and Cape Verde; but this also failed to get under way. Finally, another coalition, the Front for the Struggle of National Independence of Guinea (FLING), was responsible for several armed incidents, after which it decided to restrict its activities to the exiles in Senegal.

The war has reached the highest pitch of intensity in the Guinean territories, where military operations have been carried out on a large scale. In 1961, when the armed struggle first began, the Portuguese had 3,000 men under arms in the country; at the end of 1968 there were 30,000 and reinforcements amounting to another 10,000 men were planned for 1969. The army is backed up by an air force which has no scruples about bombing the guerilla zones with napalm. The guerilla forces number some 6,000 men. In 1964 the little island of Como was taken by the *guerrilleros*. It was recaptured by the Portuguese after sixty-five days of fighting. By the end of 1968, the PAIGC claimed to have liberated 70 percent of the territory of Guinea-Bissau.

And finally there is the island of São Tomé, discovered by the Portuguese at the end of the fifteenth century. The first freedom movements began to take shape in 1947, and in 1953, 1,300 Africans were massacred at Batepa. In 1960 the Liberation Committee of São Tomé and Principe (SLSDP) was formed, with the primary purpose of organizing strikes by the workers on the plantations, which are protected by a garrison of 3,000 Portuguese soldiers.

The movements for the liberation of the Portuguese territories, like those of other African countries, have been plagued by bitter tribal strife, the ever-present scourge of the African scene.

Almost every year since 1960 the United Nations has called for self-determination of these territories. At the General Assembly in November, 1968, it was once again voted by a majority of 93 to 3 (Portugal, South Africa, and Brazil) with 13 abstentions (the United States, Great Britain, the European Common Market countries, Malawai, etc.). The armed struggle began in 1961 in Angola, in 1963 in Guinea, and in 1964 in Mozambique. It has continued with growing intensity ever since. The Portuguese armed forces in Africa total nearly 200,000 men[6] and military service in Portugal has recently been extended to four years, two of which must be spent in Africa. In 1969, 45 percent of the Portuguese national budget was appropriated for defense, as against 23 percent in 1960. It has been estimated that 60 percent of that sum (about $140 million) is earmarked for the war in Africa. The armed struggle has gradually developed into a full-scale guerrilla war.

The Portuguese defend their presence in Africa on moral grounds, as a duty to guarantee peace, social welfare, and economic development for the African populations; to bring them the light of the Gospel, thus promoting Christian civilization and contributing to the defense of the West. There is no flagrant racism in these territories to compare with South African *apartheid;* on the contrary, the Portuguese policy of *fraternidade* is invoked as justification for a continued European presence.

Portugal, however, with its 8 million inhabitants, itself bears the marks of underdevelopment. Forty percent of the population is illiterate; the annual per capita income in 1961 was $250, approximately the same as that of Colombia and Chile; there is very heavy emigration due to a chronic shortage of jobs—in 1966 alone, 260,000 left the country—and finally there is still a quasi-feudal land-ownership system—45 percent of the land comprises only 4 percent of the land under cultivation. Under these conditions how can Portugal pretend to be able to improve the economic condition of 13 million Africans? In actual fact, the colonies serve to alleviate Portugal's own economic difficulties. The colonizers, who are usually landless peasants at home, are settled on the land. The colony provides revenues from agricultural resources and, since World War II, Angola has become one of the major oil-producing countries of the world. Local industry is deliberately kept to a minimum. In 1966 the total income of Angola was 19 billion escudos, of which 26 percent went to Africans and 74 percent to the colonizers and the Portuguese companies.

Efforts to improve the lot of the native population have been necessarily meager. In 1963 there were six secondary schools in Mozambique with 3,430 pupils, of which only about 100 were black. In Angola primary school pupils increased from 104,000 in 1960 to 255,000 in 1966, principally because of increased immigration from Portugal. (By way of comparison, in 1958, the Belgian Congo, with three times the population of Angola, had fifteen times the number of primary school pupils: 1,572,000.) In Mozambique infant mortality was nearly 40 percent in 1960, whereas in Tanzania in 1948, it ranged from 13 to 20 percent according to the regions. In 1962 there were 260 doctors in Angola, and this figure fell to 210 in 1965, a third of them in or near Luanda.

It is true that one does not meet the same kind of racism in the Portuguese territories as that which prevails in Rhodesia or South Africa. A mixing of races has always taken place between the Portuguese and the native inhabitants of their colonies; the number of people of mixed blood is a sure indication of this. But this attitude does not have its counterpart in a true social, economic, and political participation. The "assimilated" are only a tiny minority of privileged persons who are supposed to serve as intermediaries between the African masses and the colonial power. The first political movements, however, were recruited from their ranks, and at that time, they were neither violent nor racist and they advocated a gradual evolution toward greater autonomy.

The other countries of southern Africa. In South Africa, known to the African nationalists as Azania, resistance to white power began several decades ago. But before looking at the current scene, it might be useful to mention some of the salient features of the history of white settlement in the country. The Dutch settlement, and particularly that of the Boers who trekked inland from the Cape, forcing the native populations off their lands as they went, was marked by several wars. The British also waged several wars: against the Xhosas in 1818, 1877, and 1879. In 1879 the Zulus were also defeated, and 1880 saw the definitive settlement and domination by white people. Finally, in 1886 the discovery of gold was the spark that set off the Boer War.

Gradually white domination grew stronger, thanks to the policy of racial discrimination. In 1910 the Union of South Africa was created, grouping the provinces of Natal, the Transvaal, the Orange Free State, and Cape Colony. In 1926 the Labor Bar became law; in 1946 *apartheid* was officially endorsed by the passing of the "Ghetto Act" of Prime Minister Smuts. In 1950 the Population Registration Act, No. 30, established the racial categories into which the inhabitants were to be divided; in 1965 the law was amended to include the "presumption" of belonging to the category of "native" and in 1967, to provide for verification of racial lineage.

But resistance to white domination has also grown at the same pace as discriminatory legislation. As early as 1880, the year in which white colonization became firmly established, the Imbumba Yama Afrika (Union of Africans) was founded, and during the twentieth century two parallel lines of development have supported and complemented each other in organizing the struggle: the African nationalist movements and the worker movements.

The former was already at work in 1902 with the creation of the African People's Organization (APO) headed by Abdurahman. This movement, which allied itself politically with Smuts' South African Party, faded away when its founder died in 1940. In 1912 the African National Congress (ANC) was founded, and immediately after World War II the Colored People's Congress (CPC). In

1960 the ANC was outlawed. The Indians who had come to South Africa in 1860 also set up their own movements. Gandhi—who lived in South Africa from 1860 to 1914—in answer to appeals from his fellow countrymen to use his legal skills in their defense, founded the Natal Indian Congress (NIC) and the Transvaal Indian Congress (TIC), both of which later fused into the one South African Indian Congress (SAIC). In 1946 the SAIC formed an alliance with the ANC. Progressive and antiracist whites also formed a group, the Congress of Democrats (COD), outlawed in 1962. The repression against all these movements has resulted in numerous arrests and prison sentences over the years.

The labor unions also have a long tradition of resistance. In 1913 and 1914 rioting broke out among mine workers. The Industrial and Commercial Workers' Union (ICU), founded in 1919, was savagely repressed in 1920. Another revolt occurred among the miners in 1922, but the movement disintegrated in the 1930s, and not until after the Second World War did it gain a new lease on life. The Communist party, founded in South Africa in 1921, was outlawed in 1950, but reappeared in a clandestine form the same year under the name of South African Communist Party. In 1946 a strike by 100,000 miners was organized, and in 1955 the South African Congress of Trade Unions (SACTU) was formed, only to have its leaders arrested the following year. In 1960 some 200 local activists were also thrown into jail.

The nationalist and worker movements joined their efforts in concerted action. Between 1953 and 1955 a campaign was organized to prepare a common ground for their action, which culminated in the Freedom Charter, published on June 26, 1955. In December, 1956, however, 156 leaders who had been active in preparing the common platform were arrested and brought to trial. Their trial lasted four years. The outlawing of the ANC rang down the curtain on the nonviolent phase of the struggle. In 1961 the Um Khonto we Sizwe (Spear of the Nation), the military arm of the ANC, conducted a series of acts of sabotage which led to severe reprisals. In August, 1967, as a response to the alliance between the forces of Pretoria and Salisbury, the ANC entered into an agreement with the Zimbabwe African People's Union

(ZAPU) and the guerrilla war gained in intensity. The movement has foreign representation, particularly in India, and since 1967 has published a magazine from London called *Sechaba*.

South-West Africa—otherwise known as Namibia—is a vast territory as big as France and Germany combined, with a population of only 1 million people. The Germans first settled there in 1870, and the Berlin Conference gave them jurisdiction over it in 1886. They conducted systematic wars of extermination against the Namas and the Hereros, whose territory is rich in diamonds and phosphates. After the First World War the League of Nations entrusted it under mandate to the British, who administered it through the intermediary of the Union of South Africa. In 1956 the General Assembly of the United Nations voted for the independence of Namibia, but, to date, South Africa has persistently refused to put this vote into effect.

The white population, comprising only 14 percent of the total, owns 70 percent of the land. In 1957 the Owamboland People's Congress (OCP) was formed, and in 1959 the South-West African People's Organization (SWAPO), which is now carrying on the armed struggle. In 1964 the Caprivi African National Union joined forces with the SWAPO.

On July 18, 1966, ruling on a charge introduced in 1960 by Ethiopia and Liberia, the International Court of Justice at the Hague declared South Africa guilty of illegally denying independence to the territory, and on August 26 the armed struggle for which the freedom movements had been preparing since 1963, was launched. Although the SWAPO does not claim to have liberated any region fully, it does claim to have acquired partial control of some regions. Repressive measures are carried out with great brutality, either through rigorous application of the Terrorism Act of 1967, or through the army, as in the massacre of peasants at Mpacha in 1968. Since 1962 the Pretoria government has applied a policy of "separate development" in Namibia, with the creation of "homelands," reserved for the black population. But the policy seems less to promote the development of the African community than to maintain a steady supply of labor for the needs of the whites.[7]

The colonization of Southern Rhodesia—or Zimbabwe—began in 1890 with the conquest of the territory by Cecil Rhodes. Rebellions took place as early as 1893 with such intensity that a full-scale war was waged in 1896 against the two ethnic groups of the region, the Showas and the Pebeles. The struggle went on sporadically for twenty-five years. At the beginning of this century the Africans began to be pushed off the arable lands by white colonizers and British-owned companies. Two associations, originating in the two different ethnic groups, were founded as early as 1920. They were the Rhodesian Bantu Association (Showa) and the Rhodesian Native Association (Tebele). Under the influence of developments in neighboring South Africa, the African National Congress (ANC) was created in Rhodesia in 1934, at about the time the first labor unions began to take shape.

Only after World War II, however, did strikes become organized; in 1945 there was a strike against the railroads, and in 1948 a general strike. Two new interracial associations came into existence at about this time. One of them, the Capricorn Africa Society, was in favor of uniting the two Rhodesias and Nyasaland into a federation, as proposed by Great Britain in 1953, to counterbalance the overwhelming supremacy of the whites in Southern Rhodesia. The movement had a religious background and never managed to become politically effective. It ceased to function in 1958. The other movement, the Interracial Association, allied itself with the United Rhodesian Party (URP), headed by Garfield Todd, the prime minister who was defeated in 1958 because he was considered too pro-African. From that time on the movement withered and was officially disbanded in 1960.

The first movement for African autonomy, the City Youth League, was formed in 1955; among other activities it organized the bus boycott in Salisbury in 1956. In 1957 it affiliated with the ANC, which was outlawed two years later. Immediately the National Democratic Party (NDP) was formed to carry on the struggle, but it enjoyed a precarious existence for only two years and was outlawed, in its turn, in December, 1961.

The constitution of Rhodesia, adopted in 1961, allowed for 50 white and 15 African representatives (only 1,200 Africans had the right to vote). Before the end of 1961 a new movement appeared, taking up where the NDP had left off; this was the Zimbabwe People's Union (ZAPU), and almost at once it, too, was outlawed. ZAPU was a well-organized movement with clearly defined political policies, particularly on the international level. Arrests and reprisals became more frequent. In September, 1962, the military arm of ZAPU came into being and announced its existence with a series of incidents.

On November 11, 1964, Prime Minister Ian Smith proclaimed Southern Rhodesia an independent state with the name of Rhodesia. This unilateral declaration of independence was countered with economic sanctions by Britain and later by the United Nations. Political negotiations dragged on in an attempt to find a compromise solution with Britain, but they came to nothing. In 1967 the General Assembly of the United Nations asked Great Britain to intervene more energetically, with force if necessary, but Britain refused. In the meantime ZAPU split into two groups, and in 1964 Pastor Ndabaningi Sithole founded the Zimbabwe African National Union (ZANU). ZAPU and ZANU represent fundamentally different strategies for carrying on the struggle for independence. Pastor Sithole's following is mostly among the intellectuals, whereas Mr. Nkomo, the leader of ZAPU—since renamed the People's Caretaker Council—is more of a popular leader.

From 1964 on arrests of African militants became more numerous and almost all the leaders of ZANU were imprisoned. The year 1965 was marked by widespread strikes and military incidents. In 1967 the South African ANC and the ZAPU coordinated their struggle for liberation—and Pretoria and Salisbury coordinated their repressive action. The fighting continued in 1968, and Mr. Nkomo was arrested, found guilty, and imprisoned. On March 6 the execution of three Africans, in spite of a royal pardon from the Queen of England, aroused protests from around the world, including one from Pope Paul VI. In June ZAPU announced the creation of a permanent guerrilla force. The year 1969 opened with the condemnation of Pastor Sithole to six years' hard labor. In June Ian Smith held a referendum on a proposed new constitution, designed to prevent any future possibility of a government controlled by the African majority and breaking all remaining ties with the Commonwealth. Both issues were ratified by the voters after a very skillful campaign in which the fear of "chaos" and of the "destruction of the white community" was exploited to the full. By 1970 Zimbabwe had become a republic and a South-African style policy of apartheid was rapidly being put into effect.

The Church and the
African Revolutionary Movements

South Africa. In December, 1960, the World Council of Churches organized a consultation with representatives of the South African churches. Among the motions discussed was one which condemned all racial discrimination, pointing out that there are no "scriptural foundations for forbidding mixed marriages," and that "no believer in Jesus Christ should be excluded from any church because of his race."

This motion was passed with a majority, but not a unanimous, vote. The Dutch Reformed Church maintained that "the policy of racial differentiation can be defended from a Christian standpoint, for it provides the only realistic solution to the problem of race relations." A special commission of this Church even went so far as to declare that mixed blood was "immoral and anti-Christian."[8] This was the only church, in fact, that failed to ratify the motion, and one of its branches, the Hermvorde Kerk, even withdrew from the WCC,[9] to be followed shortly after by the Transvaal Church.[10]

The Dutch Reformed Churches of South Africa could boast of 1,400,000 white and 600,000 black members in 1951. They are in favor of racial segregation, which they implement by having separate church buildings for whites and blacks.[11] The arguments they use to justify their position, however, are more sociological than theological. The Church and the Afrikaans people are one indivisible body and the Church favors apartheid just as uncompromisingly as do the people. Their position is not abstract or theoretical; it is the fruit of history and a remarkable example of confusion between the social interests of a group and its religious beliefs.

The Afrikaners, abandoned by the Dutch to the domination of the British, built up their country in the face of bitter opposition from the native population, the British Empire, and adventurers of all nations. While they built their nation, they also built their language and their church. Their religion bears the marks of this history of strife and solidarity, and for them *apartheid* means being culturally and technically different from the black man. It does not just mean segregation. It is a recognition of a specific reality. They are very much aware of their duty to help the black community to develop, but without attempting to eliminate differences which they consider to be clearly intended by God. For them segregation means "separate development," with each community developing at its own pace and respecting each other's differences. Criticism of this conception by the other confessions and by the WCC seems unrealistic to the Afrikaners, who are persuaded that *apartheid* is a form of love for the black population.[12]

Catholics and Anglicans, the latter being preponderant among the Bantus, join their voices more and more frequently in protest against the prevailing situation. They are not always completely unanimous in their opinions, however. At a press conference in 1964, Archbishop Whelan, for instance, expressed the opinion that there was nothing in Catholic doctrine opposed to the idea of a state composed of different national and racial groups; from this he concluded that a Christian is free to subscribe to the policy of *apartheid*. Although some elements in this policy seem to be immoral, "the Church has never considered democracy to be the only form of government compatible with Christianity."[13]

The Catholic archbishops of Cape Town and Durban, however, do not agree with this point of view. Archbishop Hurley of Durban is one of the most outspoken opponents of *apartheid* and he had previously declared:

> The essential principle of our legislation is concern for only one section of the population, the white section, which constitutes only one-fifth of the total population.... We know that the government identifies itself with the interests of the white people only, and that in practice it treats the Africans, Asiatics and Coloreds as subject races.... Christianity has always been a religion of salvation. Today it is the salvation of the non-Europeans which should concern us. ... We have often remained comfortably ensconced in our Christian armchairs. ... The prophetic voices that have cried aloud in the wilderness have not been ours.... What is being asked of Christians is that they give up a view of life in which they identify the Christian mystery with their own national destiny.[14]

The Anglicans are sometimes more circumspect in their attitude, and one of their bishops very vigorously reproached them for it in 1967. "I am outraged by the silence of Anglicans in this country. I know that those who speak the truth run enormous risks, but I cannot see how a Christian conscience can accept *apartheid*."[15] As early as 1965 Pastor Boyers Naude suggested the creation of a "confessing Church" after the manner of those created in Germany during the Hitler regime, saying, "We must resolve unacceptable compromises and intolerable silences."[16] And in 1966 some thirty members of the Anglican clergy publicly supported a document published by the Catholic hierarchy, declaring that "racial discrimination must disappear, for it is contrary to the law of God."[17]

In 1961 Archbishop Hurley created an interconfessional organization to study and combat *apartheid*.[18] This organization has contributed substantially to making the Church's challenge of the system more pertinent, concrete, and courageous. The causes of the situation under attack are carefully analyzed. In 1964, for instance, Archbishop Hurley spoke out against seperate development, linking it to the problem of migratory forced labor and the distribution of land: "The advocacy of seperate development seems to me like wanting to clothe a naked man by giving him a pair of gaiters."[19]

In 1962 the government passed a "law against sabotage," which was aimed at virtually any and every form of social protest. Archbishop Hurley, supported by the Anglicans, criticized the law very sharply: "Communism is a real danger and it must be combatted. But let us begin by combatting the social abuses which give rise to communism."[20] Archbishop MacCann of Cape Town declared, for his part, that "the amendment of the basic law is so broad that innocent people are in danger of being accused of communism and sabotage."

Catholics and Anglicans alike seem to be keenly aware of the religious implications of the situation of the country and ready to challenge the practices of their own Churches. The Council of Churches, an association of twenty-eight different denominations, acknowledged in 1968 that the "degree to which *apartheid* has crept into the Church shows to what extent the Church has abandoned Christ's teachings."[21] And in this connection, I would like to quote two very forceful texts from Archbishop Hurley, showing how the problem has its roots in the conservative spirit of religion. In 1963, criticizing government policy, he declared: "On the one hand we produce public declarations and laws that are absolutely reprehensible by every moral standard. On the other hand we try to justify these enormities by adopting an air of injured innocence. ... There is no political solution, and the only recourse is to violence or compromise.... There is no political solution because the problem belongs to the domain of inner conviction; I maintain that it is, fundamentally, a religious problem.... I hold organized religion in this country responsible for this racial situation that has no political solution." Of course, the archbishop recognized that nothing in the convictions of faith encourage racism, but "religion has failed to keep white people abreast of social evolution.... They have not known how to apply Christian principles vigorously to the political, economic and cultural spheres.... As for the Africans, their Churches are too closely identified with their national struggle to be free to devote themselves to more important aspects of their role."[22]

In 1965 the archbishop adverted to this question again:

> Can the religious body of South Africa claim to have summoned up all the strength of its moral powers with regard to this, the most agonizing problem of the country? Wherever there is a need of love, the Church must be actively present, more than anywhere else. ... It is up to the Church to commit itself with audacity and to play its full role in redressing moral consciences. By the commitment of the Church, I do not only mean publishing declarations and documents, but giving an effective training of conscience to the whole body of the Church, and especially the laity.... The crisis of South Africa is its racial problem and the intensity of the crisis is living proof that organized religion was not present, at least not in the right place, when the seeds of the crisis were being sown.[23]

Finally, we must observe that although this profound awareness on the part of leaders like Archbishop Hurley is of great importance, it does not seem to lead to a radical transformation of the Church itself. In 1968 an African priest, Father Mangaliso, observed: "The control of the Church is wholly in the hands of white people. . . . If no responsibility is given to the black clergy, . . . if the liturgy, theology and psychology of the Church are not Africanized, the Church will continue to be a 'foreigners' club.' "[24]

The attitude of the Catholic and Anglican churches is not at all to the liking of the government, and relations between them are strained. The Anglican bishop of Johannesburg was threatened with expulsion in 1963,[25] and the Church is frequently exhorted by the government to be content to preach the Gospel without getting involved in the temporal welfare of the Bantus. The government has even called on the churches to collaborate in the struggle against "non-Christian" ideologies such as communism and liberalism. *The Southern Cross,* an official Catholic paper, reacted to this invitation as follows: "Who is to judge what is a non-Christian ideology? Many Christians might conclude that government policy in racial matters is as non-Christian as those condemned by the authorities!"[26] In 1968 a group of Christians was formed called Obedience to God. They accuse Prime Minister Vorster of an "attitude analogous to that of Hitler toward German Christians."[27]

Rhodesia. In contrast to the South African situation, in Rhodesia the Anglican and Roman Catholic communities are approximately the same size. The Catholic Church has more African members than any other denomination, but it is still the Europeans who have the influence.[28] One out of three white Rhodesians is Anglican. However, "Catholics constitute the group with the strongest internal cohesion and have a potential influence out of all proportion to their numbers."[29] Bishop Chichester, who occupied the Catholic See of Salisbury from 1921 to 1956, had considerable influence in the country. But today the bishops seem to be ill at ease when it comes to taking a stand on political matters.

A pastoral letter from the Catholic hierarchy in 1961 was presented by a section of the press as a justification of colonialism, but Bishop Lamont of Umtali energetically protested that this was a distortion of the bishops' thinking and stated that, on the contrary, they had compared the racial policy of Rhodesia with that practiced by the Nazis.[30] An Anglican bishop came to the support of this position shortly after, and advised his clergy to read the Catholic bishops' statement, adding: "It is true that the laws of this 'free' African nation are very similar to those of the totalitarian states we fought against."[31]

The situation became more ambiguous when in 1962 the African nationalist movement, the Zimbabwe African People's Union, sharply attacked a letter from Bishop Markall in which he reminded Catholics of their duty in the forthcoming elections: "By asking the faithful to vote, isn't the bishop placing himself on the side of those who have organized this election and who are destined to benefit from it? Whereas the African nationalist parties are calling for a boycott."[32] Fortunately the bishop in question dissipated all ambiguity when, a few months later, he joined with some Protestant personalities in publicly protesting a proposed law aimed at curbing the political activity of African nationalists.[33]

The role of the Christian churches in the field of education is considerable in Rhodesia and most of their work benefits the Africans: 88 percent of black school children are in Christian institutions and, of these, 23 percent are in Catholic schools.[34] This work with the Africans is frowned upon by the Smith government, however, which in 1967 cut off all subsidies to church-run schools in the hope of making it impossible for them to reach required standards and obtain official recognition. Since 1963 three Catholic colleges in Salisbury have accepted black and white students in the same classes.[35] In 1967 the bishop of Umtali urged a fundamental change of direction in the education of young Europeans. Speaking to the students at a prize-giving ceremony, he told them: "Your education is not attuned to African life. It prepares you only to live somewhere else. . . . It is essential to try and reorient all European education in order to meet the needs of Africa."[36]

At the time of the break with Britain, more than one hundred representatives of Christian communities criticized the methods used by the government to proclaim independence: Among the black population only the chiefs were consulted. As "servants of the government" they could not represent the opinion of the African masses. According to those who signed this protest, it was obvious that independence meant nothing more than "the will to establish the supremacy of the whites."[37]

Independence was proclaimed on November 11, 1965. No later than the fourteenth, the Anglican Bishop Alderson declared in a sermon: "Christians are not morally bound to obey the illegal laws proclaimed by the new government. . . . It is not enough to submit under protest. Christians have the right, and perhaps the duty, to disobey."[38] The bishop was of the opinion, however, that the moral conditions for the legitimate insurrection were not present, and consequently condemned the use of violence.

The Catholic hierarchy joined their voice to the debate on November 28. In a joint letter they observed that "many Rhodesians are fiercely opposed to independence and are especially exasperated that it has been proclaimed on the pretext of safeguarding Christian civilization. . . . The silence of its opponents is the silence imposed by fear. . . it is a dangerous silence. When racism and the interests of special groups become the guiding force of a nation, immorality reigns." But, like their Anglican counterparts, the Catholic bishops refused to entertain the notion of recourse to violence, and "ordered" the faithful to "abstain from it. . . however serious the provocation might be." This attitude was particularly momentous in view of the great majority of Africans in the Catholic Church.[39]

In Great Britain, with the government hesitating about the attitude it should adopt, the archbishop of Canterbury took a bold stand: "I believe that if the British government thought it necessary to use force to protect the rights of the majority of the Rhodesian people, we, as Christians, would agree that it is right to use force for this purpose."[40] Dr. Ramsey's statement was greeted by a storm of protest from certain groups.

In any event, these declarations, limited as they were, came a little late, but the churches have remained faithful to this stand. For the first anniversary of independence, Catholics and Anglicans alike refused to have special prayers of thanksgiving. The Anglican bishops even took advantage of the occasion to issue a public reminder: "Christians are far from agreeing unanimously that Christian ideals were the motive for this independence, or that since then our country has been governed according to the law of God."[41] The Catholics, for their part, observed: "We have several times... clearly defined the principles and fundamental demands of Christian social justice, without which we believe that there can be no equitable and lasting solution to our country's problems."[42] And finally in 1967 the Catholic bishops were openly critical of the law of racial segregation in housing. "We consider," they said, "that the proposed legislation is in fundamental opposition to the clear teaching of the Christian Gospel; for that reason it must be condemned in a Christian country."[43]

In June, 1969, the new constitution proposed by the Smith government was condemned by the Catholic hierarchy as "contrary to Christian teaching in many respects.... Catholics must reject those elements and publicly condemn them." The bishops expressed the opinion that if the constitution were adopted, it would become very difficult for them to continue to "counsel moderation to a people which has been so patient in face of arbitrary laws and which is now offered such provocation." Rhodesia was declared a republic in the beginning of 1970. On March 17 the Catholic bishops published a severe criticism of the racial policy of the Smith regime.

The Portuguese colonies: the weight of history. Portuguese colonial expansion began in 1415 with the capture of Ceuta. Missionary work began only five years later, with the arrival of missionaries in Madeira in 1420 and in Guinea in 1446. Under the patronage of Henry the Navigator, the Order of Christ penetrated deeper and deeper into African territory. The papal bulls of Martin V in 1430 and Nicholas V in 1452 gave Portugal the exclusive right to develop the missions and to carry on commerce and the slave trade in Africa. Disputes arose with Spain over the territories that were to be evangelized, and once again the Church intervened to resolve the dispute: The Treaty of Tordesillas in 1495 applied the principle established the year before by Alexander VI, giving Portugal undisputed jurisdiction over all the lands that lay to the east of a line running north and south slightly to the west of the Cape Verde Islands, whereas Spain was assigned everything that lay to the west.

After 1560 Angola became the principal center of interest of the Portuguese crown, and the trading posts established in the area for more than seventy years became the chosen land of the Jesuits and the slave traders. The Society of Jesus was the declared champion of the "expansion of the faith and the empire," and legitimated by its evangelizing activities the conquest of the land and the sale of Africans to Brazil: "The best way to convert the blacks [being] to sell them so that they can be introduced to Christianity through the dignity of their labors in the American plantations."[44] Even as late as the nineteenth century, the Bishop of Luanda still gave collective baptism to the cargos of slaves; the ceremony was known as the "baptism of freedom."[45]

Pope Paul III's interdicts on slavery in 1537 and 1547, Pius V's condemnation of unjust war against the pagans in 1567, and the decrees forbidding missionaries to have any part in the slave trade did not prevent the Jesuits and Dominicans from increasing the size of their properties, raising taxes, and selling slaves. In the eighteenth century Portuguese missionary and colonial expansion was on the wane, and Spain took up the cause. The Jesuits were expelled from Portugal in 1759 and all religious orders were suppressed in 1834. The final reckoning of this long period of Portuguese colonization shows that the expansion of trade had fared far better than that of the Church: Between 1580 and 1836 an estimated 15 million Africans had been "exported," whereas in Mozambique in 1825 there were only ten priests and a few hundred Catholics. In Angola in 1854 there were only five priests.[46]

Around 1840 the traditional clerical order was restored in Portugal and there was a corresponding renewal of interest in the missions and in Africa. In 1911, with the laws of separation of Church and State, the old agreements were suspended; but the crisis was short-lived and everything returned to "normal" when Salazar came to power. The Concordat afforded a legal basis for mutual assistance between Church and State. The Church provided the ideology (Salazar's corporatism openly took its inspiration from Leo XIII's *Rerum Novarum* and Pius XI's *Quadragesimo Anno*), and in return accepted aid—and orders—from Salazar's party. In 1940 a missionary agreement allowed the Church to take part in the colonial revival; it regained its old influence—and new sources of wealth—in the colonies, where it responded to the "patriotic cry of alarm" published in 1919 by the clergy of Mozambique, calling for aid in resisting "the destructive influence of foreign missions." In that document evangelization was seen not as an "end in itself, but as a means in the work of civilizing the African races."[47]

It must be noted that in the terms of the Concordat the Portuguese missions escaped from the direct jurisdiction of the Congregation for the Propagation of the Faith in Rome. All the clauses of the agreement served to establish administrative bonds and facilitate mutual assistance between the Church and the Portuguese state. Diocesan boundaries corresponded to the boundaries of administrative districts; prelates were required to report on their activities to the government and to pass on to it any information that came into their possession; the teaching in the seminaries was subject to government control; only Portuguese citizens had the right to be in charge of ecclesiastical territories or institutions in the missions; education of the Africans, which was entrusted to the Church, had to abide by government rulings and was primarily nationalistic (Portuguese) and practical; missionary work was considered a public service of civilization; missionary personnel received special allocations for their travelling expenses; the Church's assets were included in the provincial budgets and the Church was exempt from property taxes.

Commenting on this agreement in 1961, the patriarch of Lisbon, Bishop de Cerejeira, declared: "Anyone who is sensitive to the acute colonial problem being played out on the international chessboard, and particularly if he is a Christian, who has felt the responsibility of the salvation of the native souls that must be conquered for Christ and his Church, is capable of understanding the full import of the Missionary Agreement for the propagation of the faith and the empire overseas."[48] And a theologian, professor of missiology, had this to say: "It was only in 1940 that, with the signing of the Concordat and the Missionary Agreement, we entered frankly and firmly into the era of real accomplishments; a few years later we had already come to the end of the first phase of our ambitious plan for Christianization: religious occupation."[49]

Some current problems: education. In virtue of the 1940 agreement, the Catholic missions are responsible for all education in the

Portuguese colonies. In conformity with government instruction in educational matters, the Church collaborates, therefore, in a policy of assimilation which aims at turning the Africans into a class of rural laborers and craftsmen. Since African students are obliged to spend more time in the fields than in the classroom, it is almost impossible for them to get into secondary schools. Education for Africans also suffers from a dearth of teachers, money, and equipment. The missionaries' monopoly in the field has turned out to be an immense failure; the proportion of illiterates is enormous—99 percent in Angola.[50] Statistics show evidence of a rudimentary system thinly spread and absolutely disproportionate to the real needs of the population.[51] Also, the Second Congress of African Artists and Writers, held in Rome in 1959, made the pessimistic observation: "We would like to believe that the Church was being abused when it was employed by the Portuguese colonizers in the sinister work of destroying the native culture, stifling African languages, depersonalizing the African man and educating Africans for servile labor in the colonies."[52] Even the political and religious leaders in Portugal recognize the superiority of the work done by the Protestant missions in the field of education: "If present conditions continue to pertain. . . tomorrow's African elite will be of the Protestant persuasion, and this represents a political danger."[53]

Social problems. Some people prefer the euphemism "obligatory work."[54] But whatever one is pleased to call it, the harsh reality of forced labor which still prevails in the Portuguese territories, largely due to cultural underdevelopment, is the foremost social problem. Official statistics for 1954 mention, in Angola alone, 379,000 forced workers and 400,000 voluntary workers. The forced workers are recruited for public works and as laborers on the plantations by the settlers who own the most fertile lands, acting with the support of the government. They are often sent far away from their families and villages, and the result of this migration is disastrous to the family situation. The existence of agreements between Portugal, South Africa, and Rhodesia means that the situation is becoming inexorably worse.

Interventions by the bishops regarding this problem have been very cautious, merely evoking the principles involved without really calling into question the policy that is being carried out daily. The most outspoken declaration so far is that of Bishop Resende in 1953: "Work must be free so that the specter of obligatory labor will finally cease to exist.... If industry gave their native workers what they now spend on their recruiters, they would never lack for workers; the natives would come of their own accord."[55]

On the other hand, in 1958 the Portuguese bishops declared: "As for works that are considered to be of public utility, everything is duly controlled by laws inspired by Christian and humane principles."[56] In 1961, however, Cardinal Gouveia of Mozambique deplored the existence of "obligatory" work,[57] and in 1969 the bishops' conference of Angola noted the disastrous consequences of this practice.[58]

Racism and the myth of "assimilation." In 1959 the bishop of Malanje observed: "Racism does not exist in our legislation but, in practice, it continually creates difficulties and runs counter to the formation of Christians fully conscious of their social rights and duties." President Salazar declared in an interview in the French paper *l'Aurore* in 1954: "We thought for a long time that the white man could be replaced in every circumstance by the black man. But that is not true. Whites are the only ones capable of planning an action and organizing their work.... Nor should I be taxed with racism because I say that the blacks do not have the same aptitudes as the white man. It is a factual observation which comes from experience."

The assimilation of blacks is carried out at the cost of their depersonalization. A few privileged men who can read and write have been given an identity card and are allowed to frequent certain restaurants and movie theaters that are forbidden to their "uncivilized" brethren. According to the Reverend Malcolm McVeigh, "A woman who wears the native dress is obliged to travel third class on the railroads, but Africans who dress and behave like the Portuguese can take the train and go in and out of hotels and restaurants quite freely. Africans who show their papers proving that they are 'assimilated' are allowed into the cinemas."[59] The legislation is not racist, perhaps, but police regulations uphold attitudes which, by any standard, are racist.

What is the thinking of the Church on all this? In 1958 the bishops recommended that black and white families should inter-mingle in the plantations so as to avoid the formation of two impenetrable blocs.[60] And in a document submitted to the apostolic nuncio in Lisbon in 1964, the following pessimistic observation can be found:

> In all our missionary activity, the principle of assimilation, which we are obliged to put into effect, becomes fundamental, along with all its attendant ills: depersonalization and the creation of inferiority complexes and feelings of incompetence. These complexes are reinforced by a false notion of humility which is really servility, and because of the ascendancy of a stifling community, [the Africans] lack the elements of balance that come from truth, mutual respect, justice and charity.[61]

The structure and habits of the missionary Church contain some disquieting aspects. During their first assembly in 1957, the bishops of the Portuguese colonies admitted that, in spite of Pius XII's insistence on the need to train native clergy,

> We shall have to have recourse to a non-African clergy for a very long time to come; the formation of a native clergy is very slow work; before... there must be Christian families; without missionaries, Portuguese Africa will never be able to extricate itself from the centuries-old lethargy which has kept it chained to barbarism.[62]

Since 1961 and the beginning of the struggle for liberation, there has been a growing climate of suspicion surrounding the black and mulatto clergy. Although it is true that there is no ideological racism here, like that of South Africa, it permeates the social, economic, and cultural system as well as the religious establishment. It goes disguised as "*fraternidade.*"

The struggle for liberation and the repression. The magazine *Novidades,* of April 7, 1961, contains the following passage: "Portuguese blood is flowing in Africa... at the same time as the blood of the natives who have paid for their crimes with their lives. ... Many pages of Portuguese history have been written in blood... it was thus in the past... it is thus today... it will continue to be so."[63]

The Church is often invoked as the moral justification for this type of "supernationalism." Without raising its voice to give them the lie, it has permitted campaigns which poison the public mind, accusing the Africans of "racism" and the Protestants and Communists of promoting the freedom movements. Except on very rare occasions, it has remained silent in spite of the arrests of several priests and the cruelty of the repression.

The exceptions are a few Portuguese priests and the Protestants. The latter enjoy little freedom in the Portuguese colonies where their influence in the educational field is feared. They have never been backward in defending the local population, and today there are even some Protestant missionaries in positions of responsibility in the freedom movements. This is the case of the Reverend Pereira, president of the action committee of the MPLA.[64] Whereas Catholic priests are often looked on as representing the government, Protestant pastors are still esteemed and defended by the population. A case in point was Agostinho Neto, who is the son of a pastor: When he was arrested at Luanda, the population of his village demonstrated for his release. The repression that followed took twenty lives and left one hundred wounded.

As for the Catholic hierarchy, a few quotations will suffice to demonstrate its timidity and its fealty to the regime. On January 13, 1961, the Portuguese bishops declared:

> The expansion of the Portuguese fatherland in different parts of the world has been faithful to the ideal of human, brotherly communion contained in Christian civilization. In this hour, when the West seems to have lost all consciousness of its own identity, Portugal is aware of its evangelizing and civilizing mission.... It is illicit for any Catholic to join in a political venture with those who deny Christ. At this moment, other values are at stake for every Portuguese, and, in particular, the value of the fatherland; to vote for God is to vote for these values.[65]

At about the same time the archbishop of Lourenço Marques warned the faithful of his diocese:

> Do not allow yourselves to be seduced by fantasies, or led astray by evil counselors who feed your dreams of independence or utopias of economic and cultural prosperity. As citizens of the Portuguese nation for the last four centuries, it is within the framework of that nation that you should aspire to material, cultural and moral progress by cooperating honestly with the Portuguese authorities and obeying their orders.[66]

The established order was similarly sacralized by Bishop Alvim Pereira on April 18, 1961:

> The peaceful message of Jesus Christ has not yet penetrated the hearts of all human beings... but even worse is the fact that one finds baptized Christians

who are traitors to the fatherland. This can only mean that first they have been traitors to Christ and his Gospel.[67]

In the meantime, native Protestant missionaries and catechists are being massacred or expelled from the country—between 1961 and 1968 their numbers were reduced from 286 to 60. Priests who have sided with the emancipation movement—or who have not explicitly declared their support of the government—are being imprisoned and silenced. The accusations against them are diverse: One is accused of training guerrillas; another was never heard to speak of "our" government, "our" country, etc.; Father de Andrade, chancellor of the Luanda diocese and a brother of the nationalist leader, is presently in exile in Lisbon for the crime of saying he was opposed to the use of violence, but that he understood his fellow Africans.[68] Bishop Mendes das Neves, vicar-general of the same diocese, was arrested on suspicion of nationalism (African) and repudiated by his superior, Bishop Pinho.[69] He died in exile.

In April, 1961, the bishops of Angola denied to any but the authorities the right to kill, and condemned the nationalists whose "acts are beyond imagining."[70] When the Baptist missionaries raised an outcry against the massacre of Africans by the Portuguese army,[71] the government replied by denying the accusations of "certain religious sects," by putting all the blame on the "terrorists," and by expelling the missionaries.[72]

At the beginning of 1962, the World Council of Churches called for autonomy for Angola; its appeal went unheard. It was only in 1965 that Portuguese Catholics first condemned the policy of their country in a text that came to be known as the "Manifesto of the 101," which aroused all the reactions one might expect in the orthodox circles of the community.

In 1964 the archbishop of Lourenço Marques published ten "theses" on the political situation. In the second he states that "as long as the necessary conditions for independence are not present, it is an act contrary to the natural law to belong to an independence movement." In other passages one finds recommendations such as: "The Africans should be grateful to the colonizers for all the benefits they have received from them," and "Those who have been educated must warn those who are less advanced against any illusions concerning independence." Finally, the newspaper *La Hora*, of April 9, 1966, published an article which declared:

> In this dreadful duel between Christ and Satan, Portugal's role has always been primordial. It is an astonishing sight to see this race of theologians and warriors, after struggling for centuries against the enemies of religion and the fatherland, still keeping its frontiers intact in Africa, thus accomplishing the greatest feat in the history of humanity since the Redemption.... Since we are the right arm of God, we cannot allow barbarism to reign over even the smallest portion of our fatherland.[73]

During the Vatican Council, a letter to the Holy See from some of the exiled Angolan priests elicited no response.[74] The bishop of Luanda did publish a note on the situation in his country, but only in an attempt to justify his attitude to the nationalist movements; he made no mention of the priests' letter.[75] It was left to a French-speaking African archbishop, Archbishop Tchidimbo of Conakry, to come to the defense of the exiled and imprisoned priests. In a forceful article written in 1967, he gave a detailed account of the facts and defended the aspiration for independence, denouncing in particular the "total confusion between the Cross and the Flag" exemplified in the present situation.[76] A bishop from Angola answered him: "The Portuguese hierarchy in Angola has never made common cause with any government or political party. But, loyal to the doctrine of the Church, it has always shown itself deferential and respectful toward the authorities.... One could hardly find anything else in the pastoral letters of the Angolan bishops than the preaching of the Gospel and the teachings of Holy Mother Church, especially as it was expressed by the recent popes."[77]

From that time on the expulsion of foreign missionaries has become more frequent: Belgian White Fathers from Mozambique and Italian Holy Ghost Fathers from Angola. In 1968 the major seminary in Mozambique was taken out of the hands of non-Portuguese White Fathers and entrusted to Portuguese Jesuits. Two-thirds of the seminarians left and a number of them joined revolutionary groups.

In October, 1968, during the general chapter of the Holy Ghost Fathers in Rome, some members of the order gave devastating reports of the situation. One passage in particular should be quoted: "The official attitude of the Portuguese province [of the order] is absolutely anachronistic and erroneous: they are still living in tune with a colonialist and constantinian era. . . ." And the report goes on to give examples of the theology underlying their missionary policy: "The Holy Ghost missionaries are the vanguard of the Portuguese empire. . . . Oh missionary! oh missionary! Do not abandon your noble ideal of bringing the good news of Christ to all men in the name of Portugal." This quotation is from the missionary magazine, *Portugal in Africa,* a title which is in itself revealing, as the authors of the report point out. And they add: "The natives consider the missionaries to be agents of the Portuguese government. . . . Missionaries who do not carry out government policy (who, for example, promote the use of the African languages or call for respect for the rights of man) are labelled antipatriotic and are expelled."

On April 13, 1967, the Cooperative for Community Information and Action, PRAGMA, wrote to the Portuguese bishops: "We believe that the time has come for our bishops to declare unequivocally whether *Pacem in Terris,* the Second Vatican Council, Paul VI's declaration to the United Nations and *Populorum Progressio* . . . can also be applied to Portugal or whether, on the contrary, truth, justice, liberty and love have definitively and irremediably become subversive values for us." Not long after, another document, originating in Angola in April, 1968, declared: "A free Church is a Church that has renounced once and for all every form of theocracy and every form of Holy Roman Empire; it is a Church that has ceased to be 'Portugal in Africa' and become the 'Catholic Church in the world.' The Catholic Church in Angola is in no way a free Church in the sense of the Gospel."

In October, 1967, the police forbade publication of a short work by Father A. F. Santos Neves, entitled "The Presence of the Church in Angola Today." In it the author discussed democracy, development, peace, dialogue, active nonviolence, the social doctrine of the Church, ecumenism, noncolonialist missionary attitudes, the dignity of the human person, anthropology, and sociology—highly subversive subjects indeed. In September, 1969, a brief report from an Angolan Catholic stated:

Education is geared to the preservation of the status quo. It is totally alienating. The fundamental values of the African population are rejected in the present situation. Anyone who stands up for them is accused of being a communist. In order to avoid possible ideological conflicts, the teaching at the university of Angola is purely technical. Anyone who wants to study the humanities has to go to Lisbon. It is impossible to have scholarships for study abroad.

The report then goes on to detail the birth of OSPIDA (Secret Organization for the Defense of Portuguese Interests in Angola), a movement similar to the OAS in Algeria and France during the late 1950s. It concludes: "How is the Church going to behave during the terrible crisis that is building up?"

Paul VI's pilgrimage to Fatima. Another element which must be mentioned is the pope's visit to Fatima in 1968. The Vatican has steadfastly refused to consider objectively its political implications, which are considerable. The pope's decision to go to India for the Bombay Eucharistic Congress shortly after Goa had been reassimilated into India raised a storm of indignation in Portugal, and the press consistently ignored his visit. When he went to Fatima, therefore, albeit for purely religious reasons, his visit was taken to be a gesture of reconciliation. The astonishing thing is that Paul VI failed to say one single word about a people's right to freedom— although he was in a country living under a dictatorship—and contented himself with deploring conditions in countries where "religious freedom has been practically suppressed," and condemning those "who entertain plans for revolution and subversion."[78] Portuguese Catholics of the opposition were astounded to hear the pope talking "like a Portuguese bishop," and praising the work of Portugal in Africa. The cruellest blow, however, was his willingness to confer decorations on one of the heads of the political police[79] and on one of the principal military authorities.

Here and there, however, when the pope's intended visit to Portugal had first been announced, groups of Christians had expressed their concern. A group of students and professors of Louvain University, for instance, wrote an open letter to the pope, in which they posed the question of the meaning that might be read into his visit with respect to the situation inside Portugal and its commitment in Africa. The Belgian primate, Cardinal Suenens, called the letter "impertinent and cavalier."

Judging from the reactions of some members of Portuguese Catholic Action groups, the pope's pilgrimage was a sad event for those concerned with renewal and social justice. One must not forget that Fatima is a symbol, in Portugal even more than in other countries, of both religious and social "integrism." The help of Our Lady of Fatima is invoked for the armed forces defending Christian civilization in Africa. Some time before the pope's visit a group of Portuguese Catholic women had subscribed to the cost of distributing medals of Our Lady of Fatima by plane over the rebel zones of Angola. And after Paul's visit one of the major daily papers of Lisbon carried the headline: "A great victory." No doubt the hundreds of thousands of pilgrims to Fatima did not perceive all this clearly, but many others did.

The attitude of the churches. If, however, there is a gulf between the Roman Catholic hierarchy and the laity, that which divides the different Christian confessions is no less profound. As we have already seen, Protestant missionaries in the colonies are regarded with deep distrust, and blamed for "not educating the natives according to the policy of integration."[80]

The churches in the rest of the world are virtually unable to obtain information about the Portuguese colonies. An attempt to collate public statements of the various Christian communities in reaction to the question yields only a very meager harvest. We can quote only two isolated items: The Council for Christian Social Action of the United Church of Christ (U.S.A.) endorsed the "legitimate claims of the liberation movements in Angola, Mozambique and Portuguese Guinea."[81] Cardinal Alfrink, international present of Pax Christi, speaking at a meeting of that movement in Louvain in April, 1969, stressed the urgent need for a critical analysis of the "unknown question" of the Portuguese colonies.[82] Bound to the terms of the Concordat, the official Church in Portugal, as we have seen, cannot raise its voice. Bishop Gomez of Porto, who had the audacity to claim the right for the Church to teach its social doctrine freely, paid for it by being exiled, and was allowed to return to Portugal only after the political eclipse of Dr. Salazar.

In December, 1961, at the beginning of the revolution and just after the Indians had taken over Goa, Portuguese soldiers declared that they would not allow themselves to be killed to the last man as Salazar had advocated. Thereupon the Portuguese hierarchy published a very revealing statement in which they deplored the fact that "so much of the country's youth was so lacking in heroic ambition. We would like to see it always singing, eyes alight, a pure, strong and joyous youth in the service of the great ideals for which it is good to die, in the vanguard of Portugal which is awakening to its mission to renew Christian civilization by spreading it and bringing it to flower overseas."[83]

The African Bishops' Conference at Kampala and Pope Paul VI's Visit

At the end of July, 1969, the first Pan-African conference of the Catholic hierarchy was held in Kampala, Uganda, preceding a visit to that country by Pope Paul VI. Each local church in Africa had delegated one or two bishops, except the churches of Angola, Mozambique, and Guinea-Bissau. One bishop from Mozambique had, in fact, announced his intention of participating, but had desisted upon the discrete insistence of the Holy See, which had been warned by the FRELIMO that it would organize protest demonstrations if the Uganda government did not revoke its decision to accord the bishop a visa.

When the other bishops arrived in Kampala, they were greeted by an open letter from the leaders of the liberation movements of Portuguese Africa: FRELIMO, MPLA, and PAIGC. Sent from Dar es Salaam on July 5, the letter began with a description of the situation in the Portuguese territories.[84] It then went on to say:

> To carry out these wars Portugal invokes the reason of the defense of the West and of Christian civilization. Cardinal Gonzalvez Cerejeira himself, head of the Roman Catholic Church in Portugal, declared in Lisbon in 1967 that the Peace Day proclaimed by Paul VI in the encyclical *Populorum Progressio*[85] should not be interpreted in any way as an invitation to pacifism in Africa, for that would mean an abject abdication of Portugal's sacred duties.... The war that Portugal is waging in our three countries, therefore, can count on the explicit support of the Roman Catholic Church in Portugal. Collective massacres, assassination, deportations, the imprisonment and torture of thousands upon thousands of men, women and children, constant air attacks, napalm bombs, crops burned and poisoned—all these crimes carried out day after day

in our countries and against our people, are carried out with the blessing of the Roman Catholic Church in Portugal.

Repressive measures even extend to the African priests who share the daily suffering of the people. We, the people of the Portuguese colonies, can understand that these crimes are in outright contradiction to the principles of Christian morality as taught by the Roman Catholic Church. The truth is that many Christian voices have already been raised in protest against the barbaric colonial war which the Portuguese government is waging. In Portugal itself, Portuguese Catholics, openly opposing the Catholic hierarchy, have conducted various forms of demonstrations against the colonial war.

But it is no less true that we cannot dissociate Rome from the Catholic Church in Portugal if Rome itself does not do so. That is why we are addressing ourselves to Your Most Reverend Excellencies. It is our sincere conviction that the Church, especially in Africa, bears a large part of the heavy burden of responsibility for the defense of justice and of the dignity of the peoples of Africa.

To this effect, we, the Liberation Front of Mozambique, the Popular Liberation Movement of Angola and the African Party for the Independence of Guinea and Cape Verde, in the name of the people of Mozambique, Angola and Guinea-Cape Verde, and, in particular, in the name of hundreds of thousands of Catholics in our countries, appeal to Your Most Reverend Excellencies to intercede, in the name of the Roman Catholic Church in Africa, with His Holiness Pope Paul VI when for the first time he sets foot on our continent, to take a clear and open stand in condemnation of Portuguese colonialism and to contribute to bringing about at last a negotiated solution to the conflict between the Portuguese government and the peoples of our countries, on the basis of a solemn recognition by Portugal of our people's legitimate right to self-determination and national independence.

There is no doubt that the future attitude of our people with regard to the Roman Catholic Church will depend in a large measure on the stand that the Church takes today in relation to the fundamental problem with which our people are faced: the problem of regaining our dignity and our sovereignty as African people.

We are convinced that Your Excellencies, conscious of the magnitude of the role you can play, will contribute to the realization of the profound aspirations of our people for liberty, justice and human dignity.

Shortly before the bishops' conference in May, 1969, two movements, the MPLA of Angola and the FRELIMO of Mozambique, had asked the Vatican to inform the Portuguese government of their willingness to abandon the armed struggle, given certain conditions: that a time-limit be negotiated within which both countries would achieve independence; that equal civil rights be granted to anyone who wished to be a citizen of either of the two countries, regardless of his race; and that normal relations be established with Portugal after independence. Apparently this approach received no reply.

On August 1, 1969, the day after his arrival in Uganda for the ceremonies in honor of the Ugandan martyrs, the pope addressed the parliament at Kampala and spoke of Africa. The principal topics of his address were colonialism and racial conflict, which he considered to be the two major problems in Africa today.

> In Our opinion these problems can be considered from a two-fold point of view: one being the freedom of national territories, the other being the equality of the races. What we mean now by that word of many meanings, "freedom," is civil independence, political self-determination, emancipation from the domination of other powers foreign to the African population.
>
> This is an event which dominates world history, and which our predecessor, Pope John XXIII, defined as a sign of the times (*Pacem in Terris,* # #40-41). In other words it is a fact arising from the great awareness men have acquired of their own dignity, both as individuals and as a community of people.
>
> It is a fact which reveals the irreversible flow of history, corresponding, no doubt, to a providential plan pointing out the right direction to all those invested with responsibility, above all in the political sphere.

This was a clear and unmistakable affirmation of the African people's right to autonomy with respect to the colonial powers. There is no question that this applies directly to Portugal. In a previous passage of his speech, Paul VI, referring to the Church's attitude to Africa, had already declared: "Neither colonialism nor neocolonialism is its theme, but aid and impulse to the African people that they may be able to express in their proper genius and by their own strength, those political, social, economic and cultural structures which are proportionate to their needs and coordinated with international society and modern civilization."

Later on, however, Paul VI spoke more specifically to some points in transparent reference to the Portuguese colonies, since they are the only territories still under European domination. The first question was that of violence: "We believe that today conflicts between peoples can be resolved by a better and more effective way than that of violence." He had already forcefully asserted the principle that "the Church, by her very nature, by her evangelical principle of nonviolence, cannot adopt this inhuman language."

An analysis of the Portuguese colonies, however, demonstrates clearly that the origin of violence is Portugal's refusal to allow any evolution toward independence, and its policy of integration into the Portuguese national territory of the "African provinces." As the leaders of a certain number of revolutionary movements have very aptly pointed out, it is not they who chose the path of violence.

The second point on which the pope dwelt more specifically concerned the timing of accession to independence:

> Nevertheless, in certain concrete situations, the best method of attaining it will be the method—perhaps a little slower, but surer—of first preparing men and institutions capable of true, sturdy self-government; and we want to believe that such preparation will not only not be impeded, but will be fostered by the responsible authorities with due order and in collaboration with those concerned, during a period of symbiosis between the native populations and those of foreign origin, in such a way that cultural, civil and economic structures may be fashioned, capable of making preparation at every level of society for responsibility and for the sense of the common good, in view of accession to a true sovereignty and to avoid falling, on the other hand, into the snares of other insidious enslavements.

Here again this can apply only to Portuguese Africa. But what does this theoretically reasonable attitude amount to when it is analyzed in the context of the factual situation? It is simply Portugal's own thesis: "We must remain, for the population has to be prepared gradually for autonomy, otherwise there is great danger of their falling into communist clutches. Through *fraternidade* we are accomplishing the gradual symbiosis between the black and white populations. The day will come when, under the guidance of 'those in charge,' greater autonomy will be possible." And so the pope's words contain all the elements necessary to satisfy the official Portuguese thesis, and allow it to go on as before, even if that was not the pope's intention.

This seems, at any rate, to be the interpretation put on it by President Caetano, who on April 8, 1970, declared: "Self-determination is not effected by giving some little squares of paper to uneducated tribes. It is effected by peaceful relations under the Portuguese flag, within a union in which the different races can come together in brotherhood.... In southern Africa the future must be the work of blacks and whites together. It is a crime against humanity to divide them and set them one against the other." Referring to the war going on in Africa, President Caetano added: "We are simply carrying out a police action in these territories in order to prevent the terrorists from indulging freely in their subversive activity."[86]

On the other hand, let us see how the situation stood in those territories in 1969. Three-fifths of Guinea had been liberated; vast territories in Angola and Mozambique were no longer under the effective control of the Portuguese government. Portugal was carrying out a policy of peopling the countries very rapidly with Portuguese emigrants in order to carry out its own kind of "symbiosis." The African leaders, including religious leaders, are exiled or imprisoned if they dare to claim what the pope affirms to be the right of all peoples. Economic exploitation is steadily increasing and the bonds with South Africa and Rhodesia make it impossible to have any illusions as to the sincerity of Portugal's political intentions. At the same time a colonial war is raging, a tragedy for the African people and excessively costly for the Portuguese people, who need all their resources to develop their own country.

The lack of a sociopolitical analysis of the event leads, therefore, to results which are exactly the opposite of those intended. Having stated clear and precise principles, the pope, without intending to do so, upheld the position of the oppressor exactly as he did in Bogotá, where his call for rapid social change was quite clear, but where all the strength of the principles was dissipated by his specific remarks about the pace of change and his appeals to the patience of the poor and the generosity of the rich. It seems that, on the level of social structures, this is the same error as that in the economic sphere, which consists in the purely theoretical view that the balance of monetary exchange, like water, finds its own levels—a theory which ignores the fact that the economic entities concerned are very unequally matched from the start. It has been said that nonviolence is a gift from the oppressed classes to their oppressors. It is certainly true that the Christian tradition encourages a nonviolent attitude. But when, in practice, the dominating powers use this language to maintain the status quo, then the affirmation of theoretical truth can very well lead to its opposite in practice.

Once again, having arrived at the end of this analysis, we are compelled to ask why it is that majority churches, which enjoy the political and economic support of the established power structures, always seem to legitimate the latter's policies. We have seen this in the case of the Dutch Reformed Church in South Africa and with Catholicism in Portuguese Africa, where Church and State collaborate in sacralizing the social and political order, thereby effectively reinforcing the role of the institutions. On the other hand, the minority Protestant churches in the Portuguese territories contribute to the struggle for emancipation.

Most of the leaders in the freedom movements mentioned in this chapter are, or have been, Christians. This is so today because all the African intellectuals have had at least some contact with the missionary educational institutions. It is a sorry commentary on the situation if the only memory they have is that of an institution bound to a tyrannical power.

We have mentioned the work of the World Council of Churches in the sphere of racial problems. But the silence of the official voice of the Roman Church raises a question: Is it trying to preserve its presence and its freedom of action to the detriment of its prophetic role? The pontifical Justice and Peace commission should surely be in a position to take some initiative in such an important area. But the problem is always the same: The lack of any sociopolitical analysis restricts the Catholic Church to ineffective and largely meaningless abstractions.[87]

The whole situation is all the more serious in that it has far-reaching international implications. The solidarity of the countries of southern Africa has established a very powerful economic and military complex which is gradually consolidating the exclusive and violent mastery of the white race within its own boundaries and new forms of imperialism which menace the other African countries. The solidarity of the NATO countries with Portugal contributes to continuing the colonial war and maintaining "white power" in southern Africa. The Third World War has begun here as well.

It remains to be seen whether recent developments in the Vatican attitude should lead us to modify or to confirm our present judgment. On July 1, 1970, Pope Paul gave an audience to three leaders of nationalist movements from the Portuguese territories in

Africa meeting in Rome. It must be remembered that John XXIII had refused to receive a delegation of the freedom movements of Angola in 1962 and that Paul VI himself had refused to see priests from the Portuguese territories while he was in Africa. His present position, therefore, is in stark contrast to the attitude he had adopted previously.[88] It is true that *Osservatore Romano* spoke of the "rebels" who had been received by the pope, and that Vatican sources were careful to point out that "the interview was not a political gesture." The fact remains that this sort of moral support, even when it comes so late, can have considerable repercussions on public opinion and—as on previous occasions, but in the opposite way—can go far beyond what the pope intended. Will public opinion now begin to take notice of the war of liberation that is raging in Africa? In spite of the silence of the Portuguese press, those in Portugal who oppose the colonial war have been greatly encouraged by the event, and government propaganda attempting to show it as a defense of Christian civilization has lost a great deal of its credibility. The fact, also, that the Portuguese government recalled their ambassador to the Holy See is some measure of the political importance of the pope's gesture.

CHAPTER EIGHT

The Events of May, 1968, in France

Were the events of May, 1968, in France the first symptoms of a new type of social conflict peculiar to "postindustrial" society?

These "events," as everyone in France now euphemistically calls them, provoked a flood of literature and a flurry of hypotheses in which the quarrels of different schools of thought were given a free rein. It would be presumptuous to attempt yet another interpretation here. Only the future of the social movement of May will reveal where it sprang from, but an analysis at this point can at least help to highlight the new tendencies, relate them to the whole, and in this particular case clarify the reasons for the ebb tide that ensued.

Analysis of the Events

General characteristics. Like all the other countries of Europe, France is in the first stages of a type of development which is characterized by an increasing rationalization of the economic function and a noticeable improvement in the standard of living, but which has led to disruptions and dislocations between the different sectors of the economy. These, in turn, lead to a structural crisis, then to a conflict in value systems, and finally to a cultural crisis. The eruption of May, 1968, was born of the conjunction between French society's lack of adaptation to its production methods and the sudden emergence of a new kind of social movement.

Different analyses of modern society define their object in very different terms, according to whether they take a functional or a structural point of view: "industrial" or "postindustrial";[1] "technical" or "productivist"; "affluent" or "society of leisure," or again "repressive" or "terrorist."[2] Following John Kenneth Galbraith's

265

analyses,[3] I would like to outline the basic characteristics which technological development confers on society.[4]

Technological growth, deliberately pursued, leads to the economy being founded on the vitality of a limited number of large firms. As production cycles become longer and more complex, they require more and more stable, noncirculating capital and greater technical skills. This leads to the increasing specialization of workers. Work becomes more fragmented, requiring complicated coordination, and the workers have to adjust themselves to the production system more and more frequently.

This complicated machinery leads to longer delays between the decision to produce something and the time when it is finally put on the market. The decision to start production, therefore, requires a tremendous fund of foresight and information, and is entrusted to smaller and smaller teams of experts, which Galbraith calls the "technostructure." The guiding principle of this type of management is efficiency. Since the complexity of the instrument makes the undertaking so hazardous, it is essential to have complete mastery of the market. And so the technostructures do not limit their operations to the purely internal technical domain of a given industry; in order to control the market they also develop a powerful apparatus of persuasion to promote sales.

From studying consumer needs it is a short step to influencing those needs which, since they have been artificially stimulated, also have to be maintained at a level slightly above that of the purchasing power of the individual consumers. The prosperity of the workers, therefore, is inextricably bound up with the general prosperity of society. They are encouraged to identify with the needs created for them and with the economic goals set for them, in other words, with the "imperatives of growth." At the same time their skills and their relative security weaken both their ambition to set their own objectives and their identification with the goals set by their unions—at least it seems that one can logically presume this to be so.

Finally industry seeks support from the state, welcoming its intervention in maintaining fiscal balance, product orders, capital investments, and regulation of salaries and prices. It is also expected to keep unemployment within socially acceptable limits. The state, on the other hand, finding itself faced with increasingly complex technical problems, is inclined to leave more and more initiative to its partners in private industry, in such a way that there is a growing conjunction between government decisions and the goals of large sectors of industry which is constantly being reinforced.

One might get the impression that the economy is becoming socialized with state intervention apparently guaranteeing the concurrence of the collectivity in the decisions that are made. But the appearances are deceptive: Everything is geared to assimilating individuals, ideologies, and politics into the "industrial system." It can legitimately be called a "postindustrial society," for the strong man of the system is no longer the wealthy capitalist; self-financing increasingly provides the principal wealth of industrial firms. Authority has slipped from the hands of the capitalist into those of the manager, the technocrat, whose goals are no longer accumulation of wealth and maximum profit, but growth.

As the system develops, it "produces," as it were, a whole series of "dropouts": small producers (farmers, craftsmen) and all those who have insufficient training to integrate. The only needs stimulated are those which industrial production can fill; many others are completely neglected: housing, for instance, and leisure and cultural activities, both of which have become marginalized luxury goods for the spectator or "esthetic consumer."

The inherent contradictions of the system can be seen in the area of education and culture. The technostructure, of course, tends to make education the source of its knowledge and power, a profitable producer of technical know-how. But in the first phase of the system (and that is the phase we are in now; no one can predict what the second phase will be), the ingrained bourgeois habits of the educational system contribute paradoxically to its defense against the inroads of technocracy. University teaching is failing to adapt and is suffering from hardening of the arteries.[5] The industrial system, therefore, finds itself thwarted by the very people who should be its key elements[6] and who are best equipped to perceive and implement the instrinsic logic of the system. In addition, these people are alienated because the system has transformed their form of work, which should be the backbone of production, into a marketable factor of productivity to be bartered in exchange for consumer goods. This is the political role of scientists and technicians.

Thanks to this brief analysis, we are now in a position to understand the social movements peculiar to this new industrial society, which is that of most of Europe and of France in particular today.

The notion of technocracy, however, is an inadequate expression of the uneasiness, the menace that hovers over society because of the technostructure. Technocracy is not a doctrine according to which power belongs to the technicians. In the present stage of development in France one cannot say that the university has become completely "technocratic" or that political power has totally given way to economic power. Galbraith's analysis applies more, for the time being, to trends than to facts. The social and cultural consequences of this phase of development have made themselves sufficiently felt, however, to have given rise to a new social movement. One cultural result of technological development is already visible: The "utility value" of things is tending to become more widely differentiated from what could be termed their "development value."[7] In other words, we can already see the effects of a nascent technocratic system, which reduces the notion of development to its dimensions of growth and productivity. Social life has been invaded by the organization of profit; spare time is sold as working time in exchange for the possibility of "consuming."

The aim of the new social movements is to unmask the consumer society, to show that, concealed behind the ideology of progress, the relationship between the rulers and the ruled, the profiteers and the consumers, is as it has always been. In dismantling the integrating power of the vast cartels and institutions, they are expressing the revolt of those who are determined to effect change and not merely to submit to it.

The conflict which erupted in France in May, 1968, brought "those who confuse social progress and their own private power" face-to-face with their adversaries who "demand, through the defense of their own interest, a democratic control of social and economic change."[8] It broke out in all the different sectors of French society because the transformation that is going on in all sectors is governed by the same imperatives. The stakes in the social conflict today are no longer limited to industry or the owner- ship of the means of production; they also include the university, urban life, leisure, and culture.

And so the conflict is cultural, social, political, all at the same time, and it is extremely difficult to put a label on it, to determine the one cause, the one objective it is pursuing. As Alain Touraine writes,

> The May Movement cannot be reduced to a formula. Analysis has nothing to gain from talk about an uprising of youth or a malaise of the consumer society. The more vigorous image of a revolutionary movement would be preferable to vague expression of that kind. In a society in which the system of production no longer embraces only one sector of social life but includes everything ... this movement is an attack against the power system which is not only the control exercised by capitalist profits, but which controls increasingly all fields of activity. All sectors of human activity give rise to new forms of resistance in response to new forms of domination. People no longer resist in the name of labor rights; they now resist in the name of culture and the human person.[9]

The May Movement has forged a new political struggle by restoring meaning to a struggle for goals and values, whereas technocracy had reduced it to a debate about the means.[10]

The May Movement has also forged a new class struggle in the form of a challenge to the technocracy of "professionals."[11] The traditional proletariat has become too marginalized to be capable of offering any resistance to the new forms of domination, but those who now have a role in society equivalent to that of the nineteenth-century skilled workers are in a position to resist. Their technical skills give them a central role in the process of produc- tion (whether of things or of knowledge), but they are excluded from decision making. This is the new revolutionary "class"[12] and it includes technicians, research workers, highly skilled workers in key industries, teachers, and students. This is the class that launched the movement and succeeded to a certain degree in remaining in control and in radicalizing it, whereas the workers in the classic branches of industry wanted, for the most part, nothing more than to reproduce the 1936 movement and force management to concede the kind of advantages that are best won with a show of force.

The new revolutionary class does not belong to the traditional labor or political organizations, which are too strongly reminiscent of the old industrial society which gave them birth. It does not play the part of an "intelligentsia," but acts as a group with its own identity and its own interests. The real originality of the movement is that it succeeded in giving a new language and a new objective to the revolutionary forces latent among the younger generation of the worker movement. It remains to be seen why this revolutionary movement developed without effecting a revolution.

We must now look at some of the salient features of French society which could account for the sudden appearance of the movement. As we have already mentioned, the marks of the new industrial state were not all to be found in France in 1968. The universities are not characterized by technocracy so much as by the conflict between the need to modernize and their conservative social models.

This dilemma is characteristic of the majority of French institutions. "The models and forms of education in both schools and families are, like the relationship to authority in business and the administration, very archaic. Their function is to safeguard traditions and principles rather than to prepare and allow for change."[13] Production methods have been modernized, and this has upset patterns of consumption and the relation between work and the standard of living, but existing sociocultural models remain an obstacle to a change of structures.

The major topics of discussion in postwar France were not the traditional rifts in society, but the international role of the country in the context of decolonization and the Cold War. Political life tended to be reduced to the merry-go-round of elder statesmen in a rapid succession of governments and ministries. The emergence of great masses of young people in a society in which education and socialization are completely out of date has—as the demographer, Albert Sauvy, predicted ten years ago—given a new lease on life to the basic conflicts.

The mass of young people, attracted to higher studies in a technical and "meritocratic" society, came up against old, inflexible institutions and found themselves helplessly mired in society instead of actively participating in it.[14] They had entered a new world which they could understand but which they could not control. If I may risk a too mechanical comparison, French institutions of socialization are like a pipeline that is being forced to carry ten times the flow for which it was built. This is why the May Movement erupted so violently.

But there were other bottlenecks which contributed to making the events so explosive, and one of these was the Gaullist style of government. It has sometimes too hastily been said that de Gaulle's government cared more for France than for the French. A more penetrating analysis would perhaps show that it was at the service of a ruling class which is highly competent and efficient and which has a tremendous capacity for foresight. Another roadblock was the authoritarian and archaic mentality of management, a victim in its own way of the imperatives of technology and often quite out of touch with new conditions. Finally, there was the administration, competent—at least in the upper echelons—but immersed in its own ritualism, and authoritarian in its methods, directed by men of superior intelligence but who are very conformist.

And so, in the one sector that was the least institutionalized and organized, a center of antipolitical opposition grew up, torn between the desire to modernize and the utopian dream of a new society. It was the resistance of the state and institutions which led to this opposition breaking out in the form of a movement. But, as we shall attempt to explain, the movement disintegrated into groups of reformists and became a parody of revolution because of its inability to administer change.

A chronological account of the events. In May, 1968, there were three leading protagonists on the scene. The first was the "movement" launched by the students of Nanterre,[15] which spread to the majority of university students, then to secondary schools, and, after May 13, was taken up by the young workers and a great number of adult workers. This movement was carried forward under its initial impetus until May 27, the day on which the strikes and the political impact of the conflict were at their height. But the political and labor organizations withdrew their support progressively, and May 27 is also the day on which the Communist party and the General Confederation of Labor (CGT) broke off completely. However, the National Union of Higher Education (SNES) and the French Democratic Confederation of Labor (CFDT) gave their support to the movement almost all the way through. The only political party which actually endorsed the platform of the student movement was the United Socialist Party (PSU).

The second protagonist on the scene was the French Communist party and the CGT, which were initially taken by surprise by the movement. They very soon recovered their balance, however, and did their best to gain control of it. They "politicized" its claims, and after the workers had refused the first proposed agreement between management and the government, they attempted to steer it toward a "people's government." But within forty-eight hours they abandoned this tactic and agreed to the elections proposed by de Gaulle on May 30.

The final protagonist was the government. In the absence of the prime minister, Georges Pompidou, who was out of the country, everybody seemed to lose their heads and pulled themselves together only when he returned to Paris. General de Gaulle, gravely miscalculating the strength of the phenomenon, believed he could control it by announcing a referendum. But a renewed call to the strikers, the confusion that reigned in the majority party, and the panic in the Cabinet made it seem possible that the government would be toppled. Internal divisions in the movement, however, and the attitude of the Communist party gave the government the time it needed to pull itself together after de Gaulle's speech of May 30.

To these three principal protagonists we should also add the mass of "honest folk" who, in their mounting fear, gave de Gaulle the support he needed to regain control of the situation. Although the Communist party had also given very considerable support to the government, the latter managed to mobilize the "party of fear" against the spector of "totalitarian communism."

Some key dates[16]

November, 1967. Strike at the University Faculty at Nanterre, organized to protest the educational reform bill (known as the Fouchet reform). The form and the violence of this protest indicated a state of crisis disproportionate to the declared objectives. An arbitration committee was formed in the Department of Sociology.

March 22, 1968. One hundred and forty-two students occupied the administration building at Nanterre. The Movement of March 22 was formed, led by Daniel Cohn-Bendit. It combined three political themes: rejection of the university institution; protest against the war in Vietnam (which reveals the true nature of society); and a call to student solidarity.

April 22. The Faculty Council at Nanterre adopted, by a large majority, a proposal of strong measures to maintain order.

April 30. Legal proceedings were initiated against Daniel Cohn-Bendit.

May 1. Students and CGT security forces clashed during a worker demonstration.

May 2. Nanterre Faculty was closed and eight students received notice to appear before a disciplinary committee.

May 3. Student organizations held a meeting in the courtyard of the Sorbonne in Paris. The vice-chancellor called in the police to evacuate the university, and contrary to their promise, the police arrested the students. When their friends tried to set them free, the police reacted with brutality. The minister of education decided that the Sorbonne should be closed. The UNEF and the SNES called a strike.

May 4 and 5. A large contingent of police surrounded the Sorbonne. The May 3 demonstrators were tried and sentenced by a court specially convened on Sunday as an emergency measure.

May 6. The eight students appeared before a disciplinary committee. The UNEF and the SNES called for demonstrations, which culminated in violent clashes with the police. General de Gaulle appealed to the population to maintain order. Strikes began in some of the public secondary schools.

May 7. The UNEF organized a mass demonstration in the form of a march from the Latin Quarter to the Arc de Triomphe. In the late evening there were more violent clashes.

May 8. The Communist party, which had been hostile to the students up to then, became more conciliatory. The minister of education announced measures that would make the system more flexible. Student demonstrations took place in the major cities of the West.

May 9 and 10. Unrest was still on the increase with the formation of spontaneous groups. Strikes and the marches were being organized in the provinces. The minister, after promising to reopen the Sorbonne, went back on his word and the students occupied the Nanterre Faculty. On the evening of the tenth, after a demonstration, the police raised barricades confining the demonstrators to the Latin Quarter.

Negotiations began between the students and the professors and the vice-chancellor of the university. The students demanded the liberation of those who had been convicted on May 4, and the reopening of the faculties as well as the withdrawal of the police. When the authorities refused, they broke off negotiations.

May 11. At 2:15 A.M. the chief of police received orders to tear down the barricades and the whole Latin Quarter became the scene of violent police repression with the use of tear gas. Prime Minister Pompidou, returning from an official visit abroad, announced that measures would be taken to satisfy the students' demands. The latter, however, maintained their strike order.

May 12. Labor unions announced a general strike and a demonstration for the following day.

May 13. Strikes and demonstrations took place all over France. In Paris about 800,000 students and workers demonstrated together. But after the demonstration, when the students wanted to continue a joint action, the unions refused. That evening the Sorbonne, which had been evacuated by the police, was reoccupied by the students. An atmosphere of festivity reigned and discussions went on in small groups all night long.

May 14. The Sud-Aviation factory at Toulouse was occupied, and the Renault workers at Cléon followed suit. More and more university faculties were occupied and discussions began about the problem of examinations. The Communist party warned its members against "adventurism."

May 16. The Sorbonne was still in a state of ferment. Growing numbers of workers came for discussions with the students. A delegation of students went to the Renault factory at Boulogne, but the CGT, which had taken control of the occupation movement, prevented all contact with the workers. The government announced that it would "do its duty."

May 17. Occupations of factories spread, both in Paris and in the provinces. The CFDT declared its support of the student movement, whereas the CGT reiterated its own demands and refused to concur in a general strike. Journalists at the ORTF (government-sponsored radio and television network) moved tentatively in the direction of emancipation from the government. The Communist party called on all leftist groups to unite to elaborate a platform for government.

May 18. While the official organ of the Communist party, *Humanité,* published an attack on the student movement, the CFDT came out in favor of union control in industry and assured the student movement of its support.

May 19. General de Gaulle condemned the disorders in no uncertain terms and Pierre Mendès-France published a declaration criticizing the attitude of the government over the past ten years. The following day de Gaulle announced a referendum to decide the question of "participation." The UNEF and the CFDT held a joint press conference.

May 21. Public schools came out on strike. The divergencies between the demands of the CGT and the CFDT became more and more apparent.

May 23. The political crisis appeared to be more acute than ever after a motion to censure the government was defeated by only eleven votes. Skirmishes took place in the Latin Quarter in spite of the declared policy of the student organizations against further violence. The next day General de Gaulle outlined the main points of his plan for "participation." The reception it received was frankly unfavorable.

May 25. Negotiations began between the unions, management, and the government. On May 27 an agreement was reached which provided for substantial salary increases and more voice to the unions in running the factories. Most workers, however, stayed out on strike.

May 28. François Mitterand acted as spokesman for the non-Communist parties of the left in proposing a transitional government under Pierre Mendès-France. The Communist party was reticent about this and talked of a "people's government." The sole representative of the Gaullist government was now the prime minister, who was in constant touch with the unions. The same day General de Gaulle cancelled a cabinet meeting and disappeared for several hours. It was later learned that he had been in touch with the heads of the armed forces. Mendès-France declared himself ready to take over the responsibilities of government, but the Communists still held back.

May 30. After a day in which uncertainty was at a paroxysm, de Gaulle gave a speech in which he took the offensive, denouncing subversion by "totalitarian communism." He dissolved parliament and postponed the promised referendum. More than 500,000 people acclaimed him in the streets of Paris.

The following day revealed the Left's inability to parry the attack. New negotiations began, and very shortly the factories began functioning again. The student movement had finally been isolated and was soon to be divided in itself. The political parties set about preparing for the elections and the unions declared themselves satisfied with what they had obtained.

On June 6, *Humanité* heralded a "victorious return to work in unity!" The government began a discreet program of repression, which affected, among others, the journalists of the ORTF, 150 foreigners who were compelled to leave the country, and eleven revolutionary movements which were disbanded. On June 16, the police reoccupied the Sorbonne, and on June 30 the runoff elections for the legislature gave Gaullism a resounding victory.

The meaning of an insurrection. We must now attempt to formulate an opinion about the whole movement, the reasons for its failure, and its future prospects.

Every political plan is made up of knowledge and action. Politics, according to Hegel, "is the science of the will." To formulate a project for society and put it into effect is, indeed, to choose. And to choose presupposes knowledge of what is possible. To choose also presupposes will: the will to do one thing rather than another, to decide upon one objective rather than another.

The distinction between the two elements is the fruit of abstraction, but each element calls on a completely different level of intelligence. In giving the primacy to knowledge one can fall into the pseudo-rationalizations of technocracy and, in fact, serve unacknowledged values. If, on the other hand, one gives the primacy to the will, one can fall into the kind of dogmatism which chooses to ignore the fact that the content of values always stands in relation to a condition of human knowledge. These basic theoretical considerations can guide us in analyzing the May Movement.

To begin with an example: The students who occupied the Sorbonne were acting on two entirely different levels. One was dramatic, festive, spontaneous, and poetic—at times even delirious. The other had a "reformist" air to it, with the constitution of committees and earnest discussion of university reform. The first aspect, which is a language form, served to give concrete expression to the opposition to the system by its "crisis behavior." It was the first breakthrough which set the rest of society in motion. It was the acting out of an inner frustration and an "exemplary" action in that it opened people's eyes to the possibility of change. The second language form profited from the breakthrough operated by the first and surged into the breach with new values.

The antisociety created by the first mode can be credited with bringing out into the open social conflicts that had been glossed over by the status quo. But there is always a danger of stagnating, of provoking a backlash, and of creating new alienations if this type of action is not subject to criticism and if it is not channelled into concrete campaigns.

The elaboration of reforms, on the other hand, is always in danger of drifting into "reformism" if it does not maintain a vivid awareness of the revolutionary goal of the movement. Thus the workers' strikes in May led to the recognition of the union's part in industry and other reforms, which are significant only if they are seen within the revolutionary goal of eliminating the old forms of authority and decision making.

Similarly, it was easier for the students to restrict their movement to the university and, as it were, to shut themselves up in it in order to elaborate and obtain reforms which would not have been repugnant to the technocrats, adversaries of the old liberal universities.[17] But if the whole system of men's training in society and the whole system of production of knowledge is to be called into question, then another dimension is necessary.

These examples help us to formulate some questions about the May Movement: Was its revolutionary "knowledge" adequate to the situation of society? Was its "will" sufficiently vital to keep the changes on the path of revolution? And, finally, was its will sufficiently controlled and enlightened by its knowledge to avoid the pitfall of millenarianism?

We must first note one positive result: The repressive measures used by the police against the students served to catalyze the movement. It was a clear demonstration of the repressiveness of society—so clear, in fact, that those who were still wavering were drawn to the movement and the workers came out on strike two days later. The movement thus overflowed the boundaries of the university and began to move toward wider goals. Public opinion was aroused and this was indispensable to consolidate a movement which, since May 22, no longer thought of itself as a university reform, but as a challenge to the whole of society.

At that moment the movement benefited from a combination of important conditions. The students had been mobilized and were ready to take the step that would lead from an awareness of a state of crisis to the will to transform the social structuration of learning. The workers were in occupation of the factories with the new watchword of self-management. They had gone on strike at a time when there was no serious economic crisis in France. They had taken up arms not just to improve their existence, but to change it.

"A social force has been born . . . a social movement, that is, a group defending its own interests against an adversary and threatening to compromise the orientation of society... finding a response even in places other than where the action began."[18] The shock wave reached out not only to groups but to institutions; the negation of the social system was alive and beginning to be articulated.[19]

But the revolutionary trajectory faltered and declined for lack of a thorough rationalization. Several factors contributed to this. Although the movement had designated its objective and adversary as the Gaullist state, and although at one period this political dimension of its action served to liberate it from the confines of its reformist demands, the resistance offered by the state in the person of the prime minister, and later of the head of state, provoked a kind of backlash which revealed the lack of any coherent plan. The slogan "imagination is in power" does not, unfortunately, mean that one is exercising anything but "imaginary" power.

The fact that the government pulled back in face of the students contributed to shutting them up in the university where "student power" reigned only on the walls. Those who had hesitated initially and then rallied to the revolution, fell back on reforms and the Commission of University and Secondary School Students was formed. In the meantime, within the walls of the Sorbonne, there was taking shape what one journalist called "the intoxicated boat" of a utopian antisociety.

When the government opened negotiations with the labor unions, it was seeking to keep the economic repercussions of the crisis to a minimum. It also contributed to dividing the social movement. In this it had the support of public opinion, which is never very fond of uncertainty and always prefers negotiation to upheaval. A study of the reactions of Christians gives some idea of the measure of this support. The unions, better prepared for this type of conflict than for the type which some of their lower-echelon militants were advocating, entered into the process of negotiations. It was at this point that a second split occurred in the movement; Some union officials negotiated for immediate demands, while others were seeking long-term changes in the social functioning of the factories.

This second division in the ranks was directly linked with the attitude of the Communist party, which had staked its all on a struggle against the political superstructures and a legal take-over based on a favorable balance of forces. The French Communist party was too deeply involved in the political control of the population to adapt itself to new social conflicts or even to conceive that they could exist.

Finally, the fact that there was no political movement capable of formulating both short-term and long-term policies and, above all, of assuming power, had serious consequences. But more serious still was the inability of the student movement to regulate its own internal problems of democracy. Of course the immediate circumstances—improvisation and uncertainty about government tactics—did not make this any easier. But unrealistic outbursts like "CRS = SS," or "de Gaulle = Fascist" show an infantile political judgment and shed some light on the reasons for their failure, even if they do not completely overshadow some exemplary actions and analyses along the lines of those by Daniel Cohn-Bendit and others.

At this point we must look at the other pole of the question. It is true that the creation of an antisociety contains its own revolutionary dynamism. Daniel Cohn-Bendit saw this clearly when he said,

> The important thing is not to carry out a reform of capitalist society, but to launch an experiment which is a complete break with that society, which will not last but will give a glimpse of what might be possible. Something can be glimpsed before the light flickers out. That is enough to prove that this something can exist.[20]

The lyricism that was splashed all over the walls of the Sorbonne still has its necessary utopian value.[21]

However, as Alain Touraine says,

> Not everything that has been repressed by society can be transformed into a movement for a new society. Revolutionary action is not the affirmation of an antisociety but a revelation of contradictions within society and, therefore, the separation within that society of the "progressive" from the reactionary. If social life were reduced to alienation, then the natural man could be set over against society, as the principle of pleasure is set over against the principle of reality. But in this case no transformation of society could be effected by man, for he would be imprisoned in a vision of society that might nourish despair or celebration, but certainly not political action. In the case of the student move-

ment, the expression of refusal and revolt regularly went beyond the revolutionary project. . . ."[22]

This facet of the May Movement was in danger of turning into a
"religion" through political sterility and irrationalism.[23] The utopian vision that was a necessary part of the movement remained a
prisoner of irrationalism. The movement was virtually transformed, therefore, into an object of esthetic consumption, and n
some ways, it even revived certain forms of terrorism and totalitarianism.

What conclusions can be drawn from this? The Revolution of
1789 was prepared by a century of intellectual and practical
change. The theoretical and practical work of Marxism has been
going on for more than a century. The May Movement, however,
was both scientifically and ideologically weak. One commentator
cynically wrote it off as a "psychosomatic pregnancy,"[24] but it is
perhaps nearer the mark to say that it achieved in France something that has already surfaced in other societies of the same type:
a first expression of the class struggle in a postindustrial society.

Its weaknesses, however, make it vulnerable to attack from two
directions. The first is the danger of a regressive trend toward the
millennialist heresy of total change. The second lies in the tactics
of the authorities, who will almost certainly attempt to isolate the
extremists and guarantee the stability of society by bureaucratic
protectionism with such measures as "participation." Such reforms
could well head off the Socialists and those of the social Christians
who have not already fallen into the slough of systematic contestation.

The most important question still remains: What was glimpsed
in the flickering light of the events? The May Movement destroyed
the illusion of a society at peace with itself through growth and
prosperity. It replaced the mirage of the common good and of
rationality with a reminder of the contradictions and clashes in
society. It reinvented class warfare.[25]

Finally, although the novelty of the situation could excuse certain errors, one lesson must be learned from the events: A political
struggle cannot be improvised. When one considers how long the
Vietnamese struggle has been going on, the slow maturation of the

revolutionary movements in Latin America, and the decade of existence of the fight for freedom in the Portuguese colonies, one can see, in spite of the obvious differences in the circumstances, that the dynamism of profound social change has its roots in lengthy historical development. If the abortive May Movement does its theoretical and practical homework, and if it manages to steer clear of the seductions of either joint management or revolt, then it may still have a future.

The Church in the Event

Like any other institution in society, the French Church experienced the May Movement as a surprise and, before long, as a shock. We must look not only at the Church's attitude in face of the events, and its judgment of them, but also at its position in the events, as part of the social system that was shaken.

In this section we shall attempt to define the Church's attitude when it found itself faced with the events. In another section we shall look at the problems which were so brutally brought out into the open in May, 1968, and how they tie in with recent history. For this we shall use two different methods. For the second aspect we shall take into account the history of the last thirty years: World War II and the postwar period, the evolution of the apostolate and of theological reflection, and Vatican II. For the Church's reaction and adaptation to the events which broke out so suddenly had their source in its recent history. In the light of that study we shall be in a better position to speak of the language and attitudinal problems which face the French Church in the dynamic of the society in which it lives.

First of all, however, in order to get a clear view of the questions that arise, we shall analyze the statements of Christians during the "events." The texts we shall be using were published by groups (both Catholic and Protestant) of laymen, priests, and bishops as well as by official movements.[26] Our reading of them will attempt to find the answer to four questions: (1) How did Christians analyze the event, its causes, its nature, and its implications? (2) What image or interpretation did they have of it, and what was their frame of reference? (3) What kind of partial or total solidarity did they develop with the groups involved in the movement? (4) How did they express the impact of the event on their own institutions, their faith, and their cultural system?

The perception of the events. Even before the events, in a climate already overcast with the malaise of the universities and social conflicts, a symposium organized by *Témoignage Chrétien* and *Christianisme Social* and similar movements, on March 24 and 25, 1968, deplored "the violent conditions which reign throughout the world because of the ascendancy of, and the exploitation practiced by, the capitalist system." The participants in the symposium emphasized that the impossibility of changing this system constituted "the objective conditions necessary for revolution."[27]

On May 7 the official publication of the Young Christian Students (YCS) analyzed the causes of university unrest. According to them, the "structure and content of higher education is ill-adapted, material conditions are inadequate, future employment is uncertain, the students are allowed no part in decision making."[28] On May 15, two YCS leaders, writing in a magazine published by the movement, expressed "serious misgivings about the success which is offered to us but which will be denied to millions of other young people." And they went on, "We have to call the whole system into question ... and reinvent structures of dialogue and participation."[29]

The next day the director of Men's Catholic Action (*Action Catholique Générale des Hommes*), a movement based on parish groups, pronounced their own diagnosis: "Frequently, technical and economic imperatives alone determine decisions and lead to contempt for the dignity of persons and the common good of society."[30] On May 17, the chaplains of the Student Mission and the University Catholic Action expressed their reluctance to give any conclusive analysis. They note that "the widespread demonstrations reveal a deep unrest" which demands a university reform but which must be seen in the overall context of a crisis of the regime and of civilization.[31]

On May 21 a text was drawn up by the Bishops' Commission of Schools and Universities. It saw the movement as the "refusal of a ready-made future in a society which enslaves men. . . . Present-day society has a tendency to reduce man to his function as a cog in the system whose aims are not of his choosing. He feels deeply mutilated in a society founded on the quest for profit."[31]

Bishop Frossard, auxiliary bishop of Paris, attempted an analysis of the social movement as a whole in a letter to priests dated May 22. He says: "Many students were stirred by a question about their future and their refusal to be trapped in a consumer society which does not correspond to their youthful aspirations. They saw that what matters is man and the meaning he gives to his own existence. This is the understanding which has made it possible for them to encounter the working world, for the latter has never ceased, for decades, to fight for man . . . a solidarity is taking shape between students and workers which goes far beyond mere tactics for concerted action."[32] This text already introduces an element of interpretation and one must admit that Bishop Frossard's sketch of the situation is a little too reassuring; the complexity and the novelty of the movement would have emerged more distinctly from a more objective analysis.

On the same day various leading Catholics and Protestants condemned "the latent violence in state institutions and, more deeply, in a society dominated by the spirit of power and of pleasure." In the budding revolution they see "a revolt of liberty against bureaucratic organization."[33] On May 24 one hundred priests of the Paris area declared that it was the "paternalistic conception of politics, economics and the university that is being called into question."[34] On May 28 the Liaison Committee for Informal Groups of Christians Involved in the Revolutionary Struggle adopted a "Marxist analysis of society" and gave it as their opinion that the "events taking place are signs of a period of revolution."[35]

On May 31 the ACI (*Action Catholique des Milieux Indépendants*) published a declaration in which they condemned the "consumption used by the forces of production for gain."[36] This declaration would seem utterly commonplace if one forgets that the ACI[37] was mandated by the hierarchy precisely for an apostolate among the owner-classes of society ranging from small business people to the very wealthy.

The two last texts are in close agreement: For the archbishop of Toulouse "the structures inherited from the past are no longer adapted to present-day needs. . . . It is flagrantly true that, instead of liberating men, techniques all too often crush them."[38] To this one might be tempted to retort that this was not what the demonstrators were saying. The members of the University Parish, on the other hand, believed that "we are at the beginning of a long overdue mutation. . . . Has a society which fails to foresee the future of its secondary and university students done its duty? . . . The students are painfully aware of the gulf between spiritual values and a society which can offer them only means in the place of a goal."[39]

All these statements call for some critical commentary. It is interesting to note that almost unanimously the main thesis of the analysis is the spiritual shortcomings of society; they all emphasize man's subjection to his function as producer and consumer. The Christians seem to be particularly aware of the crisis insofar as it affects the finality of industrial society. However, the analyses rarely go far enough to put their finger on the real causes of the prevailing unrest. A veritable challenging of the system is rare.[40] A "crisis of civilization" is blamed more often than the internal contradictions of the economic and social system.

With regard to a perception of the aims of the movement, at first sight there seem to be few divergences in the texts. For all, or almost all of them, the movement aims at giving everyone greater responsibility and more participation in his own particular social domain.

The magazine *Christianisme Social,* however, calls for a far-reaching "questioning of the social role and of the finality of the university and, hence, of the structure of contemporary society."[41] But the YCS was content to recognize the "justification of the demands of the students and other organizations: against selectivity. . . for real guidance. . . for job opportunities after school."[42]

Elsewhere it was stated that the goal of the working-class struggle was "the power of decision making in the factory and in the state, by methods which still have to be defined."[43] The ACO (Workers' Catholic Action), for its part, affirmed that the "working class is manifesting its need for respect. . . . It wants to have a share of responsibility."[44]

In Bishop Frossard's view, what is most needed is that all sides "accept participation. . . . Those responsible for the economic life" feel that it is the "one condition for greater efficiency and, even more, that respect for persons demands it."[45] For the bishop of Le Mans, on the other hand, it was evident that the demand was for "the possibility of growth through the exercise of responsibility."[46] On June 20 the Bishops' Permanent Council synthesized it as follows: "It is a grass-roots movement . . . a call to build a new society in which relations between human beings will be established in new ways; the Council already had the presentiment of the urgency of this task."[47]

One of the striking aspects about all these pronouncements is that they do not seem particularly concerned about clarifying the concepts they use or making them operative! It is also interesting to note the key words to which these witnesses seem to be particularly sensitive: responsibility and participation. The revolutionary significance of the movement is barely mentioned, and when it is, it is only in declarations by groups which have no official link with hierarchical structures.[48]

Movements such as the ACO and the ACI even believed that it was a bourgeois revolution, incapable of transforming the conditions of the working class. The latter movement declared: "The events clearly reveal a new dynamic among young people; they reveal especially, by a bare account of the facts, that the organized working world has refused to be drawn into a revolt in which it would not be a basic partner, with its own concrete claims."[49] And the ACO could not conceal its embarrassment and concern: "The students are challenging society in their own way. And although there are still very few sons of workers among them, these join hands with the struggle of the working class."[50]

In fact there was even an incident between student- and worker-chaplains which evidenced their divergent analyses of the events. On May 14 the student chaplains published a statement intended as a warning about the "gravity of what has just begun," and they spoke of a crisis of civilization and a "cultural revolution." Reflecting on the Church's attitude, they said: "A century ago the Church missed out on the Industrial Revolution, the moving force of which was the working class. . . . But a new revolution is beginning, and this time it is the student world that will be the moving force; today's new mission territory is this new world which bears the mark of the human sciences. . . ."[51] The chaplains of the young workers replied to this statement: "The hesitancy of the worker movement today is due to a historical experience of which it bore the brunt. In other words the working world runs the risk of being used as a tactical instrument in the maneuvering of a revolution whose fruits will, once again, fall to the bourgeoisie."[52]

Except in a few, rather more exhaustive studies, the element which seems to have captured the attention of most Christians is the explosive, conflictual nature of the events (often seen as a generational conflict). In other words they elaborated on the most obvious characteristics of the phenomenon without analyzing or understanding them. A vocabulary with strong emotional overtones, general statements, and preconceived ideas were all served up instead of a critical evaluation of the situation. This is particularly true of the bishops' statements. Many of them took the precaution of saying that they were speaking as pastors, not as sociologists and economists, and were content to remind individuals of their duty to inform themselves and to reflect on the situation with other members of their community.

Later on we shall try to understand the reasons for and the consequences of this lack of analysis. In any event, the predominance of value judgments and interpretations over explanatory statements indicates that it is necessary to take a closer look at the "image" Christians had of the events.

The image of the event. At this stage the texts can give us an indication of the significance which Christians attributed to the events in the context of their religious or ethical view of the world. We must first try to determine what values they consider to be important, the reasons they give in support of their readings of the events, and the ideological pattern in which that reading was made. This second phase of our study is, without a doubt, more important than the preceding phase, for it is on this level that the

attitudes and behavior of individuals and institutions are determined.

The very first fact to be noted is the striking unanimity of the
views expressed about the meaning of the events, although, in fact,
this is not astonishing if we remember the unanimity of opinions
about the causes. The reading of the events as a "crisis of civilization" is thereby reinforced. "The materialism in which men live
today estranges them more and more from the message of Christ.
The meaning of poverty, effort, sacrifice, humility, respect for and
love of others, all these profoundly Christian values are esteemed
less and less, and yet true progress is possible for human persons
only if they are respected.[53] This text is significant in that it diag-
noses an unrest in society for which the cure is "more soul," and
declares that it can be obtained only through Christian "values."

It seems that the events were being observed and interpreted on
two different levels—social and spiritual—whence they are seen as
a "crisis of growth"[54] or a "crisis of conscience."[55] As the archbishop of Paris said on May 22, "Our uncertainty in face of the
future incites us to hope."[56] Later in the same day he said to some
journalists, "Christians are asked to be witnesses to a hope which
goes beyond even the most ambitious human hopes and which
penetrates and purifies them."[57]

And so, aroused by the "aching of the spiritual void"[58] which is a
characteristic of our times, Christians "will know how to awaken
men's consciences and not confine themselves to reforming structures."[59]

In these texts we can hear an echo of the spirit of the Vatican II
Pastoral Constitution on the Church in the Modern World, and we
shall have occasion to return to this point in more detail later on.
One can also see in them the expression of an "ethic of conviction"
calling on an "ethic of responsibility,"[60] in the name of a type of
man still to be realized. But at this stage it is clear that this attitude
must withstand two criticisms. One is "external"; it requires that
the practical attitudes of the members of an institution be compatible with its public pronouncements. The second criticism is "internal"; it compares the attitudes as expressed in public statements

with objective conditions and the critical function of the ideology with the religious group.

For the time being, continuing our inventory of the published texts, we can now list the moral values which Christians seemed confident were to be found in the May Movement and which they hoped would be brought to fruition. If we take only those passages which explicitly recognized certain values in the movement, we arrive at a list of twelve different terms, the most frequent being *responsibility* (twelve times), *liberty* (ten times), *participation* (eight times), *justice* and *dialogue* (six times).[61] And for this, as we have said, we have counted only those passages which declared positively that the events contained some "values." The same words can be found on every page, with the same trust and the same hopes. This phenomenon seems to be a characteristic of contemporary Christian reflection. In the opening chapters of the Vatican Council's *Pastoral Constitution on the Church in the Modern World,* we find an archetypical reading of events in terms of positive and negative values.[62] Whether participants or onlookers in the events of May, 1968, Christians, especially the bishops, seemed to share this viewpoint. All the religious interpretations of the events followed a common schema with clearly discernible elements:

(1) " *God speaks through events.*" This is often the starting point of an exhortation to be attentive to the signs of the times. "Every event bears a message from God."[63] "The Holy Spirit intervenes in the history of mankind."[64] "The events are a challenge from God."[65] "The Holy Spirit is on our side, he dwells on man's earth. We are not alone, God is with us."[66]

(2) *Christians can take an active part in introducing change.* God is telling us that "the world as we know it is passing away." "Only God is absolute, the structures of this world are relative."[67] "God is no conservative; change and transformation are not a priori contrary to God's will."[68] Or, to put it more specifically, is the Christian message not a message of liberation? "A society in which man is considered as nothing more than a producer or a consumer. . . is in direct contradiction with the message of Jesus Christ."[69] "We must side with this revolutionary movement; it is

the party of the oppressed and, therefore, the party of Christ and his followers."[70]

(3) *Christians must live in harmony with their faith.* Although, as we shall see, indications as to the practical comportment of Christians lack precision, there is unanimous agreement on the need to harmonize one's faith with one's life. For the members of the ACO this means "living our faith in solidarity with all workers."[71] Other declarations announce that "our commitment is motivated by our faith."[72] During an open meeting at the Sorbonne, with the theme "From Che Guevara to Jesus Christ," one of the participants declared that "the Christian faith begins with faith in man."[73] The bishops of the Paris region, however, are less specific: "This attitude of being present to the world is in conformity with the Council, and all Christians are urged to reflect upon what they are doing and should be doing in the circumstances."[74] Later on they add: "The principles of the Gospel must be integrated into the realities of life."[75]

(4) *Faith enables us to see the plan of God and the kingdom increasingly present in this world.* The faith must, therefore, take heed of the world. "What can we, who are present in this crisis, say about it? That it is profoundly Christian."[76] "The revolution allied to the values of the Gospel is, as it were, the onward march of the kingdom of God."[77] The social movement seems to be accomplishing what is, fundamentally, the Christian project for society: "A shock from without has shown us what we bore within us. . . . Isn't this a sign of the Holy Spirit at work in the hearts of men?[78] Christians believe in any event that "the kingdom of God is being built on earth."[79] And "if social relations are profoundly changed by this crisis, toward greater freedom, God's design will have been furthered."[80] In the midst of the crisis, on the feast of Pentecost, the bishops reminded the faithful that they are "called to construct a more fraternal world, more in keeping with God's will."[81] This is the message of the Spirit, inviting us to recognize him at work in the world today and to join with him and collaborate in his action."[82]

(5) *If the faith gives priority to any of the options before us, it is to those which favor the most deprived. But political pluralism is*

perfectly legitimate. "The very poor are the suffering Christ among us."[83] "Our solidarity with those who are most bitterly oppressed is neither demagogy nor sentimentality; it is a simple duty."[84] But "the Gospel does not propose concrete solutions; it has no magic formula to offer."[85] "There is no direct way of interpreting the Gospel that would lead us all to action under the same banner."[86]

This is the frame of reference which is used all the time by the bishops. Other groups who want, and who are in a position, to identify themselves with certain concrete goals, use the same frame of reference, but less frequently. But even when the frame of reference used is not explicitly theological, the message of the events is universalized in terms of "values." In their effort to see only the "underlying significance" of the social movement, the bishops sometimes failed to see its real significance. Their use of generalizations and universal concepts such as justice and liberty avoided any indictment of the capitalist system or the political regime, and referred only to "a sickness of civilization" or a "sickness of souls" seeking a salvation which this world cannot give them.

A summary account of the facts, especially in statements emanating from the hierarchy, is coupled with an overabundance of value judgments. And this fact raises several problems which we shall examine later on. To what extent did the overwhelmingly ideological interpretation put on the events tend to free Christians from anxiety and dispense them from action? In their haste to pronounce value judgments—whose significance was greatly diminished by their lack of precision—was the Catholic hierarchy not assuming the role of guardians of orthodoxy? Were the bishops not anxious to conceal the divisions in the ranks of the faithful by drawing a veil over some of the conflicts? Finally, the haste with which some of them made the transition from a simple statement of the facts or an attempt to understand them to a theological interpretation shows how artificial that interpretation must be. The fact that the faithful were more than usually attentive to their words, owing to the novelty of the situation, served perhaps as a pretext to reiterate a ready-made doctrine.

The options made by Christians and their solidarity with the movement. The pursuit of our analysis leads to an examination of the total or partial solidarity forged between Christians and the protagonists in the events. Where do Christians stand with regard to the goals of the groups involved in the May Movement? Most bishops and priests seem to have adhered in a general way to the movement and its inherent values. The specialized groups, however, formulated their options and qualified their solidarity with greater care. The bishops seemed mainly concerned not to take sides and not to alienate anyone, and this often led them to speak in defense of abstraction. After May 30, for instance, one bishop declared that "the return to work must not make us forget whatever was legitimate in the workers' demands."[87] And on June 19, in the context of a general resumption of work, another bishop declared: "Each in our own place, including those who control the means of production, and whose problems of conscience are often painful and difficult, we must engage in a peaceful combat in which all men of goodwill can join together: the building of a society of free men, equal in their rights and duties. . . ."[88] Or, again, we have this very revealing text: "It is not easy for us Christians to find the happy medium between ingenuous optimism and systematic opposition, between an effort of participation and the imperatives of our development today. . . . Without succumbing to a partisan choice we shall choose the path of a conversion of hearts and of dialogue."[89] On May 24 one hundred priests of the Paris region declared that they could no longer use "language that spares all parties," but, they add, "we choose to be on the side of this great movement of solidarity which is springing up and which seems to us to be more in conformity with the Gospel than the individualistic world of the consumer society."[90]

Groups of lay people defined their options a little more explicitly. The YCS, for instance, on May 7 declared their solidarity with the UNEF over the questions that had to be dealt with before classes could be reopened.[91] Some militants of the YCW, who were students at the university, emphasized that young people of the working classes should have access to higher education and that their own culture should be respected.[92] The ACO took issue with capitalism,[93] and on May 31, after de Gaulle's speech, published a statement strongly critical of "the contempt" which the head of state had shown for the workers' claims.[94] But it would be difficult to find a political blueprint in the vague calls to "participation" issued by the French Scouts or the General Catholic Action movements.[95]

It is particularly interesting to see what the various public statements had to say about two important points: the existing political regime and the question of violence. We have found only three texts which call into question the political regime. One, already quoted, was issued by the ACO, and even it does not go to the point of calling for an end to the present regime. Another was published by a group of prominent Christians: "The Gaullist regime must move over. But there are many others who are also responsible for this failure. It would be useless to change the regime, therefore, if society were not changed as well."[96] The third statement was by the Liaison Committee of Christians Involved in the Revolutionary Struggle and it declared: "We refuse to be subject any longer to a power which founds our society on the interests of the ruling classes and on capitalism."[97]

The problem of violence, on the other hand, was the object of much debate and uncertainty. Two texts quite explicitly envisage it as a means in the struggle and see no contradiction between the faith and violence on this level.[98] But most of the texts which deal with the problem repudiate violence; they opt for the alternative of dialogue,[99] seeing violence as a "nonvalue" in the movement and a painful transitional phase.[100] And, finally, we find only four instances of a reflection on the violent condition in which certain classes or groups are enmeshed through the fault of the existing social system.[101]

Here again, the lack of any analysis of the situation makes itself felt. The hierarchy was anxious to show its impartiality: "Apart from the bluff, the remote control, and the underlying political ambitions concealed behind it, this is a legitimate revolt," declared the bishop of Nancy. "But the young would be making a mistake if they believed that the world they want to build will please those who come after them. They will feel exactly the same toward that world as the young of this generation feel toward our world. This is the human condition which is basically unstable." The bishop of Limoges, on the other hand, asked "what will be the use of the reforms that need to be carried out if relations between men continue to be governed by sin?" And the bishop of Saint Flour considered that it was very difficult to make any option as long as the situation was so confused: "As the situation becomes clearer we must all attempt to look at it lucidly, without passion or partisanship, and make our own particular contribution to the common good according to our own role and responsibility."

These observations are so general they could not possibly offend anyone. Calls to prayer, for instance, are often coupled with a veritable appeal to remain neutral. Christians must be the "artisans of a true encounter and constructive and fraternal dialogue, from which a new order of justice and respect for liberty can spring." "Our country is in danger of being split into two camps. Our unanimous prayers and our fidelity to the Spirit of Love can prevent legitimate and fruitful tensions from degenerating into fratricidal conflict and sterile opposition." And, finally, "Every man must be able to hear us speaking to him in his own tongue"; "As Christians, we are artisans of peace in the midst of turmoil."

This investigation, then, brings to light a good deal of optimism about the movement and no defense of the established order, but, on the contrary, a desire to participate in building a new order. However, it must be noted that for several weeks in May all public opposition to the movement seemed to be paralyzed. It was heard only after May 30. Only in June did publications like *La France Catholique, l'Homme Nouveau,* and even the newspaper *La Croix* express reticence and even some frankly hostile opinions, which we have not, therefore, mentioned. It is certain that the statements of the specialized groups of the lay apostolate showed far more progressive attitudes than those held by the general run of Christians.

*The impact of the events on the institutional Church.*The Church lived through these events not only as an onlooker but also as a protagonist. Those for whom the French Church had seemed a peaceful oasis in the turbulence of the Universal Church before May, 1968, suddenly found quite a different state of affairs after the events. The shock to the social system loosened many tongues, causing an upheaval in men's relations with authority and uncovering many repressed problems.

During the events the bishops themselves wrote: "A certain type of relationship between lay people and the clergy, priests and bishops, and between lay people and Christian organizations, has been called into question in such a way that we cannot evade the issue."[102] And a group of priests, making it clear that the Church was not excluded from their criticism, wrote: "In every domain today we challenge the way in which things are thought out and decided for us."[103]

An appeal to all Christians, signed by both Catholics and Protestants, poses the problem explicitly: "The presence of the Church in the revolution supposes and demands the presence of the revolution in the Church, in its way of life and mental habits and in their collective and individual expression."[104]

This wish was soon fulfilled, and an even more radical text declared:

> The established Churches give objective support to the capitalist system. . . . The Church approves the oppression which is a fact of capitalism and which it is unwilling or unable to analyze or challenge. The structures of the Church are alienating: They lead Christians to hand over their responsibilities to the hierarchy who live on the fringe of society. These powerful organizations are simply superstructures which no longer correspond to the needs of the Christian community today. The other structures of ideology and theology which expatiate about the world all the more readily because they never get involved in it are also alienating and alienated.[105]

The same accusation is made by the students at the Protestant faculty of theology. They refused, as students, to be consumers of theology and later, as pastors, dispensers of the same theology for the alienation of the faithful who "consume it passively." They reject an institution whose silence or conciliatory attitude "contributes to maintaining the status quo. . . . Theology simply ratifies the internal contradictions of the capitalist system, in which the ecclesiastical institution is a partner, by taking refuge in its traditional polarities: Kingdom of God-pagan world, Church-society."[106] Finally we must mention this declaration of war: "Let us overthrow the priestly caste. That is what it wants. Let us reject the mandarins. . . . What we are living is no longer expressed by the present structure of the Church. We challenge it; we want to reinvent it."[107]

From the above texts it is clear that the Church is going through the same cultural problems as the rest of society. In challenging their Church in May, 1968, many young people—and some not so young—were building an antisociety similar to that which was built in the Sorbonne. And this symbolic activity does not make it any easier to advance a judgment about the future of the challenge or the validity of its analyses and its projects. What is true of the social movement holds good for the Church; we have to ask the same questions about the movement of challenge in the Church as we asked about the May Movement.

In concluding we must point out the relatively clear perception in many groups of the disintegration of the "community" of the faithful. The bishops, especially, came up against this problem: How could they speak to the Church, and in the name of the Church, when some Christians were manning the barricades and others taking part in the Gaullist demonstrations on the Champs Elysées? "The difficulty," as Pastor Westphal confessed, "is that the faithful of our Churches are divided as much as the rest of the population, and so any text which takes a clear position is liable to sow discord. . ."[108]

"There are Christians among the students, the teachers, and the police," said Bishop Marty. "United in one faith, they are committed, nevertheless, to different, sometimes opposite, goals. This is normal, yet all of them must receive the same Gospel and live according to the law of God."[109] And another bishop suggested: "I encourage you to persevere in a dialogue between Christians, to help each other shed light on the true Christian motives for your action."[110] But is this a solution or simply the same old problem all over again? For what does one mean by "Christian motives" for political action? We have here a living example of the difficulties involved in trying to determine the nature of the bonds between faith and politics. In the interventions of the hierarchy can be seen a general tendency to make a distinction between politics in the generic sense: the definition of values; and in the strict sense: the achievement of goals. They constantly note that they are not qualified to speak about politics in the strict sense; the problem is too complex and they wish to avoid any form of clericalism. When the hierarchical Church intervenes, it does so in order to remind people of the values of the Gospel. It speaks in the name of principles and leaves Christians and those in charge of the political sphere free to follow their consciences in the options they take.

This is indeed a far cry from the attitude of the Portuguese bishops in Africa and that of some members of the French hierarchy in the nineteenth century. But it remains to be seen whether the repudiation of clericalism is not largely a bluff. It may well be that in spite of it the bishops still have a certain conception of the Church and of Revelation in which the faithful, and society as a whole, are seen as being in a situation of dependence. And it is this conception that led them to offer a ready-made interpretation of personal and social life.

But there is another question. We have already suggested that the bishops' cautiousness was dictated by their fear of dividing the Christian community. Their frame of reference has its good points: It was open-minded and optimistic and it encouraged the quest for a very demanding concrete application of justice. At the same time it made a show of unity on the ideological level and on the level of the options which transcend the divisions, while acknowledging the diversity and even the antagonism existing in the ranks of the faithful. The result was that not only were the bishops powerless to offer any opinion in operative terms, but they found themselves in the cross fire of pressure from contradictory tendencies: some urging them to speak out in defense of law and order, others in condemnation of repression; some were scandalized by their silence, others wanted them to remain silent so that the grass-roots level could make its voice heard over that of the "dignitaries." This splintering of the Church's façade of unity is one of the principal aspects of what Christians experienced in May, 1968.

With this inventory of texts we can now indicate some general tendencies and raise certain questions. The very open-minded attitude generally expressed in these statements can almost certainly be explained by the desire to be "present to the world," which had been so unequivocally endorsed by Vatican II. But this observation raises even more questions than it answers.

At first sight, the very general terms of the statements would seem to be a result of the ambiguity of the situation, but then one wonders to what extent other factors came into play: the incapacity to offer any concrete political solutions, for example, or the hesitancy about assuming a political stance incompatible with the evangelizing mission of the Church, or the fear—especially in the case of the hierarchy—of taking sides. We shall have to probe these questions, which raise the problem of the political maturity of French Christians.

Another aspect is very evident in the texts, and that is the connection between faith and ethics. In the vast majority of them, a reminder of the demands of the Gospel is coupled with an analysis of the events, not founded on any coherent doctrine of the relation between faith and politics. To put it frankly, it seems that Christians approved the changes that were taking place with as much Christian conviction as they had dedicated, not so long before, to maintaining the established order. This attitude, which was not created but only confirmed by what happened in May, also needs to be analyzed in greater depth.

The Church After May, 1968

Christians and political analysis. One noteworthy aspect of the texts quoted above is the abstract nature of the analysis they offer. It would seem that the only language they know is that of moral "values." They readily take up the defense of justice, liberty, responsibility, and participation, but one rarely—and then only dimly—glimpses the rational foundations of their stance or the method in their plans. In this sense it seems that they are unfamiliar with political analysis.

This is in no way peculiar to the Catholics and other Christians of France. The encyclicals and the Council documents reveal the same difficulty in arriving at "even a remotely exact and, above all, operative understanding of socioeconomic realities."[111] Perhaps René Rémond is correct in blaming intellectual lethargy for the fact that in Christians circles there is endless talk about building the world but very little about analyzing it.[112]

True, one often has the impression that many Christians, when faced with political problems, hold to the principle that it is impossible to judge the roots of political questions, and so they refuse to make any judgment that would seem partisan or that would bind them to some interests and oppose others. We have already mentioned this difficulty in relation to the Vietnamese war, and it is, perhaps, the reason why the statements of Christians in May, 1968, leave one feeling somewhat dissatisfied.[113]

However, as René Rémond remarked in 1963, a change can already be seen in the fact that Catholics "who used to think in terms of authority, order, and tradition are now far more attached to the values of justice, charity, and freedom."[114] The question remains whether they have not simply switched from one level of abstraction to another.

One is compelled to make this reservation in view of the absence of analysis in the texts we have studied. A concern for values is necessarily abstract if it has no way of investigating reality. One is left only with the possibility of judging means—since one has no understanding of the causes of a phenomenon—or of drawing absolute comparisons between moral values (freedom, justice, respect for others, etc.) or abstract norms (violence or nonviolence, etc.). How can one have a clear view of one's goals—justice for the poor, for instance—if one fails to analyze the causes of their present situation? It is not that the technical side of the problem should intimidate us so much that we dare not mention the political nature of economic options. But if we are going to challenge the system, we must do so with some positive and substantial elements in hand; we must fight it with a *praxis,* which means the implementation of a *theory,* an alternative project. In the absence of any such alternative project René Rémond is justified in thinking that there "is less difference than appears between permanent legitimation and universal condemnation."[115] And, as Jean-Marie Domenach says, it is not enough for Christian charity to "take up its abode in the abandoned home of revolutionary socialism and start regilding its signboards." The temptation is to adopt only the language: "One can latch on to general slogans without worrying about their content or the likelihood of their being fulfilled."[116] We saw the same phenomenon in Latin America.

And so the political attitudes of Catholics evolve, vacillating between moralism and sacralization. In both cases they neglect far too easily to take political phenomena for what they are and to attack them with adequate conceptualizations, and, above all, they neglect to work out a praxis.

The roots of this attitude are, of course, historical.[117] History has piled up layers of prejudice which now influence the behavior of many Christians who are too ready to identify politics with corruption or violence. For fear of having to sacrifice their moral scruples and their sociological unity, many Christians have abandoned politics and turned all their energies to the "social" sphere. But even in this area their incorrigible lack of any real analytic thought has often led them to making guiding principles out of elements which were simply cultural patterns in such areas, for instance, as the family and education.

During the Second World War and the Resistance, French Catholics seemed to have finally become reconciled to the Republic and, with the MRP party,[118] they gave a fleeting impression of being ready to cooperate effectively in establishing a socialist democracy. But the bulk of their intellectual heritage (Emmanuel Mounier and Marc Sangnier) soon disappeared in the quicksands of party politics.[119]

In view of the tremendous gulf between ideology and practice, the most important question—above and beyond all circumstantial reasons—is that which concerns the system of action that Christians seem obliged to adopt and which, in spite of the various forms it has taken in the course of history, has proved so inadequate to effect change for lack of effective, scientific analysis.

"God is not a conservative." In view of the image Christians had of the May Movement and their declarations concerning it, the question arose as to whether the confessing communities in France today had any hope of spreading an authentic "ethic of conviction." What theoretical elements of the problem can be discerned in the present situation, not only in respect to the Christian ethic but in respect to all ideologies?

French society is dominated less by a class than by a model of rationalization: "growth" and the needs of expansion. Ideologies have been disarmed by this domination, and hopes for a qualitative change have been defeated by a new political philosophy in the service of development, production, and consumption. May, 1968, was a revolt against this newly established order. It was a resurrection of ideology, which had already been pronounced dead by so many analysts. But for want of a political rationale and the will to exercise power instead of simply challenging or refusing it, for want of a theoretical and practical means of influencing the established power, the revolt was stillborn.

There is a lesson here for any group which intends to work for the affirmation of the spiritual element in society: In order to win recognition of the goals and meaning of industrial society and bring them to fruition, it is indispensable to accept the mediation of short- and medium-term policies coupled with ideology and a long-term interpretation of history. But it is equally indispensable that the two aspects be combined with critical judgment.

The Church wanted to join in the affirmation of the spirit in May, 1968. It felt at home with the movement. "We too challenge a society which neglects men's highest aspirations" (Bishop Marty). But the Christians' feeble capacity for analysis has always been a handicap in formulating a challenge to society. Now any challenge they make will also have to prove its worth in the face of an "internal" and an "external" critique. The former "demystifies" the Christian argument by confronting it with the facts: What good does it do to assert that God is not a conservative if the vast majority of Christians continue to be sytematically opposed to progress and reactionary in their politics? And what is the point of preaching a God who favors change if their exhortation refuses to take the necessary means to be a critique of a system specially designed for its own self-preservation?

The second critique is one which demythologizes. It could be formulated in the question: Under what conditions can a call to social change "in the name of God" avoid being simply a subtle reiteration of a mythical discourse, a holistic notion of history which has given rise to nothing but conservatism or imaginary revolutions?

The political attitude of French Catholics. After World War II the MRP thought it could carry out a leftist policy with a rightist electorate. This illusion was very quickly exploded. The vast majority of the rightist electorate was truly Catholic, and not only in name. To quote Gabriel Le Bras, they were "fervent Catholics." In 1952 a poll revealed the level of religious practice among voters registered with the various political parties. The results showed MRP voters as 73 percent "fervent," 23 percent "practicing," 2 percent with no exterior practice, and 2 percent with no practice at all.[120] Fervent and practicing Catholics, incidentally, provided the majority in the political center and the RPF.[121]

In 1965, after the first ballot in the presidential elections, a poll revealed that out of one hundred persons who had described themselves as practicing Catholics, the votes were divided as shown in this chart:

POLITICAL LEANINGS	CANDIDATE	DISTRIBUTION OF CATHOLIC VOTES	PERCENTAGE OUT OF ONE HUNDRED REPLIES
	de Gaulle	55%	66%
Left	Mitterand	7%	8%
Center	Lecanuet	17%	20%
Right	Tixier-		
	Vignancourt	4%	6%
Other	Barbu		
	and		
	Marcilacy	1%	
	No reply	16%	
		100%	100%

The comments of those who published the polls are worth quoting. Having studied various correlations between the voters' option and their religion, age, sex, and profession, they conclude:

> Although the four criteria envisaged seem to have some significant relation to the vote, the religious criterion is by far the strongest. This is the criterion which can be considered as giving the most easity predictable results.... It is their religious situation as it is defined by their beliefs and their degree of practice

which, on the sociological level, can best account for the electoral choice of the French people on December 5, 1965.[122]

A later inquiry, conducted in 1966 by the *Nouvel Observateur*,[123] revealed that out of one hundred practicing Catholics or, rather, out of seventy-seven who expressed an opinion, sixty-eight showed a preference for central or rightist political groups.

All these findings are, of course, of only limited value. For instance, is religious practice a sufficient criterion for determining what is meant by "belonging" to the Church? One might also question whether equating right with conservative and left with progressive is sufficiently accurate to justify classing all Catholics who voted Gaullist as conservatives. Although these polls make it clear that it would be an exaggeration to speak of a Catholic "landslide" to the left, they also show that there is no monolithic conservatism. Changes are beginning to take shape even if they are still not visible under the scrutiny of electoral sociology. Maurice Duverger wrote recently: "French Catholics no longer form the kernel of a pure, hard-line, unyielding right. They no longer think in terms of delivering France from the Republic in the name of the Sacred Heart or of combatting communism to the death. . . . They have become moderate conservatives, somewhat pacifist in international questions and fairly open-minded in interior affairs." But this qualitative portrait does not invalidate the essential points of our analysis.

Only an influential and active minority has shown any tendency to move to the left. "Within the main body of Catholicism, the center of gravity for militants might be said to be left of center; for the bishops and other authorities, more right of center and, for the average Church member, on the right." And René Rémond, who made this diagnosis,[124] emphasizes the serious problems this situation entails for the institution as the imbalance is accentuated between the progressiveness of the advance guard and the relative inertia of the masses. Such circumstances can only serve to reinforce the status quo of the institution as such and the rigidity of the authorities, as is the case in all that concerns the internal structures of the Church since Vatican II.

And, finally, we must mention one last limitation to the progressive orientation of a minority of Catholics. The political parties of the left in France have had great difficulty in understanding that politics also has something to do with controlling government. They have constantly retreated into narrow-minded empiricism, parochial squabbles, or moralizing dreams of ineffectual purity. It is the quest for purity which seems to ensnare so many militant Christians of the left. Is this an ultimate example of their propensity for thinking of politics in terms of loyalty to absolute principles? However that may be, many of them plunged enthusiastically into the "antipolitics" of the May Movement, which, as we have see, remains ambiguous. On the other hand, a clear picture of the May events has been made almost impossible by the extreme disparity of the leftist groups, the incredible number of "sects" and revolutionary publications,[125] the fact that they expressed themselves sometimes with emotion and sometimes with explosive anger and their characteristically esoteric language, and, finally, the very efficient role that some of them played. Many Christians found they could go just so far in accepting these ambiguities, which were, incidentally, carefully fostered and even exaggerated. But all this is, surely, a normal characteristic of any social movement.

We now have some elements of an answer to the question: What good does it do to assert that God is not a conservative if the vast majority of Christians continue to be political reactionaries, systematically opposed to progress? The evidence we have does not allow us to affirm that Christians are, as a body, conservative, so much as to see more clearly the limitations of their progressive tendencies.

The annexation of the social critique. As for the second subhypothesis of what we called an "external" critique, that is: Is not the preaching of a God who favors change rendered invalid by the Church's incapacity to criticize a system organized for its own self-preservation? What conditions are necessary if this position—which we believe to be the position of the average Christian—is not to be defeated and even annexed by the dominant ideologies of "growth" and used by them to their own ends? To what extent do Christians avoid falling into the trap of modelling their own argument on the dominant values? An analysis of the reactions which greeted the French bishops' statement in March, 1966, *Reflections* on the Present Economic and Social Situation, indicates how very ambiguous the situation is.

In response to an article in Le Monde of March 5, entitled "The Bishops Question the Foundations of Capitalism," the magazine published by the French Center of Christian Employers wrote: "The mind of the Church is indivisible and nothing could be further from the truth than to see a break with the traditional thinking of the Church in the French bishops' declaration." And the Gaullist paper, La Nation, stating its belief that the bishops were not condemning "capital, which has brought so much new well-being to so many men in the fullest freedom, but its abuses and failings," feels it has the right to conclude: "More than ever we have the profound feeling that we are working in the direction recommended by the Church."

The magazine Frères du Monde,[126] on the other hand, was strongly critical of the bishops' statement and concluded that "the reflections of the French bishops endorse an adhesion to contemporary economic theories.... The real problems are not resolved simply by focussing on the main topic of discussion."[127]

In their statement the bishops dealt with the problem of the "waste products" of growth: close-outs, layoffs, etc., seeing them as elements in the context of "radical mutation of our civilization."

Gilbert Blardone, writing in Le Monde, gave voice to the divergent reactions to the bishops' text:

> Some people think that the Church has once again reminded us of the principles which it believes should guide our action and make it possible to conciliate all our legitimate interests, without calling into question social relations or the structures of economic life. And, some with relief and others in despair, they will conclude that once again a conceptual and moralizing outlook on reality has led to judging results in the name of principles without touching on their causes, that is, the organizational structures, and to guiding our action in the direction of a superficial readjustment of our environment instead of a radical transformation.[128]

Blardone rejects both positions and insists that there has been an attitudinal change in the Church since the Council, and that it now looks at the inner aspects of things and seeks to arouse individual consciences. As an example of this he cites Paul VI's speech before the United Nations and his attitude toward the Vietnamese war and Dom Helder Camara's stance!

If we are to take them at their word, then, the bishops not only point out painful truths; they make a direct attack on "the real, organic causes of the evil, that is, the contradictions of a mutative society."[129] Noting men's will to arrive at a "fuller mastery of the universe and its resources" through "generalized and systematic development of production, under pressure from demographic growth and technical and scientific progress," they adopt an "existential and intrinsic approach" which enables them to point out the inherent contradictions in the situation.

But the bishops' statement also elicited recriminations from within, this time from Father Calvez,[130] who accuses it of attaching insufficient importance to "the social and mental transformations entailed by growth." In his view, the contradictions exposed by the bishops are not simply the consequence of structural defects, but of the fact that mentalities and attitudes have become stuck in a rut, thereby making the necessary mutations even more arduous. In spite of this Father Calvez seems to see some value in an authoritative condemnation of the marginal situations caused by progress: the destitution of the "dropouts" of the affluent society, the pockets of poverty in the midst of prosperity. In other words the Church must have a "special concern for those who have difficulty in keeping up with the crowd," but it would be a mistake for it to try to change the rules of the game.

If it shows nothing else, this rapid view of different opinions shows how difficult it is for the Church to say anything about economic matters. From what we have seen of the reactions and commentaries which greeted the bishops' reflections, the Church lays itself open to criticism from all sides whenever it attempts to analyze a situation "from within." Some criticize it for aligning itself with the dominant values—and their criticism is valid; others, equally validly, regret that its analysis is not sufficiently grounded in the realities of life for it to be of any scientific value.

During the nineteenth century, as we have seen, the Church envisaged the social problem exclusively in the terms imposed on it by liberalism and sought to remedy a new situation without realizing that the novelty lay, not in poverty, but in the class struggle. Hence the ultimately conservative stand of Leo XIII.

The question in our day is whether the Church is in the process of renewing the appeals it addressed at the beginning of the Industrial Revolution to static capitalism to the new, dynamic, and generalized economy. The tendency to react primarily to the "ills of civilization" entails the danger of camouflaging the real phenomena. Since every political undertaking is a combination of knowledge and will, for the Church to limit itself to the former is to run the risk of providing arguments for those who, consciously or unconsciously, can profit by imposing their own norms and values and of providing them with a ready-made legitimation. A concrete example points to the necessity of taking this possibility into consideration. On April 12, 1969, Georges Pompidou, addressing a gathering of "young Gaullists" at Strasbourg, analyzed the problems of young people as a "calling into question of our civilization" and observed that "the traditional framework... on which society and individuals used to lean has been broken down, or, at any rate, the power has gone out of it." Condemning, simultaneously, refusal of progress, anarchy, and Marxism, the Gaullist leader pleaded for "progress with order. . . ." But he added that the basic problem "is the contrast between the immense power that man has acquired over the universe through scientific and technical progress on the one hand, and, on the other, the moral stagnation of individuals. . . ." And he went on to conclude: "In an admirable pastoral letter, the bishop of Strasbourg has said: 'We must reintroduce the notion of sacredness.' As far as I am concerned—and I am talking here on the political level and, therefore, as a layman—I would say that we must reintroduce the notion of an ideal. We must learn that it is only by going out of himself that man finds himself... and, incidentally, this is probably the most lofty moral teaching that the Christian European tradition has handed down to us."

The quest for a theological language. We must now explain the second aspect of our critique: The internal critique, which questions the validity of a religious reflection on change, arises from a formal analysis of the relation between faith and ideology, and faith and ethics. Here we would simply like to shed some light on a historic period in the evolution of the problem of the Church and revolution, and once we have placed it in context, to emphasize the ideological aspect of the problem.

The novelty of Catholic theology within the last generation, and especially since Vatican II, lies principally in an effort to "theologize history." It is a healthy reaction from earlier theology which "either reduced history to the status of the leftovers of eternity... or else sublimated failure in history as an achievement in eternity."[131] But one might still wonder whether the Church has not simply assimilated an old argument that was originally elaborated outside and against it, particularly in the nineteenth century.[132]

However that may be, one of the facts we have to record is that Christians today have acquired an optimistic attitude toward the world, seeing scientific and technical tasks as lying within "God's plan,"[133] while holding firmly to the principle of the autonomy of the created order.[134] This reconciliation with "the world" is also a reconciliation with history and historicity. The encyclical *Pacem in Terris* is one sign of this and, admittedly, this change of attitude clears away a considerable number of obstacles. Analysis of the statements by Christians during the events of May, 1968, showed that the organized forces of the Church and their leaders were open-minded about the future and ready to welcome innovations and reforms. This attitude could be called the "Vatican II trend" in contemporary Catholicism.

Bishop Marty's declaration, "God is not a conservative," is probably fairly typical of the average point of view, which is why we took it as the main object of our analysis. But we also noted two other trends. One, a regressive trend, which is still very active even though it did not appear very openly in May, still links the faith to counterrevolution. The other, which is gradually gaining ground, seeks to reconcile the faith with revolutionary practice, although it does not "ideologize" its attitude.

There is something very "Barthian" about the desire Christians have to read events in the light of God's word. The pretensions of man and his works are reduced to more modest dimensions by the majesty of the divine call heard in history. Since "only God is absolute," neither the conservatives nor the revolutionaries win their case. The former are rejected because the structures of the world are relative; the latter because nothing definitive is ever achieved on the purely structural level if the problem of reforming hearts and "consciences" is not also tackled.

The underlying anthropology of this position is open to criticism. But it is obvious that it is a very balanced position, which can, therefore, be extremely useful to an institution which, having renounced its role as supernatural guarantor of the established order, now finds itself the guardian of the "signs of the times," but in danger of failing to call itself into question and of dominating the debate from the lofty heights of the "Absolutely Other"—unless, of course, its apolitical nature be openly used to legitimate some third possibility.

But this position could also mean something else. It could mean the end of theocracy and, thereby, the free quest for the human finality of society. The critical aspect of faith and its function of service could be invaluable in establishing within society a permanent critical pole for its options and ideologies.[135] To say that God is not a conservative is to say, in a sense, that God has his place in a view of the world, but that it is not such as to suppress the finality of the world, rather to give it its full, human finality and autonomy.

I feel, however, that we should guard against the reintroduction of a causalist mentality to which this type of language lends itself. It is very difficult to have no absolute on which to found change. By this I mean that we are justified in suspecting theology of functioning in the realm of the imaginary—which does not mean in error—when it seeks to justify every change and every contingent option. This is my reaction to the "presence-of-the-Spirit-in-the-world" passages which abound in the texts we analyzed as well as in much of the "theology of revolution" both in certain Protestant traditions and among Catholics.

The disintegration of symbolic systems means, of course, that values lose their sacredness as objects; they always stand in relation to a state of knowledge or of practice. Thus disenchanted, as Alain Touraine has it, "man is obliged to turn in on himself, not in the deeper framework of an interior life in which, as though on the wall of a deep cavern, he can hope to see the shadows of a superhuman world and metasocial protagonists, but in the creative gesture of a personal subject."[136]

This recourse to a "subject" will no doubt oblige the would-be "theology of social change" to take an inductive approach, which means that the problems of the relation between ethics and faith can no longer be treated as simply part of a synthesis from which behavior can be deduced. Instead, the faith will have to be studied in the light of options and structures which have not been determined by it.[137]

The believer of today, therefore, should be distrustful of his own system of thought, which is like a "locomotive pushing the train of history, with an engineer on board who has a map of the railroad system."[138] And we would do well to include in our distrust the "theologies of revolution," and not only those—less numerous— which legitimate the established order. For even when theology deals with revolution there is still a danger that it will be a case of the institution reasserting its cultural role for itself; it is a step in the direction of sacralizing human options. So often in the past this has simply served to justify a refusal to commit oneself to any undertaking which was autonomous in its criteria and responsible for its own results. It could well be an unconscious preparation for the annexation of revolution by a "Christendom of the left"— which is still a form of Christendom.

Sociology can certainly help the theologian to see if his own way of envisaging social change is anything more than "a system of concepts which, recognizing no scientific criterion other than semantic coherence, takes itself as the yardstick rather than measuring itself against facts."[139]

I would like to conclude this critique with a quotation from the Jesuit theologian, Pierre Antoine. Noting the contemporary Christian's desire to "find God in human relations," he reminds his readers that, first of all, "we have to understand that history is the terrain of freedom and not look for a divine immediacy, . . . which used to be seen in nature, and not consult the signs of the times as one used to interpret the signs and portents of nature." (In passing we might recall that the French Church in the nineteenth century believed it was meant to "read" the events of the Paris Commune as a sign of God's wrath against the iniquity of France.) "The event," continues Father Antoine, "is not the word of God. And the understanding of history as Sacred History is tied to the existence of a group of inspired people, ... but revelation came to an end with the death of the last Apostle." The time of the Church is, perhaps, "the time for God to be silent and for man to work."[140]

The Church Challenged

The phenomenon triggered in the French Church by the events of May, 1968, the challenge which erupted so suddenly from within, is quite understandable if it is seen in the light of the recent history of both the French and the universal Church.

Even a "prophetic" figure like Cardinal Suhard admitted, after the war, that he had been "greatly mistaken" in his attitude under the German occupation. Many French bishops could say as much. This is important because of the consequences his attitude entailed and which are still alive. "The French Church lost something of its substance and much of its cohesion in this experience."[141] Many adult Christians today remember having begun their public life with a gesture of disobedience or of unhappy submission. The result has been a new kind of relationship between the hierarchical Church and its members. The latter learned to make their own judgments in conscience. And today the hierarchy sometimes seems to establish this as a principle in which they find a strange justification for their own silence in embarrassing situations.

The events of May, 1968, induced a sudden acceleration of this process. We said that the Church found itself challenged during these events, but it was in a way which had nothing in common with what occurred in 1789 or during the nineteenth century. The Church in 1968 was challenged not so much by the revolution as by itself. "The Catholic community is exploding under pressure from the political and social currents of thought and action," declared the French bishops in November, 1968.[142] The texts quoted earlier gave us some indication of the diversity and depth of the rethinking that was going on. But we must now try to explain this.

One of the first things we see is that the Church's problem is not so very different from that which confronts all societies. Under pressure from change, social and cultural systems have to adapt themselves and evolve. For some this consists simply in adapting institutions to the environment and to production methods in order to strengthen their capacity for decision and execution. This position, which is not necessarily conservative, leaves out all consideration of the goals of their system of work and, to the extent to which it considers only the norms, it ignores the whole question of the cultural system. The notion of "participation" can be very convenient for this type of project because of its potential as an integrating force. The most dynamic and significant elements of the May Movement refused to take this path. They sought to destructure the socioeconomic models which had been considered absolutely natural, and challenged the whole orientation of society, that is, its culture.

These few points can help to clarify what happened in the Church and to show what problems the institution comes up against once it begins to revise the system. To begin with, it must be sufficiently aware of the world in which it is living to want to transform itself. It must be aware of its own irrelevancies. For the most part this was already the case in the French Church during the war and the first few postwar years.[143] Vatican II was the expression of the same awareness on the part of the universal Church.

In this sense the worker-priest mission was originally an effort to "explore the possibilities and limits of reconverting the ancient institutions of the Church in a world which is being transformed."

The very expression "worker-priest" was significant of an attempt to adapt norms, an attempt which was triggered by the discovery of the industrial society growing up around and outside the Church. But what did the experience show?[144] Wanting to adapt its norms, the Church created an institution which was better adapted, with the result that the crisis flared up on the level of values. It became clear that the experiment had posed a challenge to the accepted notions of the priesthood and of evangelization, had challenged the very content of the message. In the eyes of the authorities, those who had been sent on this mission—envisaged simply as an improved strategy—seemed to be questioning all the rules of the game. The Church suddenly felt anomic, and the faithful, instead of feeling themselves stimulated, felt harassed. The attempt to overcome the antagonism between the Church and the proletariat, between the Church and the world, turned against the institution by calling into question its goals. "By moving to the other side of the barrier, the worker-priests only deepened the feeling of separation between the two worlds. The ghetto walls which separated the Church from the world. . . now arose within the Church, dividing left from right, conservatives from progressives. . . ." What was intended as an experiment and an attempt to adapt created a movement of challenge among those outside the Church who had discovered another aspect of the reality. And, in turn, this provoked a defensive reaction on the part of those who identified themselves very closely with the Church: the hierarchy and priests and the ruling classes.[145]

Fear of the unknown brought the whole problem back again full circle: In order to safeguard the unity of the Church the question was again posed in terms of adapting the existing structures. It was decided that parishes were to be "missionary communities," Catholic Action received a new impetus, ecclesiastical bureaucracy was given a face-lifting, and the authorities took on the delicate task of maintaining the balance between contradictory tendencies.

The experience of the Vatican Council and ensuing developments can be understood along the same lines. Gathered to "update" an outmoded institution, the Council consisted, for the most part, in a reexamination of norms and functions. In this respect, in spite of the Curia, it could not fail to be more than a parenthesis. It opened up a new era of change. It attacked some urgent problems and solved them by elaborating new structures such as collegiality, the synod of bishops, episcopal and presbyteral assemblies, etc. Instead of making the institution function more smoothly, however, instead of adapting it to the modern world, Vatican II has precipitated a crisis of values. Priests' councils, for instance, have not stemmed the mounting tide of discontent among the clergy, nor prevented it from taking a more and more anti-institutional turn, toward a conflict on the level of values.

The dichotomy which dominated the Council, between those who favored reform and those who clung to the status quo, is no longer relevant. The freedom of expression which was won at the Council has already borne fruit. No one complains any longer that established norms prevent the Church from responding to a need. The complaint is now addressed to the gap between experience and the language the Church proposes for its expression. What is the point of forming a presbyterium if the question at issue is the very nature and meaning of the priesthood? Why reform the liturgy according to archaic norms if the issue is, henceforth, that of the relation between the eucharistic experience and social practice? All the effort now being spent on renewing structures conceals the problem of the yawning chasm between the language of religion and the language of experience. And so there are seminarians who express respect for the scientific knowledge of their professors, but who tell them candidly that it does not interest them. According to Jean Mansir, this is the most general topic of complaint: The Church is too self-centered, too concerned about its spirituality and its unity in the faith, in the name of which it carefully avoids any reexamination of historical reality in the light of the Gospel.[146]

To put it briefly, more and more Christians find that the efforts the Church is making to adapt itself to modern conditions are useless on its present terms. They lose interest and, without waiting for the institution, they make their own interpretation of the whole system.

The May Movement precipitated this phenomenon in the French Church. Traditional factions challenge the bishops' attitude, which they consider to be too accommodating to subversion. They condemn the ambiguity of their open attitude toward the world, which they see as almost a subtle form of communist infiltration. At the other end of the spectrum, as we have seen in the texts we analyzed, there are Christians who challenge even the post-Vatican II structures of the institution. They express their attitude in various ways, ranging from "symbolic" gestures, such as protests in churches or at the Bishops' meetings, as at Pentecost,

1969, to the elaboration of parallel structures. In this respect, the service of intercommunion celebrated on Pentecost Sunday, in the midst of the events, is especially significant. Christians are openly going further than the prudence—or the ecumenical audacity—of theologians or the hierarchy would allow. This is a particularly clear instance of change being sought not through reforms, but starting from basic human and Christian experience. This was clearly expressed by the YCS National Council in March, 1970: "Our liturgical functions will be permeated with our commitments, our analysis, and the options we have made."[147] At the same time the YCS emphatically declined to be "the Church in the schools." It declared itself to be a movement of Christians, basing its claim on a Marxist analysis: "As long as we judge a theoretical or practical means to be liberating we shall use it to its fullest capacity. As soon as it becomes an ideology we shall criticize it."[148]

Between these two poles lies a mass of troubled Christians. Many middle-class people, who are not at all *intégristes* or anxious to disrupt everything, apply the decisions of the Council, just as they applied the decisions of the Church formerly. In fact they are more inclined to agree with the reassuring middle-of-the-road attitude of Rome than with the pronouncements of some of their own bishops.

The bishops, for their part, are caught between two rival tendencies. From time to time they call someone to order, but on the whole they seem to be more concerned with maintaining unity among those who cannot make up their own minds. They are also deeply influenced by the reformist spirit of the Council and rely heavily on adapting structures. It is quite possible that they will soon find that this is not sufficient; recent events have forced them to realize the urgency of the basic problems concerning priests, for instance, and the fact that the institutional procedures, even if they are changed, will not be adequate to the situation.

Although one cannot speak of an "underground Church" in France in the same way as in the United States, it is nevertheless striking to see to what extent questions which had been bypassed by the Council reforms are now being openly and vigorously debated by groups of priests and laymen who are not content to verbalize.[149]

It is not yet a question of "the street in the Church" as the title of a recent book would have us believe.[150] But there is a growing hope that new forms will soon be seen in which the theoretical and practical work which awaits the Church may be effectively carried out.

CHAPTER NINE

The Church and Revolution:
A Sociological Study

The preceding chapters have described a certain number of specific situations through which we have been able to study the reactions and arguments, the endorsements and oppositions that have marked the relations of the Church with the revolutionary movements. At first sight the reactions are so many and various that it seems impossible to make a systematic synthesis without oversimplifying the question. And yet it is possible to distinguish a certain number of invariables.

We have already had recourse to sociological terms in the preceding chapters, but in this chapter we must use them more systematically. The analysis of a social reality can be approached on three different levels. One can study the *social system,* that is, the interaction between *individuals and groups* and its organization into a formal system. Or one can study the *cultural system,* which includes the *values* or collective goals to which a group is emotionally committed and which are never questioned in the short term; the *norms* or means which the group uses to attain its goals; the *legitimations* or mental content which give rational support to group values; and finally the *empirical knowledge* that is the fruit of reason and the scientific method. One can also approach the question by way of the *personality system,* in an attempt to see how the influence of the cultural and social systems in which individuals live become their own.

These concepts are all useful on the level of analysis, but one must not forget that the reality itself is always complex and that there will be constant interaction between all the above aspects.

In an attempt to avoid identifying the Church with its organizational aspect, the positions taken by different categories of Christians have been described in each of the revolutionary situations

317

studied. However, it is true to say that the ecclesiastical institution as such has habitually been opposed to revolutions, and revolutions, in turn, have considered institutionalized religion, and the Catholic Church in particular, as an obstacle to social change. It is evident that the conflict has not been confined to the choice of means; more fundamentally, it concerns social values, that is, the collective objectives of society as they are perceived and embodied in the lives of men. One of the questions we have to ask ourselves, therefore, is why this conflict has arisen.

Our attempt to answer this question will include a study of four different aspects of the Church: the Church in society; the Church as an institution reacting to social change; the ecclesial system in itself; and finally some contemporary theological trends.

The Institutional Church in a Changing Society

Our point of departure in this phase of our study will be the same as that which underlies the whole of our study: an analysis of social change in itself. The events we have been studying are all part of one basic movement which can be detected in all the successive upheavals of history. We have to remember that the Renaissance signified the disruption of the *Corpus Christianum* which formed the warp and woof of the European cultural universe of the period. Through Western colonial conquests the other continents were also caught up in a process of social change, the full consequences of which cannot yet be measured. In order to understand the repercussions these phenomena had on the institutional Church, it might be well to mention some of the basic principles of religious sociology.

Religious sociology and social change. In traditional societies the symbiosis of nature and society meant that the latter was naturally integrated into the process of cosmic determinism. This, in turn, led to the elaboration of a system that explained natural phenomena by creating a mythical universe which reflected and guaranteed the social system. The worlds of the living and the dead, of the spirits and divinities were closely interwoven, and the hierarchy of human society was established in accordance with a real or mythical power over natural and social phenomena.

Human groups had practically no possibility of formulating and pursuing their own collective objectives. Social behavior consisted almost exclusively in the observation of norms whose conformity was guaranteed by the social system and particularly by the power system. The integration of nature, society, and the mythical universe invested the guarantors of social organization and its symbols with a sacred character. Conversely, this interpretation meant that nature itself became a social category.[1]

One can, therefore, readily understand that it was considered sacrilegious for man to conquer nature unless he did so by means of magic rites which put him in possession of certain sacred powers. The symbiosis of the natural universe—charged with sacred meaning—and the organization of social life was such that all the events in the lives of human communities were presided over by gods and spirits. In a system of this kind the natural and social orders are homogeneous and based on the observance of common norms.[2] Much of the content of traditional religious myths express this reality and they can be found in many different contexts.

There is some room for change in this type of world-view as long as it takes place within the basic framework. Civilizations, dynasties, and political systems appear and disappear in successive waves, the one element of continuity always being the relation with the sacred, considered under multiple and ever-changing forms as immanent to the physical, social world. A "desacralized" view of things, in which man is seen as autonomous in his use of nature and his organization of society, signifies, therefore, a clean break with the traditional view.

One might be justified in thinking that a civilization which valued man's responsibility should have won ready acceptance in the Judaeo-Christian tradition. After all, most contemporary theologians claim that the true roots of the long history of secularization are, in fact, to be found in the Bible. This, at any rate, is what Arned van Leeuwen affirms, in his *Christianity in World History*.[3] According to van Leeuwen, all the great civilizations of the East were "ontocratic," that is, founded on a vision of the universe as a "cosmic whole." The Bible is the only instance in which this view was discarded and replaced by a theocracy. Greek thought also freed man from an ontocratic vision, but in a quite different way. The Judaeo-Christian tradition, therefore, can be said to be at the origin of the process of secularization which brought forth Western civilization.

We might feel that this is a theologian's view, rather than that of a sociologist or a historian, even if it is plausible that the conjunction of Greek and biblical thought was a decisive factor in the development of the West. For even before a rational explanation had been found for the laws that govern the cosmos and social change, Christianity had taken over the function filled by the earlier religions as guarantor of the social order and by their symbolism. This was the role it assumed in the Roman Empire, in which it replaced the prevailing system of legitimation and the elaboration of collective symbols. And when the social fabric of the Roman Empire disintegrated, it managed to survive as a cultural system in a new society, which, in spite of very different circumstances, molded itself along fundamentally identical lines.

One might wonder why religion has always supplied a system of legitimation whose main purpose is to maintain the cohesion of a society. Peter Berger affirms that religion has been the most common and effective instrument of legitimation because it links the precarious social structure to an absolute reality.[4] But, on a deeper level, in a framework that sees nature and society as a homogeneous whole, a religious legitimation is essential. It is what could be called *sacral totalitarianism:* Reference to the divine is the decisive element in the system of legitimation of both natural and social mechanisms.

With the Renaissance the laws of the physical universe began to be better understood. Thomistic philosophy, which had revived the scientific Aristotelian view, paved the way for these new discoveries which presupposed the recognition of a natural world free from the influence of sacred immanence. The new world-view with roots in the biblical tradition recognized the existence of a transcendent God who, having created man, endowed him with lordship over nature. It was inevitable that such discoveries should have repercussions on the level of social structures, for they undermined the cosmosociological integration on which society was founded. Although the consequences on the social level were felt only after a long time, the first breach was opened in the overall cultural and social system, and institutionalized Christianity, the guarantor of the system, was bound to react.

In this new perspective the principle of causality was endowed with new content: the notion of law. It was no longer a normative regulating disposition which conditioned phenomena according to whether men observed or failed to observe it. The notion of a scientific law implies constant causal connection, and once it is introduced into a culture it is impossible for society to continue to be governed according to a body of divine precepts. In a society governed by divine precept not only was authority the guarantor and foundation of social order, but truth itself was the expression of social authority.[5] From the sociological point of view one can say that in such a system legitimations and values bow to the norms: The system as a whole is normative. Even the laws have a sacral and religious origin.

The new situation was one in which sacral norms governed society alone. Religious legitimation governed a narrower field, but at the same time it asserted itself more vigorously than ever. Even those who rejected a religious explanation of nature, still judged a religious legitimation of society to be essential. For instance, this was the case for Voltaire.

The laws of social development were discovered gradually in a second phase, largely as a by-product of historical studies and the discovery of other cultures. The study of society abandoned the deductive method characterized by philosophical projection of an ideal society and became an analysis of social processes modeled on the analysis of natural processes. This approach made it possible to develop a critical point of view and, then, to desacralize the power structure and the whole of the social symbolism. It was a prelude to the social changes that were becoming more and more necessary because of concurrent developments in production methods.

The process of social desacralization began with the utopians of the sixteenth century, when Thomas More published his *De optimo Reipublicae Statu deque Nova Insula Utopia,* and with the

Dominican monk Campanella, in the seventeenth century, who wrote the *City of the Sun* and paid for his temerity with twenty-seven years in prison. The major precursors of the movement were Montaigne with his *Essays* and above all Montesquieu with his *l'Esprit des lois* and Jean-Jacques Rousseau with his *Contrat social*. Rousseau's discovery of the autonomy of society, combined with the Encyclopedists' notion of a twofold unity of human knowledge—objective unity or that of the universe it expresses and subjective unity or that of the mind which knows—led to adopting the methods of analysis used to study natural phenomena in the analysis of social phenomena. This was the current which served as the matrix for the work of Saint-Simon, August Comte, de Tocqueville, and later Marx and Engels.

In spite of the differences in historical timing and the tremendous variety of situations covered by the concept of revolution, most of the events we have described in this book took—or are taking—place at the meeting point between a "sacral" and a "modern" society.

The Church in the midst of change. In Western societies and their colonies, before the transformation of the traditional sociopolitical systems, the Church had a near-monopoly in the definition of values and a total monopoly as a system of legitimation or explanation. In this sense it was the guarantor of the social system and that is why religious unity was so important in the political sphere. When the Reformation took place, it led, inevitably, to wars of religion in which political power grafted itself onto religious unanimity. The social movements of the Middle Ages inevitably had religious connotations and in many cases the Church was active in repressing them. The Waldenses, the Albigenses, and the Lollards were repressed by the Catholic Church; the peasant revolt under Munzer was repressed by the Lutheran Church. And the nineteenth-century messianic movements in Northeast Brazil and the twentieth-century Kibangist movements in the Belgian Congo had a great deal in common with those of the Middle Ages.

The gradual transformation of values, or of the cultural system, led some individuals and groups to defect from the religious body, thereby exercising a form of cultural leadership outside the

Church. The result was an intransigent reaction on the part of the Church, of which the Inquisition was only one example. Christianity in its institutional aspect, therefore, had every appearance of being closely bound to civil society. By its monopoly in the definition of values, it choked off all new values, making it impossible for them to express themselves freely. The institutional Church was the guarantor of the social system; its own system of legitimation, the doctrinal content, seemed irrevocably bound to that system. There was also a sort of osmosis between religious language and the justification of powers delegated by the religious institution (the anointing of kings, the consecration of feudal overlords and knights).

As for the lower strata of society, they were integrated into the social values through the religious institution whose rituals, for example, all expressed the dominant values and encouraged uniformity by attributing transcendent meaning to them. The Marxist analyses sees this very clearly: "The dominant religions in history are religions of the dominant class (or nation or civilization)."[6] According to Engels, the revolutionary classes opposed the dominant class by producing a subversive or revolutionary religion up until the French Revolution. According to Marx, the novelty of contemporary history "consists precisely in the fact that the mystery of the historic process of revolutionary change has been elucidated and consequently, instead of sublimating this practical, 'exterior' process in the transcendental form of a new religion, the people have rejected all religion."[7]

In these circumstances it was inevitable that the breakdown of the social system should affect Christianity itself. By its ratification of the established order, Christianity fostered an attitude toward God that prevented the emancipation of individuals and groups, which was the goal of the social movements. These movements, therefore, struggling against everything that upheld the social system, struggled also against its most solid bulwark, religion.

The Church as an organization opposed the revolutionary movements as though it believed that the only possible relation between revealed religion and the social and cultural system was that which had existed in the *ancien régime*. Generally speaking, as soon as a revolutionary movement begins to lose its virulence, the model to which the Church tends to revert, or at least to refer as a frame of reference for the future, has always been that which it had known prior to the revolution. This was the case in France as well as in Latin America where there have been various periods of "restoration." The French case is sufficiently well known. In Latin America, after the profound crisis which accompanied the accession to independence and the disintegration of the ecclesiastical institution which followed, the process was similar to that which prevailed in France. As we know, almost all the bishops were expelled after independence because they were Spanish, and the hierarchy was restored only very gradually, due to the fact that Spain invoked its right of patronage and opposed the nomination of new bishops. At the same time the religious orders were laicized in most of these countries: Educational institutions, particularly the universities in which clerics received their training, were abolished, and Church properties, which in some countries were considerable, were confiscated. Once the political situation had regained a certain stability and the relations between Church and State had improved, the only frame of reference for renewed relations was that of the colonial era. Hence the demands for ecclesiastical privileges, the union of Church and State, and a concordat assuring Church control of education.

The conflict was all the more intense in those cases in which the Church had played a predominant role in the elaboration and legitimation of the sociocultural system being overthrown. There was a great difference in this respect, for example, in the case of the French Revolution and in what took place in May, 1968, in France. And it is extremely interesting to see, in this connection, how the uncritical acceptance of a social system can distort the moral judgment. An example of this can be seen in the pessimistic judgments pronounced on the use of violence: Established violence is ignored because it is legitimate (or legalized, as Max Weber has it), while revolutionary violence, which is not legitimate, is treated with extreme wariness.

The conflict has also been more intense when the transformations being effected in the social system appealed to a rival system of legitimation opposed to the Christian system. This was the case of the revolutionary ideology in France at the end of the eighteenth century as well as of the Marxist ideology in the nineteenth century, and it is the case of contemporary revolutionary movements in Latin America, Vietnam, and Africa. Many people see atheism as the only possible form of total challenge to the old regime, bourgeois society, or political and economic colonialism. The passage from a sacral to a semisacral situation, and subsequently to one in which all reference to the divine is eliminated from the explanations of nature and society, seems to correspond to the different phases of the situation in which the Church finds itself in the process of sociocultural change. We must now take a closer look at the reactions of the institutional Church during this process of change.

The Reaction of the Institutional Church to the Changes in Society

As we have had occasion to mention already, the Church is not a monolithic entity. It would be misleading to speak of the Church's attitude to revolution as though there were only one model within the institution.

The Church as institution. The Church is an institution with its own values and norms, its own system of legitimation, and its own organization. The characteristic feature of its values is that they are focused on the ultimate meaning of human existence as it is lived by the individual and the group. The system of legitimation is based on divine revelation. The organization of the Church must be adequate to its obligation to transmit these values and translate them into the concrete facts of culture and society and to foster their inward integration on the personal level. It must also have the flexibility of a social movement and give institutional form to collective expression, as in the liturgy.

It would be a mistake, therefore, to envisage the Church as an institution exclusively from the point of view of its cultural and social functions, as though these were only secondary manifestations; but it would be an even greater mistake to reduce the whole institution to this one type of function. The relations the Church has established with society result from the way it envisages the pursuit of its particular objectives. When it defends a given society, it is very rare that it is simply defending a system as such. More often than not, it does so because it sees that system as one which provides it with the possibility of communicating the message which it believes to be essential to man. The Church, then, will resist change all the more strongly if it has reason to fear being deprived of its means of action.

It is inaccurate, however, to speak of "the Church's resistance" to change. For we must distinguish not only different functions in the institution but also different social strata. The teaching authority and the government of the Church belong to the hierarchy. There is a clear distinction of official positions and of the function of authority within the group. The persons to whom these tasks are entrusted form, for historical reasons, a clearly delineated social stratum within the institution. The clergy forms another stratum and the laity a third—albeit far more sociologically diversified than either of the other two. And, as we have seen in some of the cases studied, different points of view about the way in which the Church's objectives should be pursued often correspond to this interior social stratification.

In general, it would be true to say that the hierarchy, as the guardian of the integrity of the institution and also, therefore, of its relations with the social system, reacts more strongly than the rest of the Church against social change. And this opposition is all the more accentuated when the relationship between the religious institution and civil society is one of reciprocal guarantees. In this case, those in charge of the ecclesiastical institution are not in a position to take a stand of critical opposition to the existing regime except on the level of secondary norms, whereas they must be fundamentally opposed to the introduction of a new regime. The majority of the clergy, in most instances, reacts in the same way as the hierarchy, which acts as a control group for either religious or social reasons. There have been, however, a number of cases in which a large percentage of the clergy did not follow the lead of the hierarchy, especially when their social origin bound them to one group and that of the hierarchy to another, as was the case during the first phase of the French Revolution. At other times, their differing positions have been based on conflicting values, giving rise to a struggle between two contradictory conceptions of the Church's role.

Among the laity, which is more in touch with the values of society, one can usually find the same diversity of options as can be found in society as a whole. The pattern of distribution, however, is not at all the same; usually a large percentage of those who can be classed sociologically as members of the institutional Church rally to the side of the hierarchy in opposing change.

To put it briefly, the higher an individual ranks in the internal stratification of the instituion, the more chances there are of his being opposed to social change. Moreover, the closer the parallel between the ecclesiastical and social structures, the more similar the reactions of the hierarchy to those of the elite groups in power.

Peter Berger speaks of the structure of reliability indispensable to the religious world. By this is meant a social basis on which religion can count in order to continue to exercise its function in society, in particular its function of supporting the social reality. This function, says Berger, needs a basis and that basis is nothing more than "the continual process by which a particular 'world' is constantly rebuilt and maintained."[8] Thus the religious universe of pre-Colombian Peru stood firm as long as its structures of reliability, Inca society, remained intact. This is valid both objectively, for collective activity, and subjectively, for the individuals integrated into that activity.

If we apply this concept to the different phases described in the preceding chapters, we might say that scientific investigation destroyed a first structure of reliability based on a homogeneous explanation of nature and society (a mythicosociological world, as Levy-Bruhl expresses it). Social analysis and its concrete application in the transformation of society destroyed a second structure of reliability, that which legitimated the power structure by divine intervention. As we have said, this process entailed the passage from a wholly sacral situation to one which was only partially sacral, and finally to one in which all influence of the sacred was rejected both in the natural and in the social orders. Today we have a situation of residual sacredness, in which the sacred seeks refuge in the institutional Church.[9]

Peter Berger's thought merits further development. It seems that there is a dialectical relation between religious reality and social reality, at least if we look at the example of Christianity. In Latin America it is through concrete application of Christian values coupled to a sociopolitical analysis that a radical critique of society has been produced. Such a critique, in turn, necessarily poses a challenge to the institutional Church both in what concerns its relations with society and in its internal organization. However, this phenomenon is certainly a product of society and of the perception of social reality by means of an analysis, however rudimentary.

The causes of reaction and its mechanism. In the descriptions of the different cases studied—and many other examples would have given the same results—one observation is particularly striking: the incapacity of the ecclesiastical hierarchy, with very few exceptions, to grasp the dynamics of history. Because of the function of the hierarchy within the Church, this incapacity leads to many difficulties for the institution as a whole. Is it possible to uncover the mechanism that operates in this situation and attempt to explain it without falling into the simplistic trap of seeing only the reflection of the class struggle in the ecclesiastical institution?

As I mentioned at the beginning of this chapter, Christianity took over the function of guaranteeing the social order, and by so doing the Church won a monopoly in the definition of social values and in their explanation and systematic legitimation. But this development was probably more than a sociological accident; it was in conformity with a doctrinal conception of divine action intervening from on high in the history of mankind and guiding it toward its goal. Reference to God in a religious-cultural model of this type quite naturally leads to the Church's acting as intermediary between God and human society and conceiving its role to be the definition of collective goals or social values on the basis of the body of doctrines entrusted to it.

This conception corresponded to the cultural and social situation of society prior to the Renaissance. But the situation changed:

Nature first of all, then society itself, became the objects of autonomous analysis and explanation when men discovered that they functioned according to their own mechanisms. The old system of explanation (and the social values upheld by it) no longer coincided with the new conditions. There were only two possible solutions: Either theology, understood as a discourse on revelation, finding itself faced with a new reading of the universe, would have to fall into step with the general movement and elaborate a corresponding symbolic model of explanation, or the conflict would break out into the open.

A scientific reading of the physical, social, and psychological universe developed gradually through a cumulative process. Over a long period it had developed in spheres that presented no threat to a mythicosociological explanation of the world and the organization of society. But there came a point when this scientific reading of the universe could no longer be ignored, and its emergence constituted a challenge to society. Either this new understanding had to be legitimated or it had to be rejected.

Three different types of attitude developed as a result. Some people gradually elaborated a new world view, based on a reference to God's action in history, which recognized and respected man's responsibility for his physical and social environment. This view, in which man is a responsible protagonist, completely upset the traditional cultural and social model. Others—including the majority in the institutional Church—remained firmly attached to the old model. Still others rejected all reference to God and even saw this rejection as a necessary condition for the legitimation of the new cultural and social model.

Many centuries were to pass before the new world view was sanctioned by Catholicism. The Second Vatican Council unquestionably constituted an important phase in this process, but the concrete consequences implied in the intellectual steps taken at Vatican II are still very far from being fully operative on the level of the interior integration of social values. Many contemporary examples studied in this book demonstrate this contention.

It might be well at this point to enumerate some of the social consequences of the traditional conception described above which acted, and acts still, as a cultural brake. One of the first things to note is that the evolution of biological and social facts is of very minor importance in such an outlook. For in this view all the norms orienting the functioning of physical and social life flow directly from the system of legitimation, which, linked as it is to a certain religious conception of divine action, leaves no room for autonomous norms. Empirical knowledge is not considered significant or capable of orienting certain areas of these norms autonomously. Biological and social facts, therefore, can have no bearing on the basic model imposed by this view of nature and society. As far as society is concerned, only the pyramidal model of organization is relevant in the traditional system. Some minor adjustments on the level of functional norms might be acceptable, but never on the level of values. This explains why there is no room in this system for real sociopolitical analysis.

As for any possible transformations of society, it is obvious that they would have to be imposed from above. They could not come about through pressure from below. To be legitimate, they must be directed by the power structure. When the situation becomes too deplorable and concrete conditions too far below the standards required for decent human existence, an appeal is made to those in power to act with justice—or to the rich to act with generosity.

Also, the closer the original schema came to a sacral model, as was the case in the first type of reaction we described in Latin America,[10] the stronger the resistance to change and the more total the lack of any analysis. All energies are concentrated on the morality of the means rather than on the legitimacy of the ends. Violence, for instance, becomes the main issue in the process of social change and the pivotal point around which options are taken. Any intervention on the part of the Church in the field of social conflict is intended as prophetic rather than political, for the ecclesial institution aspires to the role of mediator and, for this, it must be sure of its audience in both parties to the dispute.

Another feature is that it is virtually impossible for such a system to accept the proposition that men can pursue values identical to its own within the framework of other systems of legitimation, and this gives rise to what Leslie Dewart, in his analysis of the

Church in Cuba, has called a tactical inflexibility. But it also happens that the Church is almost totally ignorant of all realities exterior to itself and is exclusively concerned with its own internal problems or with so-called purely spiritual affairs. This attitude is equivalent to endorsing the existing relations between the institutional Church and its social environment, and it usually goes hand in hand with a conservative attitude. The result is, also, that those Christians who participate in the new social values and are active in promoting social change, are rejected explicitly or implicitly by their Church, and many of them, tiring of the fruitless struggle, cease to have any interest in the institutional policy pursued by the Church.

There is, however, another attitude, diametrically opposed to this first view, and it is based on another conception of divine action. It accepts the fact that the Church does not have a monopoly in the elaboration of social values. Even when this is the prevailing attitude, however, the reactions of the ecclesiastical hierarchy are still very much the same as in the past. Two hypotheses could be put forward to explain this phenomenon, both of which take the Church as a social system as their frame of reference.

For historical reasons, the ecclesiastical hierarchy has, in fact, been assimilated in almost all contemporary societies, into the elite groups in power—into the "establishment." Its social prestige and its status symbols, its way of life and its social relations, all contribute to making it a part of the upper classes of society even in countries where Christians are in a minority. It is, therefore, absolutely normal, from a psychological point of view, that it should react to events in the same way as the political and social elite, and although it is theoretically possible, it is extremely difficult for it to be critically detached. This is the first hypothetical explanation. The second is that the Church, having so much highly institutionalized activity, counts on a certain degree of goodwill on the part of the political authorities in order to continue to carry it out. Schools, health services, salaries for the clergy, the construction of churches, tax exemptions, etc.—all these are signs of the Church's condition of dependence. As Leslie Dewart puts it: "It is difficult to take risks, as one sometimes must, or to assume them with wisdom when one is dominated by a desire for security."[11]

All this helps to explain the paradox of a doctrine of liberation which, in its institutionalized form, opposes the concrete applications of freedom. Alexis de Tocqueville declared that Christianity contributed to democratic ideas (what he called the immaterial sphere), but that it was the revolutions that provided their translation into concrete reality. Because of the Church's role as an institution in society, it could perceive revolution only in the light of its inherent ambiguities, whereas the established regime is clothed in the robes of legitimacy; whence its antagonism and an attitude of suspicion and distrust.

It would be an oversimplification, of course, to explain everything by one single factor, or to pretend that the Church's reaction to social change has always followed the same identical pattern at all times and in all places. And yet it is striking to observe that there is, as it were, a constant thread running through all the different circumstances. This alone is an invitation to delve deeper for an explanation. The pattern that prevailed at the time of the upheaval in European society seems to be the same as that which prevails in the contemporary upheavals in international society. It seems that the Church always has the same difficulty in recognizing the phenomena of domination—of class in the one case, and of economic, political, and military imperialism in the other.

There is, however, an evolution taking place in the Church's attitude. That is undeniable. We have already mentioned the Second Vatican Council and could quote a certain number of instances in which the Latin American, Asian, or African hierarchies have taken a new stand or initiated some concrete programs or, again, certain major documents such as *Pacem in Terris* and *Populorum Progressio*. But all this still seems very general, far removed from concrete conditions and, to be quite frank, sometimes quite unreal. As soon as concrete applications are attempted, the flood of qualms and hesitations is such that one wonders whether the ecclesiastical documents were ever really meant to be applied. And even when some progress is achieved on the level of the system of legitimation by the acceptance of certain values as, for instance, in the case of the social situation in Latin America or in that of colonialism in Africa, the concrete application of these values still seems to fall short of expectations. This is the problem that the third part of this chapter will attempt to explain, after a summary discussion of the role played by ideology in the process.

The role of ideology. The sociologist Adam Schaff defines ideology as "a system of opinions founded on an accepted value system which determines men's attitudes and behavior with regard to the goals hoped for from the development of the society, the social group, or the individual."[12] This is a sociological view of ideology. To put it differently, ideology consists of a system which enables the members of any given society to legitimate the norms and values of that society. This legitimation is never absolutely logical, but contains emotional elements which are capable of motivating men and giving them a feeling of security simply because they contain a summary of the past, explain the present, and foresee the future.

According to this definition, ideology is a fundamental element in the culture of every human, ethnic, social, or even religious group. But—and this is even more fundamental—an ideology is a synthesis which is necessarily provisional, linked to a specific historical situation. As a legitimation of norms and values, ideology always stands in relation to the level of knowledge and science and the methods of production, and this is why it enters into conflicts of interest between different groups; it is one of the keys to political problems. On the other hand ideology is itself "produced" and controlled, at least partially, by the group whose objectives it crystallizes. It is a mode of knowledge more formal than empirical knowledge, but no more scientific than direct perception. And this is why, although ideology has practically disappeared from our representation of nature in modern societies, it is still the principal mode of representation of social life. Racism, authority systems, and models for family life are a few of the instances in which ideological elements are still abundantly, if not exclusively, present.

This leads to an important point: Ideology has not only an overt, tangible role to play but also a latent function which is no less real, for on the basis of the division of labor or the distribution of power, it provides the dominant group with a sort of second language, a reading of history which can be imposed on the whole of society and which can be used to conceal the true nature of social relations. In this case it not only serves to integrate the various groups of society around common objectives, it also mobilizes all the different groups for the pursuit of objectives which are in the exclusive interest of the dominant group. It thereby becomes a "counterfeit conscience," freezing the relations of domination-subjection by justifying them. And so the dominant group produces an ideology which is capable of endorsing its domination and of giving those dominated a higher motivation, a metasocial guarantee which persuades them to accept the social system. In the name of the benefits of free enterprise, private property, even of progress, private interests are being defended.

This phenomenon is particularly visible in periods of rapid social change, in revolutionary periods. The bourgeois classes overthrew the old regime in France, which was a political obstacle to their supremacy, and established their own domination in the nineteenth century on the slogans of "liberty" and "democracy." In other places and at other times the defense of the "Christian West," or of the white race, has been invoked to legitimate situations such as we have described in Vietnam, the Portuguese colonies, South Africa, etc. An intensive use of ideology, therefore, tends to preserve the status quo and to objectify a given situation; this is the point at which ideology degenerates into myth. The internal contradictions of societies are built up in this way; the sociopolitical practice repudiates, in fact, the ideology which justifies it. Whether one looks at the United States or at the People's Democracies of the East, one can see many elements in these societies which do not correspond to their declared ideals. The "American way of life" and the "workers' internationalism" often remain empty articles of faith.

Religious myths and institutionalized religion play a large part in this mystifying function of ideology. The preceding studies have shown this clearly enough: sacralization of the old regime, excessive valorization of the workingman's condition in the nineteenth century in the name of a God-given social order and of charity, etc. The revolutions which fall back on religion and the milleninalist utopias can also be put in the same category.

After this brief discussion of ideology we can now attempt a sociological approach to the relation between faith and ideology. We shall take two different aspects of the question: first, the relations between faith and ideology properly so-called, and then the particular situations of ideology in our society today. Sociologists who set out to study possible homologies in a body of beliefs and an ideology must take into account what the believer has to say about his faith. He must, therefore, listen to theologians and use their discourse as material for his analysis.

By Christian faith we mean, then, a personal attachment to God's revelation in Jesus Christ concerning the meaning of human existence, both individual and collective, a personal welcome to a Word which bears a message about the world community and the individual person.[13] Accepting this theological definition as his starting point, a sociologist can, without necessarily reducing faith to just one more ideology, study three possible aspects of the relation between faith and ideology: on the plane of their respective world views; on the plane of their relation with other ideologies; and on the plane of the activities of religious institutions and their history.

Let us look, first of all, at their world-views. "The decision of a believer, that is to say, a truly wise decision, is an act of *charity* in the present, rooted in *faith* in an event constantly before our eyes, in the *hope* of an unfailing promise."[14] André Manaranche, who gives this definition of faith, immediately adds that "God's plan. . . does not abandon our temporal liberties to the power of a Transcendence completely exterior to us and which has already foreseen, organized, and prefabricated every possible contingency." This point of view enables us to see the position of faith in relation to ideology. On the one hand it is a wise or sensible decision, which introduces order into one's attitudes and behavior while giving direction and meaning to action by interpreting history, and in this way it can be said to be an ideology; at the same time, however, faith contains within itself that which it needs to avoid

the danger that lurks in every ideology of degenerating into historical determinism. Faith can be said to be the meaning of a task
which has to be accomplished in a context of contingency and risk.
"God's word changes man," writes another author. "Theology is a
kind of anthropology; however, faith does not say that history is
the effective realization of what it declares about man, nor can it
make it so."[15]

Faith—according to contemporary theology—must exercise a
critical function with regard to world-views, human projects, and
ideologies. "Faith," writes Pastor André Dumas, "is a warning to
the ideologies not to set themselves up as idols by becoming 'faiths'
... instead of being content to be a methodology of rational
interpretation and historical transformation." And he adds, "Faith
is a vocation accepted by a person, not an interpretation arrived at
by deduction."[16] In other words, when Scripture says that faith is
"beyond flesh and blood," we must accept the logical consequences of this and not confuse the kingdom of God with "Christian civilization." Furthermore, faith's intrinsic reference to a dimension beyond history, the "beyond" of unity in Christ of which
St. Paul speaks referring to the conflict between Greeks and Jews,
means that its intention is the dissolution of all human exclusives
and partisan group interests. The scope of faith is the whole of
humanity reconciled; it describes the figure of the perfect Man to
come. But it is precisely at this point that what can be a potent
demystification of ideologies in the name of a higher Truth, also
runs the risk of forcing history into the well-worn channels of a
unity prefabricated or even imposed by force—one only has to
remember the Inquisition.[17]

And yet "the Sabbath is made for man, not man for the Sabbath." Even in its institutional aspects Christian faith reverses the
norms. It cannot be contained by any moral precept: "Be perfect
as your heavenly Father is perfect." These, then, are the main
features of the ethicoreligious vision of contemporary Christianity,
and the sociologist has to determine how that vision evolved and
where it stands in relation to the cultural transformation of society.

The historicosocial relationship has been examined in detail in
the preceding studies, each of which explained the ideological

position of the institutional Church when it attempts to act within a cultural and social system by molding the behavior and representations of individuals and groups. It is in the area of institutional relations that the homologies in faith and ideology seem to be most visible. No doubt this is one of the dilemmas of the institutional process, for "unadulterated faith" is found only in theological textbooks.[18] Many deviations which are not always recognized as such by those who practice them are revealed by the facts in the history of the institution. The sociologist has to recognize that the institutionalized faith (i.e., the Church) sees itself as having a role as critic of society, and he will try to identify the mechanisms involved when it exercises or fails to exercise this function.

The question is particularly acute today in view of the new conditions imposed on ideologies in societies undergoing rapid change. We can now sketch some of the salient features of the phenomenon and the consequences they entail in our area of concern.

When a society evolves from one in which work is segmented and many people have multivalent roles to one which valorizes and favors autonomous groups with specialized goals, more groups develop an awareness of their own interests and become capable of envisaging the goals of society as a whole with a certain detachment. This new phenomenon makes the survival of a holistic ideology very precarious and sometimes quite impossible. It is true that the rational model to which our producer society is obliged to conform can also be analyzed as an ideology, but the progress of knowledge makes it very vulnerable, since it can be understood and criticized from within by those who should be its faithful servants. Instead of reaching stability through the pursuit of apparently rational goals, our society seems in some ways to be increasingly subject to conflict.[19]

The relativizing of ideologies, however, is counterbalanced by another phenomenon: When a society evolves from a subsistence level to a level of relative abundance in which advance planning is possible, more possibilities are open to choice and the problem of justifying one's choice becomes more complicated. The need to combat the tendency to see everything in terms of economics, the

increasingly obvious ethical dimension of economic options bring
a new sense of urgency to the ideologies. This is especially true in
the case of economies which are still developing. When it adopts
modern production methods, is a society obliged to assimilate
technical values into its cultural system, that is, to adopt the
culture of the dominant countries? Should it not, rather, create its
own values by rediscovering its own cultural origins and by a
rebirth to its own authentic identity? And in this case do not
ideological factors become fundamental in giving meaning to the
past and in formulating a projection for the future? Moreover,
does not the choice of a specific "way" of development always
involve ideological elements, whether in an advanced or an underdeveloped society?[20]

These first two features have important consequences for religious groups. The religious outlook loses its monopoly on legitimation and finds itself in competition with ideologies which experience the same difficulties. Does this mean that it is bound to lose
all its power to energize the common project and that it will have
to content itself with a residual role in the private lives of individuals? Inversely, where does it stand in the laborious task of defining
the social project and what can be the basis of its intervention in
this task?

A third fundamental feature—the passage from a sacral to a
desacralized world—has equally momentous consequences. This
process renders utterly meaningless any recourse to a holistic explanation of the world in which faith fills the gaps of men's knowledge. Man no longer believes that the natural order is taboo or
that the social order is the expression of God's will. Once this
transformation has been accomplished in men's minds, it is irrevo-
cable, and it will not be long before it spreads throughout the
world.

Believers will have to accept this desacralized view of the world
if they are going to take an active part in social change and adhere
to the ideologies of progress. It will oblige them to reexamine their
notion of authority and the political order; it will oblige them to
accept its own interpretations of themes in Scripture on those
subjects.[21] Similarly, Christians will have to acquire a positive

attitude—for which they seem to have little disposition, judging from history—toward the conflicts which social systems inevitably go through.[22]

These are very fundamental questions. The elements which history contributes to the answers tend to emphasize the ambiguous position of Christianity during periods of revolution, whether because it sacralizes the established order, or at least proves itself a willing handmaid in an attempt to do so, or because it brands the notion of social conflict as culpable.

The Internal Sociocultural System of the Church

Very early in its history, in the fourth century, Christianity became the guarantor of the cultural and social system of Roman society, and as a matter of course adopted its patterns of interior organization, as evidenced by the present juridical system as well as by the administration and the authority system. The symbols of prestige, titles, clothes, and buildings are all signs of the social image with which the Church identified itself. The fact that Christianity took on this function of guarantor had consequences which were certainly not all negative. It ensured the cohesion of European culture for a thousand years or more—something that was probably a necessary condition for the eventual flowering of a totally new cultural system—and it provided a basis of continuity in the social system when the Roman and Byzantine empires collapsed.

But at the same time the identification with the state molded the Church on a specific model in terms of its value system and its organization. The great theological syntheses of the Middle Ages, by the very power of their intellectual constructs, only served to reinforce this identification. In other words, the Church based its interior organization on a model of traditional society, that is to say, a society that was sacralized (with an authority system patterned on an immutable pyramidal organization reflecting the notion of divine authority), compartmentalized (with relatively simple and autonomous social units), and segmented (repeating the same model of organization on the different levels and within its secondary institutions).

There is no question but that the Counter-Reformation influenced the Church in such a way as to reinforce this system. Roman centralism, which began to be more marked after the Council of Trent, really came into its own after the First Vatican Council. And it was only with Vatican II that the new values could be officially introduced, that is, accepted by the system of legitimation, into the Church. It is these new values which, as critical decisions, were to trigger the process of destructuration now going on.[23] But it should be noted that many persons who have posts of responsibility in the Church have still not assimilated these newly legitimated values into their own mental schemas even if they have accepted the verbal endorsement of the system of legitimation. And this is why they are still opposed, for example, to a translation into concrete terms of a new conception of authority, of "participation" within the ecclesial institution, or, again, to the recognition of culture as a value and of solidarity with those who bear the burden of a politically and economically oppressive society. This is very manifest in the first draft for the revision of canon law which expressed a pyramidal concept not only of the organization of the Church but also of relations between the Church and society.

Throughout all this period the Church necessarily appeared as the upholder of values inherent in the traditional social structure. It is hardly astonishing, then, that it always attracted the conservative social forces and that, as an institution, it generally felt a greater affinity for them than for the forces of change. When some members of the hierarchy did begin to take a stand in favor of changes in society, those same conservative classes were scandalized and very quick to express their hostility. It is quite clear that they saw the Church as the guarantor of their own social status. Where social stratification had already been organized along new lines, the Church could not play the role of guarantor for the whole social system, but it could continue to do so for one segment of society—for the new bourgeoisie, for instance, that had grown out of industrialization and the colonial administrations in Asia and Africa. This has also been the pattern in the developing countries in which the Church exerts its influence in favor of the traditional elite or of the new elite groups arising from the growth of the administration and the economic relations with foreign powers.

It is striking to see how the cultural model of authority and power in traditional society still seems to underlie the bourgeois and colonial societies and to influence the new elite groups of the Third World. Its changelessness in the midst of changing societies explains a certain number of contradictions between the collective behavior of the power elites and their explanation of democratic society. It is at this point that the latent function of ideology comes into its own as the justification of power. The durability of this cultural model can also be seen in the case of the institutional Church. Throughout events and in spite of many distressing experiences above and beyond the legitimation of new positions, the same patterns of behavior recur, bound as they are to the function of guaranteeing traditional society. The "two societies" theory, reiterated in the draft revision of canon law, can only lead to the Church's upholding the political and social status quo.

What we have just said cannot, of course, account for all the different situations that arise and that are often highly complex and full of nuances. Rather, what we have described is a process which, in the infinitely various circumstances of societies undergoing change, takes on many different forms. And yet the recognition of this process will perhaps help us to understand three facts which seem to me to be at the heart of contemporary socioreligious situations.

The first fact is that of an overemphasis on the hierarchical character of the Catholic Church by comparison with its character as a communion. This is obviously linked with the fact that the internal social system of the Church is identified with that of traditional society. But it also explains the protective attitude of the Church as an organization with regard to its members, manifested most notably in its multiplication of temporal institutions.

The second fact is the way in which the hierarchical Church now takes a stand on social problems, especially in Latin America. Society is criticized and even roundly condemned for its injustice and its failure to provide for the essential needs of human subsistence. But judgment is usually pronounced as from without. There is no self-examination or self-criticism within the Church; hardly any of its relations with the society of which, after all, it is an integral part; and none at all of its own interior social system. Its judgment of society, therefore, even when it is relevant, seems more like a political than a prophetic act. The same can be said of the international organization of the Church and its declarations condemning liberal capitalism, prestige spending, and colonialism.

Finally, the third element which remains to be explained and which is closely bound up with the second is the fact that a serious social critique always and inevitably leads to a critique of the Church itself as a social system. It is not possible to accept the former, with all its logical implications, without arriving at the latter. It is a certainty, therefore, that the development of social criticism, which is part and parcel of the prophetic role of the Church, will lead to a fundamental reexamination of the Church's existence as a sociocultural system.

Throughout the course of man's social metamorphosis, of which we have studied only a few episodes, the organization of the Church according to a model of traditional society has strengthened it in its role as an institution which guarantees the society—or those segments of society—which held the reins of power. And this function, in turn, has tended to strengthen the internal patterns of the ecclesial institution. The acceptance of a new cultural model, its legitimation, and the gradual elaboration of a new symbolism are the necessary conditions for a change of attitude. Is this a possibility as things stand now? It is often very difficult to say. But what can at least be said is that it will not occur without some very profound upheavals, and the acceleration that is presently taking place in various internal and external processes relating to the ecclesial institution makes it conceivable that substantial change is possible. It will not take place spontaneously, however, for even after far-reaching transformations there is still a very strong tendency to strive for "restoration." This is something that has already happened in Mexico and it seems to be taking place now in Yugoslavia and even in Cuba. New models do not yet exist. They still have to be invented.

Contemporary Theological Trends

By way of conclusion I would like to take a brief look at the political theology of Johannes Metz.[24] Metz is not the only contemporary theologian to open up new avenues of study. A complete picture would have to include mention of the work of many Protestant theologians as well as, for example, the numerous attempts to elaborate a theology of revolution. However, since our purpose is sociological rather than theological, this will suffice to give an idea of the new research that is going on.

Political theology as elaborated by Metz takes as its starting point a critical reflection on the modern and contemporary history of Christianity. After a period in which the faith was politicized, that is, in which the ecclesial institution intervened actively and directly in the sphere of political organization, there followed a period of privatization of Christianity. In other words, the sphere of public affairs, the practical and theoretical construction of society no longer claimed the attention of theology. It was supplanted by the private sphere. The inner sanctum of individual consciences and the family became the favorite, almost exclusive, object of theological concern.

From this comes the dilemma; politicized Christianity or political abstention. It is no solution to politicize the faith all over again today. This would only compromise the autonomy of the sociopolitical sphere, now acknowledged by most theologians. The goal of political theology is to change the terms of the problem, by starting with a sociopolitical critique of society and of Christianity. For Christianity acts within specific social structures and it is often one of the elements in a repressive society.

In this sense the political order includes the whole public sphere, whether secular or religious, and herein lies the originality of Metz's initial hypothesis: The political order is not reduced to an instrument for the legitimation of power. As one of Metz's disciples puts it:

> Political theology hinges on the political order understood henceforth not as the sphere in which sovereignty, power and domination are grounded, but as the public sphere of democracy, the mediation of freedom and the liberation of men (an interest of the whole of society, not only of the Church). Once the options for the freedom of all individuals and of the whole individual are the constitutive and constitutional basis for the structures of social relations, it follows that

no discipline of the social body (such as theology) can fill a valid political function without basing its action on that freedom of man.

Political theology, therefore, cognizant of the structures destructive of the common good or the social body, concealed on the one hand in an identification of the religious and the profane and, on the other, in their total dissociation, has no ambition to restore the political theology of the past—by an ecclesial or christological-theological definition of the goals and means of the political order such as can still be seen in some "regional" theologies of politics, work, development, etc. Nor does it wish to assume the function of legitimating the modern "schizophrenia"—by elaborating models for Christian action as though the sphere of faith were, in its origins and its ultimate reality, independent of the sociopolitical mechanisms which determine modern and contemporary man.[25]

Political theology sets out to be not only a theory but also a praxis. If it remained on the purely theoretical level, it would be in danger of becoming the plaything of the dominant political practice. And the question arises, then, as to the locus of its praxis, and the answer is the Church; the Church as institution whose role is to criticize society. This function of social critic is essential to the Church, which exists not "in-itself" but for the parousia. It is in view of future reality, announced by Jesus Christ, that the institutional Church has the obligation to be a witness of hope and, therefore, a tangible, effective sign of hope. This means that it has the obligation to organize itself in such a way as to be the institution of critical freedom.

Throughout this book we have seen how the Church has often had a negative role in relation to movements of liberation. Political theology recognizes that this has often been so because the Church was trying to save itself and ensure its survival as an institution, and that it used the ambiguities of the revolutionary movements to justify its distrust and its attachment to the established order. But, in practice, how can it be brought to change this attitude? Is not this the dilemma of every institution? A subtle dialectical mechanism leads every institutionalization to secrete within itself the seeds of a negation of values.

It is not the task of theology to resolve this question. All it can do is to bring it out into the open and point to its fundamental connection with the message of Jesus Christ, thereby fulfilling its function with regard to itself: a critique of the Church's function in society and in its own interior organization. This type of theology, however, is inconceivable without a sociopolitical analysis, that is, without a scientific approach to its critical function. If it has the ambition to develop a praxis, it must come down from the olympian heights of general constructs and come to grips with processes and mechanisms. Political theology, therefore, must give a central place to sociopolitical analysis, and this casts an entirely new light on the relation between theology and the human sciences. Both have a hermeneutic function and neither can fulfill it without the other, for meaning is revealed not only in verbal expression and overt functions but also—and perhaps above all—in hidden functions and in the implicit discourse of ecclesial institutions.

The subject needs further development, and this is happening gradually. From our point of view, however, the important thing is to recognize that there is a current of contemporary theological reflection which is, at last, facing up to the questions raised in this study. And, as we have seen, this current exists not only in theory but also in practice. Only the future will tell whether it can be anything more than the theoretical reflection and inspiration of a minority. One thing we can already see, however, is that it seems to be sufficiently dynamic to have persuaded some people to continue their struggle for man's liberation now and in the future within the framework of the Church.

NOTES

Chapter One

1. J. Baechler, *Les phénomènes révolutionnaires* (Paris: Presses Universitaires de France, 1970); Frantz Fanon, *Sociologie d'une révolution, L'an V de la révolution algérienne* (Paris: Petite Collection Maspero, 1967); André Decouflé, *Sociologie des révolutions* (Paris: Presses Universitaires de France, 1968); Jules Monnerot, *Sociologie de la révolution* (Paris: Librairie Arthème Fayard, 1969).

2. Régis Debray, *Révolution dans la révolution* (Paris: François Maspero, 1967).

3. Lucien Sébag, *Marxisme et structuralisme* (Paris: Editions Payot, 1968).

4. M. de Certeau, *La prise de parole* (Bruges: Desclée de Brouwer, 1968); A. Decouflé, "La révolution et son double," *Cahiers Internationaux de Sociologie,* vol. XLVI, 1969, pp. 27-36.

5. Decouflé, *op. cit.,* p. 16.

6. G. Bouthoul, *Variations et mutations sociales* (Paris: Editions Payot, 1968), p. 53.

7. A.Kroeber, *Anthropology* (New York: Harcourt, Brace & Co., 1948), p. 408.

8. Karl Marx, *Zur Kritik der politischen Oekonomie,* Dietz, p. 13. (English translation, *Contribution to the Critique of Political Economy,* New York, International Publishing Co., 1970.)

9. Several authors propose different typologies according to their different points of view: juridical, philosophical, or sociological. H. D. Wendland, for example, speaking at the Church and Society conference in Geneva in 1966, enumerated the following types: *political revolution,* in the strict sense, i.e., simply a change of power; *social revolution,* a change in social stratifications and, consequently, in the power structure as well; and *total revolution,* or a global change in society. Umberto Melotti, in *Revoluzione e Società* (Milan, 1965), proposes the following: *political* and *social* revolution, cf. Marx; *major* and *minor* revolutions, the former being a change from one juridical structure to another, the latter being simply the effects of the resistance encountered in applying new principles; *bourgeois* and *proletarian* revolutions, cf. Marx; and *regressive* revolutions. See also Carl Friedrich, *Revolution* (New York: Atherton Press, 1969), "Revolution—Typology and Process," pp. 10-33.

10. Karl Marx and Friedrich Engels, *German Ideology* (New York: International Publishing Co., 1971).

11. *Ibid.*

12. Karl Marx, *Contribution à la critique de la philosophie de droit de Hegel* (Molitor's translation), vol. I, p. 101.

13. *Ibid.*

14. Marx and Engels, *German Ideology.*

15. Decouflé, *op. cit.,* pp. 23 ff.

16. Lanternari, *Les mouvements religieux des peuples opprimés* (Paris: François Maspero, 1963). A critical analysis of various studies of messianism can be found in M. de Certeau's article, "Religion et société: les millénarismes," in *Etudes,* April, 1969, pp. 608-616.

17. Louis Althusser, *Pour Marx* (Paris: François Maspero, 1966), p. 94.

18. "A class must be forged with radical chains, a class of bourgeois society which does not belong to bourgeois society, a class which is the dissolution of all classes, a sphere marked by a universal character because of its universal suffering and which does not claim any specific rights since it has suffered no specific wrongs, only a wrong in itself; a sphere which cannot lay claim to any historical rights but only to its human rights, a sphere which is not opposed to any particular consequence of the political system but is generally opposed to its presuppositions ..., a sphere which can no longer emancipate itself without emancipating all the other spheres of society and which, in a word, is the complete loss of man and which, therefore, can only reconquer itself by the complete revival of man. The decomposition of society in the form of a class is the proletariat." Karl Marx, *Contribution à la critique de la philosophie de droit de Hegel p. 106*.

19. "For the proletariat, the conditions of the old society are already virtually swamped. The proletarian is without property; his relation to his wife and children has no longer anything in common with the bourgeois family relations; modern industrial labor, modern subjection to capital, the same in England as in France, in America as in Germany, has stripped him of every trace of national character" (*Communist Manifesto*).

20. "Because of its economic vocation and the development of the economy, the bourgeoisie cannot but refuse to provide the proletariat with the economic conditions which would ensure them a certain standing, a place and role in society. Capitalism cannot exist without the proletariat ..., but it does not need them; it is constantly rejecting them from economic society by unemployment. If the proletariat is the negative of society it is because it is the fruit of society's active and effective negation of itself... above all the bourgeoisie is producing its own gravediggers" (*Communist Manifesto*).

21. *Ibid.*

22. "In all previous revolutions the mode of activity remained unchanged, and it was only a question of a redistribution of activity and a new distribution of work among different people. The Communist revolution, however, aims at destroying the previous mode of activity; it does away with work and abolishes the domination of all classes by abolishing the classes themselves" (Marx and Engels, *German Ideology*).

23. Marx and Engels, *Communist Manifesto*.

24. Pierre Naville, "Les mouvements révolutionnaires actuels et le marxisme," in *L'Homme et la Société*, vol. I, no. 1 (October, 1968), p. 42.

25. *Ibid.*, pp. 43–44.

26. Herbert Marcuse, "Réexamen du concept de révolution," *Diogène,*, 64 (October-December, 1968), p. 42.

27. *Ibid.*, pp.23–24.

28. Naville, *op. cit.*, p. 47.

29. Marcuse, *op. cit.*, p. 26.

30. Alain Touraine, *Le mouvement de mai ou le communisme utopique* (Paris: Editions du Seuil, 1968).

31. Rudi Supek, "Marx et la révolution," in *L'Homme et la Société*, 10 (October, 1968), p. 220.

32. Karl Marx, *Fondements de la critique de l'economie politique* (Paris: Anthropos, 1968), vol. II, pp. 221-222.

33. Supek, *op. cit.,* p. 224.

34. Marcuse, *op. cit.,* p. 29.

35. P. Hare, "Nonviolent Action from a Social-Psychological Perspective," *Sociological Inquiry,* vol. 38, no. 1, 1968, pp. 5-12.

36. S. I. Perloe, D. S. Olton, and D. L. Yaffe, "The Effect of Nonviolent Action on Social Attitudes," *Sociological Inquiry, loc. cit.,* pp. 13-22.

37. *Ibid.,* J. Stikem, "Nonviolence Is Two," pp. 23-30.

38. These ideas are largely borrowed from an analysis presented by Sternstein during a meeting of the International Movement of Reconciliation at Vienna in April, 1968.

39. Decouflé, *op. cit.,* p. 91.

40. *Ibid.,* p. 94.

41. Document of the political commission of the national committee of the MIR, dated April 9, 1966, *Venezuela—La Violencia, IV—MIR,* Cidoc Documents, 35 (Cuernavaca, 1968), pp. 4-46.

42. *Guatemala—La Violencia III,* Cidoc Documents, 21 (Cuernavaca, 1968), pp. 5, 18, 19.

43. H. Desroche, *Sociologies religieuses* (Paris: Presses Universitaires de France, 1968), pp. 56-74.

44. H. Lefebvre, *La somme et le reste* (Paris: Nef, 1959), p. 83.

45. G. Girardi, "Philosophy of Revolution and Atheism," *Concilium,* 36, 1968, pp. 109-122.

46. P. Blanquart, *A la recherche d'une théologie de la violence* (Paris: Les Editions du Cerf, 1968), pp. 138-155.

Chapter Two

1. Albert Soboul, *1789, l'an I de la liberté* (Paris: Editions Sociales, 1950), pp. 13-16.

2. J. Leflon, *La crise révolutionnaire* (Paris: Bloud et Gay, 1949), p. 25.

3. *Ibid.,* pp. 31-32.

4. *Ibid.,* p. 31.

5. Bossuet, *Complete Works,* vol. II, 1; vol. III, 1-2; vol. IV, 1.

6. Massillon, "Sermon on What the Mighty Owe to Religion," *Petit Carême.*

7. Soboul, *op. cit.,* p. 23.

8. Beaumarchais, *The Marriage of Figaro.*

9. René Descartes, *Discourse on Method,* Part 6.

10. Pascal, *Fragment of a Treatise on the Void.*

11. Bossuet, *Letter,* May 21, 1687.

12. D'Holbach, *La Contagion Sacrée* (1768), Preface.

13. A. Sorel, *L'Europe de la Révolution Française* (Paris: Librairie Plon, 1885), vol. I, p. 107.

14. Leflon, *op. cit.,* p. 39.

15. La Fayette, *Mémoires,* vol. III, quoted by Leflon, *op. cit.,* p. 80.

350 THE CHURCH AND REVOLUTION

16. A. Soboul, *Précis d'histoire de la Révolution Française* (Paris: Editions Sociales, 1962), p. 175.

17. Leflon, *op. cit.*, pp. 107-108.

18. Soboul, "Sentiments religieux et cultes populaires pendant la Révolution," *Archives de Sociologie des Religions*, 2 (July-December, 1956), pp. 73-89.

19. Soboul, *Précis d'histoire de la Révolution Française, op. cit.*, p. 289.

20. A. Aulard, *Le culte de la Raison et de l'Etre Suprème* (Paris, 1892), p. 19.

21. A. Mathiez, *L'Origine des cultes révolutionnaires* (Paris: 1904).

22. D. Guerin, *Les luttes de classes sous la Première République* (Paris: Editions Gallimard, 1946).

23. Soboul, "Sentiments religieux," *op. cit.*, p. 79.

24. Quoted from the newspaper *Le Patriote* by Régine Pernoud, in *Histoire de la Bourgeoisie en France* (Paris: Editions du Seuil, 1962), vol. II, p. 370.

25. See Peter Berger, *The Social Reality of Religion* (London: Faber & Faber, 1969).

26. See F. A. Isambert, *Christianisme et classe ouvrière* (Tournai-Paris: Casterman, 1961), pp. 149-150.

27. See F. Engels, *La Guerre des Paysans* (Paris: Costes, 1936); also E. Bloch, *Thomas Munzer, théologien de la Révolution* (French translation, 1964).

Chapter Three

1. Régine Pernoud, *Histoire de la bourgeoisie en France, op. cit.*, vol. II, p. 477.

2. *Ibid.*, p. 480.

3. Adolphe Thiers, *De la Propriété*, in Pernoud, *op. cit.*

4. Henri Lefebvre, *Le droit de la ville* (Paris: Anthropos, 1968), pp. 16-20.

5. Edmond Goblot, *La barrière et le niveau* (Paris: Presses Universitaires de France, 1968).

6. F. Ponteil, *Les classes bourgeoises et l'avènement de la démocratie* (Paris: Albin Michel, 1968), pp. 20-57.

7. Pernoud, *op. cit.*, p. 479.

8. Sebastien Charlety, *Histoire du Saint-Simonisme* (Paris: Hachette, 1896), p. 14.

9. Pernoud, *op. cit.*, p. 495.

10. F. A. Isambert, "Foundateurs, Papes et Messies," *Archives de Sociologie des Religions*, 5, 1958, pp. 96-98; "Religion et développement dans la France du 19e siècle," *Archives de Sociologie des Religions*, 15, 1963, pp. 63-69.

11. J. de Maistre, *Soirées de Saint Pétersbourg* (Paris: 1821), vol. II, pp. 317-318.

12. Saint-Simon, *Oeuvres choisies* (Brussels: 1859), vol. III, p. 382.

13. Saint-Simon, *Le Nouveau Christianisme* (Paris: Editions du Seuil, 1969).

14. See J. Vidalenc, "Les techniques de propagande saint-simonienne à la fin de 1831," *Archives de Sociologie des Religions*, 10, 1960, pp. 3-20.

15. René Rémond, *La droite en France, de 1815 à nos jours*, 1st. ed. (Paris: 1954), p. 26.

16. *Ibid.*, p. 83.

17. See, for example, Louis Althusser, *Pour Marx, op. cit.*, especially the note on socialist humanism.

18. Rémond, *op. cit.*, p. 19.

19. René Aubert, *Le pontificat de Pie IX* (Paris: Bloud et Gay, 1952), p. 43.

20. Pernoud, *op. cit.*, pp. 537-538.

21. Aubert, *op. cit.*, p. 52.

22. *Ibid.*, pp. 113-118.

23. Aline Coutrot and François Dreyfus, *Les forces religieuses dans la société française* (Paris: Armand Colin-Bourrelier, 1965), p. 16; Aubert, *op. cit.*, pp. 374-375.

24. An inquiry undertaken by the magazine *Le Mouvement Socialiste* in 1902 and 1903 among the leaders of European socialist movements. For an analysis of the answers, see E. Poulat, "Socialisme et anti-cléricalisme: une enquête internationale," *Archives de Sociologie Religieuses*, 10, July-December, 1960, pp. 109-131.

25. "The anticlericalism of the new breed of radicals is the other facet of replete bourgeois clericalism, . . . bourgeois idealism, with its lay priests and its divinities, is far more dangerous than Christianity." (Lafargue's reply.)

26. For similar analyses concerning the Belgian scene, see P. Joye and R. Lewin, *L'Eglise et le mouvement ouvrier en Belgique* (Brussels: Société Populaire d'Edition, 1967), pp. 33 ff.

27. Quoted by P. Droulers, "Des evêques parlent de la question ouvrière en France, avant 1848," *Revue de l'Action Populaire*, April, 1961, p. 443.

28. Pastoral letter for Lent, 1838, *ibid.*, p. 446.

29. The same bishop wrote: "This immoderate thirst for wealth sacrifices those in its employ to its fury. . . leaving them only a small proportion of what they produce as their reward." *Ibid.*, p. 446.

30. "By keeping men continually next to machines which are made to function by mechanical necessity, it is almost as though they hoped to make them understand that they themselves are nothing but machines. . . ." Bishop Belmas, *ibid.*, p. 446.

31. The reference is to child labor.

32. Pastoral letter for Lent on "Keeping Sunday holy," 1842, Droulers, *op. cit.*, p. 452.

33. Pastoral letter for Lent, 1841, *ibid.*, p. 454.

34. Bishop Affre even criticized with astuteness, in 1843, the idea that salary simply serves to reproduce the workman's labor force, but failed to draw the conclusions of his argument. Droulers, *op. cit.*, pp. 454-455.

35. Pastoral letter by Bishop Giraud, January 19, 1845, Droulers, *op. cit.*, p. 448.

36. Aubert, *op. cit.*, pp. 44-45.

37. *Ibid.*, pp. 44-46.

38. For the religious themes in the press during the July Monarchy, see Isambert, *Christianisme et Classe Ouvrière*, *op. cit.*, pp. 217-235.

39. Aubert, *op. cit.*, p. 121 ff.

40. Joye and Lewin, *op. cit.*, pp. 63-64.

41. R. Rezsohazy, *Origine et formation du catholicisme social en Belgique* (Louvain: University of Louvain, 1958), p. 74.

42. Cf. *l'Avenir*, February 2, 1830; M. J. Le Guillou, "The Mennaisiam Crisis" *Concilium*, 27 (1967), pp. 109-118.

43. Aubert, *op. cit.*, pp. 28 ff.

44. *Ibid.*, pp. 245-248.

45. *Ibid.*, p. 301.

46. Jean Lacroix, *Vocation personnelle et tradition nationale* (Paris: Bloud and Gay, 1942).

47. Aubert, *op. cit.*, p. 213.

48. Adrien Dansette, *Histoire religieuse de la France contemporaine* (Paris: Flammarion, 1948) vol. II, p. 426.

49. See, for example, R. Ledrut, *Sociologie urbaine* (Paris: Presses Universitaires de France, 1968), pp. 73-100.

50. Alain Touraine, *Sociologie de l'action* (Paris: Editions du Seuil, 1965), pp. 128-133.

51. *Ibid.*, pp. 133-134, 151-152, 295 ff. Cf. M. Montuclard, *Conscience religieuse et démocratie* (Paris: Editions du Seuil, 1965), pp. 210-211; G. Balandier, *Anthropologie Politique* (Paris: Presses Universitaires de France, 1967), ch. 4, 5.

52. But this progress can be achieved only at the expense of a weakening of the metasocial guarantees.

53. Touraine, *op. cit.*, p. 133.

54. *Ibid.*, pp. 160-163.

55. *Ibid.*, pp. 282 ff., 395 ff.

56. F. A. Isambert, *De la Charbonnerie au Saint-Simonisme; Etude sur la jeunesse de Buchez* (Paris: Editions de Minuit, 1967).

57. *Ibid.*, p. 193.

58. F. A. Isambert, *Buchez ou l'age théologique de la sociologie* (Paris: Cujas, 1968), pp. 133-195.

59. Cf. Isambert, *Christianisme et classe ouvrière, op. cit.*, pp. 183-184.

60. *Ibid.*, p. 220.

61. *L'Atelier*, November 30, 1843.

62. *Ibid.*, April, 1844. Cf. F. A. Isambert, *Christianisme et classe ouvrière, op. cit.*, pp. 222, 241.

63. F. A. Isambert, *Buchez or l'age théologique de la sociologie, op. cit.*, p. 154. Cf. Buchez's declaration: "It is useless to try to find Christian thinking in the midst of all that boastful and empty Italian chatter!" Cf. also p. 162.

64. All these texts have been collected by F. A. Isambert in *Christianisme et classe ouvrière, op. cit.*, pp. 238-256.

65. Pierre Joseph Proudhon, *Qu'est ce que la Propriété?*, p. 122. Cf. also P. Haubtmann, *Proudhon, genèse d'un anti-théiste* (Paris, 1969).

66. Karl Marx, *Critique de la philosophie de droit* (Paris: Costes, 1946), p. 106.

67. *Ibid.*, p. 16.

68. See Karl Marx, *Oeuvres choisies* (Paris: Gallimard, 1963), vol. I, pp. 212-213.

69. Letter to Ruge, November 30, 1842.

70. Isambert, *Christianisme et classe ouvrière, op. cit.*, pp. 217-235.

71. Desroche, *Sociologies religieuses, op. cit.*, p. 69.

72. Isambert, *Buchez or l'age théologique de la sociologie, op. cit.*, p. 164.

73. Montuclard, *op. cit.*, pp. 62-63.

74. H. de Lubac, *Proudhon et le christianisme* (Paris: Editions du Seuil, 1945), pp. 83-138.

75. *Ibid.,* p. 130.

76. E. Pin, "Hypothèses rélatives à la désaffection religieuse dans la classe populaire," in H. Carrier and E. Pin, *Essais de sociologie religieuse* (Paris: Spes, 1967), pp. 295-328.

77. Although the practice probably goes back as far as 1825, with the first social services.

78. Aubert, *op. cit.,* pp. 487-490.

79. M. Vaussard, *Histoire de la démocratie chrétienne* (Paris: Editions du Seuil, 1956), vol. I, p. 62.

80. Joye and Lewin, *op. cit.,* p. 94.

81. *Ibid.,* p. 96.

82. G. Hoog, *Histoire du catholicisme social en France* (Paris: Domat, 1946), pp. 43-49.

83. J. Y. Calvez and H. Perrin, *Eglise et société economique* (Paris: Fernand Aubier, 1959), pp. 109 ff.

84. Hoog, *op. cit.,* pp. 57-123; Montuclard, *op. cit.,* pp. 21-57.

85. Montuclard, *op.cit.,* p. 26.

86. This analysis completes what has already been said in the second section of this chapter.

87. Montuclard, *op. cit.,* pp. 191-200.

88. M. Montuclard, "Aux origines de la Démocratie Chrétienne," *Archives de Sociologies Religieuses,* 6, July-December, 1956, pp. 47-90.

89. Cf. supra, the second section of this chapter.

90. Cf. supra, letter condemning *Le Sillon.*

91. J. B. Metz, "The Church's Social Function in the Light of a 'Political Theology,' " *Concilium,* 36 (1968), pp. 2-18.

92. Isambert, *Buchez ou l'age théologique de la sociologie, op. cit.,* pp. 151-152.

93. Giuseppe Toniolo, "Programma di Fronte al Socialisme," reproduced in *Saggi Politici* (Rome: 1957), p. 43.

94. At the turn of the century children in the Catholic schools were taught to recite this prayer: "Let us pray for the benefactors who give work to our parents."

95. P. Bastien, S. J., spiritual adviser of the Association of Catholic Employers, in Montuclard, *op. cit.,* p. 66.

96. In 1848, 12.5 percent of the schools were run by religious orders. In 1882 the proportion had risen to 64.6 percent.

97. Canon Fichaux, *Conférence d'Etudes Sociales,* a magazine published by the Jesuit advisers of the Catholic Employers, November, 1893, p. 115, quoted by Montuclard, *op. cit.,* p. 64.

98. *Conférences d'Etudes Sociales,* May, 1896, p. 439, in Montuclard, *op. cit.,* p. 64.

99. H. de Béthune, *Conférences d'Etudes Sociales,* July, 1895, pp. 38-49, in Montuclard, *op. cit.,* p. 64.

100. Abbé Leman, *Conférences d'Etudes Sociales,* July, 1894, p. 150, in Montuclard, *op. cit.,* p. 64.

101. Montuclard, *op. cit.,* p. 64.

102. Letter from F. le Play, in Montuclard, *op. cit.,* p. 77.

103. Montuclard, *op. cit.*, p. 77.

104. *Conférences d'Etudes Sociales,* June, 1897, in Montuclard, *op. cit.*, p. 73.

105. *Ibid.,* November, 1893, in Montuclard, *op. cit.*, p. 73.

106. *La Justice Sociale,* December, 1893, in Montuclard, *op. cit.*, p. 66.

107. *Ibid.,* February, 27, 1897, in Montuclard, *op. cit.*, p. 68.

108. *Ibid,* October 24, 1896, in Montuclard, *op. cit.*, p. 69.

109. L. Ollé Laprune, in Montuclard, *op. cit.*, p. 79.

110. Abbé Naudet, in Montuclard, *op. cit.*, p. 80.

111. Montuclard, *op. cit.*, p. 80. The reader can judge for himself the truth of this from the following "analyses" of the class struggle written by two different popes: "The Church recognizes . . . that inequality exists between men who are naturally dissimilar in the powers of their bodies and their minds. . . ." Leo XIII, *Quod Apostolici Muneris,* December 28, 1878.

"It is impossible to reduce human society to a level. The socialists may do their utmost, but all striving against nature is in vain. There naturally exist among mankind innumerable differences of the most important kind . . . the inequality in fortune is a necessary result of inequality in condition." Leo XIII, *Rerum Novarum,* May 15, 1891.

"The Church teaches that the different social classes remain as they are because it is obvious that nature demands it." Leo XIII, March, 1902.

"It is in conformity with the order established by God in human society that there should be princes and subjects, employers and proletariat, rich and poor, instructed and ignorant." Pius X, December 18, 1903.

112. Maurice Merleau-Ponty, *Sens et Non Sens* (Paris: Nagel), pp. 305-321.

Chapter Four

1. Fidel Castro is an alumnus of Belén College.

2. See Leslie Dewart's excellent book. *Christianity and Revolution: The Lesson of Cuba* (New York: Herder & Herder, 1963), pp. 109-110.

3. *Bohemia,* January 18, 1959.

4. *Ibid.*

5. *Ibid.,* April 5, 1959.

6. Dewart, *op. cit.,* p. 149.

7. This is Leslie Dewart's thesis in *Christianity and Revolution.*

Chapter Five

1. The term "myth" is used here in the sense of an interpretation of reality which becomes a substitute for reality.

2. *Populorum Progressio,* #26.

3. Mwalimu Julius Nyerere, *The Arusha Declaration* (Dar es Salaam, 1967).

4. *Populorum Progressio,* #61.

5. *Ibid.,* # # 50, 64.

6. *Ibid.,* #51.

7. Eugene V. Rostow, "The Hard Realities of Power Demand That We Must Fight On," *Life,* July 2, 1965, pp. 40B-40C.

8. *Pacem in Terris,* #5, pastoral instructions.

9. Rostow, *op. cit.*

10. *Ibid.*

11. *Populorum Progressio,* # #8 and 26.

12. *Ibid.,* #58.

13. Rostow, *op. cit.*

14. He is referring to the guerrilla war.

15. Rostow, *op. cit.*

16. *Ibid.*

17. *Aggression from the North: History of the North Vietnamese Campaign for the Conquest of South Vietnam* (Washington, D.C.: State Department), Appendix c, p. 33.

18. Douglas Pike, *Viet-Cong* (Cambridge, Mass.: MIT Press, 1966).

19. Arthur M. Schlesinger, *Bitter Heritage: Vietnam and American Democracy* (Boston: Houghton Mifflin Co., 1966).

20. A striking example of this is contained in the declaration signed by 2,400 prominent religious personalities: *The Religious Community and the War in Vietnam,* February 1, 1965.

21. Cf. Celso Furtado, "Les Etats-Unis et l'Amérique Latine," in *Esprit,* July-August, 1966; Claude Julien, *L'Empire américain* (Paris: Grasset, 1968).

22. *Tin Tuong,* 56, December, 1969, p. 2.

23. My principal sources for this part of the study, in addition to the American press, are *Informations Catholiques Internationales* (Paris, 163 Boulevard Malesherbes), indicated as *ICI,* and *La Documentation Catholique* (Paris, Bonne Press, 5 rue Bayard), indicated as *DC* followed by figures indicating issue and column.

24. Allocution to Catholic Union of the Italian Press, January 29, 1966, *DC,* # 1465, col. 291-293.

25. Encyclical *Mense Maio,* April 20, 1965, *DC,* #1448, col. 865.

26. Allocution to the Cardinals, June 24, 1966, *DC,* #1475, col. 1257. Cf. also the encyclical *Christi Matri,* October 2, 1966, *DC,* #1479, col. 1633-1637.

27. Letter to the Vietnamese bishops, *DC,* #1480, col. 1741-1746. Cf. also homily of October 4, 1966, *DC,* #1481, col. 1837-1842; Christmas Message, 1966, *DC,* #1486, col. 109-114; Allocution to Vietnamese pilgrims, *DC,* #1496, col. 1065.

28. Letter to U Thant, September 22, 1967, *DC,* #1506, col. 2020. Cf. also Message for a World Peace Day, *DC,* #1509, col. 97 ff; latest synthesis on the subject of peace, January 1, 1969, *DC,* #1533, col. 102-104.

29. *La Libre Belgique,* Brussels daily paper, April 5, 1968.

30. *DC,* #1476, col. 1365.

31. Article by Claude Julien in *Le Monde,* December 16, 1966.

32. *Ibid.,* December 22, 1967.

33. *Ibid.,* April 20, 1965; cf. also *DC,* #1448.

34. *Ibid.,* October 25, 1966; cf. also *DC,* #1486.

35. Pope's Christmas Message, 1965, and replies of those concerned, *DC,* #1463, col. 177-178. It should be noted that the incident is repeated in almost exactly the same terms in 1967, *DC,* #1489.

36. *DC,* #1508, col. 4.

37. *DC,* # 1491, col. 668–669.

38. *Ecumenical Press Service,* May 4, 1967, p. 2.

39. *Information Bulletin of the WCC,* December 15, 1967.

40. The council represents 42 million Christians belonging to 34 different churches or denominations.

41. *DC,* # 1485, col. 41–44.

42. *National Catholic Reporter,* June 9, 1965.

43. *Ibid.,* August 18, 1965.

44. Address to the Catholic Daughters of America, Boston, August, 1966, *ICI,* September 15, 1966.

45. February 1, 1965, *ICI,* February 15, 1966, p. 21.

46. *Ibid.* Cf. also a declaration by the chief editor of *Ave Maria:* "I would prefer to leave the responsibility for a precise policy in the hands of men who have been elected for that purpose," September 25, 1965.

47. *ICI,* February 15, 1966, p. 21.

48. *Catholic Worker,* October, 1965.

49. Letter to *Ave Maria,* December 18, 1965.

50. *National Catholic Reporter,* September 8, 1965.

51. *Ibid.,* August 11, 1965.

52. A political trend defended by some Senators, such as Mansfield and Fulbright.

53. *Christianity and Crisis,* June 17, 1965.

54. *ICI,* February 15, 1966, p. 22, quoting from the *National Catholic Reporter.*

55. *National Catholic Reporter,* September 8, 1965.

56. Pax is an association founded in 1962 which includes Catholics and non-Catholics.

57. These resolutions were called for by Gordon Zahn, February 11, 1968.

58. *Catholic Messenger,* October 20, 1965.

59. *Time,* January 12, 1968, pp. 9–10.

60. A national campaign for new initiatives aimed at stopping the war.

61. March, 1967.

62. *ICI,* November 15, 1966, p. 17.

63. According to the text in *Ave Maria* mentioned above. Cf. also *ICI,* February 15, 1966, p. 22.

64. Cf. a statement to this effect in *ICI,* January 1, 1968, p. 30.

65. *ICI,* October 1, 1967, p. 16.

66. Statement of a priest of Dalat, reported in *ICI,* February 15, 1969, p. 28.

67. *Ibid.,* p. 29.

68. Statement by a Catholic writer, *ICI,* February 15, 1969, p. 32.

69. E.g., in March, 1965; cf. *ICI,* April 1, 1965.

70. *ICI,* February 15, 1967, p. 15.

71. *Ibid.,* June 1, 1967.

72. *Ibid.,* January 15, 1966, p. 11.

73. *Ibid.,* January 1, 1968, p. 32.

74. *Ibid.,* February 15, 1969, p. 32.

75. *DC,* # 1453, col. 1412–1414; *ICI,* July 1, 1965.

76. *DC,* # 1481, col. 1849; *ICI,* November 1, 1966.

77. *ICI,* February 1, 1968, pp. 6-7.

78. *Ibid.,* February 1, 1969, p. 13.

79. In spite of pressure from President Diem, the Holy See never named Archbishop Ngo Dinh Thuc to the see of Saigon. He was archbishop of Hue before his brother returned from exile in the United States and he was elected president of the bishops' conference by his fellow bishops.

80. *DC,* #1479, col. 1687-1692.

81. *La France Catholique,* February 23, 1968, reported and endorsed the stand taken by an editorial in the Catholic paper of Saint Etienne, France.

82. Public campaign to send a ship to Vietnam with a cargo of food and medical supplies.

83. Cf. Chapter Eight about the events in France in May, 1968.

84. Declaration made on January 1, 1967.

85. *ICI,* January 15, 1967, p. 9.

86. *Le Monde,* November 1, 1967.

87. Letter from ninety Christians to the French bishops, concerning the pope's message for an ecumenical Peace Day.

88. Conférence Chrétienne de la Paix, resolution on Vietnam, January 22 and 23, 1967.

89. *Croissance des Jeunes Nations,* September, 1967, p. 42.

Chapter Six

1. Marcel Niedergang, "Military and Economic Pressure Groups Determine United States Policy in Latin America," *Le Monde Diplomatique,* November, 1968. Cf. Niedergang, *Le Monde,* June 4, 1969, writing about the failure of Nelson Rockefeller's mission to Latin America. Cf. also Julien, *op. cit.,* pp. 98-124, 244-245.

2. *Venezuela—La Violencia—IV—FLN-FALN,* Cidoc Documents, 36 (Cuernavaca, 1968), pp. 4/61-62.

3. *Ibid.,* vols. I, II, III, IV, V.

4. *Ibid.,* vol. IV, pp. 4/86-107.

5. Cf. Eduardo Galeano, *Guatemala pays occupé* (Paris: François Maspero, 1968); Julien, *op. cit.*

6. *Ibid.,* p. 144.

7. *Guatemala—La Violencia—III,* Cidoc Documents, 21 (Cuernavaca, 1968), pp. 5/75 ff.

8. *Ibid.,* p. 4/276.

9. *Ibid.,* p. 4/303.

10. *Ibid.,* p. 4/308.

11. Luiz Mercier Vega, *Guerrillas in Latin America—The Technique of the Counter State* (London: Pall Mall Press, 1969), p. 129.

12. Galeano, *op. cit.,* pp. 139-143.

13. Hugo Neira, *Los Andes—Tierra o Muerte* (Madrid: ZYZ, 1968), pp. 178-179.

14. *Ibid.,* p. 181.

15. *Ibid.,* p. 241.

16. F. Houtart and E. Pin, *The Church in the Latin American Revolution* (New York: Sheed and Ward, 1966), p. 214.

17. Letter to the Italian committee of Europe-Latin America, *Le Monde,* March 29-30, 1970.

18. *Le Monde,* March 29-30, 1970.

19. Gérard Chaliand, "La Colombie ne peut devenir un nouveau Vietnam," *Le Monde Diplomatique,* November, 1968, pp. 11-13.

20. In the form of equipment and advisers. The other five countries are Argentina, Brazil, Chile, Venezuela, and Peru.

21. Gérard Chaliand, *op. cit.,* notes that the price of coffee fell from 80¢ in 1954 to 48¢ in 1964.

22. G. Pérez, *La Iglesia en Colombia* (Bogotá: 1962).

23. Cf. G. Guzman and O. Fals Borda, *La Violencia en Colombia* (Bogotá: 1962), which deals with this period of *la violencia.*

24. "Movement of Workers, Students and Peasants," cf. G. Guzmán, *Camilo Torres* (New York: Sheed & Ward, Inc., 1969), p. 213.

25. Revolutionary Armed Forces of Colombia.

26. The Army of National Liberation, cf. Guzman, *op. cit.,* p. 215.

27. It won about 10 percent of the votes. Diplomatic relations between Colombia and the USSR were reestablished in 1968.

28. We shall analyze the Church's place in Colombian society when we study the case of Camilo Torres.

29. At Cardinal Mercier College, Braine-l'Alleud.

30. This college is for priests who will be working in Latin America.

31. E.g., a study of radio schools published in 1960 by FERES (International Federation of Institutes for Social and Socioreligious Research), *Las Escuelas radiofónicas en Colombia* (Bogota: 1960).

32. An autonomous, government-recognized organization, directed by Dr. William Nanetti.

33. He represented Catholic apostolic movements.

34. Guzman, *op. cit.,* p. 29.

35. *Ibid.,* p. 64.

36. Alberto Prades, "Camilo Torres en tant que Sociologue," in François Houtart, Alberto Prades, and Fabio Gutiérrez Correa, *Camilo Torres en tant que Prêtre, Sociologue et Colombien* (Louvain: Cercle des Etudiants Colombiens, 1966), p. 8.

37. Address to Pro Mundi Vita convention, Louvain, 1964.

38. Platform of the United Front of the People. Cf. Guzman, *op. cit.,* p. 96.

39. Talk at Inca University of Colombia, September 21, 1965.

40. Guzman, *op. cit.,* pp. 196-198.

41. *Frente Unido,* September 23, 1965, p. 1.

42. *Ibid.,* September 9, 1965.

43. *Cidoc Information,* #17, September, 1965, vol. II, p. 246.

44. In a speech to workers published in *Vanguardia Sindical* (Bogotá), July 23, 1965.

45. Guzman, *op. cit.,* pp. 99-100.

46. *Ibid.,* pp. 142 ff.
47. Cf. "Message to the Oligarchy," Guzman, *op. cit.,* pp. 57-59.
48. *Ibid.,* pp. 133-135. General Assembly of Bishops' Conference, July 7, 1965.
49. *Ibid.,* pp. 135-138. Cardinal Concha, pastoral letter of August 15, 1965.
50. *Ibid.,* p. 112.
51. Speech at First National Sociology Convention, "Violence and Socio-Cultural Change in the Rural Areas of Colombia" (Bogotá: Iqueima, 1963), p. 137.
52. "Comunismo en la Iglesia?" *La Hora* (Bogotá: May, 1965).
53. Guzman, *op. cit.,* p. 112.
54. *Ibid.,* pp. 125-128. Letter to Bishop Isaza, auxiliary bishop of Bogotá.
55. *Ibid.,* p. 123. March 20, 1965.
56. *Ibid.,* p. 124. May 25, 1965.
57. *Ibid.,* pp. 128-129. May 28, 1965.
58. *Ibid.,* pp. 129-130. June 9, 1965.
59. *Ibid.,* pp. 130-131. June 18, 1965.
60. *Ibid.,* pp. 132-133. June 24, 1965.
61. *Ibid.,* p. 138. Cf. Cardinal Concha's final statement, September 20, 1965.
62. Orlando Fals Borda, "The Significance of Guerrilla Movements in Latin America," *Cross Currents,* 18, 1968, pp. 451-458.
63. Chaliand, *op. cit.*
64. Fals Borda, *op. cit.,* p. 454.
65. Cf. Maria Isaura Pereira de Queiroz, *O Messianismo no Brasil e no mundo* (Sao Paolo: 1965); Eric Hobsbawm, *Primitive Rebels* (Manchester: 1959).
66. Cf. the two basic books: Régis Debray, *Révolution dans la révolution* (Paris: François Maspero, 1967), and Ernesto C. Guevara, *Guerrilla Warfare* (New York: Monthly Review Press, 1961). Cf. also Marcelo de Andrade, "Considérations sur les thèses de Régis Debray," *Temps Modernes,* 275, May, 1969, pp. 2008-2036. The author questions several of the French thinker's central ideas: he believes that Debray underestimated the necessity of preparing the "matrix" of guerrilla action; it is not simply a question of training an effective guerrilla band, but of preparing a war in which the whole population will be involved. On the other hand Debray's book, *Révolution dans la révolution,* overestimates the effectiveness of armed propaganda. Even though propaganda cannot be envisaged in the present situation without the accompaniment of an armed struggle, Debray opposes the political and military domains in too abstract a manner. See also Norman Gall, "L'Héritage de Che Guevara," *Esprit,* September, 1969, pp. 195-218, and in the same issue H. Jaguarribe, "Les voies d'un mouvement populaire," pp. 218-230. The author makes an in-depth analysis of populist movements and the position of the Christian Democrats in Latin America.
67. E.g., in Colombia with the Peasant Republic of Marquetalia.
68. Chaliand, *op. cit.*
69. Not a single member of the central committee of the NLF has fallen into enemy hands. Cf. Chaliand, *op. cit.*
70. What happened in Colombia is a case in point.
71. Houtart and Pin, *op. cit.,* p. 97.
72. *ICI,* # #317-318, August 1968, p. 11.
73. *Between Honesty and Hope: Documents from and about the Church in Latin America* (Maryknoll: Maryknoll Documentation Series, 1970) p. 211.

74. *Secunda Conferencia General del Episcopado Latinoamericano,* II, Conclusiones, CELAM, Bogotá, 1969.

75. *Between Honesty and Hope, op. cit.,* p. 228.

76. *Ibid.,* pp. 3-12.

77. *Ibid.,* p. 85.

78. *Ibid.,* p. 91.

79. *Ibid.,* p. 141.

80. *Ibid.,* p. 144.

81. *Ibid.,* p. 83.

82. Audience of August 21, 1968, during which the pope explained the significance of his journey, *DC,* #1524, col. 1582.

83. Speech to the peasants, August 23, 1968, *DC,* #1524, col. 1545.

84. *Ibid.*

85. *Ibid.* "We know that, today, you are aware of the inferiority of your social and cultural conditions and that you are impatient to obtain a more just distribution of economic benefits and greater recognition of your numbers and the place due to you in society."

86. *Ibid.,* col. 1546.

87. *Ibid.*

88. August 23, homily during a Mass for development, *DC, ibid.,* col. 1554.

89. *Ibid.,* col. 1547.

90. *Ibid.,* col. 1551.

91. Audience of August 21, 1968, *ibid.,* col. 1582.

92. This is the case in Colombia, but, as we have seen, one can analyze the question from a quite different point of view, as did Camilo Torres.

93. Candido P. Camargo de Pereira, "Essai de typologie du catholicisme brésilien," *Social Compass,* vol. XIV, nos. 5-6, 1967, pp. 339-342.

94. G. Gutierrez, "Apuntas para una teología de la liberación," *Liberación, opción de la Iglesia Latinoamericano en la Década del 70* (Bogotá: Presencia, 1970), pp. 33-34.

95. *Ibid.,* p. 49.

96. *Ibid.,* p. 50.

97. *Ibid.,* p. 51.

98. *Ibid.,* p. 53.

99. *Ibid.,* p. 55.

100. *Ibid.,* p. 54.

101. See R. Shaull, "Consideraciones teológicas sobre la liberación del hombre," *IDO-C,* #68/17, April 28, 1968.

102. Letter of eighty Bolivian priests, "The Church in Bolivia." *Between Honesty and Hope, op. cit.,* p. 141.

103. G. Gutierrez, Introduction, *ibid* ., p. xvii

104. *Ibid.,* p. xxii.

105. CELAM, *op. cit.,* pp. 73-76.

106. Luis Carlos Bernal, *La violencia, planteamiento moral del problema en America Latina,* unpublished text, Faculty of Theology, University of Louvain, Louvain, 1970, p. 38.

107. Robert Bosc, *La violencia y la no violencia en el pensamiento de la Iglesia*, Faculty of Theology, University of San Miguel, Buenos Aires, 1968, CIDOC, #68/112, p. 12.

Chapter Seven

1. Until 1961 the *assimilados* were the only Africans with rights equivalent to those of white people. After that date every African who could read and write and who had a fixed income had the right to vote. About 10 percent opted for the Portuguese system; blacks and whites, however, still have different types of identity cards.

2. Roberto Holden's movement has encountered various difficulties. In the early days it was supported by the Congo-Kinshasa and by a trend in American opinion, led by Dean Acheson, in the days when the United States was in favor of decolonization—which explains, no doubt, why it also received help from the CIA. But when Moise Tshombe became Prime Minister, the movement's continued existence was threatened. Tshombe's ties with South Africa were such that he could not continue to support Holden.

3. A number of tribal organizations have been created among the Angolan refugees, most of them aimed at offering social assistance.

4. The exact number of people of mixed races is unknown. In 1955 official estimates of the "nonindigenous" population put their number at 29,507. Some sources claim that there are as many as one million, but this seems improbable in spite of the fact that there are certainly people of mixed blood among the "natives" and that there is a financial bonus for mixed marriages in Mozambique.

5. In April, 1969, it was announced that Lazaro Kavandam, a tribal chief from the northern part of the country who had fought independently of FRELIMO since 1964, had defected to the Portuguese.

6. In March, 1969, Mr. Caetano declared to the Brazilian paper *O Estato de Sao Paolo* that Portugal had 130,000 troops in Africa. No doubt this figure included only the regular metropolitan forces.

7. Cf. *Le Monde Diplomatique,* July, 1969, p. 3.

8. *ICI,* January 1, 1961, p. 44.

9. *ICI,* April 15, 1961, p. 15.

10. *ICI,* May 1, 1961, p. 16.

11. *ICI,* May 15, 1961, p. 15.

12. *ICI,* December 15, 1961, pp. 4-6.

13. *ICI,* March 1, 1964, pp. 5-6.

14. *Ibid.; ICI,* May 1, 1961; *ICI,* July 1, 1961, p. 12.

15. *ICI,* March 15, 1967, p. 15.

16. *ICI,* September 1, 1965, p. 14.

17. *ICI,* September 1, 1966, p. 13.

18. *ICI,* May 15, 1961, p. 15.

19. *ICI,* July 15, 1964, pp. 14-15.

20. *ICI,* July 1, 1962, p. 14; *ICI,* June 15, 1962, p. 13.

21. *ICI,* October 15, 1968, p. 17.

22. *ICI,* September 15, 1963, pp. 12-13.

23. *ICI,* February 15, 1965, p. 12.
24. *ICI,* March 14, 1968, p. 7.
25. *ICI,* November 15, 1963, pp. 21-22.
26. *ICI,* September 15, 1967, p. 10.
27. *ICI,* October 15, 1968, p. 17.
28. Tony Nockler, *Catholic Herald* (London), November 5, 1965.
29. *Ibid.*
30. *ICI,* August 1, 1961, p. 12.
31. *ICI,* October 1, 1961, p. 14.
32. *ICI,* May 15, 1962, p. 12.
33. *ICI,* November 1, 1962, p. 23.
34. *ICI,* February 15, 1967, p. 13.
35. *ICI,* March 15, 1963, p. 13.
36. *ICI,* February 1, 1968, p. 9.
37. *ICI,* December 1, 1964, p. 30.
38. *ICI,* December 1, 1965, p. 25.
39. *ICI,* December 15, 1965, p. 24.
40. *ICI,* November 15, 1965, p. 20.
41. *Ibid.*
42. *ICI,* November 15, 1966, p. 17.
43. *ICI,* July 15, 1967, p. 8.
44. S. Cerqueira, "L'Eglise Catholique Portugaise," in *Les Eglise chrétiennes et la décolonisation* (Paris: Armand Colin-Bourrelier, 1967), p. 468.
45. J. Duffy, *Portugal in Africa* (London: The Penguin Press, 1967), p. 54.
46. Cerqueira, *op. cit.,* p. 469.
47. *Ibid.,* p. 471.
48. *ICI,* July 1, 1961, p. 20.
49. S. Rego, *Liçoes de Missionologia* (Lisbon), pp. 342-343.
50. *ICI,* June 1, 1961.
51. *Boletin de Informaçao Pastoral,* #59, March, 1969, p. 27. The authors mention 4,958 schools with 546,156 pupils in all the mission territories.
52. *ICI,* June 1, 1961, p. 21.
53. S. Rego, *Alguns problemas sociologico-missionarios da Africa Negra* (Lisbon: 1960), pp. 105-106.
54. S. Rego, quoted by S. Cerqueira, *op. cit.,* p. 475.
55. *ICI,* June 1, 1961, p. 23.
56. Cerqueira, *op. cit.,* p. 477.
57. *ICI,* April 15, 1961.
58. *Boletin de Informaçao Pastoral,* #59, March, 1969.
59. Cerqueira, *op. cit.,* p. 496.
60. *ICI,* October 15, 1958.
61. "Situation de l'Eglise en Afrique Portugaise," *Frères du Monde,* #48, 1967, p. 59.
62. Cerqueira, *op. cit.,* p. 478.
63. *ICI,* May 1, 1961.
64. Robert Davezies, *La Guerre d'Angola* (Paris: Ducros, 1968).
65. Cerqueira, *op. cit.,* p. 480.

66. *Ibid.*, p. 494.
67. "Situation de l'Eglise en Afrique Portugaise," *op. cit.*, p. 52.
68. *ICI*, September 1, 1962; *ICI*, February 15, 1963.
69. *Ibid.*
70. Cerqueira, *op. cit.*, p. 482.
71. *ICI*, July 1, 1961, p. 14.
72. *ICI*, August, 1961.
73. "Situation de l'Eglise en Afrique Portugaise," *op. cit.*, p. 35.
74. *ICI*, November 1, 1962.
75. *ICI*, February 15, 1963.
76. *ICI*, November 15, 1967.
77. *ICI*, April 15, 1968.
78. "Situation de l'Eglise en Afrique Portugaise," *op. cit.*, pp. 6–7.
79. Henri Fesquet, *Le Monde*, May 13, 1969.
80. Cerqueira, *op. cit.*, p. 493.
81. *SOEPI*, # 16, February 13, 1965 (Ecumenical Press and Information Service).
82. On April 18, 1969.
83. Cerqueira, *op. cit.*, p. 492.
84. *Dossier sur les colonies portugaises* (Brussels: Edition Vie Ouvrière, 1970), pp. 74–76.
85. The document in question was, in fact, that in which Paul VI called for January 1 to be recognized as World Peace Day.
86. *Le Monde*, April 11, 1970.
87. At its meeting in November, 1969, the Belgian Justice and Peace commission took a stand on the question, calling on the Belgian government to reexamine its political position, to break off all military ties with Portugal, and to publish a list of Belgian financial interests in the Portuguese colonies. It also called on the Belgian hierarchy to intercede with the Portuguese religious authorities to put a stop to the use of Christianity to legitimate the colonial war. *Dossier sur les colonies portugaises, op. cit.*
88. *Le Monde*, July 4, 5, 6, and 7, 1970.

Chapter Eight

1. Cf. R. Aron, *Dix-huit leçons sur la société industrielle* (Paris: Gallimard, 1964); Alain Touraine, *Sociologie de l'Action* (Paris: Edition du Seuil, 1966); and *La Société Post-Industrielle* (Paris: Denoël, 1969).
2. Herbert Marcuse, *One-Dimensional Man* (Boston: Beacon Press, 1964); H. Lefebvre, *La vie quotidienne dans le monde moderne* (Paris: Gallimard, 1968).
3. J. K. Galbraith, *The New Industrial State* (New York: New American Library, 1968).
4. *Ibid.*, pp. 24–29.
5. Here we are, of course, referring to the situation in the European countries.
6. C. Gruson, *Origine et espoirs de la planification française (Paris:* Dunod, 1968). Cf. especially, "When those who feel they are being held on a tight rein are

students who are receiving training that is poorly adapted to future economic needs, in universities still strongly influenced by ancient traditions, and who, in addition, are learning to be critical of the rigors and vanities of societies too exclusively subject to technical imperatives and commercial interests, then the limitations imposed on their freedom by social structures and the discipline they are forced to accept, become a servitude against which they are bound to revolt."

7. Touraine, *op. cit.*, pp. 467–468.

8. A. Touraine, *Le mouvement de mai ou le communisme utopique* (Paris: Editions du Seuil, 1968), p. 10.

9. *Ibid.*, p. 38.

10. *Ibid.*, p. 16.

11. *Ibid.*, pp. 9–62.

12. In the strict sense of the class concept, determined by the place one holds in the production process.

13. Touraine, *Le mouvement, op. cit.*, p. 27.

14. *Ibid.*, p. 28.

15. Liberal Arts Faculty, located to the west of Paris.

16. Principal abbreviations used:

CFDT: French Democratic Confederation of Labor

CGT: General Confederation of Labor (Communist-inspired)

FEN: Federation of National Education

ORTF: Office of French Radio and Television

PSU: Unified Socialist Party

SNES: National Union of Higher Education

UNEF: National Union of French Students

17. Touraine, *Le mouvement, op. cit.*, p. 54.

18. *Ibid.*, p. 145. Cf. also p. 148: "The absence of political reactions on the part of the government seemed to reinforce the movement. Authority which made itself felt only through the police took on a new connotation of repression, whose effects were felt by everyone."

19. The emotional energies usually invested in social systems were withdrawn. This seems to be true of the university, businesses, schools, and the Church, also in areas such as the information media and in institutions such as the magistrature, medical boards, etc.

20. Daniel Cohn-Bendit, interview with J.-P. Sartre in *Nouvel Observateur*, May 20, 1968.

21. A few quotations from the walls of the Sorbonne give some idea of this phenomenon: "It is forbidden to forbid," "The act founds the consciousness," "Forget everything you have learned," "Begin by dreaming," "Change is revolutionary," "Be realistic, ask for the impossible."

22. Touraine, *Le mouvement, op. cit.*, p. 217.

23. We quote from the inscriptions on the walls of the Sorbonne again: "To create death is to create life," "Enjoy yourself here and now," "Make love and then begin again," "The more I make love the more I want to make a revolution, and the more I make a revolution the more I want to make love."

24. René Rémond, "Etait-ce une révolution?" *Recherches et Débats*, 63, 1969, pp. 81–89.

25. Touraine, *Le mouvement, op. cit.,* p. 13.

26. For this purpose we shall use the texts collected in three separate publications: Robert Serrou, *Dieu n'est pas conservateur* (Paris: Robert Laffont, 1968); the magazine *Christianisme Social,* 3-4, 1968). Robert Davezies, *La rue dans l'Eglise* (Paris: Editions de l'Epi, 1968). This sampling has no claim other than that it is a collection of official pronouncements intended for public consumption and published between the beginning of May and June 26. An appendix to this chapter (pp. 368-370) provides a list of the texts used, and the numbers mentioned in these footnotes refer to that list.

27. #1.

28. #28.

29. #30.

30. #21.

31. # #31 and 35.

32. #42.

33. #4.

34. #5.

35. #6.

36. #17.

37. ACI, i.e., *Action Catholiques des Milieux Indépendants.* This movement groups members, ranging from small business people to the very wealthy, on the basis of their not belonging to the working class.

38. #49.

39. #34. *La Paroisse Universitaire* (University Parish) is a nationwide movement of Christian university professors.

40. But see # #15, 6, and 30.

41. #25.

42. #18.

43. #3.

44. #16.

45. #42.

46. #46.

47. #63.

48. E.g., # #1, 6, and 25.

49. #17.

50. #15.

51. #31.

52. #18.

53. #17.

54. #36.

55. #38.

56. #40.

57. #41.

58. #50.

59. #59.

60. Following the distinction formulated by Max Weber to indicate the gap between theoretical goals and concrete decisions.

61.   Responsibility: cf. # #5, 17, 19, 39, 48, 41, 42, 47, 59, 60. Liberty: cf. # #3, 5, 6, 17, 19, 21, 43, 53, 59, 60. Participation: cf. # #17, 19, 39, 41, 45, 59, 60. Justice: cf. # #3, 5, 19, 21, 43, 53. Dialogue: cf. # #21, 22, 38, 41, 45, 49. Promotion: cf. # #17, 19, 53. Dignity; peace; sharing; encounter; self-expression; solidarity.

62.   The Council texts always speak of "values" within the context of historical becoming. Values come from God and are, therefore, good and desirable, signs of the times, and a call from God. But the corruption of sin destroys this harmony (*The Church in the Modern World,* #11). The Christian transformation of the world reintegrates values in the total context of man, transformed by Christ (*ibid.,* #61). We shall recover them fully purified and transfigured when Christ hands over the accomplished kingdom to the Father (*ibid.,* #39).

63.   #47.
64.   #57.
65.   #58.
66.   #56.
67.   #38.
68.   #40.
69.   #5.
70.   #6.
71.   #16.
72.   #7.
73.   #13.
74.   #39.
75.   *Ibid.*
76.   #7.
77.   #14.
78.   #41.
79.   #43.
80.   #62.
81.   #59.
82.   *Ibid.*
83.   #45.
84.   #55.
85.   #43.
86.   #27.
87.   #55.
88.   #62.
89.   #59.
90.   #5.
91.   *Union Nationale des Etudiants de France* (National Union of French Students).
92.   # #18, 19.
93.   #15.
94.   #16.
95.   # #20, 21.
96.   #4.

97. #6.
98. # #1, 27.
99. # #39, 44, 59, 62, 63.
100. # #22, 40, 56, 57.
101. # #1, 4, 13, 33.
102. #35.
103. #5.
104. #3.
105. #6.
106. #30.
107. #10.
108. #26. Pastor Westpahl is president of the Federation of French Reformed Churches.
109. #43.
110. #60.
111. Cf. F. Houtart and F. Hambye, "Sociopolitical Implications of Vatican Council II," *Concilum*, #36, 1968, pp. 85-96.
112. René Rémond, "Les Catholiques Français manquent-ils de maturité politique?" *Projet*, 16, 1967, pp. 657-670.
113. P. Y. Jolif, "Foi et Politique," *Lettre*, 116, 1968, pp. 2-4.
114. Strasbourg Symposium on "Religious Forces and Political Attitudes in Contemporary France," published in *Cahiers de la Fondation des Sciences Politiques*, 1963.
115. Rémond, *op. cit.*, pp. 668-669.
116. J. M. Domenach, "Pour une éthique de l'engagement," *Christus*, 52, 1966, pp. 466-477.
117. R. Rémond, "La politique des chrétiens," *ibid.*, pp. 439-440.
118. *Mouvement Républicain Populaire* (Popular Republican Movement), founded after the war and composed for the most part of "social Christians."
119. Georges Bidault, one of the founders of the movement, said cynically, "The women will vote and we shall have one hundred deputies . . . in the name of the Father and of the Son and of the Holy Spirit!" Cf. Jacques Duquesne, *Les catholiques français sous l'occupation* (Paris: Grasset, 1966), pp. 370-382.
120. By "fervent" Catholic is meant one who not only believes and practices his faith regularly (Sunday obligation, sacraments, etc.), but also takes active part in Church organizations. By "practicing" Catholic is meant one who believes, and in theory at least, practices his faith regularly. By a Catholic "with no exterior practice" is meant one who believes and is baptized and married in the Church, but who does not practice his faith.
121. *Rassemblement de Peuple Français* (Gathering of the French People). This was the first tentative Gaullist party after the war. Cf. Aline Coutrot, "L'attitude politique des catholiques français d'après les sondages," *Projet*, 16, 1968, p. 672.
122. *Ibid.*, p. 674.
123. *Nouvel Observateur*, October 26, 1966.
124. Cf. Strasbourg Symposium (1963).
125. *Le Monde*, April 3, 1970, "La Gauche révolutionnaire."

126. Magazine put out by the Bordeaux Franciscans. *Frères du Monde* publishes sociopolitical and theological studies based on socialist options.

127. *Frères du Monde*, supplement to #39, 1966, "Conscience chrétienne et néocapitalisme," pp. 15–17.

128. *Le Monde*, March 23, 1966. Gilbert Blardone is director of the *Chroniques Sociales de France* and *Croissance des Jeunes Nations*.

129. Cf. introduction to the bishops' statement.

130. J. Y. Calvez, S.J., *Projet*, April, 1966, pp. 395 ff.

131. Henri Desroche, *Sociologies religieuses* (Paris: Presses Universitaires de France, 1968), p. 199.

132. See Chapter Three.

133. *The Church in the Modern World*, #34, para. 2.

134. *Ibid.*, #36, para. 1.

135. J. B. Metz, "The Church's Social Function in the Light of a Political Theology," *Concilium*, #36, 1968, pp. 2–18.

136. A. Touraine, *Sociologie de l'action* (Paris: Editions du Seuil, 1966), pp. 419–420.

137. M. de Certeau, "Construction révolutionnaire et violence," in *Christianisme et Révolution*, supplement to *Lettre*, 119, 1968, p. 116.

138. Eric Weil, "Politique et Morale," *Cahiers de l'ISEA*, 14, June, 1962, p. 14.

139. Bourdieu and Passeron, *Le Métier de sociologue*, vol. I (Paris: Mouton-Bordas, 1968), p. 54.

140. Pierre Antoine, S.J., "Démystifier la politique," *Christus*, 60, October, 1968, pp. 463–474.

141. Duquesne, *op. cit.*, p. 447.

142. *Jésus-Christ Sauveur, Espérance des hommes aujourd'hui* (Jesus Christ Savior and Hope of All Men Today), report of the 1968 bishops' Plenary Assembly (Paris: Editions du Centurion, 1969). Cf. Bishop Matagrin's report, pp. 54–55.

143. Cf. Y. Daniel and H. Godin, *France, Pagan?* (New York: Sheed & Ward, 1949).

144. Cf. E. Poulat, *Naissance des prêtres ouvriers* (Tournai-Paris: Castermann, 1965); G. Siefer, *La mission des prêtres ouvriers* (Paris: Edition de l'Epi, 1963).

145. Siefer, *op. cit.*, p. 205.

146. J. Mousir, "Les chrétiens de France dans une situation révolutionnaire," *IDO-C*, 68/48, November 17, 1968.

147. *Le Monde*, March 27, 1970.

148. *Ibid.*

149. Groups, for example, such as *Echange et Dialogue* or *Liens*.

150. R. Davezies, *La rue dans l'Eglise, op. cit.*

Appendix to Chapter Eight

List of texts analyzed in chapter eight:

1. March 24 and 25. Resolutions of a symposium organized by groups such as *Témoignage Chrétien, Christianisme Social, Economie et Humanisme, Lettre, Frères du Monde, Terre Entière, Ido-c*, etc. See Robert Serrou, *Dieu n'est pas conservateur, op. cit.*, pp. 69–70.

2. May 6. Statement by *Témoignage Chrétien* groups.

3. May 21. "Appel à tous les chrétiens" (A Call to All Christians), signed by Catholics and Protestants. See *Christianisme Social,* 3-4, 1968, pp. 223-224.

4. May 22. Appeal of some prominent Christians.

5. May 24. One hundred priests of the Paris region. *Ibid.,* pp. 162-164.

6. May 28. Liaison Committee for Informal Groups of Christians Engaged in the Revolutionary Struggle. Cf. *Christianisme Social, op. cit.,* pp. 233-234.

7. May 28. In answer to an appeal by a group of young people, four hundred people gathered in a Paris parish. Cf. Serrou, *op. cit.,* pp. 77-93.

8. May 31. The Priests of the 19th district of Paris. *Ibid.,* p. 164.

9. June 1. Paris Presbyteral Council. *Ibid.,* pp. 219-223.

10. June 2. Pamphlet distributed in Saint Séverin parish (Latin Quarter), Paris, by members of a "working commission on revolution of the Church." Cf. R. Davezies, *La rue dans l'eglise, op. cit.,* pp. 18-19; *Le Monde,* June 4, 1968.

11. June 6. Letter distributed to members of Saint Séverin Parish. Cf. Davezies, *op. cit.,* p. 36.

12. Statement by those who celebrated a service of intercommunion on Pentecost Sunday. Cf. *Le Monde,* June 4, 1968; Davezies, *op. cit.,* pp. 37-38.

13. June 8. A forum organized at the Sorbonne with the theme: "From Che Guevara to Jesus Christ." Cf. Serrou, *op. cit.,* pp. 93-113.

14. June 26. Manifestos issued by a "working commission for revolution in the Church." Cf. Davezies, *op. cit.,* p. 123.

15. May 20. Communiqué from the ACO. Cf. Serrou, *op. cit.,* p. 151.

16. May 31. Communiqué from the ACO. *Ibid,* p. 155.

17. May 31. Statement by the ACI. *Ibid.,* p. 95.

18. May 12. National Council of the YCW. *Ibid.,* p. 130.

19. May 18. A YCW team at the university of the Paris region. *Ibid.,* pp. 144-145.

20. May 14. French Scouts. *Ibid.,* p. 131.

21. May 16. Statement by Men's General Catholic Action. *Ibid.,* pp. 143 ff.

22. May 20. Same group, women's branch. *Ibid.,* p. 149.

23. May 18. Students of the Protestant Theological School of Paris. Cf. *Christianisme Social, op. cit.,* pp. 247-249.

24. May 29. Meeting of Protestant pastors and laymen of the Paris region. *Ibid.,* pp. 229 ff.

25. May 12. Declaration of the Protestant movement, *Christianisme Social, Ibid.,* p. 221.

26. May 22. Declaration of Pastor Westphal, president of the Federation of French Reformed Churches. Serrou, *op. cit.,* p. 37.

27. Interview with Jesuit scholastics from Chantilly. *Ibid.,* p. 46.

28. May 7. Official publication of the YCS. *Ibid.,* p. 70.

29. May 8. Leaders and chaplains of Christian communities of the university faculties of Nanterre, Sorbonne, and Censier. *Ibid.,* pp. 71-72.

30. May 15. Two leaders of the YCS in the official publication of the movement. *Ibid.,* pp. 137-143.

31. May 17. Chaplains of the Student Mission and University Catholic Action. *Ibid.,* p. 131.

32. May 29. Forum held at the Catholic Students' Center at the Law School, with the theme: "Christians and the Revolution." *Ibid.*, pp. 93-113.

33. May 20. Chaplains and leaders of the University Parish. *Ibid.*, p. 145.

34. May 28. Same. *Ibid.*, pp. 113-118.

35. May 21. Text prepared by the Bishops' Commission for Educational Questions, in collaboration with lay members of specialized Catholic Action movements.

36. May 16. Archbishop Guyot of Toulouse. *Ibid.*, p. 36.

37. May 10. Bishop Marty. *Ibid.*, p. 192.

38. May 18. Interview with Bishop Marty, over Radio Luxembourg. *Ibid.*, pp. 193 ff.

39. May 19. Bishops of Corbeil, Pontoise, and Versailles. *Ibid.*, p. 198.

40. May 22. Bishop Marty, letter to priests. *Ibid.*, pp. 199 ff.

41. May 22. Bishop Marty explained to journalists why he had kept silent. *Ibid.*, p. 36.

42. May 22. Note for the clergy by the auxiliary bishop of Paris, Bishop Frossard. *Ibid.*, pp. 203-207.

43. May 23. Bishop Marty, homily for Ascension Day. *Ibid.*, pp. 207 ff.

44. May 25. Bishop Marty, radio appeal. *Ibid.*, pp. 212 ff.

45. May 31. Bishop Simonneaux of Versailles. *Ibid.*, p. 214.

46. Bishop of Le Mans. *Ibid.*, p. 215.

47. Bishop Schmidt of Metz. *Ibid.*, pp. 215-216.

48. Bishop Vial of Nantes. *Ibid.*, p. 216.

49. Bishop Guyot of Toulouse. *Ibid.*, p. 216.

50. Bishop Maziers of Bordeaux. *Ibid.*, p. 216.

51. Cardinal Renard, archbishop of Lyons. *Ibid.*, p. 216.

52. Bishop Ancel, auxiliary bishop of Lyons. *Ibid.*, p. 216.

53. Bishop of Soissons. *Ibid.*, p. 216.

54. Bishop of Besançon. *Ibid.*, p. 217.

55. Different bishops. *Ibid.*, p. 217.

56. Bishop Marty, homily for the feast of Pentecost. *Ibid.*, p. 223.

57. June 2. Bishop Vial of Nantes. *Ibid.*, p. 228.

58. June 2. Cardinal Renard. *Ibid.*, p. 229.

59. June 2. Bishop Sauvage of Annecy. *Ibid.*, pp. 230-236.

60. June 8. Bishop Delarue of Nanterre. *Ibid.*, p. 236.

61. June 14. Letter from Bishop Marty to his clergy. *Ibid.*, p. 241.

62. June 19. Bishop Vilnet of Saint-Dié. *Ibid.*, p. 251.

63. June 20. Bishops' Permanent Council. *Ibid.* pp. 252-256.

Chapter Nine

1. E. Durkheim and M. Mans, "De quelques formes primitives de classification," *Année Sociologique,* 1901-1902, p. 1.

2. See Levy-Bruhl's description in *Le surnaturel et la nature dans la mentalité primitive* (Paris: 1931).

3. A. van Leeuwen, *Christianity and World History; the Meeting of the Faiths of East and West* (Edinburgh: House Press, 1964).

4. Peter Berger, *The Social Reality of Religion* (London: Faber & Faber, 1969), p. 35.

5. Henri Desroche quotes Engels as saying, "It seemed incomprehensible to us that, in England, almost all men of culture believed in all sorts of impossible miracles and that even geologists like Buckland and Mantell twisted the facts of their science with the sole purpose of not contradicting the mosaic myths of Genesis too openly." *Marxisme et Religions* (Paris: Presses Universitaires de France, 1962), p. 105.

6. Desroche, *ibid.,* p. 40.

7. *Ibid.,* p. 41.

8. Berger, *op. cit.,* p. 45.

9. We plan to develop this point of view further in a future publication.

10. See Chapter Six.

11. Dewart, *op. cit.,* p. 102.

12. Adam Schaff, "La définition fonctionnelle de l'idéologie et le problème de la fin du siècle de l'idéologie," *L'Homme et la Société,* April–June, 1968, p. 50.

13. Paul Ricoeur, "Le projet d'une morale social," *Christianisme Social,* May–August, 1966, pp. 287-291.

14. André Manaranche, *Y a-t-il une ethique sociale chrétienne?* (Paris: Editions du Seuil, 1969), p. 179.

15. Robert de Montvalon, commenting on replies to the questionnaire on the "Nouveau monde, Parole de Dieu," in *Esprit,* October 1967, pp. 640-641. Cf. also Karl Rahner, "Christianity and Ideology" *Concilium,* #6, 1965, pp. 41-58.

16. A. Dumas, "La fonction idéologique," *Eglise et Société,* vol. IV (Geneva: Labor et Fides, 1966).

17. P.Ricoeur, *Histoire et vérité* (Paris: Editions du Seuil, 1964), pp. 81-98; 193-197.

18. Although, as any history of dogma shows, the influence of political, cultural, and economic factors can easily be detected even if, at the time, they were not consciously recognized.

19. Alain Touraine, *La société post-industrielle* (Paris: De Noël, 1969), pp. 44 ff.; J. Remy, "Conflits et dynamique sociale; Interrogations rélatives à la vie de l'eglise," *Lumen Vitae,* vol. XXIV, 1969, no. 1, pp. 26-50.

20. P. Ricoeur, "Prévision économique et choix éthique," *Esprit,* February, 1966.

21. Cf., for example, P. Ricoeur, *Histoire et vérité, op cit.,* pp. 248-273.

22. Remy, *op. cit.,* pp. 45-46.

23. Cf. F. Houtart, *L'eclatement d'une eglise* (Paris: Mame, 1969).

24. These considerations have been inspired by Johannes Metz's article, "The Church's Social Function in the Light of a 'Political Theology,'" *Concilium,* #36, 1968, pp. 2-18, and by the unpublished work of M. Xhaufflaire, "La théologie politique selon J. B. Metz," *Document CEP/01* (Justice and Peace Commission, Brussels, 1970).

25. Xhaufflaire, *op. cit.,* p. 9.